Recreation Programming

Designing Leisure Experiences

FIFTH EDITION

J. Robert Rossman
Barbara Elwood Schlatter

Illinois State University

SAGAMORE PUBLISHING, L.L.C.
Champaign, Illinois

SAGAMORE
PUBLISHING

© 2008 Sagamore Publishing, L.L.C.

Publishers: Joseph J. Bannon/Peter Bannon
Production Manager: Laura Podeschi
Interior Design: Nic Mulvaney
Cover Design: Joseph Brumleve
Cover Illustration: Lori Walls

Library of Congress Catalog Card Number: 2007940364
ISBN 978-1-57167-573-6
Printed in the United States.

Sagamore Publishing, L.L.C.
804 North Neil Street
Champaign, IL 61820
www.sagamorepub.com

For

Linda Rossman

_____

Tom Schlatter

Contents

Preface

The first edition of this book was published over two decades ago. When it was first released, it included many innovative concepts, and a few risk takers adopted it. Since then, the book has been adopted for use at over 100 universities in the United States, Canada, Australia, New Zealand, Thailand, Taiwan, and other countries.

The profession and its knowledge base have continued advancing. We have incorporated into this fifth edition the implications of the latest research in leisure behavior, as well as the latest professional practices. It is gratifying that much of the research completed during the past two decades has continued confirming the theoretical base of this book. Leisure is a phased, sequential experience resulting from interaction. How this experience is produced determines the quality of leisure experience an individual will have. Staging this experience through managed programs is a complex undertaking, and there is a continuing need for well-educated programmers who can organize and deliver excellent services.

Leisure remains a desired human experience. There is no doubt in our minds that people will continue to demand leisure experiences and services. Who supplies them will shift to those suppliers who are able to deliver the types and formats of experiences and services desired. Thus, programming will continue to be an important, primary function in all leisure service agencies.

Acknowledgments

We are grateful to the many colleagues and students who have shared their thoughts about how to improve the book and programming. We welcome their contributions and any you may add. We want to thank the following colleagues who have given us feedback useful in developing this fifth edition of the book.

Dale Adkins, Western Illinois University
Larry Allen, Clemson University
Brent Beggs, Illinois State University
Jim Busser, University of Nevada–Las Vegas
Peter Burley, Christchurch, New Zealand
Harvey Feldman, University of Minnesota
Dovie Gamble, University of Florida
Daniel Gibble, Urbana Park District
Jean Keller, University of North Texas
Deb Kerstetter, Penn State University
Sandra Little Groves, Illinois State University
Melanie Morson, Stanhope, Australia
Marta Moorman, University of Nebraska at Kearney
Carol Peterson, University of Nevada-Las Vegas
Jane Pike, Clark County, NV, Parks and Recreation

Rob Stiefvater, Jr., North Carolina Central University
Laura Valerius, University of North Texas
Brendon Ward, Wellington, New Zealand
Peter Witt, Texas A&M University

Students from the University of North Texas, Southern Illinois University, Virginia Commonwealth University, the University of Florida, Indiana University, the University of Nevada–Las Vegas, and Illinois State University have all provided valuable feedback about the book.

Practitioners and agency directors from around the country were generous in providing us with photographs of excellent programs. We received more photographs than we could use. The agencies providing photographs and, in most cases, the photographers, are cited with each photograph.

We also want to acknowledge the help provided by the staff at Sagamore Publishing. Joe Bannon, Sr., Publisher of Sagamore, has provided ongoing support for the book for over two decades and was instrumental in encouraging development of the original volume. Doug Sanders, General Manager, and Laura Podeschi, Production Manager, have both made significant contributions to producing this edition. We are grateful to all of them for their dedicated, professional work on this book.

J. Robert Rossman
Sedona, AZ

Barbara Elwood Schlatter
Normal, IL

November 2007

Publisher's Note: Sagamore would like your feedback on the coil binding of *Recreation Programming: Designing Leisure Experiences (Fifth Edition)*. Since this publication is used in the classroom and the field, it is our hope to make it as user friendly as possible. Please e-mail your comments and suggestions to books@sagamorepub.com.

Introduction

A recreation programmer works out the final details of a new geocaching program for families whereby Global Positioning System (GPS) units are used to find hidden treasures in a local park. A therapeutic recreation specialist arranges to take children with physical disabilities to a therapeutic horseback riding center. A kickboxing instructor plans daily classes for college students that include warm up exercises, a series of kickboxing routines, and relaxing cool down exercises. A programmer plans a camp for baby boomers to live out their dream of becoming rock stars.

An event planner works with staff to design a website, posters, flyers, and newspaper advertisements to promote an upcoming music festival. Programmers in retirement communities plan computer classes for senior citizens on using email and webpage design. In a skilled care facility, an activity director organizes a reminiscence program for Alzheimer's residents. During the planning process, a recreation professional visualizes how to improve the upcoming slow-pitch softball tournament by taking the perspectives of players, umpires, coaches, and spectators.

Recreation professionals design, implement, and evaluate a myriad of different recreation programs at commercial, public, and quasi-public agencies across the country. A therapeutic recreation specialist in a rehabilitation unit creates an individual program plan for a recovering stroke patient that will allow her to resume her favorite pastimes with modifications. A children's discovery museum worker plans a "Passports of the World" program where children create unique artwork from different countries and get their passports stamped each day. Counselors arrive at their wilderness camp two weeks early to design a wide range of exciting recreational activities for the campers.

Designing and delivering recreation and leisure services is programming. Programming is a major responsibility in all leisure service organizations. Edginton and Neal (1983) have empirically confirmed that producing quality programs was one of the most highly rated organizational goals of municipal park and recreation executives. LaPage (1983) has also suggested that, "Providing the environment for a 'high-quality outdoor recreation experience' is a goal of most recreation resource managers—public and private" (p. 37). Programming, then, is regarded as a central concern of managers in all leisure service agencies, and is usually an identified part of a leisure service agency's mission.

PROGRAMMING: THE FOCUS OF THE PROFESSION

Designing and delivering recreation and leisure services is the major function of the leisure service profession. Leisure experiences are the basic units of service that the leisure service profession provides. This engaged experience is the vehicle through which other outcomes are accomplished. It is not beyond fun and games in the sense of bypassing them, but through the contexts and interactions of fun and games. The context of leisure interaction facilitates unique access to leisure experiences, and this experience facilitates the accomplishment of additional desirable outcomes. Professional practice is based on the recreation and leisure discipline, which seeks to understand the antecedents to leisure, the phenomenology of experiencing leisure, and the results of participating in leisure. Programming is the reason the profession and leisure service organizations exist. Programmers, better than any other professional group, should understand the phenomena of leisure, how humans engage in and experience leisure, the results of this experience, and how to facilitate an individual's experience of leisure. Our professional responsibility is to manipulate environments to facilitate leisure experiences for patrons. Albert Tillman (1973, p. ix) characterized the centrality of programming to the profession when he declared, "Crown program. Long live the king!"

Over the past 20 years, programmers' responsibilities have expanded greatly. They can include operating special events, contracting for services with external vendors, developing program services from a marketing approach, organizing leagues and tournaments, developing socially purposeful programs, and others. Additional developments are the infusion of computer technology into the management of program services, the need to provide inclusive services, and the need to manage risk in program operations. Today, programmers are involved in an increasingly complex set of delivery formats and techniques.

Most literature about programming has been published in books on the subject (Carpenter & Howe, 1985; DeGraaf, Jordan, & DeGraaf, 1999; Edginton, Hanson, Edginton, & Hudson, 1998; Farrell & Lundegren, 1991; Kraus, 1997; Russell, 1982; Tillman, 1973). Many of the programming practices recommended have not been logically derived from current knowledge about experiencing leisure. Consequently, practice has not been tied to theory, and techniques for successful programming have been somewhat nebulous. How programmers actually develop programs has not been well documented. In this edition, the authors report results of their research on programming practices, providing some of the first insight into techniques programmers actually use to develop programs.

Numerous techniques have been proposed for developing successful programs, including planning, brainstorming, needs analysis, community surveys, evaluation, systems analysis, and marketing. All of these techniques can certainly be used in developing successful programs. But none addresses leisure program development directly, comprehensively, and uniquely. They are all only piecemeal techniques that fail to provide the comprehensive insights into programming that are necessary to develop successful programs. We are convinced that information and techniques based on current information about experiencing leisure are needed to develop successful programs. Thus, the profession must reframe concepts about the role of programs and programming.

One of the difficulties in writing a programming book is drawing the boundaries around the various functions that are needed to manage leisure services and leisure service agencies. The delivery of good leisure services requires that all management functions be performed properly, including leadership, supervision, programming, and management of services, agencies, and facilities. In preparing this text, we have tried to restrict its content to the essential elements of programming, although there is indeed some unavoidable overlap into other functions.

In order to program, one must understand programming concepts, the theory of how recreation and leisure program services are developed, and how leisure is experienced. More explicit, theory-based information about programming has begun to appear in journals (Allen, Stevens, & Harwell, 1996; Cushman & D'Amours, 1989; Edginton & Rossman, 1988; Henderson & King, 1998; Tew, Havitz, & McCarville, 1999; Stewart, 1998; Witt & Crompton, 1996; Witt & Crompton, 1997). The programmer's knowledge base must enable him or her to operate on two levels. First, the programmer must manage the production and delivery of leisure services within a specific agency context. Second, the programmer must do this in a manner that facilitates the occurrence of leisure experiences at the behavioral level—that is, for individuals within interactions in social occasions.

In *Recreation Programming: Designing Leisure Experiences, Fifth Edition*, the programmer is taught to develop program services by learning both the theory and technique of recreation programming, including: (1) basic leisure theory that explains how leisure is experienced; (2) the generic structure of situated activity systems in which social interaction produces leisure experiences; and (3) procedures and techniques used by programmers to manage recreation programs. Providing meaningful leisure experiences is important to individuals, society, and our profession. We hope this book will provide you the ability to deliver excellent services to your participants and give you a sufficient educational background to continue being an astute student of programming throughout your career.

REFERENCES

Allen, L., Stevens, B., & Harwell, R. (1996). Benefits-based management activity planning model for youth in at-risk environments, *Journal of Park and Recreation Administration, 14*(3), 10–19.

Carpenter, G. M., & Howe, C. Z. (1985). *Programming leisure experiences: A cyclical approach.* Englewood Cliffs, NJ: Prentice-Hall.

Cushman, G., & D'Amours, M. (1989). Modern leisure management [Special Issue]. *Society and Leisure, 12*(1).

DeGraaf, D., Jordan, D., & DeGraaf, K. (1999). *Programming for parks, recreation, and leisure services: A servant leadership approach*. State College, PA: Venture.

Edginton, C. R., Hanson, C. J., Edginton, S. R., & Hudson, S. D. (1998). *Leisure programming: A service-centered and benefits approach* (3rd ed.). New York: McGraw-Hill.

Edginton, C. R., & Rossman, J. R. (Eds.). (1988). *Journal of Recreation and Park Administration, 6*(4).

Edginton, C. R., & Neal, L. L. (1983). Park and recreation directors' perceptions of organizational goals. *Journal of Park and Recreation Administration, 1*(1), 39-50.

Farrell, P., & Lundegren, H. M. (1991). *The process of recreation programming: Theory and technique* (3rd ed.). State College, PA: Venture.

Gelb, M. J. (1998). *How to think like Leonardo da Vinci: Seven steps to genius every day*. New York, NY: Delacorte Press.

Henderson, K., & King, K. (1998). Recreation programming for adolescent girls: Rationale and foundations. *Journal of Recreation and Park Administration, 16*(2), 1–14.

Kraus, R. (1997). *Recreation programming: A benefits-driven approach*. Needham Heights, MA: Allyn & Bacon.

LaPage, W. R. (1983). Recreation resource management for visitor satisfaction. *Journal of Recreation and Park Administration, 1*(2), 37 44.

Russell, R. (1982). *Planning programs in recreation*. St. Louis, MO: Mosby.

Schalock, R. (1995). *Outcome-based evaluation*. New York: Plenum.

Stewart, W. P. (1998). Leisure as multiphase experiences: Challenging traditions. *Journal of Leisure Research, 30*, 391–400.

Tew, C., Havitz, M., & McCarville, R. (1999). The role of marketing in municipal recreation programming decisions: A challenge to conventional wisdom. *Journal of Park and Recreation Administration, 17*(1), 1–20.

Tillman, A. (1973). *The program book for recreation professionals*. Palo Alto, CA: Mayfield. Witt, P., & Crompton, J. (1996). The at-risk youth recreation project. *Journal of Park and Recreation Administration, 14*(3), 1–9.

Witt, P., & Crompton, J. (1997). The protective factors framework: A key to programming for benefits and evaluating for results. *Journal of Park and Recreation Administration, 15*(3), 1–18.

Part I
Foundations for Programming

This book is predicated on the notion that programmers facilitate patrons' engagements in leisure experiences. To accomplish this, programmers must understand how leisure is experienced in social occasions, how to design programs to facilitate leisure experiences, how to stage experiences, and how leisure service organizations manage the development of recreation program services.

In Part I, a foundation for successful programming is developed. In the first chapter of this part, basic concepts of programming and operational definitions of leisure behaviors are explained. Chapter Two contains a discussion of social science theory that explains leisure behavior. This is one of the more difficult chapters in the book, but understanding its content is necessary to guide the professional programmer's development and management actions throughout the steps of the Program Development Cycle. The material in Chapter Three flows from the discussion in Chapter Two. The generic structure of the situated activity systems, in which leisure experiences occur, is explained in this chapter. Chapter Four explains the basic theories and practice of outcome-based programming. Chapter Five is a discussion about leisure service products and how they may be packaged for distribution and sale. In Chapter Six, a method for developing goals and objectives that can organize and guide the development of leisure services in an organization is explained. At the end of this section, there is a two page diagram of the Program Development Cycle. Margin notes next to the diagram briefly explain the Cycle. A more complete explanation may be found on the supporting website (www. recreationprogramming.com); however, each of the remaining chapters in the book explains and elaborates on the steps in the Cycle.

Climbing to New Heights
Photo courtesy of Bolingbrook Park District, Bolingbrook, IL
Photo by Jill Wijanco

Basic Programming Concepts

1

The ultimate goal of programming is to stage leisure experiences for program patrons. Accomplishing this requires that the programmer learn the concepts that tie together leisure experiences, program definitions, the act of programming, and the management activities that must be implemented in an agency to stage successful programs (Rossman and Edginton, 1989).

PROGRAMMING CONCEPTS DEFINED

PROGRAM

A program is a designed opportunity for leisure experience to occur. Program is an elastic concept used to describe a variety of different operations, including activities, events, or services conducted by leisure service organizations. The term program can refer to a single activity, such as a bike ride, or a class meeting over several weeks. It can refer to a collection of activities, such as the cultural arts classes operated by an organization. It can refer to a single event, such as a softball skill workshop or a week-long festival. It can refer to the services offered by an agency, such as a drop-in auto hobby shop or a desk selling discount tickets to area events. It can also refer to the total set of operations offered by an agency, including all of its activities, events, and services. Any of these may be called a program.

This definition is broad and is intended to include more than typical programs organized with a face-to-face leader. The key point is the notion of design, in which the programmer conceptualizes a leisure experience and intervenes in some way to stage it for the patron. In some instances, this intervention may be minimal, but in others it may be near total. The intervention may be through face-to-face leadership, a designed physical environment, or the regulation of leisure behavior through the development and enforcement of policies. Design always involves planned intervention, regardless of its type or magnitude.

Two assumptions in this definition need further explanation. First, the notion of design assumes that we know how leisure is construed and experienced by individuals (Mannell & Kleiber, 1997) and that we can stage experiences to facilitate its occurrence. Second, it assumes that we know the attributes of the leisure experience; that is, we know why individuals

KEY TERMS

Program
Programming
Program
    Development
Leisure
Recreation
Games
Play
Sport
Tourism

The ultimate goal of programming is to stage leisure experiences for program patrons.

label some experiences as leisure but not others. The ability to program requires a thorough knowledge of the process of experiencing leisure, how to stage these experiences, and the outcomes that define the experience. This knowledge will be introduced in the appropriate sections throughout the book.

Leisure is not a set of identifiable activities, events, or services. The attributes that make them leisure experiences are not inherent in the activities, events, or services that are usually called leisure. Rather, leisure is construed by how a participant processes his or her experiences of a program and interprets what has occurred (Csikszentmihalyi, 1991; Kelly, 1987; Patterson, Watson, Williams, & Roggenbuck, 1998). Modern programming is more than simply searching for the most popular activity that can be offered. Programmers must understand that leisure is a state of mind most likely experienced when participants enter freely-chosen programs that enable them to achieve realistic personal goals by consciously directing interaction in a social occasion. Samdahl (1988) said, "Leisure can be viewed as a distinctive pattern of perceiving and relating to ongoing interaction. That is to say, leisure is a particular definition of a situation" (p. 29). Thus, a program provides an opportunity for leisure to occur but cannot ensure that it does, since this ultimately depends on how a patron experiences the event and interprets his or her participation.

PROGRAMMING

Programming is designing, staging, and delivering leisure opportunities by intervening in social interaction; that is, by manipulating and creating environments in a manner that maximizes the probability that those who enter them will have the leisure experiences they seek. Individuals achieve satisfaction from a leisure experience depending on how they guide and interpret their participation in the leisure occasion. Because the programmer understands what patrons must experience to construe an experience as leisure and how this experience is produced through social interaction, a program that facilitates (i.e., increases) the probability of a leisure experience occurring can be designed and staged. These are key notions. The practice of all professions, including leisure service provision, is predicated on information developed through the scientific method and then applied to practical problems.

Designing social interactions that will facilitate the leisure experience must be based on knowledge about experiencing leisure and how it is produced in social occasions. Kelly (1999) has suggested that all definitions of leisure presuppose that it occurs in an action context: "Something happens in directing attention, processing information, defining meaning, and producing the experience" (p. 136). He goes on to say, "The distinctive element of leisure action is that it is focused on the experience rather than external outcomes. It is engaged in primarily for the experience of the action" (p. 136). It is the responsibility of the programmer to design programs with participation processes that will facilitate participants' opportunities to engage in actions that will result in a leisure experience. Thus, how a program is staged is more important to facilitating a leisure experience than the specific activity itself.

...leisure is construed by how a participant processes his or her experiences of a program and interprets what has occurred.

...leisure is a multiphase experience...

Exercise 1-1: Comparing Programming Concepts

Compare the definitions of program, programming, and program development.
- How do the three concepts differ?
- What is the role of the programmer in each of them?

Furthermore, programmers must understand that leisure is a multiphase experience (Stewart, 1999) and begin by planning to engage the participant through the three phases of human experience—anticipation, participation, and reflection (Busser, 1993; Little, 1993). New standards for experiential engagement, introduced with the emergence of The Experience Economy (Pine and Gilmore, 1999), suggest that programs should be staged; a theatrical metaphor indicates the comprehensiveness of the details and sensibilities the programmer must deal with if the experience intended is to be achieved by the participant. Good programming, then, is designed intervention that is staged, based on knowledge about social interaction and the social psychology of experiencing leisure.

PROGRAM DEVELOPMENT

Program development is the overall management process in which the programmer designs, stages, manages, and delivers program services within the context of a specific agency. It includes understanding and developing an agency's mission, assessing needs, designing programs, staging them, delivering them, and evaluating them to document the benefits that have been provided, as well as to determine their future. All programs are delivered by some type of organization. Therefore the programmer must learn to manage program services successfully within an organizational context. Successful program development results in programs that meet the needs of the agency, patrons, and the community. Programming is one key function in program development. The overall process of program development is diagramed in the Program Development Cycle (pgs. 92-93 in this volume). Now complete Exercise 1-1.

DEFINITIONS OF RELATED CONCEPTS

Concepts we use influence how we act. The linguistic labels attached to various forms of human behavior shape our attitudes and actions. The lack of precise definitions in the recreation and leisure field is often a cause of concern to new students. This book offers concepts necessary to understanding and accomplishing programming: leisure, play, recreation, games, sport, and tourism. Each concept refers to a different type of leisure experience; therefore, each must be programmed somewhat differently. This section will discuss the concepts in relationship to each other in order to help clarify their meanings.

Leisure, play, recreation, games, sport, and tourism must be programmed differently.

Kelly (1983) contends that leisure is central to today's society. He states that leisure is "crucial life space for the expression and development of selfhood, for the working out of identities that are important to the individual. [It is] . . . central to the maintenance of the society itself as a social space for the development of intimacy" (p. 23). Driver, Brown, and Peterson (1991) take the position that multiple behaviors or experiences (Stewart, 1999) are included under the concept of leisure. Leisure, then, is the broadest concept (Neulinger, 1981), encompassing play, recreation, games, sport, and tourism, each of which can be viewed as a form of leisure that can be distinguished by more specific, defining characteristics.

LEISURE

Leisure has been defined in several different ways. Six types were identified by Murphy (1974): classical leisure, leisure as discretionary time, leisure as a function of social class, leisure as form of activity, antiutilitarian leisure, and a holistic concept of leisure. Neulinger (1974) suggested that all definitions of leisure are either quantitative or qualitative and concluded that leisure is a state of mind characterized primarily by perceived freedom and intrinsic motivation. Often, the discipline training of the individual defining leisure will influence the definition. Thus, there are definitions provided by economists, sociologists, psychologists, and social psychologists.

The perspective used throughout this book is that leisure is a social experience constructed through interaction in social occasions (Iso-Ahola, 1999; Samdahl, 1988). Iso-Ahola emphasized this point by stating that "leisure studies is a human service field in which social interaction is the main ingredient" (1980, p. 7). Samdahl (1992) found that over 50 percent of the occasions labeled as leisure by those involved included some type of social interaction. Hamilton-Smith (1991) has also assumed leisure is best understood as a social construct that can be defined in a variety of ways, including leisure as time, leisure as action, leisure as action within time and space, and leisure as experience.

Leisure is an experience most likely to occur during freely chosen interactions characterized by a high degree of personal engagement that is motivated by the intrinsic satisfaction that is expected to result. After a first reading, this definition may seem relatively simple, but it incorporates three complex concepts: freedom, intrinsic satisfaction, and engagement.

Freedom has been a central defining element of leisure since man first contemplated the meaning of leisure. Modern research has confirmed the primacy of freedom (Iso-Ahola, 1999). Freedom from something and freedom to have or do something have been primary themes of leisure definitions (Sylvester, 1987). In our society, the obligations of work, family, friends, civic duties, and so forth can obscure the meaning of "freely chosen" or "free choice," or at least make it more difficult to sort them out. Some leisure occasions are determined by the degree to which they free individuals from social role constraints (Samdahl, 1988). The "freedom from" notion, then, occurs in situations where one is freed from social role constraints to explore and accomplish something.

...leisure is a social experience constructed through interaction in social occasions.

...leisure must be freely chosen from the perspective of the individual making the choice.

The other operant condition is freedom to have "a sense of opportunity and possibility" (Kleiber, 1999, p. 3). The notion of freely choosing something can only be determined from the perspective of the individual making the choice. Thus, the notion of freedom is a matter of individual perception (Neulinger, 1981). The evidence suggests that individuals must believe that they could have chosen not to do an activity before it meets the test of being freely chosen (Kelly, 1982). As Patterson and colleagues have explained, "Situated freedom is the idea that there is a structure in the environment that sets boundaries on what can be perceived or experienced, but that within those boundaries recreationists are free to experience the world in highly individual, unique, and variable ways" (1998, p. 425–426).

Programmers should remember that leisure must be freely chosen from the perspective of the individual making the choice. Additionally, individuals must perceive that they have options and choices in a program in order to explore, move forward in their own personal stream of experience, and "become something new" by participating in a novel experience, that is, one that is experienced in this way for the first time. Freedom experienced in this manner creates a unique condition for an optimal, self-actualizing experience to occur (Csikszentmihalyi & Kleiber, 1991).

Thus, freedom plays a functional role in construing the leisure experience. Although optimal experiences may occur in other spheres of life, they are more likely to do so when the conditions of freedom just explained occur. Over-programming, by providing too much structure to an occasion, will leave the participant few or no choices. This may destroy the very experience the programmer is trying to facilitate. Entertaining, rather than engaging participants, is a good example of over-programming to the point that participants have no choice. It is an error frequently made by individuals who stage events but have no understanding of leisure behavior. Although it keeps the programmer in control of the event, it does not allow participants the freedom needed to experience leisure.

Intrinsic satisfaction is the second major dimension of leisure. Psychologists have used several different terms to describe participating in this experience, including autotelic activities, arousal-seeking behavior, and optimal experience. "The key element of an optimal experience is that it is an end in itself," writes Csikszentmihalyi (1991, p. 67); it is intrinsically satisfying. The behavior associated with pursuing intrinsically satisfying activities has also been called "arousal-seeking behavior," based on the need to maintain optimal arousal. This theory was proposed by Ellis (1973), and it assumes that people are not normally quiescent; rather, they seek and act to increase stimulation.

Intrinsically satisfying activities provide satisfaction through the interactive engagement itself, and that satisfaction provides sufficient motivation for the individual to continue participating. Thus, no external reward is necessary. The feedback received from such participation indicates that what is occurring is congruent with one's goals, thereby strengthening and validating the self (Csikszentmihalyi, 1991). This affords a freedom from concern with oneself that frees one to focus psychic energy more intensely on the demands of the current interactive

Intrinsic satisfaction is a personally interpreted perception of a specific situation that is construed through interaction in a social occasion.

engagement. These engagements both demand and consume one's complete, focused attention. The motivation to participate in interaction to seek this experience is powerful and real (Neulinger, 1981).

Programmers should understand how this occurs. Unfortunately, intrinsic satisfaction is not wholly contained within activities themselves. In fact, people similarly describe their optimal experiences in different activities, and their descriptions are consistent across sociological and cultural variables (Csikszentmihalyi, 1991; Iso-Ahola, 1999). So, it is not a matter of prescribing a list of intrinsically satisfying activities and expecting individuals to find intrinsic satisfaction in them.

Intrinsic satisfaction is a personally interpreted perception of a specific situation that is construed through interaction in a social occasion (Csikszentmihalyi, 1991; Samdahl, 1988; Shaw, 1985; Unger, 1984). Individuals' past experiences and current expectations help them determine whether or not an activity is intrinsically satisfying. What arouses an individual today is part of a stream of interactions between the individual's natural abilities and previous experiences. Participants will conclude that they were intrinsically motivated when programs provide opportunities for developing competence, self-expression, self-development, or self-realization (Mannell, 1999). Different individuals find different activities intrinsically satisfying because of factors such as their own skill levels in an activity, their level of socialization into it, and the previous opportunities and experiences they have had with it. Although these factors initially influence their likelihood of participating, their interpretation of the interactions in an activity on a given day will determine whether or not it is a leisure experience for them.

Thus, how an activity is staged and how an individual interprets his or her participation in it are more important in determining whether or not an individual will have a leisure experience than the activity type, e.g., softball, oil painting, and so on. Programmers need to devote more attention to how activities are staged rather than continually searching for the perfect activity that will provide a leisure experience.

Finally, to experience an event requires, at a minimum, that one engage in and interpret it. Leisure occurs in an action context. As Kelly (1999) writes, "Something happens in directing attention, processing information, defining meaning, and producing results" (p. 136). Experiencing is more than a passive state of mind; it denotes processing and ordering information in one's consciousness (Csikszentmihalyi, 1991; Kelly, 1990). That is, one must engage in it. Many who are now entering the experience economy and producing events and other kinds of programs repeatedly confuse entertainment with engagement (Pine and Gilmore, 1999). They design events to entertain rather than engage. Leisure is more likely to occur when individuals play an active role in organizing and self-directing outcome; that is., they have the opportunity for positive affect (Kleiber, Caldwell, & Shaw, 1992; Kleiber, Larson, & Csikszentmihalyi, 1986). Ajzen and Driver (1992) reported that "perceived behavioral control" improved their ability to predict leisure behavior, again verifying the importance of having control over outcomes of the leisure experience.

People experience leisure by active engagement in and interaction with various combinations of elements in an environment; they thereby

To experience leisure, one must engage in, interpret, and have a role in affecting the outcome of the event.

The programmer provides form and structure to create a situated activity system that facilitates a leisure experience.

have the perception that they are directing the outcome of the event and are thus the cause of an act. This engagement can be as simple as reading a book and interpreting its meaning. In this case, the interpretation is being self-directed by the reader. It can also include participating in a lively social discussion with friends or family. Participating in rule-bounded games and sports also provides a significant number of opportunities for self-directed social interaction and self-directed outcomes. When these types of engagement result in experiences that are enjoyable, fun, or pleasurable, the event is more likely to be construed as leisure (Mannell & Kleiber, 1997). Thus, leisure experiences are those that are both interpreted in a specific way and are self-directed.

Overall, then, to experience leisure, an individual must freely choose to engage in an environment and perceive that this engagement provides intrinsic satisfaction that both rewards and sustains the engagement. Intrinsic satisfaction partly results from experiences that provide opportunities for positive affect; that is, self-directing the outcome of engagement. Experiencing leisure is something that individuals do, not something programmers do to individuals. Neulinger (1981) has insisted that leisure is not a noun, but a verb that implies action, process, and experience. Leisure is something to be consciously processed and experienced, not something that is acquired and possessed. It occurs in a social context with form and structure; that is, it is situated action (Kelly, 1999). In designing and staging a program, the programmer is providing selected elements of a situation and thereby specifying form and structure for the leisure occasion. It is the programmer's responsibility to stage the proper form and structure to situate an activity system that facilitates a leisure experience. The notion of a situated activity system will be developed further in subsequent chapters.

GAMES

Games are leisure experiences with formal rules that define the interactional content, attempt to equalize the players, and define the role that skill and chance will play in determining the outcome. Formal rules create an unknown or problematic outcome, the resolution of which can only be achieved by playing the game. This applies to table games, athletic contests, and other gaming situations.

Games are rule bounded, and the rules delineate the arena of focused reality that will be addressed during the gaming occasion (Goffman, 1961). Games are popular leisure experiences because the rules of a well-constructed game create an area of focus with a high probability for a leisure experience. To create this focus, rules must clearly define the gaming encounter and the role that skill and chance will play in determining the outcome.

Game rules must define the focus of the contest and exactly what is being contested. A game winner should have exhibited more of the particular skill being contested in the game than have other participants. In some games, the rules minimize the role of chance and maximize the effect of skill on the gaming outcome.

On the other hand, chance is solely responsible for the outcome of some games. For example, the winner of "Chutes and Ladders," a popu-

A good game is different every time you play it. (V. Postrel, 1998, p.180)

lar children's game, is determined entirely by chance. Thus, parents often play the game with young children who are not able to play a game of strategy or skill. In a game whose outcome is determined entirely by chance, the players are immediately made equal—each is equally dependent on chance.

Some games require a mixture of skill and chance. This mixture is characteristic of many table games that must sustain interest among players with unequal levels of skill. "Trivial Pursuit" is a good example. No matter how many questions are answered, a lucky roll of the die is still necessary to land in the final winning position. A more highly skilled player can answer many more questions than other players and still lose the game because of unlucky rolls of the die.

Recreation always has a morality associated with it...

The element of chance in a game is usually implemented with the toss of a coin, the roll of dice, or the use of some type of spinning device. More complex contests may begin with a coin toss or some other mechanism for determining the order of play or an initial position. In football, for example, the winner of a coin toss may choose which end of the field to defend, or to receive or kick the ball to start the game. Depending on weather conditions, this choice can affect the outcome of the game. Nonetheless, it is a matter of chance, unrelated to any of the skills that football is supposed to test. The use of chance, then, as a major determinant of the gaming outcome is often used to make unequal players equal, or to determine initial advantage totally unrelated to any game skill.

Game rules define the skills that will be contested and the role that skill and chance will play in determining the outcome. Leisure service professionals must understand the function of rules in games, because much game programming involves modifying rules or facilities to allow those with insufficient skills to participate.

RECREATION

Recreation is leisure that is engaged in for the attainment of personal and social benefits. Recreation has always been characterized as socially purposeful and moral; that is, it incorporates a rightness and a wrongness. Hutchison (1951) stated that, "Recreation is a worthwhile, socially accepted leisure experience that provides immediate and inherent satisfaction to the individual who voluntarily participates . . . " (p. 2). Jensen (1979) also commented on the inherent morality of recreation when he said, "In order to qualify as recreation, an activity must do something desirable to a participant" (p. 8). Recreation is considered to have a specific moral purpose in society.

Play is the most spontaneous form of leisure behavior...

Recreation has always been viewed as restoration from the toil of work. De Grazia (1964) assumed this view when he wrote, "Recreation is activity that rests men from work, often by giving them a change (distraction, diversion), and restores (re-creates) them for work" (p. 233). He credited recreation with having social significance by functionally relating it to work: Recreation is instrumental to work because it enables individuals to recuperate and restore themselves in order to accomplish more work.

Recreation is not only good for individuals—it is also good for society. Recreation has been used as a diversion from government repression, war, economic depression, congested urban conditions, and so forth.

Recreation always has a morality associated with it, and there are good and bad forms of recreation. For example, drug use is considered morally degenerative. Therefore, to a recreation professional, the notion of "recreational drug use" is not possible.

Moreover, organizations that provide recreation services are viewed as social institutions that espouse the positive aspects inherent in the recreation activities they offer. Specific moral ends or purposes are usually attributed to providers such as municipal recreation agencies, churches, the Girl Scouts and Boy Scouts, the armed services, and other similar organizations. More recently, recreation programs for at-risk youth have been developed to combat exposure to adverse social conditions and the general lack of positive opportunities.

Thus, recreation is a specific form of leisure behavior that is characterized as having a pervasive morality. It is an institutionalized form of leisure that is manipulated to accomplish socially desirable goals and objectives that are often defined by the sponsoring agency. It is the form of leisure behavior that programmers most often try to facilitate. In developing recreation programs, the programmer is often expected to go beyond providing a leisure experience and to also intervene to accomplish some additional socially purposeful goal.

PLAY

Play is leisure with the childlike characteristics of spontaneity, self expression, and the creation of a nonserious realm of meaning. As a specific form of leisure, play has further defining characteristics.

Play incorporates a dualism that distinguishes it from the real world. Play involves a lack of seriousness in which interaction is free flowing, and it progresses from place to place and takes on new forms as focus, needs, and demands shift (Denzin, 1975). It is an expansive interactional form that is not guided by conventional rules of interaction. Hunnicutt (1986) has suggested, "Play may well be one of those things that we do to understand other things and to create a truth" (p. 10).

Play is the most spontaneous form of leisure behavior, and its occurrence depends totally on the consent and conscious participation of the players. Lynch (1980) has shown that players recognize and signal each other when interactions shift into a play mode. The inconsequential nature of play establishes for the player a sense of self and reality that cannot otherwise be attained in daily life. To "play with" an object, person, or an idea is to experience the meaning of the object, person, or idea in a fundamentally new way. Because of this, play is one of the most difficult forms of leisure to program.

Three key concepts define sport: physical exertion, rules, and competition of physical skills.

SPORT

Sport is leisure that involves institutionalized competitive physical activity. It can be thought of as a game whose rules require physical competition. Many programmers are engaged in organizing sport competitions and managing sport venues.

In defining sport, one is faced with the question of professional athletes, i.e., is their participation leisure? Pragmatically, very few individuals are employed as athletes, although they are highly visible and well known to the wider population. Not completely resolving this issue does not influence a large number of individuals. Nevertheless, most sport scholars include professional athletes in the rubric of sport participation. For our purposes, we will assume that whether someone is paid or unpaid, it is the experience the athlete has while participating that determines whether or not an event, including participation in sport, is leisure.

Three key concepts define sport: physical exertion, rules, and competition of physical skills. Most academics who have studied sport agree that it includes only those activities that require physical exertion. They do not include activities such as card playing, chess, and others under the rubric of sport. In our sedentary world, the need to expend physical energy is one of the unique attributes of sport that separates it from everyday life.

Rules are a second attribute that define the sporting event and regulate participation: "The essence of sport lies in its patterned and regulated form. Through the social process of institutionalization—the formalizing and standardizing of activities—sport is regulated" (Leonard, 1998, p. 13). In addition to rules for actual competitions, sport as an institution is also regulated by league rules. The modification and enforcement of rules often becomes the focus of sport, attracting as much attention from the sport media and fans as the competitions themselves. Owners of professional teams will spend many hours contemplating rule changes. One is reminded of the use of instant replay in professional football. First it was not used, although the technology was available. Then it was used but later dropped. Now it is being used again in a more limited fashion.

Most sports are games with rules that function like the game rules previously discussed, except that all sport games involve physical exertion and are contests of physical skills. Rules affect the character of a game, including the strategies used to compete and the skills that may be needed to participate. Rules often differ for collegiate versus professional competitions or national versus international competitions. Programming sporting competitions will inevitably involve the programmer in rule discussions as teams try to manipulate rules to assure themselves of a competitive advantage on the playing field.

The final attribute of sport is that it involves a competition of physical skills. The rules of each sport require participants to possess and showcase specific physical skills, e.g., eye–hand coordination (table tennis), flexibility (gymnastics), strength (weight-lifting), endurance (marathon running). The most popular sports, such as basketball, football, baseball, and hockey, require athletes to possess multiple physical skills in various combinations to succeed. Often, programmers will be involved in developing rule modifications to accommodate participation of individuals in sport who possess less physical skill than needed to compete successfully in open competitions.

A significant amount of association with sport in the United States involves individuals watching others participate in sport, i.e., being a sports fan. This type of involvement does not, of course, provide the benefits or challenges of actually participating in sport. In general, it is not part of a programmer's daily tasks, except for contending with sport fans who attend sporting events organized by the programmer and occasional trips that may be organized to attend sporting events.

Additionally, much of a recreation programmer's time may be spent in organizing participation in youth sports. In many cases, the programmer will be working with adult groups who organize and operate youth sports. Currently, the focus of programmers in operating youth sports has been to improve the skills of adults coaching youth and to deal with the behavior of parents who attend youth sport games. The behavior of parents at youth sporting events has become a national problem. To ensure that children may play in a nonthreatening environment, agencies have instituted various regulating policies and practices such as "Silent Sundays," where parents are not allowed to cheer, or mandatory sportsmanship classes for parents; if mom or dad do not attend, the youngster may not play (Engh, 1999).

TOURISM

Touring is a rapidly expanding form of leisure in which individuals travel for opportunities to experience leisure. Additional defining dimensions that characterize touring are restoration, change of pace, and individual purposes. Touring for leisure is distinguished from travel for business or commercial purposes. A tourist is defined as someone who travels at least fifty miles from home and stays at least one night for the purpose of recreation or leisure. Touring is ripe with opportunities for leisure, as leisure experiences can result both from the travel itself as well as engagements during travel.

An enduring feature of tourism is its use as an escape from and renewal for work. The annual vacation is still pursued to restore individuals for work. A two-week annual vacation is often the norm for beginning employees. In North America, the number of days of annual vacation one has often increases with job seniority, sometimes reaching four or five weeks per year for employees with longevity. In other countries, annual vacation days from work frequently exceed those provided in North America. In many cases, these days are used as an opportunity to travel and get away from home and one's work locale. Leisure experiences that will refresh and restore one for work are pursued.

But tourism encompasses more than simply restoring individuals for work. Retirees, who no longer work, are a growing segment of the tourism industry. For them, touring provides a change of pace from the routine of their lives: a chance to visit new and exotic places. Thus, travel to places, with schedules and activities that are different from a routine pattern of work or routine imposed by continual interaction with the same individuals, places, and events, is pursued through traveling and becoming a tourist. Since becoming a tourist requires one to be away from home, there is a high probability that touring will result in a change of pace. With a change of pace as a benchmark for defining a touring experience, touring can provide this change through a wide va-

Leisure is considered the most general and encompassing concept; recreation, play, games, and sport are viewed as specific forms of leisure.

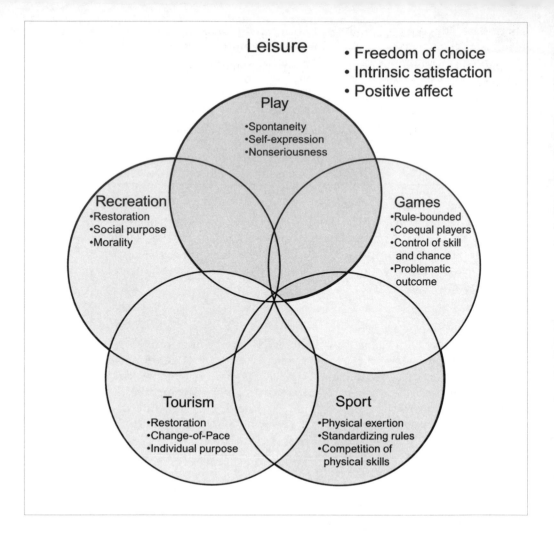

Figure 1-1: Relationships Among Central Definitions of Leisure, Recreation, Play, and Games

riety of engagements, including rest, relaxation, culture, sport, escape, adventure, and many others.

A final dimension of uniqueness in tourism is the diversity of individual purposes for touring. This diversity has resulted in emerging niche tours that include sport-tourism, eco-tourism, gambling tours, medical tourism, and many other specialized kinds of touring groups and tours. Some purposes can include specialized destinations such as golf courses, gardens, or wineries. Some utilize specialized forms of transportation such as cruises, bus tours, trekking, or a new possibility, space touring. Unique associations are the basis for some tour cohorts. For example, tours organized for university alumni, members of specific religious denominations, or tours for members of a civic organization. There are many other market segments that form the basis for organizing touring groups or themed, organized tours.

Programmers work in the tourism industry as tour organizers for the hotel industry, transportation businesses, attraction venues, or tour companies who package tours. Ironically, the attractions that are the reason for travel are often the least expensive part of a trip. The majority of tourism dollars are spent on transportation, housing, and food—not admission to the recreation attractions that are the primary reason for traveling to a specific locale. Because the total cost of travel, lodging, and food are likely to far exceed the total cost of admissions to recreation amenities or venues, the price of admission to a recreation amenity or venue is relatively inelastic and is one of the lower costs incurred when traveling.

PROGRAMMING IMPLICATIONS

Leisure is considered the most general and encompassing concept; recreation, play, games, sport, and tourism are viewed as specific forms of leisure. The central defining concepts of each leisure form and its relationship to others is illustrated in Figure 1-1. The boundaries of each form overlap, illustrating the nebulous character of each form of leisure. For example, game rules are often structured to allow players to play in a spontaneous, free-flowing, and creative manner. Nonetheless, when game players serendipitously discover a new move or game strategy that gives them an advantage, rules are modified to quash it or to accommodate it within the rule structure of the game.

When recreation activities are programmed, they are often made to appear as much like leisure as possible; perceptions of free choice and intrinsically rewarding activities are included in the program. However, the programmatic goals of the agency sponsoring and operating a program may foster an activity structure that does not permit ongoing freedom of choice in the activity. The use of prescriptive programming methods such as Benefits-Based Programming can lead to highly structured programs that impose the agency's desired outcome on participants. Programmers need to realize the central concepts of each of these forms of leisure and should design and operate programs that are least obstructive to a participant's desired experiences. Programmers often are faced with the situation in which the best programmatic manipulation is simply to avoid destroying the experience desired. In this case, the programmer must understand the experience and make sure that

Programming is the central focus of the leisure service profession and the primary mission of leisure service organizations.

the design or operation of a program does not have built-in blocks to the leisure experience desired by the participant or intended by the agency. Now complete Exercise 1-2 on page 15.

CONCLUSION

Programming is the central focus of the leisure service profession and the primary mission of leisure service organizations. Programmers stage opportunities for leisure to occur. Leisure is a primary social space in modern society for exercising free choice and the development of self. Leisure occurs through interactions in social occasions that are characterized by perceived freedom, intrinsic satisfaction, and opportunities to experience positive affect. Recreation, games, play, sport, and tourism are all specific forms of leisure with additional defining concepts.

REFERENCES

Ajzen, I., & Driver, B. (1992). Planned behavior and leisure choice. *Journal of Leisure Research, 24*, 207–224.

Busser, J. A. (1993). Leisure programming: The state of the art (Intro duction). *Journal of Physical Education, Recreation and Dance, 64*(8), 25, 33.

Csikszentmihalyi, M. (1991). *Flow: The psychology of optimal experience.* New York: Harper Perennial.

Csikszentmihalyi, M., & Kleiber, D. A. (1991). Leisure and self-actualization. In B. L. Driver, P. J. Brown, & G. L. Peterson (Eds.), *Benefits of leisure* (pp. 91–102). State College, PA: Venture.

De Grazia, S. (1964). *Of time, work, and leisure.* Garden City, NJ: Doubleday-Anchor.

Denzin, N. K. (1975). Play, games, and interaction: The contexts of childhood socialization. *The Sociological Quarterly, 16*, 458–478.

Driver, B. L., Brown, P. J., & Peterson, G.L. (1991). *Benefits of leisure.* State College, PA: Venture.

Ellis, M. J. (1973). *Why people play.* Englewood Cliffs, NJ: Prentice-Hall.

Engh, F. (1999, December 6). Out of control: Youth sports leagues tackling parents. *The Pantagraph*, p. A11.

Goffman, E. (1961). *Encounters.* Indianapolis: Bobbs-Merrill.

Hamilton-Smith, E. (1991). The construction of leisure. In B. L. Driver, P. J. Brown, & G. L. Peterson (Eds.), *Benefits of leisure.* State College, PA: Venture.

Hunnicutt, B. K. (1986). Problems raised by the empirical study of play and some humanistic alternatives. Abstracts from the 1986 Symposium on Leisure Research (pp. 8–10).

Hutchison, J. (1951). *Principles of recreation.* New York: Roland.

Iso-Ahola, S.E. (1980). *The social psychology of leisure and recreation.* Dubuque, IA: Wm. C. Brown.

Iso-Ahola, S. E. (1999). Motivational foundations of leisure. In E. L. Jackson & T. L. Burton (Eds.), *Leisure studies: Prospects for the twenty-first century* (pp. 35–51). State College, PA: Venture.

Jensen, C. R. (1979). *Outdoor Recreation in America.* Minneapolis, MN: Burgess.

Kelly, J. R. (1982). *Leisure*. Englewood Cliffs, NJ: Prentice-Hall

Kelly, J. R. (1983). *Leisure identities and interactions*. Boston: Allen & Unwin.

Kelly, J. R. (1987). *Freedom to be: A new sociology of leisure*. New York: Macmillan.

Kelly, J. R. (1990). *Leisure* (2nd ed.). Englewood Cliffs, NJ: Prentice-Hall.

Kelly, J. R. (1999). Leisure behaviors and styles: Social, economic, and cultural factors. In E. L. Jackson & T. L. Burton (Eds.), *Leisure studies: Prospects for the twenty-first century* (pp. 135–150). State College, PA: Venture.

Kleiber, D. (1999). *Leisure experience and human development: A dialectical interpretation*. New York: Basic Books.

Kleiber, D., Caldwell, L., & Shaw, S. (1992, October). Leisure meaning in adolescence. Paper presented at the 1992 Symposium on Leisure Research, Cincinnati, OH.

Kleiber, D., Larson, R., & Csikszentmihalyi, M. (1986). The experience of leisure in adolescence. *Journal of Leisure Research, 18,* 169–176.

Leonard, W. M., III. (1998). *A sociological perspective of sport* (5th ed.). Needham Heights, MA: Allyn & Bacon.

Little, S. L. (1993). Leisure program design and evaluation. *Journal of Physical Education, Recreation, and Dance, 64*(8), 26–29, 33.

Lynch, R. L. (1980). Social play: An interactional analysis of play in face-to-face social interaction. Doctoral dissertation, University of Illinois at Urbana-Champaign, 1979. *Dissertation Abstracts International, 41,* 804A.

Mannell, R. C. (1999). Leisure experience and satisfaction. In E. L. Jackson & T. L. Burton (Eds.), *Leisure studies: Prospects for the twenty-first century* (pp. 235–251). State College, PA: Venture.

Mannell, R. C., & Kleiber, D. A. (1997). *A social psychology of leisure*. State College, PA: Venture.

Murphy, J. F. (1974). *Concepts of leisure, philosophical implications*. Englewood Cliffs, NJ: Prentice-Hall.

Neulinger, J. (1974). *The psychology of leisure*. Springfield, IL: Charles C. Thomas.

Neulinger, J. (1981). *To leisure: An introduction*. Boston: Allyn & Bacon.

Patterson, M. E., Watson, A. E., Williams, D. R., & Roggenbuck, J. R. (1998). An hermeneutic approach to studying the nature of wilderness experiences. *Journal of Leisure Research, 30,* 423–435.

Pine, B. J., II, & Gilmore, J. H. (1999). *The experience economy: Work is theatre & every business a stage*. Boston: Harvard Business School Press.

Postrel, V. (1998). *The future and its enemies*. New York: The Free Press.

Rossman, J. R., & C. R. Edginton. (1989). Managing leisure programs: Toward a theoretical model. *Society and Leisure, 12*(1), 157–170.

Samdahl, D. M. (1988). A symbolic interactionist model of leisure: Theory and empirical support. *Leisure Sciences, 1,* 27–39.

Samdahl, D. (1992). Leisure in our lives: Exploring the common leisure occasion. *Journal of Leisure Research, 24,* 19–32.

Shaw, S. M. (1985). The meaning of leisure in everyday life. *Leisure Sciences, 7*, 1–24.

Stewart, W. P. (1999). Leisure as multiphase experiences: Challenging tradition. *Journal of Leisure Research, 30*, 391–400.

Sylvester, C. D. (1987, January). The politics of leisure, freedom, and poverty. *Parks and Recreation*, 59-62.

Unger, L. S. (1984). The effect of situational variables on the subjective leisure experience. *Leisure Sciences, 6*, 291–312.

Inclusive T-ball Leagues
Photo courtesy of Recreation and Park Commission for the Parish of East Baton Rouge, LA

How Individuals
Experience Leisure

The practice of a profession is based on a body of knowledge the practitioner is responsible for applying to the everyday affairs of his or her participants. The body of knowledge programmers use to accomplish this is the theory and knowledge of leisure behavior, which has increased dramatically over the past 20 years. During the past 15 years we have begun to integrate this knowledge into practice (Busser, 1993; Rossman, 1988, 1989, 1993; Rossman & Edginton, 1989).

To develop program services, programmers must understand how leisure is experienced and produced in occasions of social interaction. This requires an understanding of leisure behavior, the phenomenology of experiencing leisure, and an understanding of the structure of social occasions. These unique bodies of information provide the knowledge base that enables programmers to develop successful recreation programs that facilitate leisure experiences.

A SOCIAL SCIENCE THEORY OF PROGRAMMING

The theory of leisure programming presented in this book is based on a social science theory that views leisure as an interactional episode, consistent with the symbolic interactionist perspective of H. Blumer and N. K. Denzin. Sociological theory has three major approaches: structure-functionalist, conflict, and symbolic interactionist. Each is useful in different ways for investigating the nature of human social order. The structure-functionalist approach examines the basic structure of society, the roles and functions of its institutions, and how roles and institutions affect individual and collective action in society. Conflict sociology examines the role of conflict in a society and how power struggles affect the order of a society. Symbolic interactionism examines the "different dimensions of the construction of social reality through the seemingly autonomous activities of individuals," according to Eisenstadt and Curelaru (1977, p.46). They continue:

> [Symbolic interactionists'] . . . major contribution was in the exploration of different levels and types of "informal" and "subterranean" situations of human interaction which cut across formal arrangements and institutional settings, of the less fully organized dimension of everyday life: their phenomenology and nature; the structure and rules of interaction

KEY TERMS

**Symbolic
  Interactionism**
**Phases of the
  Leisure
  Experience**
Objects
**Self-Reflexive
Meaning**
Interaction
**Phenomenolgy
  of Experience**

To develop program services, programmers must understand how leisure is experienced and produced in occasions of social interaction.

that take place within them, as distinct from the formal institutional definition of goals; the mechanisms of interaction through which such situations are constructed and their perception by the participants in them; their impact on different levels of formal social organization. (Eisenstadt & Curelaru, 1977, pp. 46–47)

Symbolic interactionism is well established as an approach to understanding leisure behavior (Kelly, 1987; Kuentzel, 1990; Lee, 1990; Lee & Shafer, 2002; Samdahl, 1992). Lee and Shafer (2002) point out that "Leisure experiences are believed to be dynamic and to emerge through the interaction process" (p. 290). It is a relevant approach because it examines the social process of human behavior in the face-to-face interactions that constitute the bulk of leisure, play, recreation, game, and sport participation. The sole joy of leisure may be in participating in its construction (Kuentzel, 1990; Podilchak, 1991). For programmers, an interactionist approach is important for explaining how individuals structure their participation in leisure occasions and how they experience these occasions (Samdahl, 1988, 1992). Thus, it will be used as the theoretical base of recreation programming presented in this book.

...an interactionist approach is important for explaining how individuals structure their participation in leisure occasions and how they experience these occasions.

SYMBOLIC INTERACTION THEORY

Symbolic interactionism rests on three premises (Blumer, 1969; Denzin, 1978). Denzin provides a capsule explanation of the symbolic interactionist's theoretical perspective:

Symbolic interactionism rests on three basic assumptions. First, social reality as it is sensed, known, and understood is a social production. Interacting individuals produce and define their own definitions of situations. Second, humans are assumed to be capable of engaging in "minded," self-reflexive behavior. They are capable of shaping and guiding their own behavior and that of others. Third, in the course of taking their own standpoint and fitting that standpoint to the behaviors of others, humans interact with one another. Interaction is seen as an emergent, negotiated, often unpredictable concern. Interaction is symbolic because it involves the manipulation of symbols, words, meanings, and languages.

Integral to this perspective is the view that the social world of human beings is not made up of objects that have intrinsic meaning. The meaning of objects lies in the actions that human beings take toward them. Human experience is such that the process of defining objects is ever-changing, subject to redefinitions, relocations, and realignments. The interactionist assumes that humans learn their basic symbols, their conceptions of self, and the definitions they attach to social objects through interactions with others. Each person simultaneously carries on conversations with himself or herself and with significant others. Behavior is observable at the symbolic and the behavioral levels. (1978, p. 7)

Blumer (1969) distinguishes three slightly different assumptions of symbolic interactionism. When considered together with Denzin's assumptions, they present a comprehensive picture of symbolic interactionism:

> Symbolic interactionism rests in the last analysis on three simple premises. The first premise is that human beings act toward things on the basis of the meanings that the things have for them. Such things include everything that the human being may note in the world—physical objects, such as trees or chairs; other human beings, such as friends or enemies; institutions, such as a school or a government; guiding ideals, such as individual independence or honesty; activities of others, such as their commands or requests; and such situations as an individual encounters in his [or her] daily life. The second premise is that the meaning of such things is derived from, or arises out of, the social interaction that one has with one's fellows. The third premise is that these meanings are handled in, and modified through, an interpretive process used by the person in dealing with the things he [or she] encounters. (p. 2)

IMPLICATIONS OF SYMBOLIC INTERACTION FOR LEISURE PROGRAMMING

A theory that provides a basis for recreation programming should focus the programmer's attention and effort on the factors relevant to facilitating a leisure experience and thus provide direction to one's programming efforts. The symbolic interactionist perspective suggests that leisure is a unique meaning attributed to specific social occasions that are created by the individuals involved through interaction with objects in the occasions (Csikszentmihalyi, 1991; Kuentzel, 1990; Lee & Shafer, 2002; Samdahl, 1988, 1992; Shaw, 1985; Unger, 1984). Five points need to be developed for a full explanation and understanding of the implications of the theory for recreation programming: the phases of the leisure experience, the nature of objects acted on during interaction, how meaning is derived through interaction, how interaction is produced, and the phenomenology of experiencing leisure.

> There is growing evidence that leisure is a multi-phase experience.

PHASES OF THE LEISURE EXPERIENCE

There is growing evidence that leisure is a multi-phase experience (Madrigal, 2003; Lee & Shafer, 2002; Stewart, 1998b). At a minimum, it is experienced in three phases: anticipation, participation, and reflection. These are derived from Mead's (1934) concept of the "specious present"—the moment of participation. It is preceded by mental images of anticipation and succeeded by imaged reflections. This concept was applied to outdoor recreation by Clawson and Knetsch (1966), who expanded it to five phases: anticipation, travel to, on-site, travel back, and recollection.

Often, programmers only plan interventions for the participation phase and thus do not consider the total experience. This may cause the programmer to miss important opportunities for intervention and facilitation of the outcomes desired. Since satisfaction with a program is a function of fulfilling a participant's expectations, during the anticipation phase we must either discover them or try to manipulate them. For example, Skipper (1992) has demonstrated that the wording of advertising flyers can influence the number of participants who register and attend an event. McCarville (1993) found that patrons' expectations are influenced by how they are dealt with during phone inquiries about a program, registration procedures, and so on. Raymore (2002) has outlined how three types of facilitators to leisure (intrapersonal, interpersonal, and structural) are experienced or perceived by participants "...to enable or promote the formation of leisure preferences and to encourage or enhance participation" (p. 39). All of these can be known in the anticipation phase and planned for in a program's design.

Post-program interventions influence reflection on a program. The distribution and solicitation of evaluation information is both an important customer satisfaction activity and a source of information to use in documenting program outcomes and improving future operations of the program (Howe, 1993; Little, 1993). Patterson, Watson, Williams, and Roggenbuck (1998) found that participants spent the period of time immediately following an intense outdoor recreation experience sorting through and analyzing the meaning of what occurred. Kiewa (2001) found evidence that climbers reflect on their climbing experiences to reconcile how the current experience affected their narration of self. Post program debriefing, publishing photographs, staging reunions, and selling souvenirs are all interventions designed to influence the recollection phase of a leisure experience.

Thus, symbolic interaction theory suggests a need to expand the programmer's responsibility for intervention from dealing exclusively with the participation phase of an experience to also include the anticipation and reflection phases.

THE NATURE OF LEISURE OBJECTS

Objects are anything that can be indicated, pointed out, or referred to (Blumer, 1969). Objects receive our focused attention and are consciously dealt with during interaction. Human beings act toward objects on the basis of the meanings that the objects have for them, and their meaning is derived through interaction.

There are only three categories of objects: physical, social, and symbolic. Physical objects are those that may be used in the leisure occasion, such as balls, bats, craft supplies, and so forth. Social objects are other people, including leaders, friends, mothers, and other participants in a program. Most leisure occasions are participated in with family or friends (Cheek, Field, & Burdge, 1976). People are the ultimate interactive objects, because another person offers more social interaction possibilities than any other type of object. Symbolic objects are ideas, philosophies, doctrines, and they too present possibilities for interaction. That is, individuals can form a line of behavior based on them. Notions about moral or immoral recreation influence the leisure behavior of many individuals. Concepts about cooperation and competition

One must program all three phases of experience—anticipation, participation, and reflection.

Objects receive our focused attention and are consciously dealt with during interaction.

also influence interactions in leisure occasions. Programmers often program in order to reify abstract concepts, such as those associated with Valentine's Day, for example, love, Cupid, hearts, and other symbolic objects.

These three types encompass all possible objects that can be indicated, pointed out, or referred to in social occasions. They are the objects of all interaction. Programmers need to learn which objects make essential contributions to the leisure experience and which are superfluous so that decisions can be made about which of them must be included in a given program. In Chapter Three, we will focus further on the objects included in leisure occasions.

DERIVING MEANING FROM INTERACTION IN LEISURE OCCASIONS

The meaning of objects arises out of the interaction one has with them. Meaning is not inherent in an object: "Creating meaning involves bringing order to the contents of the mind by integrating one's actions into a unified flow experience" (Csikszentmihalyi, 1991, p. 216). Thus, meaning is derived through interaction with social objects. Blumer (1969) states that:

> [Symbolic interactionism] sees meaning as arising in the process of interaction between people. The meaning of a thing for a person grows out of the ways in which other persons act toward the person with regard to the thing. Their actions operate to define the thing for the person. Thus, symbolic interactionism sees meanings as social products, as creations that are formed in and through the defining activities of people as they interact. (pp. 4–5)

Meaning is produced socially through interaction with physical, social, and symbolic objects. Therefore, meaning is situationally specific, and the meaning of an object can change from occasion to occasion. For example, Mann (1973) points out that queues for leisure events have a different meaning than queues for other functions. Hunnicutt (1986) suggested that to "play" with an object is to experience it in a totally different way than through any other modes of interaction.

Furthermore, meaning is negotiated within the context of interaction. Lee (1990) has documented that leisure is situationally interpreted by individuals based on the social context in which they have the experience. It is often the case that participants, especially individuals who are new to an activity, do not have well-defined expectations about what they will derive from participating in a specific activity (Patterson et al., 1998). Meaning and expectations are negotiated and developed by participating. Hultsman (1998) found that over the course of a multi-day event, satisfied participants were those capable of coping with an event by either modifying their behavior or their expectations. Construing the meaning of a leisure experience, then, seems to occur both while an activity is being experienced (Kelly, 1999), as well as immediately after the event (Patterson et al., 1998; Kiewa, 2001).

2

Construing the meaning of a leisure experience seems to occur both while an activity is being experienced as well as immediately after the event.

Exercise 2-1: Symbolic Interaction Theory and You

1. Write down the name of an object in your life that is meaningful to you (Examples: new CD, hockey stick, backpack, swim suit).
2. Write down three ways that you "act toward that object." In other words, what do you do with it?
3. What the object means to you is related to social interactions that you have with the object. Write down two completely different social interactions that resulted in you feeling completely different about the object.
4. Wait a second! Do you suppose the "objects" we've been discussing always have to be tangible objects? Why or why not?

Meanings are situational productions constructed by individuals based on internalized conversations with themselves while interacting with physical, social, or abstract objects.

Meaning arises out of the interaction one has with objects in an occasion. Interaction in leisure occasions results in a different meaning than interaction in other occasions because of the perceived freedom of participants, the intrinsic satisfaction of participating, and finally because of the satisfaction of being the cause of an act; that is, being an active participant in creating and sustaining the interactions. Meaning occurs within and as a result of interaction (Goffman, 1983; Kelly, 1999), and the leisure experience emerges from this interaction (Stewart, 1998b). Thus, programmers must be concerned with the interactions in a program and assure the occurrence of key, meaning-deriving interactions that will result in participants construing that they had a leisure experience. How this is dealt with in programming will be discussed further in Chapter Eleven. Now complete Exercise 2-1.

HOW INTERACTION IS PRODUCED IN SOCIAL OCCASIONS

Meanings are developed and modified through a process of interpretation during occasions of interaction that demand that individuals interpret the meaning of objects encountered. Face-to-face interaction is defined by Goffman (1959) as "the reciprocal influence of individuals upon one another's actions when in one another's immediate physical presence" (p. 15). Lee and Shafer (2002) found empirical proof of this process in a recent study of trail users. Goffman (1967) goes on to describe how individuals organize their behavior in social occasions that arise from "the co-mingling of persons and the temporary interactional enterprises that can arise there from" and characterizes the comingling of individuals as "a shifting entity necessarily evanescent, created by arrivals and killed by departures" (p. 2).

Social gatherings are constructed by the interactions of minded, self-reflexive individuals who align their actions based on their interpretations of the meaning they attribute to the actions of others in the occasion. It is important to note here that symbolic interactionism has as one of its root assumptions the notion that human beings are capable of minded, self-reflexive behavior (Denzin, 1978). That is, they are capable of guiding their own behavior and developing a joint line of behavior with others through interaction with them. This notion is crucial to defining the dimensions of leisure experiences: Individuals must be actively engaged in the joint construction of the occasion, and this occurrence is a necessary condition for perceptions of competence and consequent intrinsic satisfaction with participation.

In Goffman's view, the social order created by such activity is fragile and can be sustained only by the focused attention of each participant. Leisure is experienced in social occasions where interaction occurs among individuals. The interaction requires the individuals to take account of each other's actions, interpret the meaning of each object in the occasion, and form a line of behavior based on this interpretation. This basic interaction ritual continues through repeated cycles of this same basic scenario. During instances of interaction, the meaning of objects is built up through interaction with them. During interaction, an individual engages in a process of interpretation by carrying on an internal conversation in order to identify the meaning of objects based on the immediate situation and on the direction to be taken. Meanings are thus situational productions constructed by individuals based on internalized conversations with themselves while interacting with physical, social, or abstract objects. The meaning attributed to objects in this manner shapes individual lines of behavior in social occasions, and that is how social occasions are created.

Evidence of this ongoing interaction and negotiation of meaning is beginning to emerge in the research literature (Stewart, 1998a; Lee & Shafer, 2002). Based on an investigation of rock climbers, Kiewa (2001) concludes that the notion of positive affect or control of participation in an activity cannot occur unless the participant deliberately and willingly embraces participation in an activity. She observes that a program determined and structured by another cannot provide the experience desired. The point cannot be made too often that the implication of this process for programming is the need to create opportunities for participants to engage in action. Thus, the programmer must be concerned with the process of participating; that is, the occurrence and order of interactions in a leisure event. This topic will also be dealt with further in Chapter Eleven. Now complete Exercise 2-2 on page 28.

EXPERIENCING LEISURE

How, then, do individuals experience leisure? "Experience is going through an episode or event as well as processing the perceptions of that time period," according to Kelly (1987, p. 20). More recent research has confirmed that during participation, "…people's situational identities are, in essence, constantly being tested as interactions occur" (Lee & Shafer, 2002, p. 306). "Recreation activities are behavioral construc-

…the notion of positive affect or control of participation in an activity cannot occur unless the participant deliberately and willingly embraces participation in an activity.

Exercise 2-2: Play Cards to Practice Symbolic Interaction Theory (20 minutes)

Objective:
During the card game exercise, the class will discover the things that can cause the meaning of a social occasion to be modified.

Equipment needed:
One complete set of playing cards per group of four students. Desks should be arranged into small groups accordingly.

Directions:
Each group should select a game to play (examples: Hearts, Euchre, Rummy, Go Fish) and then begin playing for approximately 10 minutes.

Discussion Questions:
1. What were the leisure objects in this exercise?
2. What was the central object?
3. Initially, what meaning did the object have for each person in the group?
4. How did the meaning change as play began among group members?
5. What events, if any, caused you to modify the meanings you had for the object?

tions that people build" (More & Averill, 2003, p. 372). Interaction in an episode is sensing one's self, the selves presented by others, and other elements in an environment. It occurs through the conscious direction and interpretation of one's behavior in response to actions encountered in the environment. It is evaluated during and after an episode by determining how one's situated self has been confirmed or altered by the experience. Order and satisfaction are achieved when we have made decisions within an episode of interaction that enable us to reach our personal goals, which may be to confirm or change our personal narrative of our self-concept. Four implications from this theory directly affect the programmer's efforts.

1. Occasions of interaction are emergent productions. Interaction is constructed in real time in which self-reflexive individuals chose the line of behavior they will follow. Despite staff efforts to plan and predict how behavior will play out in a given program, individuals who enter activities will interpret the meaning of the objects differently, and their respondent actions will differ accordingly. Programmers must understand how humans shape meaning and how that meaning shapes action. Each occasion of interaction is constructed anew each time it is experienced, and a past success is no guarantee that the same combination of circumstances will again lead to the same outcome.

2. *Occasions of interaction are fragile.* Providing the experience desired in an occasion is sometimes difficult because of the fragility of social occasions. More and Averill (2003) indicate that all recreation activities are made up of two subsystems—"...prototypic subsystems (those present in virtually all instances of the activity) and design subsystems (optional subsystems that adapt the activity to serve multiple goals" (p. 372). The prototypic are the structural elements of a given activity to be true to its form; for example, the rules of a game or sport event. Design elements are those that are more flexible and may be manipulated to meet program or participant outcome expectations. Programmers should avoid imposing structures that are so rigid that they will interfere with an individual participant's perceived freedom or the opportunity for focused experience needed to achieve intrinsic satisfaction. Programmers can actually destroy the experience they are trying to facilitate by forcing programmatic controls and manipulations to operate a program.

3. *People always play a role in constructing leisure occasions.* According to symbolic interactionist theory, individuals always play a part in shaping the direction of an interactional episode and the meaning of interaction for them. Csikszentmihalyi (1991) emphasizes this point: "It [happiness] does not depend on outside events, but rather on how we interpret them" (p. 2). Thus, optimal experience is something individuals make happen through the conscious interpretation and volitional direction of interaction. The autonomy of the individual must be respected in program development. If the programmer provides too much direction, the patron may not have a sufficient opportunity for involvement.

4. *The programmer must help situate the event by providing some form and structure to the occasion.* It is crucial to understand this concept and how

...optimal experience (leisure) is something individuals make happen through the conscious interpretation and volitional direction of interaction.

it enables those present in an occasion to be set free so leisure may be experienced. Patterson and colleagues (1998) describe this phenomena as "situated freedom," and Kelly (1999) calls it "situated action." Goffman (1983) explains that all occasions of interaction are directed by a series of enabling conventions; in other words, rules of interaction that may range from the very formal through tacitly agreed-to conventions. Participating in interaction, then, requires participants to pay the small price of agreeing to abide by the conventions, so that they may obtain the large benefit of participating in the interaction facilitated by the conventions without having to continually renegotiate the rules.

The conventions that situate a leisure event come from two sources: the relational history of participants and the rules of interaction. Many leisure experiences occur in informal interaction with family and friends where an individual's true self is already a known and accepted entity. Thus, there is no need to continually renegotiate who one is (Samdahl, 1992), and the true self can interact with a degree of freedom not possible in interactions where the self must be continually renegotiated. In a similar manner, the rules of interaction create or define a social order and the acceptable roles a person is to assume in this defined occasion of interaction. For example, in an occasion with very formalized rules, such as a game of racquetball, two players previously unknown to each other may play and know the roles and expectations each is to perform to sustain the occasion of interaction. This is possible because they both know and accept the rules of interaction in racquetball and are thus freed to attend to the defined requirements of the game. In this way, conventions of interaction create the freedom to present a known self and to interact freely. This uniqueness helps define leisure occasions.

Knowledge about the phenomenology of experiencing leisure, then, gives the following direction to programmers: To facilitate leisure experiences, the programmer must develop a situated activity system. This requires situating an occasion of leisure by providing social order (form and structure) through conventions that provide interactive social space. This space must afford participants the opportunity to actively interact in a manner that results in perceived freedom and intrinsic satisfaction for them, plus provide fun, enjoyment, and/or relaxation. Now complete Exercise 2-3 on page 29.

CONCLUSION

Professional programmers rely on the theory of leisure behavior to guide the development of program services. Symbolic interaction is a theory that attempts to understand behavior at the level of face-to-face interaction; it assumes that individuals participate in the construction of occasions of interaction and the meaning of them. The theory suggests that programmers must give increased attention to how they operate programs and how they are experienced by the patrons. Understanding how to intervene to facilitate leisure is a crucial programming concept that includes understanding how meaning is produced through interaction, and what meanings must result for an occasion to be construed as leisure.

REFERENCES

Blumer, H. (1969). *Symbolic interactionism*. Englewood Cliffs, NJ: Prentice-Hall.

Busser, J. A. (Ed.). (1993, October). Leisure programming: The state of the art in leisure today. *Journal of Physical Education, Recreation, and Dance, 64*(8), 25–26.

Cheek, N. H., Field, D.R., & Burdge, R. J. (1976). *Leisure and recreation places*. Ann Arbor, MI: Ann Arbor Science.

Clawson, M., & Knetsch, J. L. (1966). *Economics of outdoor recreation*. Baltimore: Johns Hopkins Press.

Csikszentmihalyi, M. (1991). *Flow: The psychology of optimal experience*. New York: Harper Perennial.

Denzin, N. K. (1978). *The research act* (2nd ed.). New York: McGraw-Hill.

Eisenstadt, S. N., & Curelaru, M. (1977). Macrosociology theory, analysis, and comparative studies. *Current Sociology, 25*(2), 44–47.

Goffman, E. (1959). *The presentation of self in everyday life*. Garden City, NY: Doubleday.

Goffman, E. (1967). *Interaction ritual*. Garden City, NY: Anchor Books.

Goffman, E. (1983). The interaction order. *American Sociological Review, 458*(2), 1–17.

Howe, C. Z. (1993). The evaluation of leisure programs. *Journal of Physical Education, Recreation, and Dance, 64*(8), 43–46.

Hultsman, W. (1998). The multi-day, competitive leisure event: Examining satisfaction over time. *Journal of Leisure Research, 30*, 472–497.

Hunnicutt, B. K. (1986). Problems raised by the empirical study of play and some humanistic alternatives. Abstracts from the 1986 Symposium on Leisure Research, 8–10.

Kelly, J. R. (1987). *Freedom to be: A new sociology of leisure*. New York: Macmillan.

Kelly, J. R. (1999). Leisure behaviors and styles: Social, economic, and cultural factors. In E. L. Jackson & T. L. Burton (Eds.), *Leisure studies: Prospects for the twenty-first century* (pp. 135–150). State College, PA: Venture.

Kiewa, J. (2001). Control over self and space in rock climbing. *Journal of Leisure Research, 33*, 363-382.

Kuentzel, W. F. (1990, October). Motive uniformity across recreational activities and settings: A synthesis of research. Paper presented at the National Recreation and Parks Association Research Symposium, Phoenix, AZ.

Lee, B., & Shafer, C. S. (2002). The dynamic nature of leisure experience; An application of affect control theory. *Journal of Leisure Research, 34*, 290-310.

Lee, Y. (1990, October). Immediate leisure experiences: A phenomenological approach. Paper presented at the 1990 National Recreation and Park Association Leisure Research Symposium, Phoenix, AZ.

Little, S. L. (1993). Leisure program design and evaluation. *Journal of Physical Education, Recreation, and Dance, 64*(8), 26–29, 33.

Madrigal, R. (2003). Investigating an evolving leisure experience: Antecedents and consequences of spectator affect during a live
sporting event. *Journal of Leisure Research, 35,* 23-48.

Mann, L. (1973). Learning to live with lines. In J. Helmer & N. A. Ed-
dington, (Eds.), *Urbanman: The psychology of urban survival.*
New York: Macmillan.

McCarville, R. E. (1993). Keys to quality programming. *Journal of Physical Education, Recreation, and Dance, 64*(8), 34–36, 46, 47.

Mead, G. H. (1934). *Mind, self, and society.* University of Chicago Press.

More, T. A., & Averill, J. R. (2003). The structure of recreation behavior.
Journal of Leisure Research, 35, 372-395.

Patterson, M. E., Watson, A. E., Williams, D. R., & Roggenbuck, J. R.
(1998). An hermeneutic approach to studying the nature of
wilderness experiences. *Journal of Leisure Research, 30,* 423–435.

Podilchak, W. (1991). Distinctions of fun, enjoyment, and leisure. *Leisure Studies, 10,* 133–148.

Raymore, L. A. (2002). Facilitators to leisure. *Journal of Leisure Research,
34,* 37-51.

Rossman, J. R. (1988). Development of a leisure programming theory.
Journal of Park and Recreation Administration, 6(4), 1–13.

Rossman, J. R. (1989). *Recreation programming: Designing leisure experiences.* Champaign, IL: Sagamore.

Rossman, J. R. (1993). Integrating theory and practice into leisure
program design. In A. J. Veal, P. Jonson, & G. Cushman (Eds.),
Leisure and Tourism: Social and Environmental Change. (Papers
from the World Leisure and Recreation Association Congress,
Sydney, Australia, 16–19 July 1991, pp. 485–489). Sydney, Australia: Centre for Leisure and Tourism Studies, University of
Technology.

Rossman, J. R., & Edginton, C. R. (1989). Managing leisure programs:
Toward a theoretical model. *Society and Leisure, 12,* 157–170.

Samdahl, D. M. (1988). A symbolic interactionist model of leisure:
Theory and empirical support. *Leisure Sciences, 1,* 27–39.

Samdahl, D. M. (1992). The common leisure occasion. *Journal of Leisure
Research, 24,* 19–32.

Shaw, S. M. (1985). The meaning of leisure in everyday life. *Leisure Sciences 7,* 1–24.

Skipper, B. A. (1992). The relationship between desired results and the
marketing tools used in recreation programming (Doctoral
dissertation, University of North Texas, 1992). *Dissertation
Abstracts International, 53,* 3364A.

Stewart, W. P. (Ed.). (1998a). Leisure as multiphase experience [Special
issue]. *Journal of Leisure Research, 30*(4).

Stewart, W. P. (1998b). Leisure as multiphase experiences: Challenging
tradition. *Journal of Leisure Research, 30,* 391–400.

Unger, L. S. (1984). The effect of situational variables on the subjective
leisure experience. *Leisure Sciences, 6,* 291–312.

Teen Cooking Class
Photo courtesy of City of Aurora, Colorado, Department of Library, Recreation, & Cultural Services

Six Key Elements
of a Situated Activity System

In this chapter, we will discuss the elements that situate an instance of interaction. All instances of leisure involve the interactions of one or more persons who are orienting their behavior toward themselves and other physical, social, or symbolic objects (Denzin, 1975). This co-orientation of selves occurs in a situated social system; that is, it occurs in a social occasion that has an identifiable set of elements that give it form and structure.

Erving Goffman dedicated his career to investigating and identifying the dynamics of face-to-face interaction in social occasions in an effort to identify the generic set of elements that are present in these occasions. From Goffman's work, Denzin (1975) has identified six generic elements that structure all social occasions:

> . . . differentially self-reflexive actors; place or setting itself (e.g., the physical territory); social objects which fill the setting and are acted on by the actors in question; a set of rules of a civil–legal, polite–ceremonial, and relationally specific nature which explicitly or tacitly guide and shape interaction; a set of relationships which bind interactants to one another; and a shifting set of definitions reflective of each actor's co-orientation to self and others during the interaction sequence. (p. 462)

These six elements situate instances of social interaction. In order to develop leisure services, the programmer must take account of or manage these six key elements to provide opportunities for participants to actively engage their environment. Their effect on a program is of such fundamental importance that a change in any one element changes the situation of the program. Collectively, they constitute a social system for instances of interaction to occur.

Murphy, Williams, Niepoth, and Brown (1973) state, "The basic method used by agencies to structure opportunities which encourage different kinds of recreation behaviors is the creation and/or manipulation of physical and human environments" (p. 77). The literature on leisure programming has never elaborated on the generic elements to be created and manipulated. An assumption of this text is that each leisure program is a series of interaction episodes that occurs in a uniquely configured situation of these six elements. These six

3

KEY TERMS

**Situated Activity
  System**
**Six Elements of
  a Situated
  Activity
  System**
**Social
  Interaction**
**Interacting
  People**
Physical Setting
Leisure Objects
Structure
Relationships
Animation
**Service
  Continuum**

*All instances
of leisure
involve the
interactions
of one or
more persons
who are orienting their
behavior
toward themselves and
other physical, social,
or symbolic
objects.*

are the key elements of program production because they are all that a programmer can manipulate, or needs to manipulate, in developing a leisure program.

Interaction occurs as a linear sequence of episodes, with only one episode given focused attention at any given moment by the individuals in the social occasion. Any one element can be the most important element in any single episode. The importance of any single element can shift with the transition from one episode to another. Interaction is made up of a series of episodes that occur in sequential order. Within an individual program, each element assumes a shifting role of importance as the interactions of the program progress.

The task of the leisure programmer is to identify the unique configuration of these six elements that situate a program, to anticipate how the series of episodes that make up the program will unfold, and to determine how the face-to-face interactions of a program can be manipulated to move participants through the program. The programmer anticipates and plans how the action sequences in each episode will unfold, and then puts in place the mechanisms needed to guide the occurrence of the intended interactions. The programmer does this vicariously by experiencing the program before its actual occurrence. In this process, the programmer tries to anticipate and predict the outcomes of interactions within a program and the order in which events during the interaction will unfold. The process is analogous to writing the script of a play, except that in leisure programs, the interactants are not bound by the script, but actually play a role in shaping the event. The program design process will be explained in greater detail in Chapter Eleven.

Adopting this viewpoint makes clear the problematic nature of program design, planning, and operation. Interacting individuals are one of the six elements that situate an instance of interaction. But once the individuals enter an occasion, they are not bound to follow the action scenarios designed by the programmer. The overall outcome of an individual program depends on the interactions of individuals with the other five elements, the interactions of individuals with each other, and the interaction of all six elements with each other. Pfeffer and Salancik (1978) make clear the problematic nature of interdependent events: "Interdependence is the reason why nothing comes out quite the way one wants it to. Any event that depends on more than a single causal agent is an outcome based on interdependent agents" (p. 40). This is the case when designing and operating leisure programs.

A familiarity with social interaction theory will help programmers understand how humans experience and construct their participation in leisure programs. Research on social interaction has led to the development of a generic structure of a social occasion; namely, the six elements that situate instances of interaction and provide a social system for it to occur. These are the elements that programmers can create and manipulate in order to program leisure experiences. Because of the emergent and negotiated nature of interaction (Stewart, 1998), any program plan is best viewed as a probability estimate of what the programmer believes will happen in an occasion of planned interaction. Any program plan must have a "loose–tight" notion to it. There must be a tight enough structure to move participants toward the desired goals of the program, but it must be loose enough to accommodate participants interacting and negotiating their way through the program's activities.

Although the elements that situate a program can be reduced to six generic categories, one would be deceived by believing that only six variables need to be manipulated. The number of possibilities within each element is large. Furthermore, the number of possible combinations of elements is even larger. The six elements do, however, provide a compact conceptual framework from which programmers can organize their efforts. Programmers create this situated production by understanding the existence of these elements and controlling or manipulating them. Some elements may be unalterable in some programs and therefore not subject to manipulation. In developing a program design, the programmer must anticipate the implications that an unalterable element has on the remaining elements that can be manipulated.

SIX KEY ELEMENTS

The six elements identified by Goffman and Denzin have been renamed to clarify conceptually their role in program design. The new names are the following: interacting people, physical setting, leisure objects, structure, relationships, and animation. An explanation of the role and effect that each of these elements has in a program is presented in the sections that follow.

INTERACTING PEOPLE

Leisure is a human experience created by differentially self-reflexive individuals interacting in social occasions. As discussed earlier, social occasions are constructed by interacting individuals who build a line of behavior after taking account of their own behavior and that of others in the occasion. Effective programming requires the programmer either to anticipate who the specific individuals will be and to design the program for them, or to design the program for a specific type of individual and then recruit this type of individual into the program.

When different individuals come into a program, it changes. A perfect illustration of this point is the operation of programs for youth. Often the same program can be operated successfully year after year. The configuration of the other five elements does not change—only the individuals in the program change. For example, in a typical program for youth there may be a different cohort of 6-year-old children who participate in the same program each year. Even though the basic program has not changed, it continues to be successful. What has changed are the individuals in the program. Since one of the program elements has changed, the program itself has in fact changed.

Many programmers have had similar experiences. Having operated a program that originally failed, they offer the same program a second time with no change other than the individuals; with this one change, the program succeeds. One possible reason for program failure, then, is that individuals are recruited into a program that is inappropriate for them. If a different group of individuals is recruited, the program may succeed with no other changes.

When different individuals come into a program, it changes.

Because people are one of the major elements of program design, programmers must take great care in investigating or anticipating who these individuals are and what benefits they seek from participation. A solid understanding of life span development will aid programmers in understanding the benefits participants seek from participation in leisure. To do so, it is necessary to understand the physical, social, and psychological development of individuals; to understand their gender, age, skill level, and other pertinent information about them. For example, from birth to late adulthood humans develop socially, physically, and psychologically. The preschool years are characterized by child-centered play, careful supervision, gross motor development, short attention spans, and the need for immediate gratification. The childhood years are marked by increased social skills, awareness of others, fine motor skill development, creativity, and competency (Patterson, 1991).

Adolescent characteristics include puberty, social awkwardness, and peer acceptance. A desire for autonomy often spurs conflict between adolescents and their parents. During young adulthood, finding meaningful relationships and work are central concerns. Taking risks asserts one's independence and demonstrates skill competency (Lifespan Development, 2001).

In adulthood, wisdom and expertise develop concomitantly with learning and knowledge. The need for belonging is often filled by marriage or a relationship with a significant other. The physical body gradually changes in appearance as one grows older. Social commitments may involve children, work, and civic responsibilities. In this time period, "Leisure can represent activity, status, diversion, and autonomy" (Patterson, 1991, p. 32).

Older adulthood is marked by age-related physical and biological change. One's experience in retirement is influenced by factors of socioeconomic status. Life satisfaction will often depend on staying involved with family and friends, with leisure serving as the catalyst.

These are examples of how social, physiological, and psychological characteristics intermingle, change, and influence leisure participation throughout the life span. For more information for these and other human characteristics, please consult human development literature.

Marketing literature has pointed out the need to design programs for specific individuals through market segmentation (Howard & Crompton, 1980, p. 338) and to develop services for a well-defined target market. Although agency goal statements often suggest that programs are for all people regardless of race, age, gender, ethnic origin, and so forth, we know that every program, to be successful, must be targeted for a specific group of individuals whom we can define with some precision. The programmer deals with this issue in one of two ways—either through macro or micro market segmentation (Crompton, 1983, pp. 10–19).

Macro segmentation involves developing services for a cohort of individuals who are seeking similar benefits from participation in recreation programs. The notion of a benefit package comes from the personal meaning of leisure that was discussed in Chapter One. Crompton (1983) has pointed out that the desires of each potential client are likely to be unique, but agencies cannot afford the resources to develop services

...every program, to be successful, must be targeted for a specific group of individuals whom we can define with some precision.

for each client. Because of resource limitations, the programmer is then forced to compromise and to group together individuals who desire similar benefits from participating in specific leisure occasions. These benefits may include any number of psychological outcomes, such as achievement, autonomy, socialization, or risk. Driver and Brown (1975) have identified a number of possible psychological outcomes of leisure participation. In macro segmentation, the programmer develops a service to satisfy a projected benefit package that has been identified, and then individuals who want this projected benefit package are recruited into the program.

But programmers have no assurance that such a group indeed exists for the service identified. For example, through market research one could produce evidence that a group of individuals desires physical fitness and social interaction. This is a benefit package that is sought. Further investigation identifies an actual group of mothers, 23 to 30 years of age with preschool children, who would like an aerobics fitness program in their neighborhood between 9:30 and 11:30 in the morning, with nursery service provided. The programmer then develops this service for the specific individuals identified. Sometimes, however, it is impossible to identify further the specific cohort of individuals who desire this service, so it is developed solely on the basis of data suggesting that there is a group of unidentified individuals who seek this benefit package. In these cases, programs are developed slowly through trial and error until the individuals who desire the benefits of the program can be identified.

When micro segmentation is used, cohorts of specific individuals are identified by using various traditional segmentation variables from one of three categories: geographic location descriptors (neighborhood, city, distance from program location), sociodemographic descriptors (age, income, gender, education), or behavioral descriptors (usage rates, level of specialization, psychological benefits sought; Crompton, 1983, p. 14). Once target groups are identified, the programmer develops specific services to fill the benefit package that is desired by people in the group.

The difference between these two techniques is in the timing, or the point at which one begins dealing with actual individuals. In macro segmentation, a benefit or a package of benefits is first identified, and then the programmer tries to identify the characteristics of the individuals who want the benefits. Sometimes, though, it is impossible to identify actual individuals initially. In this case, the programmer has only a projected benefit package that is desired by a group of individuals whose identity is unknown. In micro segmentation, individuals are identified first, and then the benefits they seek are identified.

The individuals who participate are thus a key element in the design of a program. All programs are either consciously or inadvertently designed to meet the needs of a specific cohort of individuals. Effective programming involves matching the right group of individuals with the correct service so that the benefits sought can be obtained. One possible reason that a program fails is that the programmer has not matched the correct group of individuals with a program design that provides the desired benefits. A principle of program design implied by this element

...the physical setting is one of the key elements that situate a program.

of place can be stated as follows: *When the individuals in a program change, the program changes. Changing the individuals in a program may be the only change needed to make an unsuccessful program successful. Further, it is essential to plan programs for the identified needs of specific individuals or the projected needs of a group believed to exist in the service community. The more information a programmer can obtain about the individuals who will actually be in a program, the better chance the programmer has of designing and operating a program that will meet the needs of the participants.*

THE PHYSICAL SETTING

The physical setting for a program is the second element to be discussed. The physical setting includes one or more of the following sensory components: visual, aural, olfactory, tactile, and taste. Each component will affect a program if it is consciously or unconsciously included in the program design or if it is inadvertently omitted from the design. The physical setting is an expansive concept, so not all possible settings can be discussed here. However, it is important to recognize that the physical setting is one of the key elements that situate a program. If the setting changes, the program itself will change. Three considerations about the physical setting for a program are especially important.

First, programmers must understand the uniqueness of a setting. Too often, they try to duplicate a program that was successful elsewhere, only to fail because they do not understand that a unique setting was the key element contributing to the program's success. For example, one military installation started a successful program in which the patrons would bring their lunch every Friday and listen to a small musical combo while eating. Several other installations tried unsuccessfully to duplicate the program. They served the same type of food, had the same type of music, and used the same promotional materials and strategy. Eventually, the success of the original program was attributed to its unique setting—an ocean side area where the combos played on a hill with beautiful waves breaking in the background. This unique setting simply could not be duplicated at other installations.

Programmers must be able to analyze what elements contribute to the success of their programs for several reasons. Knowing if a unique physical setting is the major element contributing to a program's success and whether the setting can be duplicated is a critical piece of information needed before attempting to duplicate a program that was successful elsewhere. Sometimes, if the setting cannot be duplicated, the program itself cannot be successfully duplicated.

Second, programmers must understand the limits of a setting. Too often, the setting is not adequate for a program. For example, one of the authors was once asked to operate a program with active games for elementary school children in a neighborhood recreation center that had not been designed for active play. In fact, to create an open setting, the architect had put glass walls on almost two full sides of the room to be used for active games. After replacing several panes of glass, the administration suspended playing active games "because the building was not designed for active play"! Some settings are simply not suitable for certain programs. An inappropriate setting may even detract from an event.

> Programmers must be able to analyze what elements contribute to the success of their programs...

> ...it is important to ascertain whether the program to be produced requires a unique setting for success.

Third, settings can be manipulated with decorations, lighting, and other physical alterations. Programmers should therefore realize when a unique physical setting is necessary for the success of a program. Once it is determined that a unique setting is needed, the programmer can begin to find or to create such a setting for the program. If programmers do not understand how a unique setting contributes to the success of a program, they cannot hope to duplicate the program elsewhere.

The more a physical environment is altered, the more expensive the alteration becomes. For example, an artificial ice rink can be kept frozen during the summer, although the high energy consumption that is needed to keep it frozen is expensive. Making an inadequate setting adequate is almost always possible if enough resources are available. But the cost of doing so may far exceed any potential benefit. It is therefore very important to understand how essential a unique physical setting is to the success of a program before beginning expensive alterations of the physical environment.

The physical setting is the second program element a programmer must evaluate. Although there is much to consider, it is important to ascertain whether the program to be produced requires a unique setting for success. Knowing the limits of a setting, and the many ways to alter it to make it adequate, are also important pieces of information.

LEISURE OBJECTS

As discussed in the previous chapter, there are three types of objects: physical, social, and symbolic. In programming, one must be able to identify the key objects that fill a leisure setting and are acted on when people interact during a program. Not every object needs to be identified, only the key objects that must be present for a program to occur and be successful. The question to answer that brings focus to this inquiry is: What objects are needed to support the interactions intended for the program?

For example, in Oak Park, Illinois, one author, along with other staff, was attempting to develop a different program design for the annual children's Easter Egg Hunt. Several objects were identified that were considered critical for such an event. The list included enough Easter eggs for all children to have a good probability of finding at least one egg; a beautiful park with grass, trees, and bushes for hiding the eggs; and a costumed Easter Bunny for children to visit in a surrealistic forest created with painted panels. The park itself was obviously the concern of the previous section on physical setting. However, the eggs and the Easter Bunny were important objects that would contribute to this event. They were assumed to be so critical that they could not be excluded; if these objects were not available, the event would not occur.

Too often, programmers are willing to continue with an event even though they do not have enough objects or they do not have the objects that are essential to operate a program successfully. Appropriate objects, whether they are physical, social, or symbolic, are sometimes the critical program elements. Programmers need to be able to determine which objects are essential, which are optional, and which actually detract from the event being planned and should be excluded. For

What objects are needed to support the interactions intended for the program?

The regulating effects that rules impose on a program cannot be underestimated.

*...program-
mers need to
understand
how regula-
tions im-
pinge on
perceived
freedom...*

the Easter Egg Hunt to be successful, the programmer assumed it was essential that each child find an Easter egg. If there were not enough eggs to make this possible, the event could not occur. Easter eggs are an essential object for an Easter Egg Hunt—there is no substitute for them. Special prize eggs were also provided that, if found, entitled the bearer to a large chocolate rabbit. These prizes were considered optional and were to be included as long as the budget allowed for their purchase. In previous years, the beginning of the hunt was signaled with a starting gun. During the redesign of this program, the gun was considered detrimental to the atmosphere intended for the event, so the hunt was begun with an air horn.

Programmers must identify the key objects that are essential to supporting the interactions intended in a program. Objects can be either essential to the success of a program, optional to its success, or detrimental to a program.

STRUCTURE

All programs are provided organizational structure by a set of rules and program formats that guide interactions in a program. The structure provided by the programmer determines how interactions may or may not unfold. Rules make certain interactions possible while restricting others. Here, the term rules is being used in a generic sense to include civil–legal, polite–ceremonial, and relational rules. With this conception, all of the rules—including laws, administrative regulations imposed by the agency, the codified rules of a game, the ceremonial rules of a game, and the relational rules of everyday discourse—need to be considered. How each or all of these rules will affect the interactions in a program must be anticipated and planned into the program design. At the same time, programmers need to make certain there are enough rules to direct interactions in a manner desired, but not so many rules that the freedom needed fails to emerge from the interactional episode being planned.

The regulating effects that rules impose on a program cannot be underestimated. Their cumulative effect determines how interactions may or may not occur in a program. It is known that the leisure experience is in large part determined by the perceived freedom a participant achieves as a result of his or her interactions in a program. Because of this, too many rules or inappropriate ones can destroy the experience we are trying to facilitate. A Ziggy cartoon that appeared many years ago illustrated this point very well. In the cartoon, Ziggy is shown entering a park, where he is confronted with a series of signs that say: "Keep off the grass," "No picnicking is in this area," "No swimming," "No bicycle riding," and so forth. The last sign says: "This is your park, enjoy it! Your Park Commission." It is not being suggested that leisure settings should have no regulations. However, programmers need to understand how regulations impinge on perceived freedom, and they must make certain that programs are not overregulated to the point that no freedom is perceived by participants.

*When rule
structures
are unclear
or constantly
changing,
anxiety is
introduced
and per-
ceived
freedom is
quashed.*

Well-written rules can foster perceived freedom. Rules that guide interactions create a known arena for interaction that fosters a perception of freedom for participants. For perceived freedom to emerge, structure for interaction must be present. Game rules create a known interactive structure in which specific interaction may and may not occur. Within the permitted range of interactions, game players have total freedom to act. By allowing some actions to be restricted by game rules, players are given total freedom to engage in other actions.

When rule structures are unclear or constantly changing, anxiety is introduced and perceived freedom is quashed. This point was made clear in an article one author was asked to referee. The author of the article had been a participant observer in a river float trip operated by a commercial outfitter. There were several rafts in the group, and each raft was handled by a staff boatperson. Members of the group were required to change rafts daily; consequently, they also changed boatpersons each day. Each boatperson had his own rules about how passengers were to sit in the raft when it was going over rapids, where passengers were to sit, how trash was to be disposed of, and so on. The net effect of this constant change was that the boatpersons, who were supposed to be providing patrons with a pleasant experience, were constantly at odds with them and badgering them about the proper way of doing things on "their" boat. The pleasure that would have been possible on the trip never fully emerged because of the constant badgering of patrons by the staff. In this case, requiring patrons to deal with rule changes daily interfered with their enjoyment of the event. The stable rule structure necessary for perceived freedom to emerge was never allowed to develop.

The structure that is used to organize and operate a program is also one of its regulatory mechanisms. The programmer can use several structures to operate a program. For example, softball can be offered as an instructional workshop, a league, a tournament, or a special event. Farrell and Lundegren (1978) have termed this organizing structure a program format and state that program format is the "basic structure through which an activity is presented" (p. 82). They have identified five formats: (1) clinics, workshops, and classes; (2) tournaments; (3) clubs; (4) special events; and (5) open facilities (Farrell & Lundegren 1978). In their second edition (1983), they renamed these five formats (1) education, (2) competition, (3) activity club, (4) performance or special event, and (5) open facility (p. 82). The U.S. Navy has identified five similar formats: (1) open house, (2) special events, (3) skill development, (4) competition, and (5) clubs and groups. They also add to this list a sixth format: self-directed noncompetitive, which includes many of their rental and check-out services, through which the Navy Recreational Services unit simply provides equipment of various types to sailors.

Program formats are organizational rules that structure program services. When programmers select a format, they are determining to some degree the satisfaction a program patron will have while limiting the probability that other satisfactions will be realized (Rossman, 1984). When a format is selected, then, it influences to some degree the experience the patron will have in the program. Program format is one of many rules that will situate the social system of a program and influence the satisfaction the patron may experience.

Structure situates a social system in which interaction can occur. Programmers must provide enough structure so that a program takes the form intended

3

> *Program format is one of many rules that will situate the social system of a program and influence the satisfaction the patron may experience.*

> *To design a program properly, the programmer needs to determine whether the participants have a relational history with each other.*

and the desired interactions that make up the content of the program can occur. However, overregulating, or rules that are unclear, will impinge on the perceived freedom necessary for a true leisure experience to occur and will interfere with the experience desired by the patrons or intended by the program designer.

RELATIONSHIPS

Participants in a program may have a pre-existing relationship that binds them to each other. People most frequently participate in leisure with family and friends. To design a program properly, the programmer needs to determine whether the participants have a relational history with each other. If indeed they do, it is necessary to determine the nature of this history and to assess its potential impact on the program being designed. If the interactants do not have a relational history, the programmer must determine whether it is necessary to develop a relationship during the operation of a program. Mechanisms for accomplishing this include icebreakers, first-comer activities, and other social recreation activities that can be planned into a program's design.

It may be unnecessary to create a relational history, however. Not all events require that those who attend know each other. Recreation personnel tend to force friendliness even when it is unnecessary. Forcing this issue often adds nothing to an event and can even detract from it. Individuals unknown to each other can co-experience many events without knowing the rest of the individuals who are participating. Bus trips to one-day events are one such an example. Often, pre-existing, small groups of two to five people will attend such an event, but it is not necessary to implement a program mechanism that forces all thirty participants to get to know each other. In fact, doing so may keep individuals from having valued interaction time with their own small group and may lead to dissatisfaction with the event.

It is also important not to structure events in a way that could destroy relational histories that might otherwise contribute to a participant's satisfaction with an event. For example, at one university, demand for tickets to basketball games increased dramatically because of the team's excellent record. In order to promote open access to games, athletic department officials decreed that henceforth no one would be permitted to purchase more than ten tickets at any one time. There was an unexpected outcry of protest against this policy. What the athletic department had inadvertently done was destroy the opportunity for friendship groups to attend ball games together. Many pre-existing groups from fraternities, sororities, and dorms were larger than ten individuals. Although in this instance the demand for tickets was so great that the policy could stand, clearly the interactants' relational history, which contributed to their satisfaction with an event, was not taken into account in creating the operational policies. This decision worked to the overall detriment of participant satisfaction with the event.

Understanding the role that relationships play in interactions within a program and anticipating how they may contribute to, or detract from, client satisfaction is an important element of situated activity system. Programmers cannot simply assume that the best course of action is always to foster or create relationships between individuals who attend an event.

> **It is important to understand how relationships contribute to or detract from client satisfaction.**

> **...to animate a program, the designer needs to anticipate how individuals will move through a program and how they will learn about the process and the timing of their movement.**

Animation deals with how a program is set into motion and how the action is sustained throughout the program. To animate a program, the programmer must structure it in such a way that spontaneous, natural movement is implemented. This can be accomplished in a number of different ways. Obviously, providing a leader is one solution and a possible source of action to move a program through time. How to plan and anticipate the scenario of action that will occur in a program is covered in more detail in Chapters Eleven and Thirteen. The process is analogous to action planning in other fields.

In theater, planning animation is known as "blocking." A play is blocked by describing and rehearsing where each actor will be situated at each moment, how the actors are to move through each scene, and how and where their attention is to be focused at each moment. In dance, determining the content and sequence of each movement is known as "choreographing." In sport, it is known as developing a "play."

In a similar way, to animate a program, the designer needs to anticipate how individuals will move through a program and how they will learn about the process and the timing of their movement. Additionally, programmers need to predict how the sequence of interactions that make up a program will unfold. The program designer must then provide sufficient structure and direction to animate the program so that participants will have the intended experience.

Providing a recreation leader who personally leads, and thereby animates, a program is one method for implementing animation. It is important to understand the role that one unique leader can play in a program. Programmers will be unable to duplicate a program whose success depends on a uniquely skilled leader if they do not have another leader with similar skills. One of the authors has observed this phenomenon in the production of a variety show. One agency sponsored an annual variety show modeled after the popular television program *The Gong Show*. The variety show was tremendously successful, but other agencies could not duplicate it because its success was dependent on a talented amateur comedian who was the emcee each year. The skills used to emcee the show accounted for a good deal of the show's success. Other programmers failed to understand that unless they could duplicate this animation element of the program, they would be unable to successfully duplicate the program itself, despite successfully duplicating the other five elements. The variety show's success was primarily accounted for by the unique manner in which a single individual animated the program.

Understanding this notion of being an animator can clarify the role that individuals in drop-in types of operations can play. Too often, people employed to operate a facility see their role as one of simply opening the facility, regulating its use, and closing it at the appropriate time. They never understand that they are one of the six critical elements that will determine the success or failure of a leisure locale.

Programs can often be animated without a leader. For example, in most of the attractions at Disneyland, the program is animated with mechanical and electrical devices. The program moves forward through

Animation, then, not only involves the use of a leader, but is a higher-level concept that deals with how the participant is going to be moved through a program.

Exercise 3-1: Manipulating the Six Elements

The left column of the matrix below lists the six elements that situate a program. Assume you are to identify these elements for two different Fourth of July special events. One is to operate on an Air Force base and the other at a nursing home. Complete the following tasks:

- Identify the key components for each element. What are the most defining characteristics for each element that will be present and that will need to be dealt with, or that should be present and thus will need to be created?
- Compare the two programs. What element(s) distinguish the difference(s) between the two programs?
- Discuss how the elements for either of the programs form a system for the program. If this is not apparent, consider the implications of operating either of the programs with the population for the other.

Six Elements	Air Force Base	Nursing Home
Interacting People		
Physical Setting		
Objects		
Structure (Rules and Program Format)		
Relationships		
Animation		

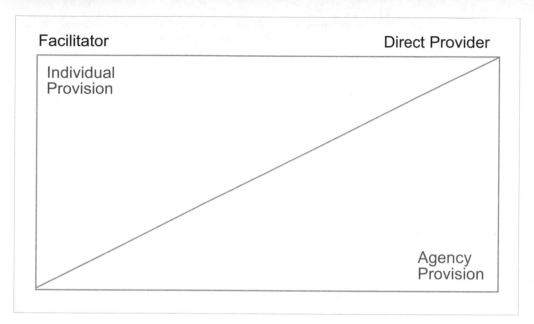

Figure 3-1: The Service Continuum

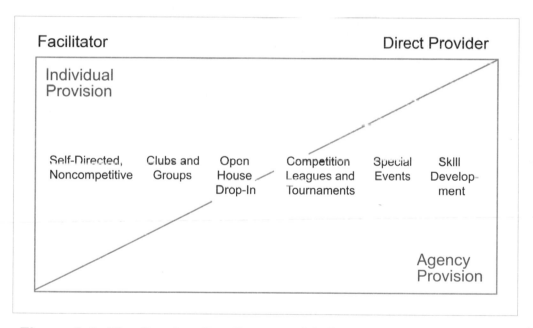

Figure 3-2: The Service Continuum with Programming Formats

time whether the patron is ready or not! Self-guided tours are also animated without a leader by using signs with instructions and arrows, recorded messages, and similar devices.

How much direction to provide in animating a program is somewhat problematic. Providing too much direction can interfere with an individual's perception of freedom and of being the cause of an act that is essential to intrinsic satisfaction. However, a lack of direction can be anxiety provoking and thereby produce dissatisfaction.

Animation, then, not only involves the use of a leader, but is a higher-level concept that deals with how the participant is going to be moved through a program. Providing a face-to-face leader is one way, but not the only way, of accomplishing this movement. The program designer must anticipate how the patron is to be moved through a program and must make certain that the devices necessary to implement this movement are in place and can be understood by the patron.

The act of programming involves developing opportunities for leisure by manipulating or creating one or more of these six situating elements. In developing programs, programmers must either control these elements by manipulating them, or they must be aware of the circumstances created by any element they cannot control. They must then take into account the circumstances of the uncontrolled element in their manipulations of the remaining elements. These six elements are the basic organizing framework around which all program services are developed. All programs are simply variations of these elements. Now complete Exercise 3-1 on page 46.

THE SERVICE CONTINUUM

The amount of a service that is actually arranged and provided can vary from program to program. Some participants want to provide some of the elements of a program themselves. It is theoretically possible for the programmer to completely provide a program so that the participants need do nothing except attend the activity, event, or service. At Disneyland, for example, participants simply pay their admission fee and get on a ride. The provider does everything else. It is also possible that individuals do not need the programmer at all and can use a service without any assistance from a programmer. We know that the majority of leisure occurs at home in self-organized activities. Although the theoretical extremes of this continuum involve unlikely circumstances (see the Addendum at the end of this chapter for an explanation of this point), the middle part of the continuum has some very practical implications for program development. Specifically, how much of a program must a programmer provide, and how much may one reasonably expect the participant to provide?

The service continuum is illustrated in Figure 3-1 on the top of page 47. On the left end of the continuum are those services that are totally provided by individuals in a program. When offering services in this mode, the agency is said to be operating in a facilitator role. On the right end of the continuum are those program services that are totally provided by the agency. When offering services in this mode, the agency is said to be operating in a direct provider role. Where an individual program is located on the service continuum is a function of the ratio of agency-provided to participant-provided program elements.

Two major issues affect whether an agency will operate in a facilitator or direct provider role. One is cost. It is assumed that, as one moves from being a facilitator to a direct provider, costs increase. Although this is not true in every case, it is generally true. Being a direct provider

Most comprehensive agencies offer multiple types of program formats to give patrons flexibility in choosing a program style that meets their preferences.

Exercise 3-2: Experimenting with Programming Formats

Directions: Select three different activities, such as volleyball, oil painting, or kickboxing, and provide examples of how each activity could be operated as six different programs, using each of the six programming formats included in the figure below. Note the guitar playing activity as an example.

Programming Formats:

Activity	Self-directed, non-competitive	Clubs & Groups	Drop-In	Competition Leagues & Tournaments	Special Events	Skill Development
Guitar playing	Guitar rental service	Rock Band	Studio practice	Finger picking contest	Guitar music festival	Intermediate guitar class

Discussion Questions:
1. How does the role of the programmer differ in each format?
2. How does the role of the agency differ in each of the formats?
3. How does the role of the patron differ in each of the formats?

of all leisure services in a community would be prohibitively expensive. Allowing the participants to provide part or all of the elements of program service is less expensive for the agency.

The second major issue is the relative importance for the participant in playing a role in the development and provision of the leisure service. Some individuals want a completely packaged service, while others want to play a major role in designing, planning, and operating a leisure experience. For example, outdoor recreation outfitters success-fully market two kinds of services: trips complete with a guide plus an itinerary, or simply outfitting groups with equipment for a specified period of time. In the latter case, the participants are responsible for designing the entire program except for the equipment.

Between the extremes, there are many organizational formats that require varying degrees of effort from both the individual and the agency. The six organizational formats discussed earlier are placed on the service continuum in Figure 3-2 in the middle of page 47. This figure illustrates that any activity may be operated in a variety of program formats that require varying degrees of agency and individual input into the program. As one moves from left to right on the continuum, the agency assumes an increasing role in developing and operating the program, while the individual assumes a lesser role.

Which type of service an agency will develop depends on the type of agency one is in and the agency's philosophy, role, and mission. Some agencies offer only one type of service. Most comprehensive agencies offer multiple types of program formats to give patrons flexibility. Now complete Exercise 3-2 on page 49.

CONCLUSION

Leisure occurs in a situated activity system that is made up of six interrelated elements. The act of programming is anticipating the circumstances of each of the six elements, accommodating or manipulating these circumstances, anticipating the scenario of actions that will make up the program, and anticipating the shifting importance that each element will assume as the program moves through time. Because these six elements situate a program, they are all that one needs to control, or can control, in designing a program. These elements are of such fundamental importance that if one of them is changed, the program is also changed. Programmers need to develop the ability to analyze their programs using these elements and to determine which element or combination of elements is central to the success of an individual program. To create, manipulate, or duplicate a program requires this level of understanding. Programmers can develop program services that require varying degrees of design input and operational effort from the agency and the individual participant.

REFERENCES

Crompton, J. (1983). Selecting target markets—A key to effective marketing. *Journal of Park and Recreation Administration, 1*(1), 7–26.

Denzin, N. K. (1975). Play, games, and interaction: The contexts of childhood socialization. *The Sociological Quarterly, 16,* 458–478.

Driver, B. L., & Brown, P. J. (1975). A socio-psychological definition of recreation demand, with implications for recreation resource planning. In *Assessing the Demand of Outdoor Recreation.* Washington, DC: U.S. Government Printing Office.

Farrell, P., & Lundegren, H. M. (1978). *The process of recreation programming: Theory and technique* (2nd ed.). State College, PA: Venture.

Farrell, P., & Lundegren, H. M. (1983). *The process of recreation programming.* New York: Wiley.

Howard, D. R., & Crompton, J. L. (1980). *Financing, managing, and marketing recreation and park resources.* Dubuque, IA: Wm. C. Brown.

Life Span Development. (2001). Lifespan Periods. WGBH Educational Foundation. Retrieved on February 10, 2007 from: http://www.learner.org/discoveringpsychology/development/dev_non-flash.html.

Murphy, J. F., Williams, J. G., Niepoth, W. E., & Brown, P. D. (1973). *Leisure service delivery systems: A modern perspective.* Philadelphia: Lea & Febiger.

Patterson, F. C. (1991). *A systems approach to recreation programming.* Prospect Heights, IL: Waveland Press.

Pfeffer, J., & Salancik, G. R. (1978). *The external control of organizations: A resource dependence perspective.* New York: Harper & Row.

Rossman, J. R. (1984). Influence of program format choice on participant satisfaction. *Journal of Park and Recreation Administration, 2*(1), 39–51.

Stewart, W. P. (1998). Leisure as multi-phase experiences: Challenging tradition. *Journal of Leisure Research, 30,* 391–400.

ADDENDUM

The two extremes of the service continuum are theoretical points. On the left side, where individuals provide the entire program for themselves, there is no need for the programmer at all. This point is on the continuum only as a point of reference to illustrate program formats that require the participant to be involved in the design and delivery of the program.

The right end of the continuum, which illustrates programs in which the participant has no role, is also a theoretical point. As discussed earlier, the leisure experience always requires the active participation of the participant in constructing the experience. At a minimum, the participant must take in and interpret the meaning of the sensory stimuli provided. Leisure is not something that is done to individuals, but rather something that they play a role in constructing. What the right end of the service continuum illustrates, then, are those programs designed and operated wholly by a programmer.

Hip Hop with a Message
Photo courtesy of Fox Valley Park District, Aurora, IL
Photos by Amy Roth

Outcome-Based Programming

Numerous philosophical orientations or approaches have been used to plan and design recreation programs. Kraus (1997) identified the following six approaches: "(1) the quality of life approach, (2) the marketing approach, (3) the human service approach, (4) the prescriptive approach, (5) the environmental/aesthetic/preservationist approach; and (6) the hedonist/individualist approach" (p. 67). Another approach, outcome-based programming, was developed to address the overall effects, benefits, and changes to individuals as a result of being in a recreation program from both short and long term perspectives (McNamera, 1997-2006). Similar to this approach are evidence-based programming and benefits-based programming, both of which are subtle derivations of outcome-based programming.

The outcome-based programming approach uses inputs, activities/processes, outputs, and outcomes to create programs that are beneficial to participants and society at large (McNamera, 1997-2006). Inputs are described as the items needed to run a program, such as staff, money, equipment, resources, etc. Activities are the processes that are used to stage a program to meet participants' programmatic needs, such as teachings, guiding, coaching, encouraging, etc. Outputs are described in terms of units of service, such as the number of people served by a program. Outcomes, the last component, illustrate the overall changes in behavior, skill, or attitude that participants experienced as a result of the program. Additional terms in outcome-based programming include outcome targets (percentage of participants expected to achieve an outcome) and outcome indicators (long-term indications that the program was successful).

A specific example of outcome-based programming is Benefits-Based Programming (BBP) which was developed by Witt (1993-1999). While no longer actively promoted by the National Recreation and Park Association, BBP is still used in municipal and nonprofit agencies around the country. Recreation professionals find that BBP provides solid evidence of the benefits of recreation, which can be easily communicated to stakeholders and to the general public.

In this chapter, we illustrate the use of BBP as an example of outcome-based programming. Specifically, we explain how BBP can help reposition agencies by detailing the history and development of BBP, and by describing a model that can be used to implement BBP. Throughout the chapter, examples of

4

KEY TERMS

Outcome-Based Programming
Repositioning
Benefits-Based Awareness
Benefits-Based Programming
Target Issues
Protective Factors
Activity Components
Benefit Outcomes

An approach that has gained increased respect and application in recent years is called Benefits-Based Programming (BBP). It was developed to address social problems, especially among youth in at-risk environments.

BBP's application in recreation and leisure settings are presented, as well as exercises for readers to gain hands-on practice.

REPOSITIONING

Positioning (Crompton & Witt, 1997) refers to the way in which local officials and citizens perceive the field of parks and recreation, especially in terms of how the field compares to other publicly funded services. According to Crompton and Witt (1997), the current view or position is that parks and recreation are relatively nonessential public services. In the minds of public and local officials, recreation and parks take a back seat to other services, such as police and fire protection. Thus, agencies need to reposition how they are viewed.

One outcome of this view is inadequate financial support for parks and recreation. Americans, tired of paying increasingly high taxes, have led a series of successful tax revolts which, since 1976, have severely cut the availability of tax dollars for governmental services (Crompton, 1998). Moreover, as many industries and middle class groups have migrated from cities to the suburbs, the tax base of many large cities has eroded. During this period of declining financial resources, services that were deemed nonessential, such as parks and recreation, did not continue to secure the necessary political support for proper funding.

In spite of these financial pressures, the demand has increased for parks and recreation agencies to provide after-school activities. This development has been an attempt to respond to the needs of an increasing number of working and single parents. The hours between 3:00 p.m. and 7:00 p.m. put school-aged children of working parents at risk not only for juvenile crime, but for getting into trouble in general (Tindall, 1998). The scope and nature of recent efforts to increase after-school programming for youth is extensive and has attracted financial support from public and private sources. But the continuation of this funding is contingent on an agency's ability to demonstrate positive results.

The major challenge faced by recreation and leisure programmers, then, is to reposition or change that view from being a nonessential governmental service to being an agency that is a positive agent of change (Crompton & Witt, 1997). Attempts must be made to demonstrate that parks and recreation services can serve as major players in promoting healthy and active lifestyles, making neighborhoods and cities safer, and advocating for a clean environment and open spaces.

One way the profession has begun to reposition itself successfully and, at the same time, address the aforementioned social and financial problems is through Benefits-Based Programming (Allen, Stevens, & Harwell, 1996a). Through the application of BBP, the profession can be repositioned in the public's mind from that of a nonessential service to that of an essential and positive agency for solving social problems and enhancing community life. Experiment with the concept of repositioning by completing Exercise 4-1.

> *The major challenge faced by recreation and leisure programmers, then, is to reposition or change the view that the public and stakeholders have of our field...*

> *Benefits-Based Programming requires that programmers take a more developmental approach by planning outcome-based programs for specific user groups.*

BENEFITS-BASED AWARENESS

Readers may be familiar with the former Benefits-Based Awareness campaign of the NRPA, known as *The Benefits Are Endless* . . . ™, shown on page 56. This component of BBP focused on communicating the benefits of parks and recreation to all audiences. A key point of this campaign was that the benefits described were based on empirical studies, documenting the personal, social, economic, and environmental benefits of parks and recreation. For example, Sefton and Mummery (1995) compiled an update from the years 1991-1994 of all research related to the benefits of recreation. One of the research conclusions stated that "regular moderate sports playing adds 1.25 years to the life expectancy of a 45-54 year old man" (Paffenbarger, Hyde, Wing, Lee, Jung, & Kampert, 1993, in Sefton & Mummery, 1995, p. 7). In a study of female smokers, Grove, Wilkinson, and Dawson (as cited in Sefton & Mummery, 1995, p. 7) found that with just 15 minutes of daily exercise, cigarette cravings were reduced. *The Benefits Are Endless* . . . ™ promotional campaign made decision makers and citizens aware of the benefits provided through recreation and leisure programs and services.

BENEFITS-BASED PROGRAMMING

Benefits-Based Programming is an outcome-based programming approach that focuses the programmer's efforts on producing identified benefits for participants as a result of their participation in specific recreation programs. It was originally demonstrated at four different sites (Illinois, South Carolina, Washington, and Maryland) between 1996 and 1997 through an initiative funded by the National Recreation Foundation (Allen & McGovern, 1997). In these four demonstration projects, programs were designed to address problems associated with youth in at-risk environments. The conclusion from these projects was that BBP works if it is implemented properly (Allen & McGovern, 1997). The BBP approach was also successful in populations other than youth in at-risk environments. One such program is the "Merry Milers," a walking fitness program for seniors in Miamisburg, Ohio (Rudick, 1998). Because

PARKS and RECREATION

BE HAPPIER · Build Family Unity · *Feel Great*
take care of latch key children · reduce unemployment
INCREASE COMMUNICATION SKILLS · *Expand knowledge*
Lose weight · diminish chance of disease · **build self-esteem**
reduce stress · *promote sensitivity to cultural diversity*
eliminate loneliness · **INCREASE COMMUNITY PRIDE** · Reduce Crime
provide safe places to play · *generate revenue* · lower health care costs
MEET FRIENDS · *educate children and adults* · **RELAX**
KEEP BUSINESS FROM LEAVING · **Elevate Personal Growth**
strengthen neighborhood involvement · *conquer boredom* · **provide child care**
BOOST ECONOMY · *curb employee absenteeism* · *increase tourism*
build strong bodies · increase property value · **attract new business**
Preserve plant and animal wildlife · *instill teamwork*
live longer · **create memories** · **PROTECT THE ENVIRONMENT**
CLEAN AIR AND WATER · *boost employee productivity* · *look better*
enhance relationship skills · *decrease insurance premiums* · **CONTROL WEIGHT**
OFFER PLACE FOR SOCIAL INTERACTION · *diminish gang violence*
TEACH VITAL LIFE SKILLS · *Provide space to enjoy nature* ...

THE BENEFITS ARE ENDLESS ...

© National Recreation and Park Association
(Used with permission)

of these successes and the need for a programming methodology that produces identifiable outcomes, BBP remains a viable example of outcome-based programming.

BENEFITS-BASED PROGRAMMING: HOW IT IS DONE

The premise of BBP is that through recreation experiences, the potential exists for addressing significant issues (e.g., social, economic, environmental) without changing the basic nature of the recreation experience. This is not to suggest that the recreation experience is not inherently beneficial or positive; rather, "recreation programs must be specifically structured" to adequately address the overall goals of the program, those being the target goals (Allen et al., 1996a, p. 11).

Providing resiliency is the ultimate desired outcome of BBP. Individuals with resiliency have developed a personal set of coping skills that provide them the personal strengths, resources, and self-image they need to avoid the pitfalls of an at-risk environment. If the goals of a program are addressed successfully, participants will become significantly more resilient than they were at the beginning of the program. Allen and McGovern (1996) identified several programming principles that they believe build resiliency among user groups. A list of these principles is included in Figure 4-1. These principles are not only applicable for youth in at-risk environments, but for all populations. When designing programs whose purpose is to build resiliency in participants, these principles should be considered.

1. Provide opportunities to create significant relationships with others
2. Provide opportunities to feel competent
3. Provide constant encouragement
4. Provide opportunities for participants to be involved in the planning and creation of experiences
5. Build in high but attainable expectations, not high standards
6. Provide opportunities to be helpful to others
7. Provide opportunities to socialize with peers and adults who can serve as role models
8. Provide unconditional support and universal acceptance
9. Build in opportunities for helpfulness to others
10. Provide opportunities to contribute to one's community
11. Encourage family support and involvement
12. Include initiative and cooperative types of frames
13. Provide opportunities to practice communication skills
14. Provide opportunities for group decision making
15. Allow participants to create experiences
16. Create opportunities to socialize with peers and adults
17. Provide opportunities to belong
18. Be caring; have respect for them as persons, listen without being intrusive
19. Provide consistent opportunities for recognition
20. Model good behavior for participants
21. Provide positive adherence to rules
22. Discipline without criticism
23. Be firm, fair, and fun

From: Allen, L. R., & McGovern, T. D. (1997). BBM: It's working. Parks and Recreation, 32(8), 48–55.
(Used with Permission.)

Figure 4-1: Programming Principles to Build Resiliency

BENEFITS-BASED PROGRAMMING: THE MODEL

In 1997, Allen and McGovern proposed the Benefits-Based Management Activity Planning Model (Figure 4-2 on page 58) that included three basic components: (1) Issues and Target Goals, (2) Activity Components, and (3) Benefit Outcomes. The authors offer a revised model (Figure 4-3 on page 59) adding a fourth component, Benefits-Based Awareness, based on the works of Forest (1999). In the remainder of this chapter, implementing each component of this Benefits-Based Programming (BBP) Model will be discussed.

ISSUE AND TARGET GOALS

The first component, issue and target goals, involves the identification of a problem or issue by stakeholders. This component corresponds to the outcome-based programming concept of *inputs* described earlier

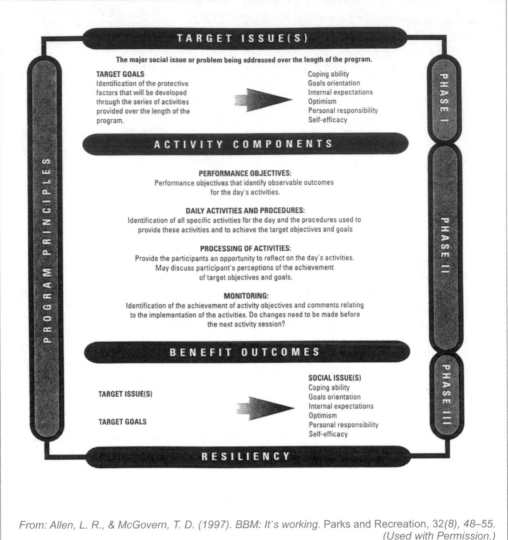

From: Allen, L. R., & McGovern, T. D. (1997). BBM: It's working. Parks and Recreation, 32(8), 48–55. (Used with Permission.)

Figure 4-2: BBM Activity Planning Model

in this chapter. The issue statement and resulting target goals become the focus of the program. In BBP, the issue is developed for a specific population cohort, such as youth in at-risk environments, senior citizens of a particular community, or single parents with elementary school-aged children. Examples of possible social issues might be to reduce gang violence within a particular neighborhood, to encourage an active and healthy lifestyle among seniors, or to improve family relations among children and their single parents. A key point to remember is that benefits-based recreation programs alone will not address the issue entirely. Widespread community involvement is required to adequately confront all facets of a social issue. But BBP gives recreation program-

Phase 1. Target Issues		Phase 2. Activity Components
The major social issues or problems being addressed over the length of the program. Selection of protective factors that will be developed through the series of activities provided over the length of the program. Protective factors include, but are not limited to, coping ability, goals orientation, internal expectations, optimism, personal responsibility, and self-efficacy.		1. Write <u>performance objectives</u> that identify observable outcomes for the day's activities. 2. Identify specific <u>daily activities and procedures</u> to be used to provide these activities to achieve the target goals. **[Program Implementation]** 3. <u>Process the daily activities</u> by discussing participants' perceptions of the achievement of target goals. 4. <u>Monitor</u> the achievement of activity objectives. Comment on implementation processes—successes and problems. Do changes need to be made before the next activity session?
	The Benefits-Based Programming Model	
Phase 4. Benefits-Based Awareness		**Phase 3. Benefit Outcomes**
Communicate the BBP successes to the general public, funding sources, and stakeholders in terms of: • Improved conditions • Prevention of worse conditions • Realization of a psychological expectation Communication methods: • News releases • Promotional materials • Newsletters • Annual reports • Speaking engagements • Web sites • Other materials		Summarize the achievement of target goals leading to increased <u>resiliency</u> among participants in terms of their: • Coping ability • Goals orientation • Internal expectations • Optimism • Personal responsibility • Self-efficacy

Adapted from the Benefits-Based Programming Model by Allen and McGovern (1997).

Figure 4-3: Benefits-Based Programming Model

The first component, issue and target goals, involves the identification of a problem or issue by stakeholders.

mers the tools they need to become a part of the community's solution. Once the issue is focused, the next step is to develop target goals that address characteristics of the issue.

Two essential features must be included in each target goal. First, the goal must validate the issue that was initially identified. It should be logically connected to the social issue. The reasonableness of this connection must be apparent to and accepted by the stakeholders of the program. Second, goal statements must be written to facilitate the devel-

1. Is knowledgeable of neighborhood resources
2. Caring adults are interested in him or her
3. Is accepted and liked by others and family
4. Has high controls against deviant behavior
5. Has an appreciation of role models
6. Has a positive attitude toward the future
7. Values achievement
8. Has the ability to work with others
9. Has the ability to work out conflicts
10. Has the perceived competence to do . . .

From: Allen, L. R., & McGovern, T. D. (1997). BBM: It's working.
Parks and Recreation, 32(8), 48–55.

Figure 4-4: Ten Protective Factors

opment of protective factors. That is, it must be clear how participating in a program with the goals specified will develop resiliency skills, attitudes, and behaviors or coping mechanisms (McMillan & Reed, 1994).

McMillan and Reed (1994) state that at-risk youth are influenced by factors that might include (but are not limited to) family structure, socioeconomic status, inadequate adult supervision, neighborhood location, possibility for substance abuse, and so on. Children who grow up in these at-risk environments have to work extra hard to *beat the odds* and lead successful lives. There are generally two explanations for those children who succeed: innate characteristics and the development of protective factors (Mundy, 1996). For our intents and purposes, we will focus on the development of protective factors (see Figure 4-4). Given that building resiliency in participants is the ultimate desired outcome of the model, it is essential to prepare target goals that develop protective factors.

Target goals should specify which protective factors will be developed for the particular population of interest. Examples might include self-control, self-discipline, positive outlook, and personal responsibility. Additional information about how to write goals is provided in Chapter Eight, Writing Program Management Goals.

Programmers should use a planning sheet when developing this first component of the BBP Model (see Figure 4-5 on page 62). The planning sheet assists the programmer in developing a clear description of the issue and target goals. Practice developing target goals by completing Exercise 4-2. Once a major issue has been identified and the target goals have been developed to address the issue, it is then time to move to the second component of the BBP Model, the activity components.

ACTIVITY COMPONENTS

In the activity components section, specific programs and activities that address the target goals are designed, implemented, and monitored. This phase of BBP is equivalent to the outcome-based programming concept of *activities*. The activity component is implemented by completing the following four subcategories: (1) Performance Objectives, (2) Daily Activities and Procedures, (3) Processing of Activities, and (4) Monitoring. Allen, Stevens, and Harwell (1996a) stress the importance of customizing programs for each specific user group. Programmers who design general programs for specific user groups may find that participants did not adequately attain the target goals. Two of the four subcategories of the activity component are covered in great detail in later chapters. Specifically, performance objectives are covered in Chapter 10, and daily activities and procedures are covered in Chapter 13.

Processing the impact of completed activities is an essential aspect of activity components, and it is carried out by the recreation staff who lead the programs. The purpose of processing is to help participants relate their feelings about what they learned in the activity to real-life situations. Time is set aside at the end of each activity session to lead discussions among participants. If participants are to truly understand the importance of the activity session and to link their experiences to the issue and target goals established at the outset of the program, it is essential that the appropriate questions be discussed. Twelve questions that programmers can use when leading a processing session are found in Figure 4-6 on page 63. Not all of these questions need to be asked during each activity session; rather, the leader or facilitator selects those questions that best relate to the activity or content material of the cur-

> *In the activity components section, specific programs and activities...are designed, implemented, and monitored.*

Program:

Target Issue:

Time:

Program Synopsis:

Facility Needs:

Supplies:

Target Goals (Protective Factors to be Addressed; * = Primary, + = Secondary):

_____ Self-efficacy		_____ Internal expectations
_____ Goal orientation		_____ Coping ability
_____ Personal responsibility		_____ Other
_____ Optimism		

Partnering Agencies (Contact Person):

_____ School		_____ Social services
_____ Law enforcement		_____ Other
_____ Church		

From: Allen, L., & McGovern, T. (1996, October). *Implementing a benefits based recreation program.* Paper presented at the NRPA Congress for Recreation and Parks, Kansas City, MO.

Figure 4-5: BBP Planning Sheet

rent program. The list of questions in Figure 4-6 is by no means exhaustive, and program leaders may need to develop questions that are more appropriate for their activities or issue and target goals.

Processing can be formal or informal, depending on the type of activity and setting. Similarly, the type of participants involved in the program can dictate limits on the conceptual depth that processing may take. For example, younger children are not as capable of articulating their feelings about an activity (other than that they liked it or didn't like it) as perhaps teenagers and adults. Also, in working with persons with disabilities, special processing guidelines may need to be developed, depending on participants' levels of cognitive functioning.

Another aspect of processing is the "teachable moment" that can occur anytime during an activity. These moments, if used properly, facilitate a shared learning experience among all participants. A camping example illustrates this concept well. One of the authors led a backcountry canoeing trip for teenagers. Prior to the trip, the teens were taught how to pitch and strike a tent. Discussions also ensued about the importance of being prepared and setting up tents upon arrival at a new site each day. One day during the trip, four campers decided to horse around instead of pitching their tents along with the rest of the group. A surprise rainstorm resulted in drenched gear and discontentment among the four negligent campers. This was an ideal "teachable moment," at

Asking the right questions is often the key to good processing. Listed below are questions that may help activity leaders become more comfortable with processing.

1. How did you feel when you had to trust someone else to keep you safe?
2. How did you decide whom you would trust?
3. What did it feel like to cooperate with other members of your group?
4. How did you (your group) make decisions?
5. How well did you do?
6. What did you say to yourself?
7. In what ways did you criticize or support yourself?
8. What type of feedback did you receive or give to others?
9. In what ways do you differ from other group members?
10. What was your greatest success today?
11. How can you use something you learned today in other situations?
12. What did you learn about yourself during this activity that you want to work on in the future?

From: Allen, L., & McGovern, T. (1996, October). Implementing a benefits based recreation program. Paper presented at the NRPA Congress for Recreation and Parks, Kansas City, MO.

Figure 4-6: The Right Words

which a brief discussion during the rainstorm helped reinforce the importance of being prepared when camping in backcountry.

Processing may also be accomplished through journal writing, whereby participants are given a set time each day to write down their thoughts and reflections about the program. They may be asked to respond to the same set of questions each day or to simply write whatever is on their mind that pertains to the activity. It is sometimes difficult to motivate people to write their feelings in a journal. The more structure that surrounds journal writing, the more likely it is to be successful. For example, if participants are told merely to write one page a day in their journals, yet no time is set aside for this activity, it probably will not occur. Similarly, having specific topics to write about or specific questions to address often makes writing easier. It cannot be stressed enough that recreation staff need to be consistent in their approach to journal writing among participants. Many participants find that, once they become accustomed to the idea, journal writing can be a rewarding and satisfying way to reflect on their feelings about an activity.

Monitoring, the last subcategory of the activity components, is a daily task that is the responsibility of the recreation staff in charge of the program. Through monitoring, programmers gain valuable feedback about the extent to which the performance objectives are being achieved. Just as recreation staff must encourage participants to write

Program Title:			Activity Title:	
Date/Time	Performance Objectives	Daily Methods	Procedures Used to Measure Objectives	Monitoring and Evaluation
Comments:				

From: Allen, L., & McGovern, T. (1996, October). Implementing a benefits based recreation program. Paper presented at the NRPA Congress for Recreation and Parks, Kansas City, MO.

Figure 4-7: Activity Report Form

in their journals, so, too, should staff set aside time each day to determine how well the performance objectives for the activity session were accomplished. Staff should also monitor whether their assumed links between the identified performance objectives and the target goals remain valid and should make any modifications needed in the program to re-establish this linkage.

Allen and McGovern (1996) recommend the use of a formalized system of monitoring that includes completing a form for each activity session (Figure 4-7). All columns except for the Monitoring and Evaluation sections should describe what is to be accomplished *during* that particular activity session. Note that those sections should be completed prior to the activity session. The Monitoring and Evaluation column is completed *at the end* of the activity session. It is a report of how well the performance objectives were achieved (e.g., "Almost everyone was able to tie at least one knot. Only 2 out of 10 were able to tie both knots."). The Comments section at the bottom of the form is for a narrative summary of how the session went and should include comments about staff as well as participants. Reminder notes may also be made about any distractions, equipment problems, or changes that should be made before the next activity session, and so on. These completed forms will provide the programmer with an important data-base to use in documenting the program's benefit outcomes. Practice this activity by completing Exercise 4-3.

BENEFIT OUTCOMES

The third component to the BBP Model, benefit outcomes, is where programmers evaluate the benefit outcomes as they relate to the issue and target goals. Outcome-based programming uses the concept of *outputs* to describe this part of the model. To implement this component of the model, a comprehensive evaluation plan must be in place. In some cases, valid and reliable instruments will be available for evaluative purposes. In other cases, instruments or other appropriate indicators will need to be developed by the programmer. Witt, Baker, and Scott (as cited in Witt and Crompton, 1997) developed the Protective Factors Scale, a valid and reliable scale for measuring protective factors as they relate to target goals (Figure 4-8 on pages 66-68). For more information on the development, reliability and validity, and use of the scale, see Witt and Crompton (1997). If it can be determined that the participants were successful in addressing the target goals, then programmers can claim that the attainment of such target goals may lead to an increased sense of resiliency among the participants.

One common evaluation method used by Allen, Stevens, and Harwell (1996a) to measure the impact of the program is to "use a control group for comparative purposes and a pre–post evaluative format" (p. 18). The control group should be as similar as possible to the participants involved in the Benefits-Based Program. If there are 20 participants in the program, all of whom are females between the ages of 60–65, 50 percent white and 50 percent Hispanic, and widows, then the control group should be comprised of persons with the same demographic characteristics. The pre-test would be administered to *both* the control group and BBP participants prior to the beginning of the program. At the completion of the program, both groups would receive

	Version A: Pre- and Post-Program	Version B: Post-Program Only
Question Format	Each statement as listed.	As result of participating in program X, I increased . . .
	7-point scale: "Strongly Agree" to "Strongly Disagree"	7-point scale: "Decreased a Great Deal" to "Increased a Great Deal"
Subscale Area		
Neighborhood Resources: Knowledge of and interest in neighborhood recreation opportunities, including organized and informal programs and opportunities.	• I know lots of safe places to play or hang out. • I know lots of activities to do in my community. • I am interested in participating in programs in my community. • I am interested in programs that take place after school.	• My knowledge of safe places to play or hang out. • My knowledge of other community activities. • My interest in participating in programs in my community. • My interest in programs that take place after school.
Interested and Caring Adults: The perception that there are adults who care about and are interested in teens, and who are available to help teens when they have problems.	• There are adults who are interested in me. • I can turn to adults for help. • There are adults who will look out for me. • Adults are willing to help me with my problems.	• My understanding that there are adults who are interested in me. • My understanding that I can turn to adults for help. • My understanding that there are adults who will look out for me. • My understanding that adults are willing to help me with my problems.
Sense of Acceptance and Belonging: The perception of being liked and accepted by other teens and family members.	• I am able to get along with friends. • There are other children who like me. • I am an OK person. • I am wanted by the people around me.	• My ability to get along with friends. • My understanding that there are other children who like me. • My knowledge that I am an OK person. • My understanding that I am wanted by the people around me.

Figure 4-8: Protective Factors Scale Subareas, Formats, and Questions (Witt, Baker, & Scott, 1996)

	Version A: Pre- and Post-Program	Version B: Post-Program Only
Question Format	Each statement as listed.	As result of participating in program X, I increased . . .
	7-point scale: "Strongly Agree" to "Strongly Disagree"	7-point scale: "Decreased a Great Deal" to "Increased a Great Deal"
Subscale Area		
High Controls Against Deviant Behavior: The understanding that it is important and necessary to stay out of trouble and obey the rules.	• I must stay out of trouble. • I must obey the rules. • I will be punished if I break the rules. • I must follow the rules if I want to participate.	• My understanding that I must stay out of trouble. • My understanding that I must obey the rules. • My understanding that I will be punished if I break the rules. • My understanding that I must obey the rules if I want to participate.
Models for Conventional Behavior: Respect for and appreciation of teens, adults, and institutions who model or reinforce appropriate behavior.	• I respect authority figures. • I respect adults. • I respect people in charge. • I respect children who stay out of trouble.	• My respect for authority figures. • My respect for adults. • My respect for people in charge. • My respect for children who stay out of trouble.
Positive Attitude Toward the Future/Future Expectations: Perception of oneself as having a positive future, including the willingness to be spontaneous and creative, and the understanding that one has some control over the outcome of daily events.	• I am creative. • I can set goals. • I can deal with problems that might come up in the future. • I like to try new things.	• My ability to be creative. • My ability to set goals. • My ability to deal with problems that might come up in the future. • My ability to try new things.
Value on Achievement: Interest in and understanding of the importance of doing well in school. Also includes the general idea of being successful and trying to do one's best in any area of involvement.	• I can succeed in life. • It is important for me to always do my best. • It is important for me to do well at school. • It is important for me to stay in school.	• My understanding that I can succeed in life. • My understanding of the importance of doing my best. • My interest in doing well at school. • My interest in staying in school.

Figure 4-8: (continued)

	Version A: Pre- and Post-Program	Version B: Post-Program Only
Question Format	Each statement as listed.	As result of participating in program X, I increased . . .
	7-point scale: "Strongly Agree" to "Strongly Disagree"	7-point scale: "Decreased a Great Deal" to "Increased a Great Deal"
Subscale Area		
Ability to Work with Others: Understand the importance of and have the ability to get along with other teens, be cooperative, and be a good member of a team or group.	• I try to treat other children with respect. • Teamwork is important. • Cooperation is important. • All players need a chance to play.	• My ability to treat other children with respect. • My understanding of the importance of doing my best. • My interest in doing well at school. • My interest in staying in school.
Ability to Work out Conflicts: The ability to deal in a positive manner with problems that arise with other teens.	• I try to solve problems in a positive manner. • I try to control my anger. • I try to listen to the opinions of others. • I can settle arguments without fighting.	• My ability to solve problems in a positive manner. • My ability to control my anger. • My ability to listen to the opinions of others. • My ability to settle arguments without fighting.
Liking and Perceived Competence: The degree to which one likes to do a particular activity and feels he or she has the skills to participate successfully.	• I want to keep playing [this activity]. • I want to improve my skills [in this activity]. • I am interested in [this activity]. • I like [this activity].	• My desire to keep playing [this activity]. • My desire to improve my skills [in this activity]. • My interest [in this activity]. • My liking of [this activity].

From: Witt, Baker, and Scott (1996), as cited in Witt, P. A., & Crompton, J. L. (1997). Invited Paper: The protective factors framework: A key to programming for benefits and evaluating for results. Journal of Park and Recreation Administration, 15(3), pp. 8–9. (Used with permission.)

Figure 4-8: (continued)

the post-test. The results would be compared between the two groups. If the program was designed, implemented, and monitored properly, programmers can expect the evaluation to document positive results. Chapter Twenty illustrates specifically how the BBP approach can be incorporated into program evaluation. Additional experience in developing control groups may be gained by completing Exercise 4-4.

BENEFITS-BASED AWARENESS

The final component in Benefits-Based Programming is Benefits-Based Awareness. The outcome-based programming approach uses the term *outcomes* for this component. According to Forest (1999), this component involves "the establishment of a comprehensive marketing ef-

Exercise 4-4: Establishing Control Groups

In groups of three, brainstorm a specific target population to participate in a hypothetical Benefits-Based Program. Then think of ways you might establish a control group for evaluative purposes.

- What factors would you focus on when determining the control groups?
- How much information would you give the control group about the Benefits-Based Program you (hypothetically) designed?
- How often would you meet with the control group, and for what purposes?

Discuss your results with the rest of the class.

fort that effectively communicates the significance of the programs and services offered by recreation service providers" (p. 42). By effectively communicating successes to the public and local stakeholders, agencies will continue to legitimize the importance of the recreation and parks field and what we do to improve communities. This final component is an essential link in repositioning the community's perception of parks and recreation agencies.

Programmers are often so wrapped up in the design, implementation, and evaluation of their programs that they may overlook the importance of the Benefits-Based Awareness phase of the BBP model. Programmers who can effectively communicate the successes and benefits of their programs to local government officials, community leaders, and the public in general will serve to reposition the field. O'Sullivan (1999) suggests that programmers create a timeline based on a hierarchy of "who knows when" (p. 94) for communicating successful program indicators. First, communicate to the internal audience, which includes the agency staff, participants, and board members. Second, successes should be communicated to your agency's partners, along with the general public. When possible, communicate these demonstrated benefits as part of the ongoing *The Benefits Are Endless...*™ campaign. Whether through documentation or demonstration, the benefits and successes must be communicated effectively to all audiences at all levels (O'Sullivan, 1999).

THE BBP APPROACH: SOME CONCLUDING THOUGHTS

Readers whose area of focus within the profession is therapeutic recreation may have already noted the prescriptive nature of the BBP approach to program planning. Prescriptive program planners are concerned with planning outcome-based recreation activities that are designed for a specific purpose and a specific user group. This approach is in contrast to the homogenized approach often used by many recreation and park agencies, where generic programs are designed for

> *Benefits-Based Awareness... involves 'the establishment of a comprehensive marketing effort that communicates the significance of the programs and services'... (Forest, 1999)*

participants in general. Allen, Stevens, and Harwell (1996a) contend that purposeful, outcome-oriented programming will result in more resilient participants, which, after all, is the overall goal of BBP. Of the five demonstration projects, four involved youth in at-risk environments. The other project involved a walking program for seniors. The point is that the BBP approach, although prescriptive in nature, can be tailored to address the issues of any user group, not just those patrons who are commonly associated with therapeutic recreation settings.

Implementing the BBP approach is labor intensive. A substantial amount of record keeping, report writing, and monitoring takes place before, during, and after BBP. Programmers who have not used this approach before may be overwhelmed at the level of depth and involvement required on their part in order to plan, implement, and evaluate effective programs. It is assumed that both new and seasoned programmers will find that specific chapters in this text will equip them with the knowledge and skills necessary to incorporate the BBP approach into their programming efforts. To assist the reader, practical exercises and discussions that containing BBP-related materials are included in relevant chapters throughout this text.

The adoption of outcome-based approaches such as BBP, although intensive and time-consuming, will benefit the park and recreation field as well as participants. The BBP approach can not only help programmers plan purposeful and successful programs, but can also help communicate the benefits of those programs to the public and thereby help reposition the field.

> *The BBP approach can help programmers plan purposeful programs and help communicate the benefits of those programs to the public.*

An underlying assumption of using this outcome-based programming approach is that programmers already possess an understanding of recreation programming. As illustrated in the first three chapters of this book, it should be apparent to the reader that designing leisure experiences requires a sound understanding of programming theory as well as competence in a variety of complex skills and techniques. In the process of describing the various aspects of recreation programming throughout this text, the authors have simultaneously woven together the components of outcome-based programming for the reader's benefit.

CONCLUSION

This chapter has provided an overview of outcome-based programming, repositioning, and the BBP model. Benefits-Based Programming was broken down into its four component parts: Issue and Target Goals, Activity Components, Benefit Outcomes, and Benefits-Based Awareness. Specific techniques for implementing each component were discussed.

REFERENCES

Allen, L. R., & McGovern, T. D. (1996, October). Implementing a benefits-based recreation program. Paper presented at the NRPA Congress for Recreation and Parks, Kansas City, MO.

Allen, L. R., Stevens, B., & Harwell, R. (1996a). Benefits-based management activity planning model for youth in at-risk environments. *Journal of Park and Recreation Administration, 14*(3), 10–19.

Allen, L. R., Stevens, B., & Harwell, R. (1996b). Purposeful recreation programming. In T. A. Mobley & D. Newport (Eds.), *Parks and recreation in the 21st century* (pp. 223–229). Arlington, VA: National Recreation and Park Association.

Crompton, J. L. (1998). *Financing and acquiring park and recreation resources.* Champaign, IL: Human Kinetics.

Crompton, J. L., & Witt, P. A. (1997). Repositioning: The key to building community support. *Parks and Recreation, 32*(10), 4.

Forest, K. K. (1999). Benefits-based Programming. *Illinois Parks and Recreation, 30*(5), 41–42.

Kraus, R. (1997). *Recreation programming: A benefits-driven approach.* Boston, MA: Allyn and Bacon.

McMillan, J., & Reed, D. (1994, Fall). Resilient at-risk students: Students' views about why they succeed. *The Journal of At-Risk Issues,* 27–33.

McNamera, C. (1997-2006). Basic guide to outcomes-based evaluation for nonprofit organizations with very limited resources. Retrieved on January 11, 2007, from http://www.management help.org/evaluatn/outcomes.htm

Mundy, J. (1996). Tipping the scales from risk to resiliency. *Parks and Recreation, 31*(3), 78–85.

O'Sullivan, E. (1999). *Setting the course for change: The benefits movement.* Ashburn, VA: National Recreation and Park Association, Professional Services Division.

Park, M., Clark, D., & Rudick, J. (1997). Benefits: Where we are at this moment. *Parks and Recreation, 32*(10), 14, 16.

Rudick, J. (1998). Benefits: Benefits-based programming—You can do it. *Parks and Recreation, 33*(5), 20, 22, 24.

Sefton, J. M., & Mummery, W. K. (1995). *Benefits of recreation research update.* State College, PA: Venture.

Tindall, B. (1998, February). Dateline: President emphasizes after-school services. *Parks and Recreation, 33*(5), 2.

Witt, P. A. (1993-1999). Development of methods to evaluate recreation programs. Funded by the National Recreation and Park Association.

Witt, P. A., & Crompton, J. L. (1997). The protective factors framework: A key to programming for benefits and evaluating for results [Invited Paper]. *Journal of Park and Administration, 15*(3), 1–18.

4

Public Swim at a Wave Pool
Photo courtesy of Blacktown Leisure Centre, Stanhope, Australia

Developing Leisure Products in the Experience Economy

5

The introduction of the Experience Economy (Pine & Gilmore, 1999) has created great interest in programming and staging experiences throughout many sectors of the economy. Conventional wisdom among leisure providers was that we were in the service sector of the economy. Although we will continue to provide services, staging experience is the next stage in the progress of economic value (Schmitt, 1999). This development demands that we re-examine what business we are in. What follows is an analysis about what this has to do with recreation programming and developing leisure products.

Today, economists classify economic value into four sectors, as outlined in Table 5-1 on page 74. Each of these economic value sectors are provided by specific kinds of economic activity that are also included in the table. These activities basically follow the historical development of economic activity, but each of them continues today. The portion of overall economic activity each represents has shifted over time. For example, human's first economic endeavor was extracting; principally mining and agriculture, i.e., harvesting activities. A great shift of human endeavor occurred when people became so proficient at farming that fewer and fewer individuals were needed to produce sufficient food. In about 1850, the Industrial Revolution occurred and there was a great migration of population from rural to urban areas. This was accompanied by a shift in how individuals participated in the economy—people now worked in factories and produced manufactured goods. Another shift occurred in about 1980, when delivering services became 50% or more of the Gross National Product. This shift to a service economy created great economic upheaval since many service jobs paid less than established manufacturing jobs. Nevertheless, as manufacturing became more and more efficient, fewer and fewer people were needed to work in this sector of the economy, and many workers were relocated into providing services. At the beginning of the twenty-first century, many are convinced that we are moving into the Experience Economy (Pine & Gilmore, 1999) wherein commodities, goods, and services are most successfully sold when they are marketed as contributing to experiences. In the title to their book, Pine and Gilmore (1999) claim *Work is Theatre & Every Business a Stage.*

KEY TERMS

**Experience
   Economy
Experience
Commodities
Entrepreneurial
Revenue Stream
Product
Goods
Services
Activities
Classification
Activities
Events
Personal Service
Supplies
Equipment
Venue**

Programmers are expected to be entrepreneurial employees in the emerging leisure service industry.

PRINCIPAL ECONOMIC ACTIVITY	ECONOMIC VALUE CREATED
Extracting	Commodities
Manufacturing	Goods
Delivering	Services
Staging	Experiences

Table 5-1: Evolution of Economic Value and Activity (adapted from Pine and Gilmore, 1999).

Although commodities were traditionally thought of as mining and agricultural products, today the term "commoditized" is applied as a pejorative term—a state of affairs to be avoided. Companies do not want their products to be considered commodities because commodities compete solely on price, not on other product features. According to Shaw and Ivens (2005), "For the first time in centuries, differentiation on price, quality, and delivery is an unsustainable business strategy" (p. xix). Commodities, for example, iron ore, have always had this characteristic. For the most part, iron ore is iron ore. There is little product differentiation and therefore iron ore competes solely on price. However, as manufacturing processes improve, many manufactured goods are similar and of high quality. There is less and less product differentiation to be demonstrated on product features alone. In a similar way, the service economy has struggled to differentiate its products as well. Until they are used, it is difficult to understand differences between services. Thus, not only are commodities commoditized, so are many products and services. Competition for customers has shifted to the customer's experience with a product or service. Shaw and Ivens (2005) assert, "The customer experience is the next competitive battleground" (p. xix).

> *An activity is focused participation in a specific occasion of interaction...*

There are several implications of this for programming. First, many other providers will now be developing experiences; we will have additional competition for our patron's attention. Second, new concepts about how to think about and develop programs are being introduced. For example, Pine and Gilmore (1999) use the theatrical metaphor of "staging" programs, and we have incorporated this concept in this text as appropriate. Third, the attributes of the leisure experience as put forth in this text describe the ultimate experience to be developed. Leisure is a "gold standard" experience, and we know how to stage it. Fourth, consumers prefer to spend their resources on services and experiences rather than on commodities and goods. Services and experiences are higher-valued economic ends. The success of mass retailers such as Wal-Mart, where goods can be purchased at a very low cost, suggest that people prefer to acquire goods at the least cost possible to free up personal assets to spend on services and experiences. Fifth, and perhaps most important, the programs we have produced for years—leisure experiences—are now a category of economic activity. Since the entire economy is shifting to providing experiences as an important economic end, surely we will not need to continually spend time justifying providing experiences!

Some have argued that experience is not a separate sector of the economy but just a variant of the service sector. We believe that it is fundamentally different. A service is a set of intangible activities carried out on the customer's behalf (Pine & Gilmore, 1999). For example, when we organize a trip for individuals, they are freed from the burden of doing it themselves. Experiences, however, are a set of events staged to engage the customer in a memorable way (Pine & Gilmore, 1999). They are created through interaction and result in pleasant memories to be recalled in the future. It is this notion of engagement and participation by the participant in creating the experience that separates a service from an experience. Engagement is a well-known phenomenon to recreation and leisure programmers, as we have been focusing on operationalizing engagement for the past 25 years.

So, we are primarily in the experience sector of the economy, although we also provide services, and in some cases, we market goods. Programmers in hospitality, event management, tourism, public agencies, and commercial recreation are expected to be entrepreneurial employees in the emerging leisure experience industry (Crompton, 1999). "The leisure services industry is that group of service enterprises whose primary aim is to serve consumers' leisure time needs," write Crompton, Reid, and Uysal (1987, p. 22). These needs are met through a variety of products that Kelly (1985) defines as "something that is designed, made, developed, and distributed" (p. 342). Programmers are responsible for developing marketable leisure experience products that will attract a participant base and provide adequate revenue streams. *A revenue stream is the income generated by a product that can be brought to the marketplace and sold.*

LEISURE PRODUCTS

As discussed in the previous section, all products can be classified as commodities, goods, services, or experiences. *Product* is the inclusive term used to identify commodities, goods, services, and experiences that may be brought to the marketplace and sold for use in leisure.

Commodities are not offered as recreation and leisure products. However, the other three are offered. A *good* is tangible; an individual has something in his or her possession after its purchase. For example, tennis rackets, suntan oil, and jet skis are all goods sold in the leisure market. A *service* is intangible. It involves an activity being carried out on the customer's behalf, but the customer does not possess a physical item as a result of the purchase. A typical leisure service would be sharpening ice skates. *Experiences* involve engaging participants in a series of staged events that result in reflective, pleasant memories. A memorable vacation to an exotic island, participation in a leisure education program, or participation in a peak experience can all be part of an individual's consciousness for many years.

GOODS

Goods are physical entities marketed for use in leisure. There are two types of goods: supplies and equipment. They can range in cost from a 50-cent table tennis ball to expensive ski equipment, and are provid-

Product Type	Activity	
	Tennis	Shooting
Goods		
Supplies	Balls, rosin	Gun powder, bullets, targets
Equipment	Racquets, clothes, and shoes	Guns, ear protectors, eye guards
Services	Stringing racquets Scheduling and renting court time	Loading shells Selling time on a shooting range
Experiences	Tournaments Fantasy camp	Instructions on gun safety and shooting Hunting trip

Table 5-2: Types of Products

ed by a wide range of manufacturers and retailers. Table 5-2 presents examples of each type of goods for two activities to help further differentiate them.

Supplies

Supplies are consumable products used while participating in leisure occasions. Because they are consumed and thus need to be continually replenished by participants, these sales represent an ongoing source of income for the agency.

Selling supplies at or near the point of use is usually a very lucrative source of revenue for leisure service agencies. In most cases, supplies offered for sale at these locations are sold at a premium price because the demand for them at these locations is inelastic. This means that within a range of prices, the supplies will be purchased regardless of price and that demand is not reduced by price. For example, after a difficult hike to the rim of the Grand Canyon, one is not likely to fail to capture the triumph on film because film costs $8.50 a roll on-site instead of the $5.50 regularly paid at K-Mart. This is price inelasticity.

There are many supplies for participating in leisure that can be provided on-site. In addition to the supplies used to participate in the activity, there is also a considerable market in associated merchandise, such as food, beverages, and souvenirs. A general principle used by entrepreneurial programmers today is to provide the supplies needed to facilitate participation in a leisure activity at a point close to use, and to use these sales as an additional revenue stream.

...the wise programmer will spend more effort on retaining current customers and trying to move those with infrequent and moderate rates of play to more frequent participation.

Equipment

Equipment is a nonconsumable product used to participate in leisure. The sale of equipment is a potential source of revenue for a leisure service agency, but the equipment inventory will not turn over as frequently as the supply inventory. Examples of equipment include fishing rods and reels, ballet shoes, scuba equipment, golf clubs, and so on. There are a variety of settings in which equipment is sold by leisure service agencies. Commercial operations almost always have a pro-shop or other retail outlet to sell equipment associated with the activity offered in the facility.

Sport and leisure equipment retailing is undergoing a polarization. Large sport equipment megastores are at one end of the retailing spectrum. They offer primarily a low price and use few knowledgeable clerks to assist. At the other end are small specialty shops with higher prices and a knowledgeable sales staff. Any decision to retail sport and leisure equipment will need to consider the local market and how the agency will position its retail operation relative to existing outlets. Regardless of the retailing strategy, equipment sales can also be an important revenue stream for an agency.

Renting equipment is considered a service and is covered in the next section on services.

SERVICES

There are two types of services that may be developed for leisure markets: personal services and equipment and venue rentals. All can be offered at multiple sites in many different formats.

Personal Services

A personal service is a helpful function related to leisure participation for which a fee is charged. Often, these functions could be completed by the customer, but for some reason, such as the lack of time, skill, or specialized equipment, they cannot or prefer not to perform them. Instead, they choose to hire someone to perform them. For example, stringing a tennis racquet requires a special machine and some skill at using it. The cost of the machine and the time it takes to develop the skill make it impractical and uneconomical for most to string their own racquets. In contrast to this, many fly fishermen would not consider using a fly they had not tied themselves even though pre-tied ties are readily available in the marketplace. Scraping and varnishing a boat is a difficult but manageable job that does not take specialized skill, just hard work. Some hire individuals to perform this service, whereas others perform it themselves. One can hunt without a guide, but a guide will usually have intimate knowledge of an area and know the recent migration patterns of the game being hunted. Thus, they offer for sale unique access to the experience sought. This last example is a good illustration of how indiscrete these categories can be. A good guide can turn a service into a memorable experience if their work is well-organized and they engage the participant in an appropriate manner to allow them to truly participate in the evolving event.

Events are a collection of activities usually organized around a theme or purpose.

THE SERVICE ENCOUNTER

Regardless of the type of service being offered, how it is offered matters. The service encounter refers to the sum of face-to-face interactions between the patron and provider that occurs in delivering a service and the emotional feelings generated by these interactions. The outcomes of these interactions endure through the recalled memories of the encounters, and these memories are the enduring product of the service encounter.

Training employees to deliver good service encounters is a major part of a programmer's job. The programmer prepares employees to deliver good service in three steps.

• Lead by example and deliver the good service you expect of your employees.

• Train new employees to deliver good service by outlining expectations, role-playing service encounter episodes, and providing on-the-job supervision and tutoring to further develop employees' skills.

• Reinforce training and establish good service providing ongoing, supportive supervision and rewarding good service delivery.

What is a good service encounter? What should employees strive for in delivering good service? As our economy has moved from a production to a service economy, these are major questions perplexing all organizations. Because of its importance, much research and writing has occurred on this topic. Distilled from this research, here are our recommendations about the most desired features of a good service encounter.

• Speedy, Prompt Service. After presenting themselves to be served, people expect to receive service promptly. How long is too long varies by individual and the service situation. But we all have a sense of how long is too long to wait for recognition by a waiter in a sit-down restaurant, and similarly, have a notion of an appropriate wait time in a variety of service situations. Waiting too long for service or having a service encounter take too long both result in unsatisfied patrons.

• Efficient, Effective Service. That staff are prepared to get it right the first time matters greatly. Not having answers to reasonable questions and not having or completing the correct forms are all seen as product defects in a service encounter. Patrons expect to have their business completed when they leave the service encounter.

• Friendly, Authentic Service. For some individuals, friendliness is the benchmark of good service; for others, it is promptness and effectiveness. The best encounters have a feel of authentic interaction and caring for the patron that results from the demeanor of service staff. As part of this general concept, patrons expect to be treated with civility, courtesy, and in a friendly manner. Expressing genuine caring and empathy for patrons' needs is also important.

There are cultural differences in how patrons view a service encounter. Some age groups and cultures expect to be treated with appropriate role distance, formality, and deference. For example, it is very unlikely that a senior citizen will find it friendly for a teenage employee to refer to them by their nickname. So, one-size-fits-all training may not work well in a heterogeneous, diverse community.

There are other situations in which friendliness of the staff is an essential part of the service. For example, the atmosphere created by staff in a health club is an essential, signature feature of health clubs and other kinds of membership operations.

Thus, the programmer needs to understand the role and function of the service encounters that they are preparing staff to deliver and to make certain that staff have appropriate training and authority to allow the flexibility needed to meet the different expectations of patrons.

Myriad services associated with leisure participation can be organized and offered for sale. Recognizing and developing these services into revenue streams is an important skill for programmers. The following are additional examples of personal services supporting leisure participation that could be for sale.

- Sale of tickets with point-of-sale convenience provided for a surcharge
- Rental of on-site storage lockers
- Sale of guide services
- Retail sales at point-of-need or -participation—for example, the sale of film on the rim of the Grand Canyon
- Repair service—ski repair offered at the base of a ski slope
- Maintenance services—racquet stringing, skate sharpening, and so on
- Activity service amenities—fish cleaning services offered at a boat dock, or golf caddies
- Personal amenities—a masseuse in a fitness club, or locker room attendant who provides toiletry articles and warm towels

When examined in this manner, it becomes apparent that the programmer has many opportunities to develop a variety of complementary leisure services that can expand current product lines. These activities will make their units a revenue contributor to leisure service enterprises.

Equipment and Venue Rentals

An important service that is often provided is the rental of recreation and leisure equipment and venue space. There are many reasons customers may desire to rent equipment. If they are beginners, they may be simply exploring the activity and will not want to invest in equipment until they are certain of their future participation. Some will want to rent different types of equipment to try it out. Others will rent equipment on-site because it is too bulky to bring to the recreation area. For example, scuba divers almost always rent air tanks, although they may bring the rest of their gear to a dive site. Renting equipment so individuals can experiment with various recreation and leisure activities at an initial low cost of investment is a significant way that leisure service agencies help individuals experiment with and learn about new pursuits. Equipment rentals can be an important revenue stream for many recreation and leisure facilities.

Venues are locales used to stage leisure experiences. They include buildings, special facilities, and park areas. Some activities require a specific, dedicated facility, whereas others can use a more general facility. The provision of venues for leisure is a major role for all leisure service agencies. Some venues, for example, a swimming pool, are owned by individuals, making them a good. Most often, because of high cost and relatively infrequent use, access to a specialized leisure venue is through paid admission. Individuals essentially rent time in a venue, and providing these venues is an important service leisure services agencies provide. The revenue from renting leisure venues is also an important revenue stream to many agencies.

There are many ways to charge fees for use of leisure venues. How these sales contribute to an agency's revenue varies with the type of agency. No single agency offers every type of venue. The same venue may have many different financial arrangements for its operation. For example, water play facilities are operated with every conceivable financial arrangement, including public and private beaches at salt and fresh water locations, free public pools, member-only private pool clubs, commercial water parks, and privately owned home pools.

The provision of recreation facilities is undertaken by all four types of leisure service agencies. The public leisure system offers many recreation venues on a no-cost basis, although it is not uncommon for these systems to charge for expensive, newly constructed, specialized facilities. In general, the public system limits its facilities to those that are relatively inexpensive to build and that serve a large number of people. They typically provide baseball, football, hockey, softball, and soccer fields; tennis, volleyball, and basketball courts; swimming pools, beaches, and marinas; and golf courses. The public system has the primary responsibility for providing communities open space, which positions them as the major provider of recreation and leisure play space. Leisure service agencies in larger cities are also involved in providing cultural and educational amenities, such as zoos, museums, and aquariums, plus regional facilities, such as arboretums and spectator sport stadiums.

Rental of specialized leisure facilities is often the major source of earned income for many commercial leisure service agencies. For example, an indoor tennis facility obtains a significant amount of its income from the rental of court space; that is, the sale of access to leisure space. Crossley (1990) has outlined how providers of commercial facilities and retailers of supplies and equipment can use multi-tier programs to expand their revenue streams. Additionally, complimentary revenue streams in such a facility could include the sale of instructions, proshop sales, nursery services, and possibly an annual membership fee.

Commercial, not-for-profit, and private leisure service agencies operate a wide variety of leisure facilities. Occasionally, their facilities will duplicate those provided by the public system, in which case they market additional features not included in public facilities, such as easier access, nicer amenities, or some other feature. In other cases, they build specialized or expensive facilities that could not be justified with public expenditures. Not-for-profit agencies, such as YMCAs, also sell access to recreation facilities and space as a major source of revenue. Private agencies are frequently formed to build a specific facility for members, for example, a private country club.

EXPERIENCES

Experiences are a series of staged events that engage a participant and re-sult in pleasant, recallable memories. Experiences occur through engaged interaction in a situated activity system as has been explained elsewhere in the text (Refer to Chapters Two and Three). They are the principal, unique product of leisure service provision, and knowledge about how to stage experiences to facilitate leisure is the unique professional ex-pertise of the programmer. Two major types of experiences are activi-ties and events.

Activities

An activity is focused participation in a specific occasion of inter-action, for example, baseball with specific objects, rules, and physical spaces. Activities are the basic unit of participation in leisure and rec-reation; therefore, they are the primary unit that may be packaged for sale. Individuals usually participate in activities with family or friends. Thus, the manager will often be marketing activities to networks of peers rather than individuals unknown to each other.

A wide variety of activities are considered leisure. Some are endur-ing and have continued to attract a significant number of participants

Arts: Performing; music, dance, drama
Visual; crafts
New arts; (technology-based arts such as computer graphics)
Cognitive and literary activities
Self-improvement/education
Sports, games, and athletics
Aquatics
Environmental activities; outdoor recreation, risk recreation
Wellness and fitness
Hobbies, social recreation
Volunteer services
Travel and tourism

Table 5-3: Activity Classifications

Exercise 5-1: Examining the Breadth and Depth of Activity Program Offerings

Obtain recreation program brochures from two leisure service agencies, such as a municipal park and recreation department and a not-for-profit agency. Examine both brochures and compare/contrast them based on the following questions:

- To what extent does each brochure offer a wide range of activities (such as those outlined in Table 5-3)?
- Which activity classifications were offered in both brochures? Which were not?
- What are some reasons why agencies do not offer all of the classifications listed in Table 5-3? In your professional opinion, do you think these are viable reasons? Why or why not?

for many years, e.g., swimming, walking, softball, and other sports. Yet many other activities attract smaller numbers of intensely interested individuals in highly specialized activities, such as snowmobiling and oil painting. Skate boarding and paint-ball battles are examples of current activities with growing participation.

The leisure service manager is left with the problem of determining which activities to offer initially and which to develop further. Unfortunately, some activities require very expensive facilities, and one is always left with the dilemma that interest may wane before the investment capital needed to build a specialized facility is recovered. To help develop an understanding of the breadth of possible activities that may be offered, a typology of activity classes, developed from classifications published by Edginton, Hanson, and Edginton (1992), Farrell and Lundegren (1991), and DeGraaf, Jordan, and DeGraaf (1999), is presented in Table 5-3 on page 81.

It is generally considered good practice in municipal leisure service agencies to offer a comprehensive inventory of activity classes. However, many leisure service organizations offer only one class or type of activity, for example, a tennis club or a country club. Explore this concept further by completing Exercise 5-1.

To provide comprehensive services that are in current demand, programmers must keep abreast of popular interest in a breadth of activities. Additionally, they must understand how activities may be delivered as a product that can attract participants. The following six methods of selling activities can be used to create revenue streams:

Venues are locales used to stage leisure experiences.

1. Selling instruction in the activity. Sales can be segmented by level of ability, including beginner, novice, advanced, refresher courses, and improvement workshops. Sales can be further segmented by how the instructional program is organized. For example, one could offer the same activity as a six-to-eight-week class, a weekend clinic, or a one-day workshop.

2. Renting equipment needed to participate in the activity. (This is discussed in more detail in the section on goods.)

3. Charging admission to unique space needed to participate in the activity. For example, fees for rounds of golf, rental of tennis courts, signing of hunting leases. All of these involve charging for access to expensive leisure space.

4. Selling equipment needed to participate in an activity. Pro-shops at a golf course are an example of selling recreation and sport equipment needed to participate.

5. Charging for organizing and arranging to participate in an activity, for example, trips and tours, or providing unique access, for example, an organized boat tour to scuba dive specific sites.

6. Selling needed ancillary supplies such as food, water, and lodging, while participating in an activity. For example, a major portion of travel and tourism dollars is spent on food, lodging, and transportation, not on the amenities that motivate individuals to take the trip in the first place.

The programmer must take a strategic approach to the marketing of activities and must match activities to specific networks of interested individuals. Often, recreation programmers spend too many resources trying to attract new participants to an activity when their best marketing strategy would be to increase the usage of infrequent users. For example, Warnick and Howard have documented that golf and tennis appeal to small cohorts of the population: "Eighty-eight percent of the

---

Softball tournaments—weekend or week-long.

Softball weekend getaway—a tournament is offered at a camp and all players stay in the camp's dorms, eat meals together, have skills improvement clinics, and so on.

Softball Fantasy Camp—a weekend or week-long camp of softball with instruction, play, videotaping of each player, and so on.

Softball Equipment Pro-shop—sell a range of softball equipment at a wide variety of price-points.

Softball Skills Improvement Clinic—with professional players as a lead draw.

Softball Diamond Rental—rent your softball diamonds for practice.

Table 5-4: Expanding the Softball Product Line

adult population reported never playing even one round of golf during 1999, while tennis had an even narrower appeal, with 93 percent indicating never playing the sport at any time during the same period" (1996, p. 74). They go on to explain that about two percent of the total population accounts for approximately 75 percent of the play in each sport. Thus, the wise programmer will spend more effort on retaining current customers and trying to move those with infrequent and moderate rates of play to more frequent participation. Expanding product lines to encourage more play is one good strategy. For example, although the agency may already offer the opportunity to play in softball leagues, sales of this product may be increased by expanding the ways it is packaged for sale. Consider the ideas included in Table 5-4 on page 83 for expanding the softball product line.

In a similar fashion, the programmer needs to continually scan other activities that are offered for ways to expand these product lines by increasing or expanding participation and thereby increasing revenues. Practice developing this skill by completing Exercise 5-2.

Format	Example
Less than one day	A parade
One day	A health fair, clinic, or workshop
Weekend	A weekend softball tournament
One week	County fair
A month	A community's centennial celebration

Table 5-5: Formats of Events

Events

Events are a collection of activities usually organized around a theme or purpose. They may become a special event if there is something unique to them. Leisure service managers are responsible for conceptualizing, organizing, and staging desirable leisure activities and events so they may be sold to create a revenue base. Their duration can vary, but five typical formats are presented in Table 5-5.

Events are financed in different ways. For example, a parade may be operated with no charge to spectators. In this case, all organizations that have entries in the parade will finance them and perhaps pay an entry fee. The parade organizers may also receive in-kind services from the city government for police to maintain crowds and control traffic. Another possible arrangement is to pay for these services with profits

5

Enduro—an endurance event.

Grand Prix—an event operated to see who can complete the course in the shortest time.

Hare and Hound—operated on a marked course over natural terrain with a mass, dead engine start.

Hare Scrambles—similar to Hare and Hound but operated over a closed course, usually as a multi-lapped race.

Scrambles—held on a relatively short, prepared course with left and right turns, hills, and usually a few jumps.

Hill Climb—a short race to see who can make it to the top of a very steep hill first.

Ice—operated on ice covered courses up to a half-mile long, with classes for studded and non-studded tires.

Motocross—usually operated on a relatively small course, entirely visible from one location by a group of paying spectators. Raced on a dirt track with various combinations of tight turns, jumps, and a few other obstacles, such as a water jump. Individual heats usually last 20–45 minutes and have 20–30 riders.

Observed Trails—this event challenges a motorcycle rider's balance and finesse and involves negotiating a prescribed course of significant obstacles.

Trail Rides—strictly fun rides with no timekeeping or racing

.

From: Motorcycle Industry Council. (1992–1993). The OHV Planner. Irvine, CA: Motorcycle Industry Council.

Table 5-6: Off-Road Vehicle Events

1. Total Audience

2. Sponsor Service/Follow Through

3. Sponsorship Fee

4. Other Sponsors

5. Name in the Event Title

6. Event History/Success

7. Right of First Refusal

8. Signage

9. Media Coverage

10. Category Exclusivity

From: Schmader, S. W. & Jackson, R. (1997) Special events: Inside and out (2nd ed.).
Champaign, IL; Sagamore.

Table 5-7: Top Ten Factors Corporate Sponsors Look for in an Event

from entry fees or other activities offered in an accompanying festival or other event.

The organization and operation of events can be very specialized. For example, Table 5-6 on page 85 includes ten events that could be operated for motorcycle enthusiasts by managers of large park areas or private land owners. This list is presented as an example of the wide variety and specialization of events that can be organized and sold.

There are many possible revenue streams from off-road vehicle events, including entrance fees for contestants, spectator admission fees, pit/garage fees, concession sales, souvenir sales, parking fees, etc. It is especially important that activities in large events be planned so that there are many free ones to draw a crowd and thereby create a critical mass of customers. However, there must be enough revenue producing activities to support the non-revenue producing activities.

Most large special events operated today must have additional financial support from corporate sponsors (Schmader & Jackson, 1997). To obtain this support, the leisure service manager will need to offer benefits to the sponsor. Schmader and Jackson (1997) have identified ten factors that corporations look for in an event (shown in Table 5-7).

Frequently, leisure service managers in not-for-profit, governmental, and private agencies will also organize and operate fund-raising events that are not leisure programs but whose purpose is to finance leisure programs that cannot be operated on a complete cost recovery basis (Busser, 1990). For example, an all-community garage sale, bake sales, car washes, and so on, may be offered.

CONCLUSION

Programmers in all agencies are expected to be entrepreneurial. To accomplish this, they need to understand the business we are in and the breadth of leisure service products that may be developed. Many ideas for packaging these products and bringing them to the marketplace for sale were discussed in this chapter. Providing a comprehensive set of leisure products will fully serve an agency's target service population and result in sufficient revenues to meet the agency's financial goals.

REFERENCES

Busser, J. A. (1990). *Programming: For employee services and recreation.* Champaign, IL: Sagamore.

Crompton, J. L. (1999). *Financing and acquiring park and recreation resources.* Champaign, IL: Human Kinetics.

Crompton, J. L., Reid, I. S., & Uysal, M. (1987). Empirical identification of product life-cycle patterns in the delivery of municipal park and recreation services. *Journal of Park and Recreation Administration, 5*(1), 17–34.

Crossley, J. (1990, March). Multi-tier programming in commercial recreation. *Parks & Recreation,* 68–72.

DeGraaf, D., Jordan, D. J., DeGraaf, K. H. (1999). *Programming for park, recreation, and leisure services: A servant leadership approach.* College Station, PA: Venture.

Edginton, C. R., Hanson, C. J., & Edginton, S. R. (1992). *Leisure programming: Concepts, trends, and professional practice.* Dubuque, IA: WCB Brown & Benchmark.

Farrell, P., & Lundegren, H. M. (1991). *The process of recreation programming. Theory and technique* (3rd ed.). State College, PA: Venture.

Pine, B. J. II, & Gilmore, J. H. (1999). *The experience economy.* Boston, MA: Harvard Business School Press.

Kelly, J. R. (1985). *Recreation business.* New York: John Wiley & Sons.

Motorcycle Industry Council. (1992-1993; Winter) Types of OHV events. In *The OHV planner* (pp. 1, 4). Irvine, CA: Motorcycle Industry Council, Inc.

Schmader S. W., & Jackson, R. (1997). *Special events: Inside and out* (2nd ed.). Champaign, IL: Sagamore.

Schmitt, B. H. (1999). *Experiential marketing.* New York: Free Press.

Shaw, C., & Ivens, J. (2005). *Building great customer experiences.* New York: Palgrave Macmillan.

Warnick, R. B., & Howard, D. R. (1996). Market share analysis of selected sport and recreation activities: An update—1972 to 1992. *Journal of Park and Recreation Administration, 14*(2), 53–79.

5

Seniors and Youth Conference
Photo courtesy of Long Beach Parks, Recreation, and Marine Department, Long Beach, CA

Using Goals and Objectives in Program Development

Leisure service agencies use goals and objectives for a variety of purposes. There are planning goals, strategic goals, outcome goals, profit goals, budget goals, income goals, learning goals, performance goals, and so on. We know students are required to develop these in many classes, and that you have likely been required to use a variety of methods that are the favorites of your different professors. Goals and objectives in various forms are used by modern organizations to organize and coordinate the efforts of their employees and varied activities. To function effectively in these organizations, you must be proficient in this process.

KEY TERMS

Goals
Objectives
Heirarchical
   Arrangement

WHAT ARE GOALS AND OBJECTIVES?

Developing goals and objectives involves writing statements that define and delimit an intended accomplishment. Simply put, one succinctly writes down what he or she intends to do. The process is implemented by developing a series of linguistic statements that are arranged hierarchically, beginning with broad statements and moving successively through more narrow and specific statements. One concludes by stating an objective so specific and clear that its accomplishment is measurable and can thereby be documented.

A goal is broad statement about what is to be accomplished. For example, a programmer may wish to develop a kayaking class for beginners. Thus, the goal may be "to develop a kayaking class for beginners." Objectives, then, are the specific statements that describe how the goal will be accomplished. In most cases, a single goal will require the development of several objectives to fully describe and document accomplishment of the goal.

In and of itself, an individual goal or objective seldom will be specific, clear, and measurable. Goals and objectives achieve meaning because they are a part of a series of statements that have been logically and sequentially developed. Examining a single goal or objective out of context cannot convey meaning any more than a single sentence taken out of context from a novel can convey the meaning of a novel. Writing goals and objectives and writing novels both require a considerable degree of writing skill and an ability to clearly express one's thoughts with written language in a well-developed, clear, and logical fashion. This skill can be learned.

Goals and objectives use linguistic statements to define and delimit an intended accomplishment.

The linguistic structure of goals and objectives can be simple or complicated. Neophytes often err by trying to write a statement that is too complicated. For beginners, it is recommended that each linguistic statement—that is, each goal or objective—be written in the following form:

Infinitive: Each statement should begin with an infinitive, which consists of the infinitive marker "to" and a verb that indicates the action to be taken. Each statement should contain only one infinitive. Measuring accomplishment is easier if there is only one action to measure. For an excellent list of verbs useful for writing goals and objectives, see the work of Gronlund (1970).

Subject: Each statement must have a subject that conveys what is going to be accomplished. There should be only one subject in each statement.

Measurement device: Each statement should have some device incorporated into the statement that makes clear how the accomplishment of the goal or objective is going to be measured and documented. Often, this measurement device is a time frame that is specified for accomplishing the goal. However, many other measurement devices can be used.

There are exceptions to this last requirement. Some goals and objectives do not contain specific measurement devices, but are simply declarations of an intention to accomplish something or point the agency in a specific direction. When this is the case, other support goals or objectives that are measurable are developed to measure the original goal.

Consider the following agency program planning goal: *To operate a women's softball league during the summer of 2010.* This goal begins with the infinitive *to operate*, which indicates an intention to accomplish it by organizing, publicizing, and running the event. *Operate* is a verb that is a summative, final action that includes all of the other actions necessary to complete the operation of the event. The subject of the goal is *a women's softball league*, which is the entity to be developed and operated. The measurement device is *during the summer of 2010*. In stating this, we have said that we will consider our goal accomplished if the league is operated during the summer of 2010. With a timeline, we have created a terminal behavior that is clear and specific enough to be measured.

What is unclear in this goal? The size of the softball league, where it is going to be held, and other details of operation. However, these details are unnecessary at this level of goal development. The specific details of league operation will be presented later in an additional series of program design goals. What is important in the current goal is that the agency has committed its resources to a specific project with a targeted completion date.

In writing goal and objective statements, one should keep the thought conveyed simple. Never use a conjunction in a goal or objective statement. If a conjunction is used, a second thought (either a second verb, subject, or measurement device) is added to the statement that will unnecessarily complicate the goal or objective. If there are two goals or objectives, then write two statements—do not try to join them together into one statement. It is also important to be parsimonious in writing

> *...goal and objective writing is a method for focusing the organization and giving it direction in accomplishing its mission.*

goals and objectives. Try to write a simple, clear, concise statement to convey what you intend to accomplish.

HIERARCHICAL ARRANGEMENT

The application of goal and objective writing in organizations is a means to an end. It is a method for focusing the organization and giving it direction in accomplishing its mission. The task, then, is to develop goal and objective statements that have *operational clarity*. These statements are operationally clear when they are clear to the staff who must implement them. They provide direction to the organization and its staff, and they can be measured so that the accomplishments of the organization can be documented. Operationally, clear goals and objectives have operational meaning and provide a way for the organization to focus, organize, direct, and document its activities, thereby helping it accomplish its mission.

The relationship between an agency's mission statement and its subsequent goals and objectives is one of a *hierarchical arrangement*. An agency's mission statement delimits, in a general way, what it is trying to accomplish. The mission statement itself is not measurable. Its accomplishment is measured by a succeeding series of goals and objectives that progressively become more narrow and specific. There can be many succeeding levels of goals and objectives between the mission statement and the final, measurable objectives. How many levels of statements there will be depends on the complexity of the organization and the complexity of the content area for which goals and objectives are being written.

Figure 6-1 on page 92 provides a diagrammatic representation of this *organizational hierarchy* with some examples. Note that the mission statement defines the purpose of the agency and provides direction about what the agency will accomplish in the larger community, but it is not necessarily measurable. Generally, the agency director, in consultation with the board, is the individual responsible for this portion of the hierarchy. The short-range planning goals are not measurable either, but they outline an area of program development and begin to state what it is the agency will accomplish. These goals are usually prepared by the agency director with the unit directors. At the next level, management by objective statements are prepared. These usually accompany budget preparation and allow program managers to provide further definition to services that will be developed. Finally, program design goals are developed by program managers (and sometimes leaders) at two levels. One level focuses on the planning and logistical aspects of the program (e.g., scheduling fields, hiring officials, ordering uniforms). The other level of goals specifies what the participants will be able to do at the completion of the program (e.g., skill attainment, attitude changes). Additional examples of these will be provided in Chapters Seven, Eight, and Ten.

FRAMING THE MISSION STATEMENT

"A mission statement is a statement of the organization's purpose—what it wants to accomplish in the larger environment," according to

The relationship between an agency's mission statement and its subsequent goals and objectives is one of a hierarchical arrangement.

A mission statement is a statement of the organization's purpose.

Hierarchy	Staff Responsible	Examples
AGENCY MISSION Not measurable, defines purpose of agency.	Director	–To ensure that all citizens of Anytown, USA, have access to comprehensive leisure services, including activities, events, and facilities, by serving as a provider, referral agency, or catalyst for their development.
3-5 YEAR SHORT-RANGE PLANNING GOALS Defines basic areas of programming effort; identifies the types of activities, events, services, or facilities that will be provided.	Director and Unit Directors	–To develop a comprehensive sports program for children.
1-YEAR MANAGEMENT BY OBJECTIVES Specifies programs to accomplish, usually tied to a budget element or work program.	Program Managers	–To develop a summer softball league for girls 12-16 years of age by May 1, 2004 with at least 10 teams.
PROGRAM DESIGN OBJECTIVES Planning statements for the manager to accomplish and performance objectives to be demonstrated by participants.	Program Managers and Leaders	Planning Objectives –To order regulation uniforms for all teams. –To hire at least two certified officials per game. Performance Objectives –At the end of the league, participants will demonstrate improvement in seven out of 10 skill areas, as evidenced by the coaches' progress forms.

Figure 6-1: Goal and Objective Hierarchy with Examples

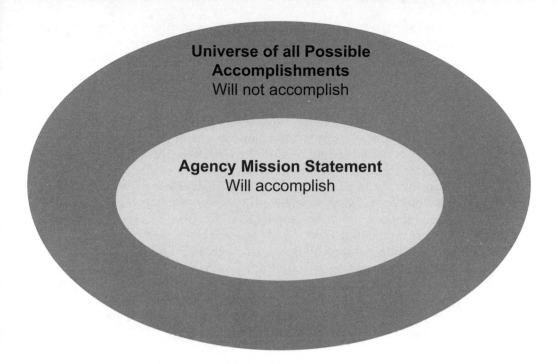

Figure 6-2: Limits Defined by the Mission Statement

Kotler and Armstrong (1993, p. 27). It provides the direction needed so that the efforts of independent work groups are focused toward the accomplishment of the organization's reason for existing. In a mission statement, it is as important to define what the agency will not accomplish as well as what it will accomplish. This notion is illustrated in Figure 6-2. For example, mission statements include the provision of recreation services and facilities. Concomitantly, they exclude other possible tasks that the agency could undertake but chooses not to for a variety of reasons.

It is also important to recognize that mission statements are somewhat elastic in what they include. They are nebulous in order to provide maximum flexibility for the agency in the future. Mission statements are considered long-term commitments of the agency and are not usually altered in the short run. A very narrow, specific mission statement would commit the agency to providing a narrow range of services to its clients. A nebulous statement gives the agency maximum leeway to respond to changing demands and needs without continuously rewriting the mission statement. Developing a mission statement, then, requires one to define some area for accomplishment without being so restrictive that the agency has no latitude for flexibility in accomplishing the mission. Additional detail about how to write a mission statement will be provided in Chapter Seven.

...the relationship between goals and objectives is determined by the position each statement occupies in a hierarchy...

GOALS AND OBJECTIVES—HOW ARE THEY DIFFERENT?

There is a great deal of confusion about the difference between goals and objectives. In this book, we will take a pragmatic approach to this problem and assume there is no practical difference between a goal and an objective. *It can thus be deduced that the relationship between goals and objectives is a syntactical one that is determined by the position each statement occupies in a hierarchy of goal and objective statements. Furthermore, objectives for some levels in an organization are goals for employees occupying the next lower level.*

However, the relationship between the goals and objectives is important. First, objectives are the measurement points for a goal. Therefore, it is accepted that if all of the objectives identified for a goal are accomplished, the goal is considered accomplished. Second, one must consider the location in the organizational structure for which the goal or objective is being developed. Very often, objectives for one level become the goals to be accomplished in the next descending level of the organization. In this way, goals and objectives network the activities of the organization and allow work activity to be unified from the highest statement in the organization (mission statement) through the activities of a part-time recreation leader; that is, an objective states what the leader intends for participants to accomplish in a program.

Two assumptions govern goal and objective theory and the development of goal and objective statements:

> 1. The accomplishment of a set of goals that support the mission statement or a set of objectives that support an individual goal will be accepted as proof of mission or goal accomplishment.
> 2. Any list of goals and objectives that we use operationally to document mission or goal accomplishment is only a partial list of the many goals and objectives that could have been developed. Selection of any goal or objective is normative; one must realize that any goal or objective selected is just a sample from a larger list of all possible goals or objectives that could have been selected. This latter point is illustrated in Figure 6-3.

REPRESENTATIVE NATURE OF SELECTED GOALS AND OBJECTIVES

Figure 6-3 is a further elaboration of Figure 6-2. In Figure 6-3, there are three types of ovals: A, B, and C. Oval A illustrates the entire universe of all possible accomplishments that the agency could undertake. Oval B illustrates the space from the entire universe of possible accomplishments that the agency has delimited with its mission statement and thereby indicated its intent to accomplish. Oval C represents the space occupied by any goal the agency has indicated it intends to accomplish.

Figure 6-3 graphically illustrates that any goal or objective is only a representative sample from the entire universe of goals and objectives that could be drawn from the universe defined by the mission statement.

All of the space outside Oval B but within Oval A represents possible accomplishments that have been excluded from the agency's mission statement. The space within Ovals C1 and C2 illustrates the accomplishments that could be achieved within the space of possible

...objectives are the measurement points for a goal.

Figure 6-3: Limits Defined by Goals and Objectives

accomplishments defined by these two goals. The space outside Ovals C1 and C2 but within Oval B includes all other possible goals that could be accomplished within the parameters defined by the agency's mission statement. Any set of goals, then, represents only a small portion of all possible goals that could be selected. The Xs within Ovals C1 and C2 represent objectives for accomplishing each goal. Again, there is room for many more Xs in each oval. This illustrates that any list of objectives identified for a goal is only a partial list of all possible objectives that could be developed to document goal accomplishment.

Selecting goals and objectives should be taken seriously. As illustrated in Figure 6-2, in using goals and objectives to demonstrate agency accomplishments, one is allowing the agency to be evaluated on only a small portion of the activity that could be used. Because of this, it is important that the goals and objectives selected be representative of the agency's total mission and typical undertakings.

STAFF PARTICIPATION IN DEVELOPING GOALS AND OBJECTIVES

The process of developing and implementing goals and objectives in an organization is extremely important to the success of their use in the organization. Where should goals and objectives originate in the organization? Should they originate at the top and be passed down through succeeding levels to the bottom-most employees? Or should goals and objectives originate at the bottom and be passed through each hierarchical stratum until they all accumulate at the top?

In the former case, employees have very little commitment to goals imposed from above. In the latter case, employees find it difficult to develop goals when isolated from any type of organizational direction. Using this latter method often results in a collection of widely diversified goals, with little of the focus needed for effective organizational action.

The most reasonable procedure is for the goals to originate from the top of the organization and for each managerial level to pass them to the employees below. Through a process of iterative negotiation, the employees will need to develop a set of objectives they intend to achieve in order to accomplish the goal. Although several iterations may be required before a final list of objectives acceptable to both employee and supervisor is developed, this process does allow for employee action and input that is consistent with the organizational mission. In this way, the activities of employees are networked and integrated in an effective manner. Additional examples that illustrate this process are provided in Chapter Eight.

CONCLUSION

Goals and objectives are linguistic statements that delimit some area of activity to be accomplished. Through goals and objectives, an agency defines what it will accomplish from the large number of possible activities it could undertake. In this way, the collective resources of the agency are focused on accomplishing tasks that demonstrate fulfillment of the agency's mission. It is important to select goals and objectives that are comprehensive and diverse enough to be representative of the agency's breadth of service responsibilities. Additional information and examples of how these concepts are used in programming are included in Chapters Seven, Eight, and Ten.

REFERENCES

Gronlund, N. D. (1970). *Stating behavioral objectives for classroom instruction*. New York: Macmillan.

Kotler, P., & Armstrong, G. (1993). *Marketing: An introduction* (3rd ed.). Englewood Cliffs, NJ: Prentice-Hall.

The Program Development Cycle

Information included thus far has provided background information needed to develop successful programs. Programs should be developed in a methodical and cyclical manner. The Program Development Cycle (PDC), a process diagram of the steps for developing programs, is presented on the next two pages. The cycle includes four major stages and nine specific steps. For a detailed explanation about the role and function of each stage and step, visit our web site at www.recreation-programming.com.

In actual practice, programs are not developed in the linear, sequential process illustrated, but rather in an iterative, interactive process requiring continued recycling of these steps until an operational program plan is completed. The process diagram gives the illusion that each step takes a similar amount of the programmer's time. Recent research has indicated that this is not the case. The amount of time programmers report spending on each step is discussed below.

Once thoroughly planned, a program is operated. Successful programs are the result of several trial-and-error developmental operations of them. Organizations acquire an inventory of quality programs by carefully planning them with the steps of the Program Development Cycle, operating them, evaluating them, and reworking them to be operated again based on their observations. Progressive program organizations have a number of new programs under development at all times. Successful programs are nurtured and developed further. Unsuccessful programs are dropped. Having to rework a program through several trial-and-error operations of the program is the normal course for successful program development, not an indication of failure.

How much time do programmers spend on each step of the Program Development Cycle? This was one of the questions asked in recent research on programming practices conducted by one of the authors. The PDC is redrawn on page 100 so the size of the boxes for each step on the diagram reflect the percentage of time programmers indicated they spent on each step. The single most time-consuming activity is Step 7, Implementation. Three steps, including Program Design, Planning, and Implementation consume almost 60% of a programmer's time. However, this does not mean they are the most important steps to successful programs, only the most time consuming.

As succeeding chapters develop, you will see that implementation is a broad activity, and thus more chapters are devoted to it than any other step. Even though some steps take more time and some are more important than others, thoroughly completing each of the steps is necessary to develop excellent program services.

The remaining chapters explain how each step of the Program Development Cycle is implemented. The Program Development Cycle is illustrated at the beginning of each chapter and the step being discussed in the chapter is highlighted. When there are multiple methods for accomplishing a step, each is explained, thereby giving the programmer multiple options for action and eventual success.

The Program Development Cycle

©2000 J. Robert Rossman and Barbara Elwood Schlatter

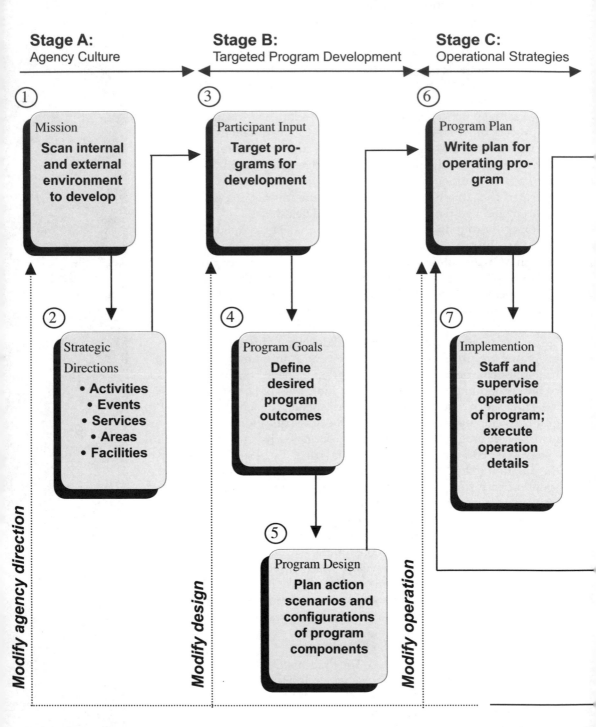

Stage A: Agency Culture

Stage B: Targeted Program Development

Stage C: Operational Strategies

① Mission — **Scan internal and external environment to develop**

② Strategic Directions — **• Activities • Events • Services • Areas • Facilities**

③ Participant Input — **Target programs for development**

④ Program Goals — **Define desired program outcomes**

⑤ Program Design — **Plan action scenarios and configurations of program components**

⑥ Program Plan — **Write plan for operating program**

⑦ Implemention — **Staff and supervise operation of program; execute operation details**

Modify agency direction

Modify design

Modify operation

For a detailed explanation, visit our website at www.recreationprogramming.com

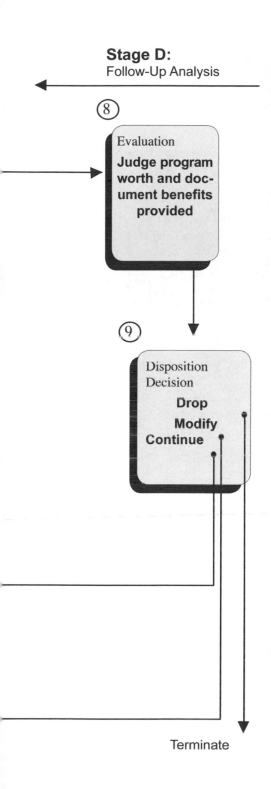

Stage D:
Follow-Up Analysis

⑧

Evaluation

Judge program worth and document benefits provided

⑨

Disposition
Decision

Drop

Modify

Continue

Terminate

Stage A: Agency Culture
In this stage, the programmer develops an understanding of the agency's programming philosophy and the overall programmatic goals of the agency. This stage is relatively static because of the stability of an agency's mission and direction. Programmers usually do not write agency missions but must understand them so the program services developed help fulfill the mission.

Stage B: Targeted Program Development
In this stage, the unique program needs and desires of specific population groups are identified, program outcome goals that are consistent with the agency's mission are specified, and a program that can meet these goals is designed. Programs developed should be desired by participants, should be within the resource capabilities of the agency, and should fulfill its mission.

Stage C: Operational Strategies
In this stage, an implementation plan is developed and the program is delivered to clients. The programmer oversees and manages the details for operating the program. Managing the implementation of program services includes many functions and is the most time consuming stage of programming.

Stage D: Follow-Up Analysis
In this stage, the programmer oversees the evaluation of the program. With this evaluation data, a disposition decision is made about the future of the program. It may be continued, dropped, or modified. Deciding to modify a program may require reworking its implementation method or its conceptualization and design, or rethinking the overall mission or goals of an agency.

Overall, although the model suggests that programs are developed in a methodical and systematic way, in reality it is an iterative, interactive process requiring continued recycling of the steps until an operational program is developed. Most often, successful programs are the result of ongoing, incremental expansion and improvement over a period of time.

ALLOCATING TIME TO PROGRAM DEVELOPMENT

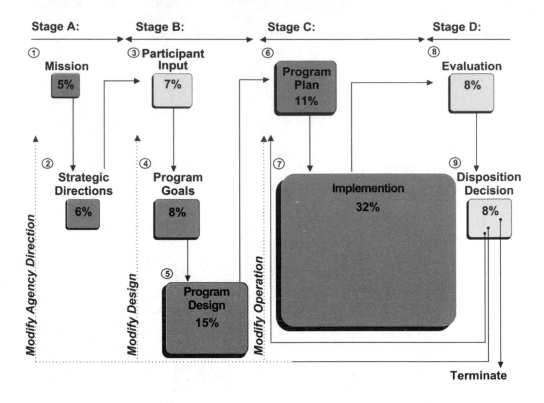

From: Schlatter, B. E. (2003). Recreation programming practices. *Research Quarterly for Exercise and Sport.* 74(1) Supplement, A-23-24. American Alliance for Health, Physical Education, Recreation, and Dance.

Stage A: Determining Agency Culture

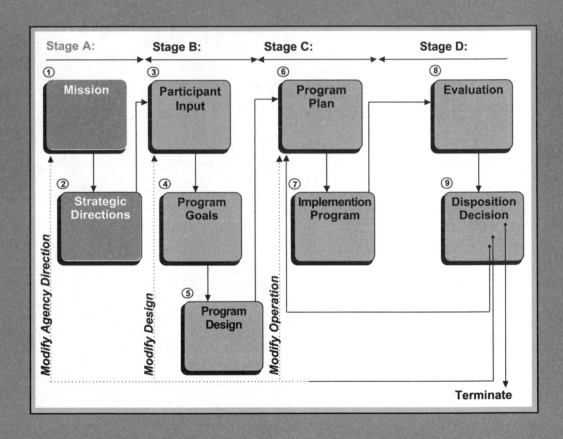

Part II
Determining Agency Culture

In Part II, Stage A of the Program Development Cycle is discussed. This stage involves assessing the culture in which the programming organization operates, developing a mission statement, and developing program planning goals for the organization. The leisure service programs discussed in this book are always designed and delivered by programmers operating in an organization. The programmer must therefore understand the environment in which the organization operates, and how this environment influences the services that the organization can develop and operate.

There are two chapters in this section. In Chapter Seven, we explain how to develop the organization's mission statement through assessing the threats and opportunities in its environment and its own internal strengths and weaknesses. In Chapter Eight, we discuss the role and use of goals and objectives in developing strategic directions the agency will pursue and provide examples to illustrate this process.

Chapter 7: Developing the Agency's Programming Mission

Chapter 8: Developing Strategic Directions: Writing Program Management Goals

Sand Sculpture Contest
Photo courtesy of Long Beach Parks, Recreation, and Marine Department, Long Beach, CA

Developing the Agency's
Programming Mission

STEP 1: MISSION

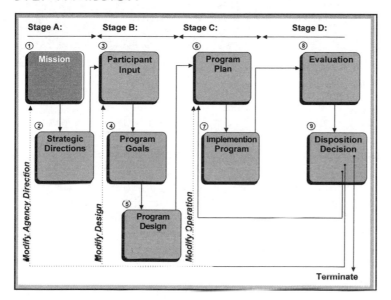

Mission
Individual Needs
Macro
Environment
Resource
Dependency
Organizational
 Needs
Community
Public Interest
Community
 Needs

As stated In Chapter Six, a mission statement defines the agency's purpose and outlines what it intends to accomplish in the larger environment. Knowles (1970) describes this environment as a "pool of needs," which include individual, organizational, and community needs. Developing successful services requires that programmers meet the identified needs of individuals and communities, and contribute to the organization's need to fulfill a purpose and role in the community. The recent effort by community recreation and park agencies to develop services that could have a positive impact on youth at risk is an example of a community purpose and role that might be fulfilled.

To succeed, programmers must understand how the conflicts and demands created by the issues surrounding these three—individual, organizational, and community needs—influence program development. Collectively, this analysis will lead to the development of a mission that will provide direction to day-to-day operations as well as confirm the need to develop some programs and restrict others. Although a mission statement is not developed every year, it will influence every program in operation. Thus, the programmer must understand the mission and its implications.

Although a mission statement is not developed every year, it will influence every program in operation.

Implementing Outcome-Based Programming

Incorporating outcome-based programming into agency mission or vision statements requires agency personnel to reposition themselves as providers of essential services with serious and important outcomes for those who participate. The San Diego Park and Recreation Department mission and vision statements included in Exhibit 7-5 on page 123 provide an excellent example of the outcomes message through its commitment to delivering services that make a difference in a community.

The remainder of this chapter deals with the issues that should be analyzed to develop a mission statement. The discussion is roughly organized around the three types of issues that must be analyzed, namely, individual, organizational, and community. These divisions are somewhat arbitrary, and there will be overlap in some cases. Furthermore, individual needs are not completely investigated at this point. The more detailed analysis that permits the development of specific, custom-tailored program services is covered at a different point in the Program Development Cycle and will be discussed in Chapter Nine.

Generally, the analysis that is conducted to develop a mission statement answers the following questions:

Individual: Who are our patrons? What kinds of services do they want? What types of services can we provide them; that is, what business should we be in?

The needs of any population are influenced by social forces that create opportunities and pose challenges for an agency.

Organizational: What are the strengths and weaknesses of our organization? What are the activities, events, services, and facilities we can develop a unique ability to offer?

Community: What are the threats and opportunities in our environment? Where can we make a difference that matters?

Figure 7-1 diagrams what is included in each of these three.

ASSESSING INDIVIDUAL NEEDS

Every organization must determine who it intends to serve, and this intention should be articulated in the mission statement. Government agencies are required to serve all who are within their jurisdiction, so their mission statements are usually inclusive. However, a commercial agency, for instance, a tennis club, may want to serve individuals in one activity who have higher than average incomes. Thus, their mission statement would narrowly define their service population. Many not-for-profit organizations may also have mission statements that reflect a more restricted target population whom they intend to serve.

If there are restrictions on the type of service the agency intends to provide, or any other similar restriction, it should also be reflected in the mission statement. For example, Little League organizations have

Individual	Organizational	Community

Macro trends
Effects on
  local community
	Resources
	Organizing authority
	Organizational strengths
	  and weaknesses
		Resources
		Community needs
		Public interest
		Assessing current
		  opportunities
		Relationships
		  among providers

Figure 7-1: Issues That Must Be Analyzed to Develop a Mission

both a restricted age group they serve and a single activity that they provide.

ASSESSING THE MACRO ENVIRONMENT

The needs of any population are influenced by social forces that create opportunities and pose challenges for an agency. These forces can be local, regional, or national in origin. Information about them and their potential effects on the leisure service agency, either positive or negative, are gathered by scanning and interpreting information about the agency's environment on an ongoing basis. Potential sources of information for this analysis include local, regional, and national print and broadcast media; government-issued technical reports; planning reports; political activity; and developments in the entertainment industry.

It is important to ascertain whether national or regional developments will actually affect the local community.

It is almost impossible to give directions about the reports, information, and so forth that one should take into account. Programmers do need to remain aware of possible threats to program continuation and seize special opportunities for program development. For example, the large percentage of working women today threatens mother–tot programs unless they are scheduled around the workday. Unless the programmer alters the scheduling of these types of programs, they are likely to fail because no client group is available to attend them.

Programmers must also remain aware of national trends and media happenings in order to seize on ideas and develop timely programs. There is a timeliness to programming that can only be achieved by scanning the external environment of the organization for emerging trends. In each case, the programmer must answer the question: *What are the specific operational implications of this, if any, for my agency?*

Programmers should prepare themselves to track systematically what is happening in five areas: demographic, social, technological, economic, and political. Developments in each of these areas are certain to have discernible effects on programming. The first three of these will have the greatest effect on individual leisure needs. The latter two could affect any of the three—individual, organizational, or community needs. Each of these trends should be analyzed from a local, regional, and national perspective. It is important to ascertain whether national or regional developments will actually affect the local community. For example, although the nation may be suffering from an economic recession, the local community may not be suffering any of its effects. A brief review of each key indicator is outlined on the following pages.

DEMOGRAPHICS

By 2015, racial and ethnic minorities are expected to comprise greater than one-third of the U.S. population (U.S. Census Bureau, 2004). Another demographic trend in our country is that of obesity plaguing our society. Nearly two-thirds of American adults are overweight, and 31% of those are considered obese (Witt, 2004, p. 28).

Programmers should analyze their service community in light of these and other reported demographic trends. For example, what ethnic groups populate the community? In which age group are the majority of community members? What effects will the increased prevalence of obesity and the trend towards sedentary lifestyles have on programming? Is obesity a concern in the local school system, or in the community overall? If so, are your program services prepared for the demands of these various groups?

SOCIAL

Are there emerging lifestyles, customs, or habits that will affect programs? What effect will single-parent families have? What will be the effect of large numbers of single people of all ages on programming? What effect do women who are working outside the home have on programming? What effect will newly-immigrated people from Hispanic and Asian cultures have on current programs? What is the educational level and social status of the clientele? What are the local customs and mores of the community? For example, the habits of 'tweens—children between the ages of 8-12, exhibit an emerging lifestyle by spending more than $1,200 a year on food, clothing, and personal care items, including entertainment and reading material (Kennedy, 2004)!

Unlike organizational and aggregated individual needs, community needs are created by social forces in society. They are also created because people live in communities with a shared value system that binds them together and because people take joint responsibility for preserving those values.

Thus, the reader should understand that the concept of community used here is inclusive and could include religious, corporate, military, or other communities with a shared value system that would need to be reflected in the development of a mission statement.

TECHNOLOGICAL

What emerging technology will have an impact on program services? The ubiquitous personal computer most certainly comes to mind. In 2003, 62% of American households had one or more computers, up from 56% in 2001 (U.S. Bureau of the Census, 2005). The most common use of the home computer among children ages 3-17 was to play games.

Among adult computer users, 88% use it for communication purposes (U.S. Bureau of the Census, 2005).

Along with personal computers come Internet access, the World Wide Web, and e-mail, just to name a few. How do these technologies impact program services? Leisure service providers increasingly use the World Wide Web to promote their agencies and services. This means that citizens, at the click of a mouse, can access information about agency hours of operation, or send an e-mail message to a park board member. Questions still remain for many leisure service providers regarding which technologies should be used and their impacts. To what extent, if any, should computer games be allowed in community recreation centers, YWCAs, or church recreation centers? With recent outbreaks of violence in schools and day care centers, the issue of security-related technology is coming into question for public and quasi-public agencies. Finally, what impact will WebTV, DVDs, iPods, MP3 players, cell phones, palms, etc. have on attendance at programs?

ECONOMIC

The United States has experienced a relatively stable economy in recent years, with growth due largely to consumer spending (Bew, 2007). It has been suggested that we are entering a new era of economic output, the Experience Economy (Pine & Gilmore, 1999), which will result in many others providing opportunities for experiences. In both strong and weak economic times, it's necessary to ask questions regarding the local economy in terms of its diversification and stability. How much annual income do the majority of patrons have? How much discretionary income do the patrons have? What percentage of the leisure service market share does the agency currently have? Is this likely to increase, resulting in increased income? Are there additional competitors who are likely to cut into the agency's market share? If so, what are the financial implications of this? What is the current tax base and tax rate? Are either of these likely to increase or decrease? If so, what are the programming implications?

It is impor tant that the organi- zation have distinctive competen- cies that result in a competi- tive advan- tage in its market.

POLITICAL

What is the political orientation of the local elected officials? Are they supporters of public recreation? How political is the administration of the agency? How many jobs in the agency are patronage jobs? How receptive are local elected officials to using the powers of government to encourage privately developed recreation enterprises? What is the political climate in the state? What is the political climate in the nation? Is it conservative or liberal, and what are either of these attitudes likely to do to funding and program operations?

ASSESSING ORGANIZATION NEEDS

Organizations are dynamic entities whose needs must be met to keep them operating. One of the most important needs of an organization is to continue its existence. This is most assured if it fulfills an identifiable role in the larger society that controls its resources. Because no agency can offer everything, it is important that the agency identify its strengths and weaknesses to discover a distinctive competence the organization possesses (Zikmund & d'Amico, 1993). Furthermore, it is important that the organization have distinctive competencies that result in a competitive advantage in its market (Kotler, 1991).

RESOURCE DEPENDENCY

Programming organizations are resource dependent: Their survival depends on successfully acquiring the resources needed to deliver services to their client groups. The level of resources available will determine, to some degree, what the organization's mission may be. Adequate or unique resources will create the differential advantage to provide some unique opportunities, but a lack thereof will be a limitation and thereby restrict what the agency can accomplish. Thus, resources are an issue at both the organization and community levels. Pfeffer and Salancik (1978) have taken the following position:

> Our position is that organizations survive to the extent that they are effective. Their effectiveness derives from the management of demands, particularly the demands of interest groups upon which the organizations depend for resources and support. (p. 2)

The organization's mission must be developed to focus organizational efforts toward meeting the needs of its relevant clients and publics. Resource dependency is complicated by the fact that no organization is completely self-contained, and organizations both compete with and depend on other organizations for resources. Pfeffer and Salancik (1978) comment on this dilemma by stating,

> Organizations are embedded in an environment comprised of other organizations. They depend on those other organizations for the many resources they themselves require. (p. 2)

What an organization may accomplish is partly dependent on what other organizations will allow it to accomplish or want it to accomplish. Organizational success, then, is partly determined by an organization's external environment.

ORGANIZING RATIONALE

Often, leisure service organizations are created to offer specific types of recreation programming and to achieve specific purposes. Kraus (1985) has identified eight different types of organizations that exist to offer recreation service: public recreation and park agencies; voluntary, nonprofit organizations, including sectarian and nonsectarian; commercial recreation enterprises; private-membership organizations; armed forces recreation; campus recreation; corporate recreation; and therapeutic recreation.

Each of these organizations has specific social ends that they attempt to promote through participation in recreation activities. An

What an organization may accomplish is partly dependent on what other organizations will allow it to accomplish.

Exercise 7-1

Identify and discuss how the same program service, such as a Fourth of July Day Special Event, would differ if organized by each of the agencies paired below.

How does the organization's mission influence the way this program would be developed?

Air Force Recreation Services.................YMCA
Public recreation agency.........................Private country club
University campus recreation.................Corporate recreation
Easter Seal (community-based)..............An institutional therapeutic
recreation setting for physically
disabled children

overriding need of such organizations is the need to accomplish the social ends identified as part of the rationale for creating the organization in the first place. As Tillman (1973) has observed, "Agencies use [a] recreation program as a tool for obtaining their objectives" (p. 19). Different agencies offer different leisure services because of the social ends they are organized to promote. For example, the Boy Scouts of America offers different programming than YMCAs. Although they may serve similar youth, their program services differ because their perceived social missions differ.

Marketing literature suggests that individual needs should be the central driving force in organizations. This is a desirable goal to strive for in all leisure service organizations. However, organizational social ends will narrow the range of programs that may be provided and thereby have an overriding influence on the organization's mission in the short run. For example, the organizational mission of campus recreation organizations limits their concern to students, faculty, and alumni from a specific university. Once this parameter is accepted, the organization becomes concerned with what its targeted client groups want, and the marketing concepts and ideas about how to determine individual wants become useful. Similarly, armed forces recreation providers are primarily concerned with active duty military personnel, their dependents, civilian employees, and retirees. All of the programming efforts in the armed services are directed toward helping one of these four groups of individuals. The organization's mission will influence the program services it delivers. Examine this concept further by completing Exercise 7-1.

ASSESSING THE ORGANIZATION

An organization can determine how well it is doing by assessing its strengths and limitations. The checklist approach for self-evaluation

To obtain a comprehensive view of the organization's strengths and weaknesses, it is essential to obtain the key public's images of the organization.

Exhibit 7-1: CAPRA Assessment Criteria

6.0 Program and Services Management
    6.1   Program/Service Determinants
           The program and services provided shall be based on:
- *Conceptual foundations of play, recreation, and leisure*
- *Constituent needs*
- *Community opportunities*
- *Agency philosophy and goals*
- *Experiences desirable for clientele*

           6.1.1   Participant Involvement
                    Development of program should involve the participants.
    6.2   Nature of Services
           Services shall be delivered in a variety of ways, such as structured leadership programs, outreach user services, and rentals.

           6.2.1   General Supervision
                    The program should provide for recreation opportunities under general supervision.

           6.2.2   Structured Leadership Programs
                    The program should provide recreation opportunities under direct, face-to-face leadership, including skills instruction.

           6.2.3   Facilitator
                    Services should be provided to individuals and small groups of individuals to stimulate and assist them to become independent of the supervision and control of the recreation agency.

           6.2.4   Services for a Fee
                    Services should be offered for a fee to augment basic recreation opportuties.
    6.3   Objectives
           Specific objectives shall be established for each program or service.
    6.4   Outreach
           The programs and services shall be available to all cultures and populations resident of and visitors to the community.
    6.5   Scope of Program Opportunities
           The agency's programs shall provide opportunities in all program fields for persons of various levels of proficiency, socioeconomic levels, racial and ethnic backgrounds, ages, and genders in accordance with the agency's statement of mission.
    6.6   Selection of Program Content
           The selection of program content, specific activities, and opportunities shall be based on an understanding of individual differences and the culture of the community.
    6.7   Types of Participation
           The program shall provide structurally for a wide range of types of participation.
    6.8   Education for Leisure
           There should be a plan of education for leisure.

From: National Recreation and Park Association, Self-Assessment Manual for Quality Operation of Park and Recreation Agencies, 2001. (Used with permission).

Exhibit 7-2: Organizational Assessment Criteria

	Strengths			Weaknesses	
	Major	Minor	Neutral	Minor	Major
Board					
Legal authority?	____	____	____	____	____
Political leadership?	____	____	____	____	____
Responsiveness?	____	____	____	____	____
Management					
Accountable?	____	____	____	____	____
Visionary leadership?	____	____	____	____	____
Flexible?	____	____	____	____	____
Staff					
Adequate number?	____	____	____	____	____
Skilled?	____	____	____	____	____
Enthusiastic?	____	____	____	____	____
Service-minded?	____	____	____	____	____
Finance					
Adequate resources?	____	____	____	____	____
Equitable resource allocations?	____		____	____	____
Reasonable program prices?	____	____	____	____	____
Facilities					
Adequate (size, number, and quality)?	____	____	____	____	____
Attractiveness?	____	____	____	____	____
Good distribution?	____	____	____	____	____
Accessibility?	____	____	____	____	____
Marketing					
Service reputation?	____	____	____	____	____
Partnering in the community?	____	____	____	____	____
Promotion effectiveness?	____	____	____	____	____

Adapted from: Kotler, (1991). Marketing management: Analysis, planning, implementation, and control (7th ed.; p. 51). Englewood Cliffs, NJ: Prentice-Hall.

of public leisure service organizations (van der Smissen, 1972) has been revised and updated by the Commission for Accreditation of Park and Recreation Agencies (CAPRA). One hundred and fifty-five standards have been established for park and recreation professionals and citizen advisory or policy boards to evaluate their agencies. Of the 155 standards, 36 have been designated as essential for accreditation purposes.

There are ten major categories of standards, of which Program and Services Management is one. Each standard has an accompanying written description and supporting performance measures that can be used to determine the degree of compliance exhibited in an agency. The Program and Services Management category is outlined in Exhibit 7-1 on page 112.

Although the CAPRA standards are designed for public recreation organizations, many of the standards in it are also important for commercial and not-for-profit leisure service organizations. The standards can be adapted and used in these two types of organizations as well.

A MARKETING APPROACH TO ORGANIZATIONAL ASSESSMENT

To obtain a comprehensive view of the organization's strengths and weaknesses, it is essential to obtain the key public's image of the organization. An image is "the sum of beliefs, ideas, and impressions that a person holds of an object" (Kotler, 1982, p. 57).

Determining the key publics to investigate is an important decision. Some publics will be more influential in determining the future success of the organization than others. In the public sector, this is accomplished by surveying the entire population of the jurisdiction. For a YWCA or other similar not-for-profit organization, one would need to examine thoroughly the views of its members and also sample nonmembers to investigate whether or not they hold views substantially different from members. Similarly, in a commercial agency, it is necessary to examine a sample of the total market; that is, all actual and potential buyers.

An instrument that could be used for this assessment is illustrated in Exhibit 7-2 on page 113. The items included are thought to be organizational assets that may result in a competitive advantage. Respondents can classify them as "strengths" or "weaknesses" and further indicate if they believe they are major or minor. Responses to this instrument will provide the agency with their public's image of them.

From these data, a picture of the organization's current strengths and weaknesses will emerge. These will influence the organization's mission in a variety of ways, depending on the results of the investigation. For example, in a large suburb of a major midwestern city, it was discovered that a unique strength of the recreation operation was its lakefront parks. Programs operated in these parks were almost sure to succeed and further enhance the residents' image of living in a unique community.

In a medium-sized southern city, it was discovered that a major limitation for the recreation organization was the image of its staff, facilities, and programs. In this instance, the organization needed a major overhaul to successfully operate programs that would attract the target market in sufficient numbers. There were too many serious limitations in essential areas of operation. It was therefore recommended that new personnel policies be implemented, that the structure of the agency's financial base and practices be reorganized, that the organizational structure be changed, and that the powers and duties of the

No organization has enough resources to operate from a position of strength in all areas...

Once a mission is written, programmers are expected to develop program services that contribute to the mission...

board be changed. In this case, the organization itself needed radical change to begin meeting the leisure needs of the community and its individuals.

No organization has enough resources to operate from a position of strength in all areas; that is, to operate all programs for which need could be demonstrated. The idea of assessment is to document organizational strengths and weaknesses in order to develop a mission that will direct organizational effort toward its strengths, and to avoid operation in areas where the organization has weaknesses. The notion of strategic planning and marketing is to match clients' expressed desires with organizational strengths and resources so that targeted markets are well served. To be significant contributors to overall organizational effort, programmers need to understand the role and process of organizational assessment and how it relates to the development of the organization's mission.

Once a mission is written, programmers are expected to develop program services that contribute to the mission within existing organizational strengths and weaknesses. Successful programming is measured, in part, by how well the services contribute to the identified organizational mission and are operated within the resource limitations of the agency. "Recreation in the Streets" (Rossman, 1973) is an example of a program whose success was partly attributable to its contribution to the overall agency mission and identified community needs. An analysis of the program is included as Case Study 7-1. The Warrior Games, developed by the U.S. Navy, is another example of a program that meets individual, organizational, and community needs. It is presented in Case Study 7-2. Both case studies are at the end of this chapter on pages 132-133.

ASSESSING COMMUNITY NEEDS

A notion of community implies a set of common ideas or shared beliefs that serve as a binding force for a group of people. Obviously, many ideas and beliefs compete for attention and resources in any larger community. The community analysis, then, focuses on identifying threats and opportunities in the environment (Zikmund & d'Amico, 1993) that will affect an agency's delivery of leisure services.

COMMUNITY NEEDS

A marketing approach to assessing community needs suggests that one should examine the organization's external environment, including its market environment, public environment, competitive environment, and macro environment (Kotler, 1982). The results of this assessment will establish the organization's functional role in a community by determining the following: what organizations and interest groups the organization must deal with in the community; the various publics and special interest groups who may influence the organization's functioning in the community; who the organization will need to compete with directly in delivering services; and the larger social forces that will influence program services and client wants.

Kraus (1985) has expressed concern about the use of marketing concepts as a major philosophical orientation for the delivery of leisure services. He states:

> At the same time, unquestioning acceptance of the marketing point of view raises a number of important issues in terms of the role that recreation and park agencies have traditionally had. When recreation is viewed primarily as a product to be sold, the issue of social value or achieving positive personal outcomes through leisure involvement becomes secondary. (pp. 70–71)

Kraus reflects the viewpoint of many recreation professionals regarding marketing as a strategy for developing park and recreation services. Their concern is that the role of recreation as a basic community service, which is made available through public financing to meet identified community needs, is being altered to one of service for a fee. These services are delivered to meet only the needs of individuals who can afford to pay to participate.

The community-need orientation of community recreation has been part of the movement since its origins at the beginning of the twentieth century and was part of the social-welfare, social-reform movement of the period. The traditional viewpoint assumes that recreation is provided to meet a greater community need, as well as individual needs. During the past 15 years, the prevalence of marketing and the concern with pricing and revenues have obscured some of the original notions of recreation as a public good.

RECREATION AND THE PUBLIC INTEREST

The notion of public interest implies a certain relationship of people to society. Friedmann (1973) describes the public interest as follows:

> The public interest is a republican idea whose origins reach back to the golden age of Greece. It has not always gone by its present designation. At other times, it has been called the common wealth, the general welfare, or the public good. All these terms express the notion of something shared or held in common. To the extent that something is held in common, that which is shared binds men to one another: The good that is shared creates a moral community whose members agree to be jointly responsible for that which is precious to them. The idea of a public good therefore implies the existence of such a community and the commitment of its members to it. (p. 2)

The notion of community need, then, is of concern not just to community recreators, but also to recreators in all organizations.

For many years, recreation was considered one of several public services (such as education, libraries, police protection, and fire protection) to be provided in the public interest. A rationale for its provision by government is presented by Peterson and Schroth (n.d.):

> Leisure, used in a constructive manner, is basic to the self-fulfillment and life enrichment of the individual and therefore

helps to strengthen the stability of the family, the community, and the nation.

How people use their leisure time is an important social question. By providing recreation resources, a community is contributing to the physical, mental, and social health of its residents.

Leisure and recreation are recognized as effective ways to enhance life in a community by developing leadership potential and stimulating popular participation for community betterment.

It is only through public recreation services that a large portion of the population will have access to many recreational facilities, such as pools, tennis courts, picnic areas, and golf courses.

Recreation and leisure services consume space. Local government is best suited to acquire, develop, and maintain that space in the best interest of the entire community.

Government sponsorship of recreation services assumes equal participation by all ages, races, and creeds, all seasons of the year; it is democratic and inclusive.

By providing a park and recreation agency, citizen participation on park and recreation boards can be assembled, and the community can focus its attention on protecting public lands and developing facilities and programs. Concentration on long-range plans will help assure proper growth of the system as the community expands.

It is only through government that equitable, fair-share financing is available for the acquisition, development, and maintenance of park facilities and programs.

A park and recreation board can, through cooperative agreements with school boards, library boards, and other governmental agencies, energize and maximize the leisure and recreation potential of a community. (p. 2–3)

Recreation is still a service to be provided by government in the public interest. What the public interest is in a specific community and what is to be included in a local government's provision of recreation services vary widely from community to community, depending on each community's identified needs and resources.

The notion of community needs also extends beyond the public interest notion of community recreation. Other organizations that sponsor recreation programs do so to serve a larger sense of community and community need. They too have a parallel notion of community need that should be met. For example, in armed forces recreation operations, the notion of organizational needs focuses on the recreation organiza-

Each community has a leisure delivery system made up of public, private, voluntary or quasi-public, and commercial sub-systems.

The public recreation organization has the unique role of assessing and coordinating the development of the community leisure service system...

Exhibit 7-3: Community Needs Assessment Agenda

Open Space Inventory
- Total amount of public park acreage in the community
- Total amount of acreage devoted to recreational use owned by other providers and an estimate of the percentage of population served by the provider
- A map indicating the location of all recreation spaces
- Knowledge about the size of each recreation space

Facility Inventory
- A list of all public recreation facilities, including type, location, and who is serviced by the facility
- A list of all other recreation facilities, including type, location, and who is serviced

Program Services
- A list of all program services offered by public, private, commercial, and quasi-public recreation agencies in the community, including the types of services offered and who is serviced by the programs

Exhibit 7-4: The Programmer's Evaluation Cube

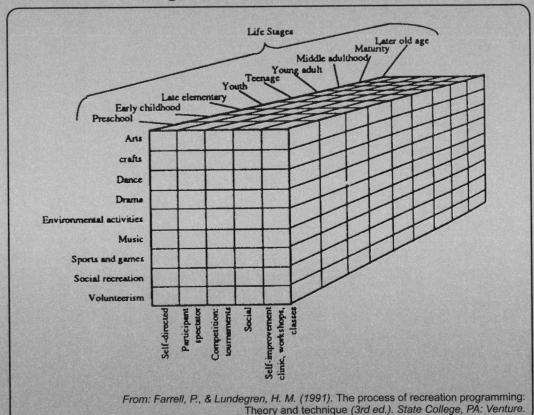

From: Farrell, P., & Lundegren, H. M. (1991). *The process of recreation programming: Theory and technique (3rd ed.).* State College, PA: Venture.

tion contained in the Morale, Welfare, and Recreation unit. The notion of community needs would be the overriding needs of the armed service community, of which the recreation organization is a part. Similarly, in a corporate recreation operation, organizational needs would refer to the needs of the recreation unit within the larger organization; community needs would refer to the needs of the larger entity—the sponsoring corporation. The notion of community need, then, is of concern not just to community recreators, but also to recreators in all organizations.

ASSESSING LEISURE OPPORTUNITIES

Assessing the needs of a community requires an assessment of the existing range of leisure options in a community, an understanding of the leisure service system, the role of each provider in the community, and an understanding of the macro environment affecting the community. Remember, the notion of community need is not simply the aggregation of identified individual needs, but the needs created by a sense of community and the moral contract between individuals who are part of the community and held jointly responsible for the overall good of the community.

Each community has a leisure delivery system made up of public, private, voluntary or quasi-public, and commercial subsystems (Sessoms, 1980). A comprehensive assessment of community needs begins with an inventory of existing service options offered by the complete leisure service delivery system. It is important to determine the scope and depth of service already available in the community (Bannon, 1976) and the individuals served and not served by the current system.

The public recreation organization has the responsibility in every community to ensure that the leisure needs of the entire population are met. This does not mean they must provide all leisure services. It does mean they are ultimately responsible for assessing community recreation needs, maintaining an inventory of the complete community recreation system, conducting individual needs assessments, interpreting needs assessment data, being the catalyst for implementing needed services, and coordinating the entire system. To accomplish this, the public system may encourage the establishment of a commercial recreation enterprise to meet an identified need or encourage the development of a YMCA or YWCA. The public recreation organization is the provider of last resort. One of their unique functions is that they are ultimately responsible for meeting the overall leisure needs of the community. To do this, they must coordinate the entire leisure delivery system. As Sessoms (1980) indicates, "Efforts are made sometimes to coordinate each subsystem without much concern for overall integration. More and more municipal leisure service agencies are beginning attempts to bring the resources of the public, voluntary, private, and commercial interests into play, but in the past these efforts were the exception, not the rule" (p. 126).

The public recreation organization, then, has the unique role of assessing and coordinating the development of the community leisure service system, including all of its subsystems. A community assessment should include the items displayed in Exhibit 7-3.

Once these data have been gathered, they must be analyzed to place the information into a meaningful pattern and permit insights into met and unmet needs. Farrell and Lundegren (1991) have proposed one method for analyzing such data—the programmer's evaluation cube, diagrammed in Exhibit 7-4 on page 118.

The evaluation cube is a three-dimensional matrix, with life stages on one axis, program activity types on a second axis, and programming formats on a third axis. In conducting this analysis, the programmer is examining current services to see if they are comprehensive and complete on a number of dimensions deemed important. The basic idea of using a cube for this analysis can be expanded by changing the variables on the cube to analyze further the comprehensiveness of services. For example, program distribution by gender, geographic neighborhoods, and family income would be a legitimate set of variables to analyze. It is axiomatic that the overall leisure service delivery system should ensure that its comprehensive services include the following:

1. A wide variety of activity types, including sports, individual activities, fitness activities, hobbies, art, drama, music, and social recreation, are available in the community.
2. A variety of programming organizational formats are available.
3. Service opportunities are available for all age groups.
4. Service is available, through some provider in the system, to all residents in the community regardless of age, gender, religion, socioeconomic class, geographical location, or other factors.

In examining these data to determine community need, the programmer is searching for gaps in existing services. These gaps may be due to resource limitations or to a lack of interest and resources, or may be inadvertent because the gap was previously unknown. In any case, some analysis of existing gaps should be conducted to determine whether they need to be filled with additional services.

COMMUNITY PARTNERSHIPS

The adequacy of cooperation and coordination among providers in a community should also be assessed. This is accomplished by examining all documents that were used to establish partnerships among agencies. Indicators of a coordinated community leisure service system include the number of joint ventures among leisure service providers; the number of joint programs; evidence of sharing resources, facilities, and staff; evidence of coordinated scheduling; and other similar types of evidence.

FOCUSING ON THE INDIVIDUAL

It is interesting to consider which of these three entities—individual, organizational, or community needs—is the driving force that determines agency direction and consequently the content and focus of program services. This dilemma has been conceptualized and discussed elsewhere as a problem of determining whether the organization will

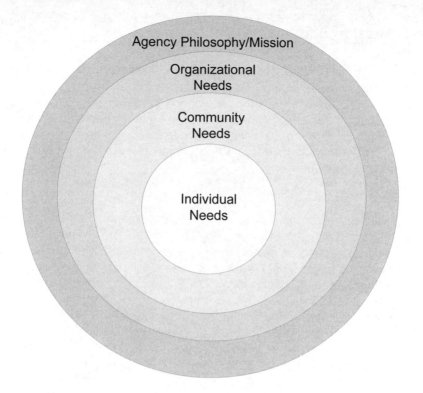

Figure 7-2: Relationship of Mission to Individual, Community, and Organizational Needs.

have a selling or a marketing orientation (Howard & Crompton, 1980; Crompton & Lamb, 1986). A sales orientation places community or organizational needs first and assumes that the organization will convince patrons to consume what they have produced. In contrast, a marketing orientation places consumer needs and wants first. In this case, the organization will first discover what patrons want, then focus on producing it.

Kotler's (1991) societal marketing concept further explains the relationship of these three need packages to each other. He states:

> The societal marketing concept holds that the organization's task is to determine the needs, wants, and interests of target markets and to deliver the desired satisfactions more effectively and efficiently than competitors in a way that preserves or enhances the consumer's and society's well-being. (p. 26)

Each mission statement initiates the process of specifying what the agency will accomplish.

With this concept, the driving force is the identified wants and needs of target markets; that is, groups of individuals the agency intends to serve. The responsibility of the program manager in this case is to

Exhibit 7-5: Mission Statements

Knoxville Bureau of Recreation, Knoxville, Tennessee

To provide comprehensive year-round opportunities for recreation and use of physical resources that are accessible to and respond to the articulated needs and desires of all residents of the city of Knoxville, with an emphasis on educating citizens on the value of learning and practicing lifetime leisure skills and appreciations, and serving as a catalyst and facilitator for the provision of recreation programs by other organizations in the community.

Discussion

The mission statement for the Bureau makes clear its responsibility in the community of serving as one of the primary providers of recreation. The Bureau has a responsibility to initiate services in areas currently being underserved and to serve as a community catalyst to get other agencies to initiate services to meet identified needs. However, the Bureau will not be able to meet all needs identified in the community, so its operational mission will, by necessity, be more strategic and selective. Currently, program operations are heavily team sports oriented. In order to meet the mission objective of offering a comprehensive program, development of recreation opportunities in other program areas will need to occur.

While the Bureau's mission statement addresses only opportunities for recreation and leisure services, in actual operation the mission will include all of the resources needed to make these opportunities available, including facilities, land acquisition, land development, adequate financing, and other resources needed to produce recreation and leisure opportunities.

From: Management Learning Laboratories. (1985). *Assessment of the management function of the Knoxville Bureau of Recreation, Knoxville, Tennessee: Report 1, Review of existing organizational structures*. Champaign, IL: Management Learning Laboratories.

St. Andrew's Parish Parks and Playground Commission, Charleston, South Carolina

Our mission is to enhance the quality of life for the people of the St. Andrew's Parish Public Service District by developing, fostering, and promoting quality parks and recreational programs, services, and opportunities. We will do so by listening to our customers' needs and by creating safe, diversified recreational and educational programs and facilities that promote fun, fitness, family, health, wellness, and individual successes to meet those needs.

We will forge cooperative relationships with like organizations to help us meet our goals. We will train, empower, and inspire every commissioner, employee, and volunteer to bring a sense of joy to the lives of every man, woman, and child who participates in these opportunities, without regard to ability, age, gender, race, religion, ethnicity, or income.

From: St. Andrew's Parish Parks and Playground Commission. (n.d.). *Our mission* [On-line]. Available: http://www.standrewsparks.com

Champaign Park District, Champaign, Illinois

Mission: The mission of the Champaign Park District is to provide quality parks and recreation for our community.

Vision: Excellence in parks and recreation

From: Champaign Park District (n.d.). *About Us* [On-line]. Available: http://www.champaignparkdistrict.com/main.htm

City of Kearney Park and Recreation Department, Kearney, Nebraska

Mission: Provide excellent recreational facilities and programs which promote healthy and diversified leisure time activities for the citizens of the Kearney area.

From: (2006-2007). Mission Statement. City of Kearney Operating Budget and Program Services. City of Kearney, Nebraska.

San Diego Park and Recreation Department, San Diego, California

Mission: To acquire, develop, operate, and maintain a park and recreation system which enriches the quality of life for residents and visitors alike, and preserves it for future generations.

Vision: "We Enrich Lives Through Quality Parks and Programs"

Come out today and play!

Be happier	Build family unity
Feel great	Reduce unemployment
Lose weight	Build self-esteem
Reduce stress	Eliminate loneliness
Increase community pride	Reduce crime
Provide safe places to play	Lower health care costs
Diminish gang violence	Boost employee productivity
Protect the environment	Live longer
Increase tourism	Boost economy and attract business
Create memories	

From: City of San Diego Park and Recreation Department (n.d.). *Mission statement and vision* [On-line]. Available: http://www.sannet.gov/park-and-recreation/general-info/mission.shtml

Westmont Park District Mission Statement, Westmont, Illinois

It is the purpose of the Westmont Park District to efficiently and economically provide safe recreation programs, quality and enjoyable leisure experiences, and improve the quality of life for individual residents of all ages and the community of Westmont as a whole. Efforts to fulfill our mission will be focused through employee collaboration, sound financial management, the updating of present facilities and playgrounds, a wide range of year-round recreation programs, and a strong belief in the following values: accountability, enthusiasm, quality, innovation, cooperation, and respect.

From: Westmont Park District. (n.d.). *Mission statement* [On-line]. Available: http://www.wpd4fun.org/index_2.htm.

Merage Jewish Community Center of Orange County, Irvine, California

The mission of the Jewish Community Center of Orange County is to enrich Jewish life and general community life through county-wide social activities, which include social service, recreational, social education, and cultural activities.

From: Merage Jewish Community (n.d.). *Mission statement* [On-line]. Available: http://www.jccoc.org/

U.S. Army Family and Morale, Welfare, and Recreation Command (FMWRC)

Mission: The FMWRC provides oversight for Army MWR operations worldwide, and is committed to providing the highest quality family and MWR programs to support soldiers (active and reserve), civilians, retirees, and their families.

- Develop and formulate plans, strategies, and standards to achieve "First Choice" MWR programs.
- Support commanders in the implementation of the Army's MWR programs
- Operate and manage assigned MWR activities.

Vision: A preeminent organization that achieves and sustains "First Choice" programs which contribute significantly to the Army's Well-being.

From: Army MWR About. (n.d.). *About Us* [On-line]. Available: http://www.armymwr.com/portal/about/

Navy Morale, Welfare, and Recreation Mission Statement

The Navy Morale, Welfare, and Recreation Division administers a varied program of recreation, social, and community support activities on U.S. Navy facilities worldwide. Our programs provide active-duty, reserve, and retired Navy personnel and their families with sports and physical fitness activities, child development and youth programs, and a variety of food and beverage services. Our mission is to provide quality support and recreational services that contribute to the retention, readiness, mental, physical, and emotional well-being of our sailors.

From: Navy Morale, Welfare, and Recreation (n.d.). *Mission statement* [On-ine]. Available: http://www.mwr.navy.mil/

Nantahala Outdoor Center Philosophy/Mission, Nantahala, North Carolina

It was Payson and Aurelia Kennedy's intention to create "something special" with NOC, a place "where the lines between work and play could merge," where individuals could share and experience the outdoors in an ultimately recreational and inspiring way. The conditions of commitment, challenge, employee control, and community are integral elements that are incorporated by staff as outlined in our Statement of Purpose:

- To provide the highest quality programs in outdoor recreation and education
- To offer a wide variety of activities
- To provide high quality equipment and auxiliary services for persons participating in these activities

- To maintain leadership in our fields with experienced staff contributing to the state of the art
- To foster in all our staff an attitude emphasizing helpfulness, personal attention, and flexibility toward our guests
- To maintain a high level of safety in our activities and to encourage safe attitudes in our guests
- To serve the interests and needs of people of different ages, sexes, races, physical abilities and income levels
- To provide these programs and services at a cost that represents good value to the customer as well as fair return to the NOC
- To carry out our programs so as to be fun and educational for all
- To observe high ethical standards, to plan and control growth so as to uphold the quality of the NOC community and programs, and to reflect NOC ideals and values
- To provide the highest quality of life for our staff
- To enrich our community through mutual endeavor, trust and understanding, and open and effective communication
- To move toward complete employee ownership and control
- To operate our programs in a manner that encourages staff involvement and pride in NOC
- To provide salaries and benefits sufficient for a simple lifestyle, to link pay with profitability, and to keep a narrow range between the highest and lowest wage
- To provide year-round employment, and to use our resources to foster off-season opportunities
- To provide opportunities for personal growth for our staff
- To participate actively and considerately in the larger community
- To serve the community through contributions of work and money, and to encourage and support individual staff contributions
- To respect and care for the environment and to foster environmental awareness in our guests
- To earn enough profit to accomplish the first three purposes and to increase the value of ownership in NOC

From: Nantahala Outdoor Center. (n.d.). *Philosophy/mission statement* [On-line]. Available: http://www.nocweb.com/whojobs/nfwhphil.htm

Cayuga Nature Center, Ithaca, New York

Cayuga Nature Center, Inc. is a not-for-profit organization whose mission is to facilitate awareness, appreciation, and responsibility for the natural world through recreation, and environmental, agricultural, and outdoor education

From: Cayuga Nature Center. (n.d.). *Mission statement* [On-line]. Available: http://www.cayuganaturecenter.org/about/mission.html

restructure *the organization as needed* to respond to identified client wants and needs. However, program services to be offered are still limited by community needs or desires because anything offered must "preserve or enhance" both the "consumer's and society's well-being." Because of this latter requirement, developing a philosophy and mission for a not-for-profit organization is somewhat more problematic than developing a philosophy and mission for a commercial recreation operation.

RELATIONSHIP OF THE THREE ENTITIES TO MISSION

Figure 7-2 on page 121 illustrates the relationship of each of these entities to the other. The agency mission is represented as the outermost ring in a series of concentric rings. As this figure illustrates, the agency mission must encompass individual needs, community needs, and organizational strengths and limitations. However, since no agency has unlimited resources, not all identified needs can be met, so priorities for the distribution of scarce resources must be established. Individual needs are seen as the centermost priority. They influence community needs, organizational needs, and agency mission. The identified needs of individuals are tempered and influenced by community needs and organizational strengths and limitations before they become part of the agency's mission. Kotler (1982) recognized this when he stated that the agency mission should be "feasible, motivating, and distinctive" (p. 36).

An agency's mission should be feasible within the limitations imposed on the agency by its own resource limits, by community needs, and by individual wants. Staff members should not be asked to accomplish results that they lack the skills or resources to achieve. The mission should motivate staff members by giving them clear direction about what they are to accomplish. Finally, the mission should be distinctive in order to separate the mission of the organization from other organizations providing similar services.

To be successful, organizations must meet organizational needs and the needs of the environment in which they operate. Determining organizational and environmental needs is antecedent to developing an agency philosophy or mission statement. One may eventually try to change the organization or community perceptions of its needs to better accommodate individual needs once identified. But one must first take inventory of the current state of affairs to have a starting point.

WRITING THE MISSION STATEMENT

The use of goals and objectives in an organization begins with the development of a mission statement. An overview of the role of an agency's mission statement was provided in Chapter Six. Thus far in this chapter, we have reviewed the issues that need to be analyzed in order to prepare to write the agency's mission statement. The analysis portion of this task is complex but necessary, because the actual mission statement must be as clear and simple as possible. There are no step-by-step guidelines to direct its preparation. The reader is reminded that its purpose is to announce to external parties the unique role and

Exercise 7-2: Mission Statements

Break into four small groups and select one of the following types of recreation and leisure service agencies: (1) municipal recreation and park department, (2) commercial recreation business, (3) community-based therapeutic recreation agency, or (4) campus intramural recreation department. Using Figure 7-1 and Exhibit 7-2 as guides, write a brief mission statement for your selection.

Use as discussion questions:
- Did the mission statements vary as a function of the agency type?
- What are the difficulties of writing a mission statement?
- What were the underlying philosophies of each?
- To what extent were the mission statements flexible?

function of the agency in the community and to provide direction to employees within the agency to ensure that their activities contribute to accomplishing the agency's mission. Examples of mission statements from different agencies are presented in Exhibit 7-5 on pages 122-125. Please read and compare the mission statements in Exhibit 7-5 and then proceed with the text below.

Each of these mission statements is different but consistent with the current trend of writing short mission statements (with the exception of the more lengthy Nantahala Outdoor Center statement). Each uses linguistic statements to define or "frame" an area of reality that the agency will attempt to accomplish. None of these statements is clear, specific, or measurable. However, they initiate the process of specifying what the agency will accomplish. From the entire realm of possibilities that the agency could do, the mission statement begins by limiting what the agency will actually do.

Notice in the St. Andrew's Parish Parks and Playground Commission mission the desire to work with "like" organizations. This terminology suggests that the Commission hopes to partner with other leisure service agencies in the future. The Champaign Park District includes a mission and a vision to be excellent in parks and recreation. The mission statement from the City of Kearney Parks and Recreation focuses on the provision of excellent facilities and programs that promote health and diverse activities. How this is to be accomplished is left open. This gives the agency maximum latitude in the future.

San Diego's Park and Recreation Mission Statement is the only example that explicitly mentions the importance of meeting the recreation needs of visitors as well as residents. Note also that their vision incorporates a list of outcome-based benefits of their programs and services. Westmont Park District's mission represents a strong commitment to sound management practices as the key to quality recreation programs and leisure experiences.

An interesting aspect of the mission statements of the Merage Jewish Community Center of Orange County and the U.S. Army Family and Morale, Welfare, and Recreation Command (AFMWRC) is the initial commitment to serving the Jewish community and active army personnel, respectively. However, the mission statements do not limit their services to those two groups. The Merage invites involvement of all community persons, regardless of their background. Similarly, AFMWRC programs are open to all members of the defense community, including family members of active military personnel, military retirees, civilian employees, and the like. Conversely, the example provided by the Navy Morale, Welfare, and Recreation mission does not indicate that its programs are open to civilian employees.

The Nantahala Outdoor Center, an example of a commercial recreation mission statement, illustrates a commitment to high quality staff as a key element for obtaining guest satisfaction and employee control or ownership of the business. The mission contains numerous goals pertaining to the well-being of staff, staff commitment to high quality programming, and the Center's concern for continuous educational training of staff. One gets a sense that NOC cares about its employees and that it might be a good place to seek employment. Finally, the Cayuga Nature Center centers its mission on facilitating personal responsibility for the natural world.

It is important to recognize that all mission statements have an underlying philosophy that serves as the foundation for action in the agency. Often this philosophy is not explicit; it is made apparent only through ongoing actions taken by the organization. Whether explicit or implicit, an underlying philosophy guides the actions taken by an agency. Now complete Exercise 7-2 on page 127.

CONCLUSION

The agency's mission statement emerges from an analysis of individual, organizational, and community needs. The issues to consider and methods for analyzing them were discussed, and sample mission statements from 11 agencies were provided. The mission statement should state the purpose of the agency and identify the population it will serve. It should be based on an analysis of the organization's strengths and weaknesses and an analysis of the threats and opportunities facing the agency in the larger community environment. For programmers to achieve ongoing success requires that their programs meet individual, organizational, and community needs. Case studies of two such programs were provided.

REFERENCES

Army MWR About. (n.d.). *About Us* [On-line]. Available: http://www.armymwr.com/portal/about/

Bannon, J. J. (1976). *Leisure resources: Its comprehensive planning.* Englewood Cliffs, NJ: Prentice-Hall.

Bew, R. (2007). Emerging and surging. *The Economist: The world in 2007*, 16.

Carpenter, G. M., & Howe, C. Z. (1985). *Programming leisure experiences.* Englewood Cliffs, NJ: Prentice-Hall.

Cayuga Nature Center. (n.d.). *Mission statement* [On-line]. Available: http://www.cayuganaturecenter.org/about/mission.html

Champaign Park District. (n.d.). *About Us* [On-line]. Available: http://www.champaignparkdistrict.com/main.htm

City of San Diego Park and Recreation Department (n.d.). *Mission statement and vision* [On-line]. Available: http://www.sannet.gov/park-and-recreation/general-info/mission.html

Crompton, J. L., & Lamb, C. W., Jr. (1986). *Marketing government and social services.* New York: Wiley.

Crompton, J. L., & Witt, P. A. (1997). Repositioning: The key to building community support. *Parks and Recreation, 32*(10), 4.

Directorate of Morale, Welfare, and Recreation. (n.d.). *Air Force Morale, Welfare, and Recreation Student Work Experience Program.* Randolph AFB, TX: Air Force Manpower and Personnel Center.

Farrell, P., & Lundegren, H. M. (1991). The process of recreation programming: *Theory and technique* (3rd ed.). State College, PA: Venture.

Friedmann, J. (1973). The public interest and community participation: Toward a reconstruction of public philosophy. *Journal of American Institute of Planners, 39*(1), 2–12.

Howard, D. R., & Crompton, J. L. (1980). *Financing, managing, and marketing recreation and park programs.* Dubuque, IA: Wm. C. Brown.

Jacobs, J. (1961). *The death and life of great American cities.* New York: Vintage Books.

Kennedy, D. G. (April, 2004). Coming of age in consumerism. *American Demographics, 26*(3), 14.

Knowles, M. S. (1970). *The modern practice of adult education.* New York: The Association Press.

Kotler, P. (1980). *Marketing management* (4th ed.). Englewood Cliffs, NJ: Prentice-Hall.

Kotler, P. (1982). *Marketing for nonprofit organizations* (2nd ed.). Englewood Cliffs, NJ: Prentice-Hall.

Kotler, P. (1991). *Marketing management: Analysis, planning, implementation, and control* (7th ed.). Englewood Cliffs, NJ: Prentice-Hall.

Kraus, R. G. (1985). *Recreation program planning today.* Glenview, IL: Scott Foresman.

Kouzes, J. M., & Posner, B. Z. (1997). Envisioning your future: Imagining ideal scenarios. *Illinois Parks and Recreation, 28*(6), 18-22.

Leisure Resource Center. (n.d.). *Student field placement manual.* Peoria, IL: Leisure Resource Center.

Madison Metropolitan School District School, Community Recreation Department. (1982). *Action plan for the 1980s: Perspectives on programs—Projections for progress.* Madison, WI: Madison Metropolitan School District.

Management Learning Laboratories. (1985). *Assessment of the management function of the Knoxville Bureau of Recreation, Knoxville, Tennessee: Report 1, Review of existing organizational structure.* Champaign, IL: Management Learning Laboratories.

Merage Jewish Community. (n.d.). *Mission statement* [On-line]. Available: http://www.jccoc.org/

City of Kearney Operating Budget and Program Services. (2006-2007). *Mission Statement.* City of Kearney, Nebraska.

Mogelonsky, M. (1998). A desk at home. *American Demographics, 20*(6), 35.

Nantahala Outdoor Center. (n.d.). *Philosophy/mission statement.* [On-line]. Available: http://www.nocweb.com/whojobs/nfwhphil.htm

National Recreation and Park Association. (2001). *Self-assessment manual for quality operation of park and recreation agencies: A guide to standards for national accreditation* (3rd ed.). Commission for Accreditation of Park and Recreation Agencies.

Navy Morale, Welfare, and Recreation. (n.d.). *Mission statement* [On-line]. Available: http://www.mwr.navy.mil/

Peterson, J. A., & Schroth, R. J. (n.d.). *Guidelines for evaluating public parks and recreation.* West Lafayette, IN: Cooperative Extension Service, Purdue University.

Pfeffer, J., & Salancik, G. R. (1978). *The external control of organizations: A resource dependence perspective.* New York: Harper & Row.

Pine, B. J., II, & Gilmore, J. H. (1999). *The experience economy: Work is theatre & every business a stage.* Boston: Harvard Business School Press.

Rockland Young Men's/Young Women's Hebrew Association. (n.d.). *Mission statement* [On-line]. Available: http://www.rocklandymwha.org/framesey.htm

Rossman, J. R. (1973, March/April). Recreation in the streets. Des Plaines, IL: *Illinois Parks and Recreation*, pp. 4–5.

Roswell Recreation Department. (n.d.). *Roswell Recreation Department mission statement* [On-line]. Available: http://www.roswell-usa.com/city/recreation

St. Andrew's Parish Parks and Playground Commission. (n.d.). *Our mission* [On-line]. Available: http://www.standrewsparks.com

Sessoms, D. H. (1980). Community development and social planning. In S. G. Lutzin (Ed.), *Managing municipal leisure services* (pp. 120–139). Washington, DC: International City Management Association.

Tillman, A. (1973). *The program book for recreation professionals.* Palo Alto, CA: Mayfield.

U.S. Census Bureau. (2004). U.S. interim projections by age, sex, race, and Hispanic origin. Published March 2004 [On-line]. Available: http://www.census.gov/ipc/www/usinterimproj/

U.S. Census Bureau. (2005). Computers and internet use in the United States: October 2003. Current Population Reports. Washington, D.C. [On-line]. Available: http://www.census.gov/prod/2005pubs/p23-208.pdf

van der Smissen, B. (1972). *Evaluation and self-study of public recreation and park agencies: A guide with standards and evaluative criteria.* Arlington, VA: National Recreation and Park Association.

Westmont Park District. (n.d.). *Mission statement* [On-line]. Available: http://www.wpd4fun.org/index_2.htm.

Witt, L. (2004). Why we're losing the war against obesity. *American Demographics, 25*(10), 27-31.

Zikmund, W. G., & d'Amico, M. (1993). *Marketing* (4th ed.). Minneapolis/St. Paul, MN: West.

7

Case Study 7-1: Recreation in the Streets

Recreation in the Streets was developed in 1973 in Oak Park, Illinois. The community is the first suburb west of Chicago's corporate boundary. During the late 1960s and early 1970s, the population in the Chicago neighborhoods east of Oak Park had changed from all white to all black. The typical pattern of racial turnover in segregated, white Chicago neighborhoods was one of increasing distrust of new neighbors (black or white) and increasing isolation of existing residents in their own homes. This isolation intensified until each resident, at his or her own breaking point, moved, and the neighborhood once again became totally segregated, this time with all black residents. Oak Park developed a community goal of establishing and maintaining racially integrated neighborhoods. To accomplish this, it was necessary to find both white and black buyers for homes offered for sale and to create open neighborhoods where residents know and trust each other.

All city departments were asked to foster and facilitate an open dialogue among residents. The goal was to encourage them to interact with each other and in doing so create a safe, stable neighborhood (Jacobs, 1961). To contribute to this policy, the Oak Park Recreation Department developed the Recreation in the Streets program with the following goals:

1. To place leaders from local, neighborhood playgrounds into neighborhoods one day per week in order to create visibility for the leaders and their program, and to foster trust in the leadership provided at the neighborhood recreation centers.
2. To create interaction among neighbors on city blocks and to create a visible program service that would enable residents to come out of their homes and meet each other.
3. To temporarily create additional play space in an urban environment by making the street into a playground.

The program consisted of having three leaders from a neighborhood recreation center visit a residential block one morning per week from 9:00 a.m. until 12:00 noon. Traffic was blocked off from the street, and a trailer filled with recreation equipment was delivered to the block at about 8:30 a.m. When leaders arrived, they set up a volleyball net, a puppet stage, and other equipment in the street. The leaders then conducted an organized program consisting of events such as parachute games, bicycle and tricycle races, street hockey, volleyball games, chalk drawing on the street, and craft projects. The morning concluded with a luncheon cookout, and the street was reopened at noon. Each of the seven neighborhood recreation centers visited a different block each week for the seven weeks of the summer program.

In addition to facilitating interaction during the event, Recreation in the Streets was designed to require the interaction of neighbors in requesting and operating the event. To be selected for a visit, a block resident had to obtain the signatures of at least fifty percent of the block residents on a petition for service to be provided by the Recreation Department. Blocks to be visited were selected on the basis of their existing service (blocks farthest from existing services received highest priority) and their previous history of receiving visits. Once a block was selected for a visit, the individual who initiated the petition was responsible for designating a home on the block where the trailer could be parked, for circulating notices that the street would be closed the next day for the event, and for obtaining a charcoal grill for the cookout. Residents clearly had to interact before the event; otherwise, it could not occur.

Case Study 7-1: (continued)

Recreation in the Streets is an example of a program that was designed to build on an existing strength of the Oak Park Recreation Department; that is, its well-distributed neighborhood recreation centers. In addition, it met an identified community need to foster interaction among residents. In this program, individual, community, and organizational needs, as well as organizational mission, were all met within the resource limits of the agency.

Case Study 7-2: Warrior Games

In 1985 a ship commander requested that Navy recreation personnel create a program for sailors who were given 24-hour duty leave from extended training missions operating out of Guantanamo Bay, Cuba. Ships operating out of the bay are sent on training missions that simulate actual combat situations for 14 to 21 days at a time. They return infrequently to base for a 24 hour leave. It was important that some type of recreation be available to provide release from the continual strain of simulated combat conditions. It was equally important that the training mission of creating esprit de corps, teamwork, and leadership not be broken during these short leaves. The recreation program, then, needed to provide opportunities for fun, teamwork, and leadership.

A series of Warrior Games was developed and was operated as competitions among units. These games presented the sailors with a problem that needed to be solved. The solution did not require superior strength or skill. To successfully solve the problem and win the competition, someone in the unit had to exercise leadership and get the unit to operate as a team. For example, in one game a unit had to submerge a large inflated ball in a swimming pool by organizing unit members to lock hands and legs to form a "human cargo net" to drape over the ball. This could be done only with the organized cooperation of the entire unit. Similarly, in each Warrior Game a different problem had to be solved quickly through the cooperation of the entire unit.

In this program, organizational needs (the Morale, Welfare, and Recreation unit's need to contribute to combat readiness), community needs (command needs to continue the themes of the training mission), and individual needs (for a playful diversion) were all met with a single program operating within the resource limits of the organization. Excellence in organized recreation programming requires that the needs of all three entities be met simultaneously.

Cinco de Mayo
Photo courtesy of Long Beach Parks, Recreation, and Marine Department, Long Beach, CA

Developing Strategic Directions:
Writing Program Management Goals

STEP 2: STRATEGIC DIRECTIONS

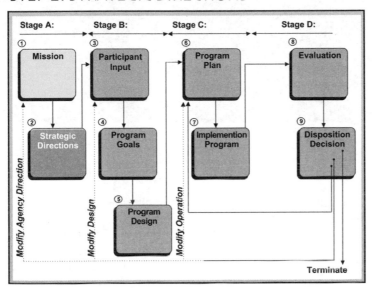

KEY TERMS

Program
   Management
   Goals
Short-Range
   Planning Goals
Networking Goals
   and Objectives
Operational
   Meaning
Systems
   Approach

Additional direction and focus are given to an agency's programming efforts by the development of program management planning goals. As indicated in Chapter Six, an organization's mission statement is not measurable. The sample mission statements included in Chapter Seven are not measurable. Therefore, a series of goals and objectives must be developed as a means of operationalizing and measuring an organization's mission statement. This is accomplished in Step 2 of the Program Development Cycle. The next level of goal development is a series of three to five year planning goals that are often followed with one-year "management by objective" type goals. These goals delimit some specific programmatic directions the agency will try to take.

The next level of goal development is a series of 3-to-5-year planning goals.

SHORT-RANGE PLANNING GOALS

An example of statements of three- to five-year short-range planning goals is provided in a planning document for the Knoxville Bureau of Recreation, Knoxville, Tennessee (Management Learning Laboratories, 1985). The bureau's mission statement, which was presented in Chapter Seven, is developed below with eight short-range planning goals:

Implementing Outcome-Based Programming

Recreation and park agencies that adopt an outcome-based programming approach will derive from its mission statement three- to five- year planning goals. These planning goals should be based on the fundamental premise that the agency envisions itself to be a key element for improving and enhancing community life. The resultant program management goals should exude these qualities.

As will be described in this chapter, outcome-based program planning goals, like any planning goals, will be networked fully into the agency from the administrative level all the way to the programming level. The further those planning goals are networked into the agency, the more directive and specific they become for programmers.

1. To enhance the quality of life for all citizens of Knoxville through the provision of public recreation services.
2. To employ a professionally-trained staff and to provide staff an environment fostering personal and professional growth.
3. To improve the efficiency and effectiveness of maintenance operations.
4. To increase revenue production and to implement a budget process at the operational level in the Bureau.
5. To be future-oriented, planned, and prepared to meet the changing needs and wants of citizens regarding recreation services.
6. To maximize citizen involvement in the planning and development of recreation programs and services.
7. To more effectively market the Bureau's services to the citizens of Knoxville.
8. To act as a facilitator or catalyst for the provision of recreation programs by other public or private organizations.

These eight goals are examples of statements that have no measurement devices included in them. Goals of this type must be specified further and given meaning by developing more specific statements that will be used to measure them. To further illustrate this process, the first goal identified—to enhance the quality of life for all citizens of Knoxville through the provision of public recreation services—will be developed further. A series of objectives for accomplishing this specific goal could include the following objectives:

1. To establish a senior citizens' program.
2. To establish an athletic facility reservation system.
3. To establish a cultural arts division.

These three objectives are still short-term planning statements; that is, they are written assuming they will be accomplished in three to five years. They are, however, objectives for the goal previously specified. For purposes of illustration, only three objectives have been developed. They are by no means exhaustive of all that the agency could do to enhance the quality of life for all Knoxville citizens; however, they do represent what could be done. (See Figure 6-3 and its accompanying explanation for a review of this concept.)

To continue with the Knoxville example, it is possible to illustrate how an objective for one level of the organization becomes a goal for the next stratum in the organizational hierarchy. For example, the chief executive officer of the organization may have the goal of "enhancing the quality of life for all citizens of Knoxville through the provision of public recreation services." This same individual may have developed the three short-range planning objectives outlined above in order to accomplish that goal.

Next, this individual passes his or her objective of "establishing a cultural arts division" down the organizational hierarchy to the director of recreation, for whom it becomes a goal to be accomplished. The director of recreation must then develop objectives for demonstrating its accomplishment. Although it is not mandatory that the director develop objectives with a one-year time frame, for purposes of illustration we will use one-year objectives.

As an example, the goal "to establish a cultural arts division" will be implemented in fiscal year 2010 with the following one-year objectives:

1. To hire a cultural arts supervisor within the first two months of FY 2010.
2. To budget $60,000 for cultural arts programs during FY 2010.
3. To develop fifteen cultural arts programs during FY 2010.

Several important dimensions of using goal and objective technology are made apparent here. First, it is clearer now that goals and objectives are not definitive categories and that a goal can often later become an objective and vice versa in actual implementation. Second, the objectives just presented do have measurement devices in them. Because they were developed by the director of recreation, we know who is to be held accountable for their accomplishment. And because they include measurement devices, we will know if they have been accomplished. For example, the director of recreation is responsible for hiring a cultural arts supervisor within the first two months of fiscal year 2010. Third, these objectives all have a one-year timeline. The time frame for accomplishment is getting more specific. In this case, the fiscal year is the time frame being used.

These examples are illustrative of the objectives typically used in a management by objectives system. They are action-oriented, specifying what managerial action is going to be taken to accomplish a task and what criteria will be used to judge its success. It is also important to note that this is where program planning activities are integrated with budgeting. The development of a specific program service has become a budget element with resources committed to its implementation.

It is assumed here that the chief executive officer and the director of recreation jointly agree that the successful accomplishment of these three objectives will be accepted as proof that the goal has been accomplished. This is the implicit assumption of the technology. We accept this, knowing that the three objectives identified are just a partial list of all that one could do to establish a cultural arts division. In this case, the three objectives are representative of what the director of recreation must accomplish in FY 2010 to establish a cultural arts division.

Goals and objectives should provide clarity and help the organization achieve and document its accomplishments.

NETWORKING GOALS AND OBJECTIVES FURTHER IN THE ORGANIZATION

Continuing with the Knoxville example, we will illustrate further how goals and objectives are networked throughout the organization and used to provide further direction and focus to program management. Once the director of recreation hires the cultural arts supervisor and budgets the funds for the year, the director will give the objective of "developing fifteen cultural arts programs for FY 2010" to the new cultural arts supervisor as a goal. The director will ask for a list of objectives outlining how the cultural arts supervisor intends to accomplish this goal. The supervisor could then develop the following list of objectives:

Exercise 8-2: Program Management Goals

Develop program management goals for the operation of a chain of commercial recreation facilities. Each facility has a nursery, a weight room, an exercise machine room, an indoor swimming pool, a running track, a concession and lounge area, twelve racquetball courts, and separate shower and locker facilities for men and women. Each facility is family-oriented; 85 percent of the membership in each facility is made up of families.

After developing program management goals, discuss the following questions:
- Are the goals comprehensive and explicit enough to guide less capable staff members? That is, if the goals are met, will a facility have an acceptable program?
- Is there enough flexibility to allow creative staff members leeway to develop a program further?
- Are the goals written to recognize differences among facilities with regard to the number of members, the number of staff, and the size of the budget?

1. To operate a cultural arts fair during the spring of 2010.
2. To operate a summer cultural arts workshop for children during the summer of 2010, with three different media.
3. To operate a concert in the park series during September 2010.
4. To offer an arts instructional program for adults during the fall (October and November) of 2010, with at least five different media.

These statements could be made more specific still with additional measurement devices. For example, the second objective could be rewritten to read, "To operate a summer cultural arts workshop for children during the summer of 2010, with three different media and an enrollment of at least 75 students." The addition of this new measurement device further defines how success in accomplishing this objective will be measured. How detailed one must be is a matter of professional practice in a specific organization. Remember, using goal and objective technology is a means to the end of developing useful programs and services and of measuring and documenting the organization's accomplishments. Goals and objectives should be developed to the point that they provide operational clarity and help the organization achieve and document its accomplishments.

It is certainly possible to develop these objectives further. For example, to accomplish the objective of offering "a summer cultural arts workshop during the summer of 2010, with three different media," this objective can be treated as a goal. The following objectives can then be prepared to document its accomplishment:

Exhibit 8-1: Recreation Center Programming Goals

V Corps Recreation Center
A Morale Support Activity
"Your Link to Leisure"

These are recommended MINIMUM programming standards for community recreation centers in V Corp, based on minimum staffing as it exists in some communities. If there [are] one full-time professional and at least two recreation aides [available], the following variety of programs can and should be offered in each recreation center. When there is more staff (a full-time program director) the number and variety of programs should be increased, reflecting the needs and interests of the constituency as well as modern trends of American life-styles. Naturally, the use of other MSA core programs and community agency staff, as well as volunteers, is urged.

DIRECTED PROGRAMS: Minimum of three nights per week.
FILLER PROGRAMS: Maximum of two nights per week.
SPECIAL INTEREST GROUP MEETINGS: Maximum of one night per week.
CLASSES: Maximum of two nights per week.
THEME PROGRAMS: Minimum of one day/night/weekend.
COMMUNITY-WIDE PROGRAM: Minimum of one per quarter.
SPECIAL ENTERTAINMENT PROGRAM: Minimum of twice per quarter.

The following definitions are offered:

DIRECTED PROGRAM: A program that requires professional staff (GS/UA 5 or above) to lead patrons (regardless of whether 1, 10, or 100 show up) in an active activity, that is, open forum discussion group with guest speaker, new games, quiz show-type games. This means the director conducts the program and participates actively; it does not mean the director passes out pieces of paper or serves refreshments only. A directed program may require props, audiovisual equipment, some decorations, and gimmicks, but not to the extent that a theme program does.
FILLER PROGRAM: A program that can be executed by trained professionals GS/PS 2–4, which usually involves passive activity such as video movies, but can also be active such as bingo, challenge-the-staff, pub night, small games, card tournaments, kitchen activities.
SPECIAL INTEREST GROUP MEETINGS: Six or more individuals who share an interest in the same activity, be it chess or mountain-climbing, constitute a "special interest group." There are no dues, no elected officers, and no constitution and by-laws. These groups usually develop around one or two highly enthusiastic individuals who attract followers—they are loosely organized but need recreation center support in order to exist. This kind of program can usually take place in another room of the recreation center while something else is going on. However, if the group grows very large, such as a computer interest group, that meeting or activity may become a valid program on its own in the main area of the recreation center, but not more than once a week.
CLASSES: Program involving six or more individuals who are being instructed by a contracted individual not on the recreation center staff. Also a program which can be conducted in another area of the recreation center in addition to other programs being conducted simultaneously.

Exhibit 8-1: (continued)

THEME PROGRAMS: A program conducted within the recreation center or other facility which contains at least six of the ten elements of a theme program. The ten elements of a theme program are:

1. Activities (active games)
2. Refreshments (food, beverages)
3. Decorations/props
4. Entertainment (live)
5. Audiovisuals (films/slides/video tapes)
6. Costumes
7. Lighting (special room arrangement)
8. Prizes
9. Music (canned, for atmosphere)
10. Gimmick, (giveaways, mystery or special guests, special effects, etc.)

All ten elements are geared toward one overall concept or idea, the most natural being the holidays that occur throughout the year. There is at least one theme to celebrate each month, and these are the most basic:

January: Ice, snow, winter
February: Valentine's Day, President's Day
March: Mardi Gras, Fasching
April: Easter
May: Spring, Memorial Day
June: National Recreation and Park Month
July: Independence Day
August: Summer
September: Native Americans
October: Halloween
November: Thanksgiving
December: Christmas, New Year

COMMUNITY-WIDE PROGRAM: A program that contains the elements of a theme program, but is coordinated with other MSA core programs and community agencies. The program can and should take place outside the recreation center facility at other locations; that is, Renaissance Faire, Winter Ski and Travel Expo, Auto Flea Market, and so on.

SPECIAL ENTERTAINMENT PROGRAM: Organic variety shows and revues, coffee-house-style in-house informal shows, talent and "no talent" shows, rock concerts, dinner theater, drama club skits, DOD touring shows, celebrity nights, improvisations, and commercial entertainment.

NOT ACCEPTABLE to stand alone as programs titled on a publicized program calendar are "food" program nights, such as "Make Your Own Sundae," "Make a Pizza," "Taco Night," or "Steak Night." These foods and the sale of those foods should be incorporated into a directed or theme program and should not appear as the sole activity for an evening.

Tour departures listed on a program calendar are misleading. Tours are not programs for patrons in the recreation center. Although the calendar square for that date is filled, there is, in reality, nothing happening in the recreation center facility.

Exhibit 8-1: (continued)

Recommend departure from the calendar style of program promotion. If every square is not filled with definitive, exciting activity, do not use that format. Empty calendar squares indicate no activity and do not motivate patrons to use facilities or attend programs.

Program titles appearing on printed publicity should have fresh, new, and interesting approaches.

From: Rice, H. (1986). Come on...Let's get with the programming! Mimeographed workshop handout, U.S. Army V Corps D.C.A. Recreation Center Training Workshop, Baumholder, Germany.

1. To offer a children's drama class during the summer of 2010, with at least 15 enrollments.
2. To offer an oil painting class during the summer of 2010.
3. To offer guitar for beginners during the summer of 2010.

Preparing concise program management goals is an important skill that programmers must develop to effectively provide direction to the development and management of program services. Remember, however, that we have not yet developed program design goals; this will be discussed in Chapter Ten. Practice developing program management goals in an organizational heirarchy by completing Exercise 8-1 on page 138.

USING GOALS AND OBJECTIVES TO ESTABLISH PROGRAMMING STANDARDS

Program management goals and objectives can also be used to establish operational standards. McCarville (1993) indicates that "Standards provide precise standards that staff members may use to monitor their own success in providing programs and services" (p. 36). Exhibit 8-1 describes program management goals for the operation of recreation centers for the Army V Corps in Germany. Using goals and objectives in this manner helps direct the program that will be developed at each recreation center.

Program management goals such as those included in Exhibit 8-1 on pages 140-142 ensure that program operations at a recreation center are organized and controlled so that a minimum level of programming is provided. They establish customer service standards. Similar types of program management goals are used to direct the management of day camps, swimming pools, craft centers, and the like. In service industries, these types of goals are analogous to the production goals used in manufacturing organizations. Program management goals are used as quality assurance guidelines to direct program production at a number of similar facilities or programming entities. Now complete Exercise 8-2 on page 139.

A SYSTEMS APPROACH

Peterson (1976) has explained how goal and objective technology can be combined with systems theory to develop a comprehensive, networked set of agency goals and objectives. The process offered by Peterson shows how to operationalize the concepts illustrated in Figure 6-3. In this system, one assigns numbers to each succeeding level of goal and objective development. The entire program of the Leisure Resource Center in Peoria, Illinois, was developed in this manner. Their program will be used to illustrate this point.

The first statement in the Leisure Resource Center's manual (n.d.) is their statement of purpose:

To provide a comprehensive system of leisure service delivery in the greater Peoria area that assists people with disabilities in the development of leisure skills, attitudes, and awareness, and promotes their personal and community leisure participation.

This statement of purpose is operationalized with the following nine goals:

1. To provide services that assist in the development of leisure skills.
2. To provide services that assist in the development of leisure awareness, responsibility, and potential for involvement.
3. To provide opportunities for ongoing leisure involvement and utilization of existing and newly-acquired leisure skills.
4. To provide services that enable the acquisition of leisure resource information.
5. To promote physical and architectural accessibility of leisure-related facilities and programs.
6. To provide training, consultation, and other resources to assist other agencies in the provision of recreation and leisure opportunities for people with disabilities.
7. To promote community awareness of the leisure needs, abilities, and rights of people with disabilities.
8. To provide development and educational services for professionals and students related to the leisurability of people with disabilities.
9. To advocate for the leisure rights of people with disabilities.

These goals define how the Leisure Resource Center will accomplish its mission. The governing board and the community accept the center's accomplishment of these goals as proof that it has accomplished its mission. Other goals could have been selected, but these were chosen for a variety of reasons, including staff skills, agency resource limits, unique opportunities available to the agency, and client needs. These goals do not have measurement devices or time limits on them. They are typical of short-range planning goals that are developed to provide programmatic direction to an agency for a three- to five-year period. Some of these same goals may continue as part of the agency mission for a number of years if periodic review and evaluation determine that they are still desirable for the agency to pursue.

In Figure 8-1, the nine goals are placed in a figure, and each is given a code number from 1.0 through 9.0. These goals thereby become the nine components of the Leisure Resource Center's program. For each of the nine components, additional goals can be developed that further define what is to be included in each component. In Figure 8-2, the support goals for component 3.0, Ongoing Recreation Participation, are placed in a figure.

From the goals in Figure 8-2, one can begin to develop annual goals for programming purposes. For example, for Films (3.1.1), it would be possible to develop the following goals:

1. To offer a film each Saturday night during October 2010, with 50 or more clients in attendance at each screening (3.1.1.1).
2. To offer a Holiday Film Festival by showing a Christmas film on each of the four Saturdays preceding Christmas 2010 (3.1.1.2).
3. To instruct a filmmaking class during the summer programming season 2010, with 12 or more enrollments (3.1.1.3).

In a similar fashion, each of the goals included for the Leisure Resource Center can be further defined and developed in the hierarchical manner discussed earlier. When a numeric coding system is added, the purpose of each activity, program, or other undertaking of the organization can be traced through the hierarchical structure of the goals and objectives that have been developed.

Using this numerical, hierarchical arrangement helps the organization in three ways. First, development of the goals and objectives helps interpret the organization's mission into desired programs for development. Second, the uncertainty surrounding the management of programs is thereby given direction and focus through a sequential, logical, and orderly process of goal and objective development. So much of what is done in a leisure service organization is normatively determined on the basis of any number of factors, including resource limitations, client interests, staff skills, abilities and interests, and unique opportunities available to the agency. The use of goals and objectives to develop program directions helps the agency interpret to its public why it exists and what it will accomplish. Third, employee effort is networked throughout the organization. Through the information and networking provided by a hierarchical arrangement of goals and objectives, em-

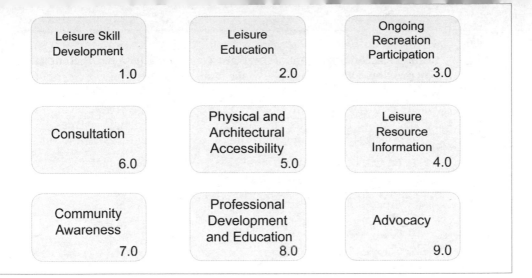

Figure 8-1: Easter Seal Leisure Resource Center Goals

Figure 8-2: Ongoing Recreation Participation Goals 3.0

ployees at all levels understand their role in helping the organization achieve its mission.

It can be confusing to develop a hierarchical arrangement of goals and objectives that is logical, that is constructed in the correct order from general to specific, and that has measurable statements. The systems approach offered by Peterson (1976) brings structure that clarifies the process. The numerical coding system used allows one to quickly identify the place of a goal or objective statement and its relationship in the overall hierarchical structure. Now complete Exercise 8-3.

CONCLUSION

Goal and objective technology is used to provide further direction to program development within a program agency. Three- to five-year program planning goals are developed to provide short-range planning direction for the agency. Each of these goals is further defined through the development of one-year management by objective goal statements. Additional development of goals with supporting objectives continues until operational clarity and direction are achieved. How program management goals can be used to establish program standards was discussed. Incorporating goal and objective technology with systems theory results in a numerical coding system for tracking the management of the agency's programs.

REFERENCES

Leisure Resource Center. (n.d.). *Student field placement manual*. Peoria, IL: Leisure Resource Center.

Management Learning Laboratories. (1985). *Assessment of the management function of the Knoxville Bureau of Recreation, Knoxville, Tennessee: Report 1, Review of existing organizational structure.* Champaign, IL: Management Learning Laboratories.

McCarville, R. E. (1993). Keys to quality programming. *Journal of Physical Education, Recreation, and Dance, 64*(8), 34–36, 46–47.

Peterson, C. A. (1976). *A systems approach to therapeutic recreation program planning.* Champaign, IL: Stipes.

Rice, H. (1986). Come on. . . . Let's get with the programming! Baumholder, Germany: U.S. Army V Corps D.C.A. Recreation Center Training Workshop, Baumholder, Germany. Mimeographed workshop handout.

8

Stage B: Targeted Program Development

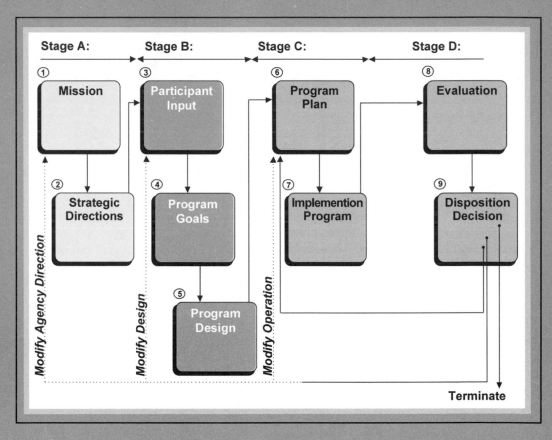

Part III

Targeted Program Development

In Part III, Stage B of the Program Development Cycle is discussed. This stage involves obtaining participant input into programs through a variety of techniques, identifying the market segments to serve, developing operational program goals and objectives, and using data generated in the first parts of the cycle to creatively design programmed experiences for patrons. The programmer's responsibility is to design and develop programs based on demonstrated patron needs and wants.

Part III includes four chapters. In Chapter Nine, a variety of techniques for obtaining input from participants are discussed, including needs assessment and marketing assessment. In Chapter Ten, writing program design goals is covered. In Chapter Eleven, a technique for designing programs is discussed, as is how participant input is used in program design. In Chapter Twelve, techniques for applying creativity and innovation to program design are explained, and several practice exercises are provided.

Skate Park
Photo courtesy of Long Beach Parks, Recreation, and Marine Department, Long Beach, CA

Obtaining Participant Input

STEP 3 : PARTICIPANT INPUT

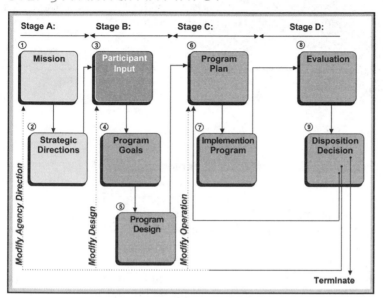

KEY TERMS

Participant Input
Social Policy
   Literature
Political Science
   Literature
Need
Interest
Want
Intention
Normative Need
Felt Need
Expressed Need
Comparative Need
Citizen Advisory
   Committees
Public Meetings
Interviews
Focus Group
   Interview
Surveys
Marketing
Exchange
Segmentation
Target Marketing

In this step, participant input into program development is sought. Throughout the development of the park and recreation field, practitioners have been admonished to seek input from those they serve in developing parks, facilities, experiences, and program services. Today, this is still sound advice. Although the programmer may, through trial and error, serendipitously develop a successful program, the more information he or she has about the needs, preferences, and habits of potential participants, the higher the probability for developing a successful program.

Several mechanisms for obtaining input from participants and other stakeholders have been developed. These include input from citizen board members who may be elected or appointed to governing or advisory boards, needs assessment strategies, and market assessment methods provided by marketing techniques. Usually, governing boards of most recreation enterprises will not be involved in providing input into program development. However, they will be involved in setting policies that govern participation in various program services, as well as in determining resource allocations that will determine which program services may eventually be developed. Advisory councils and other similar citizen advisory groups are usually more focused and organized to give direct input into specific activity or facility development.

Implementing Outcome-Based Programming

Once the agency mission statement is completed, it is then possible to begin creating programs using outcome-based programming. There are four components to the BBP model: (1) inputs, or in BBP, issues and target goals; (2) activities, or in BBP, activity components; (3) outputs, or in BBP, benefit outcomes; and (4) outcomes, or in BBP, benefits-based awareness. The portion of the model that is accomplished in this chapter is the first portion of the first component: *inputs*. In this chapter, we discuss how to assess the needs from the community to help determine program inputs for the participants. This step ties in directly with Knowles' (1970) notion that programs must meet the needs of individuals, the community, and the agency.

...the more information we have about the needs, preferences, and habits of potential participants, the higher the probability for developing a successful program.

Following is a more detailed explanation about how programmers conduct needs assessment and market analyses to obtain participant input into program development. Carpenter and Howe (1985) state, "In leisure programming, needs assessment performs two major functions: the generation of program ideas, and the facilitation of input from constituents and responsiveness to constituents by service providers" (p. 77). Embodied in this definition are two major objectives of needs assessment: (1) helping the agency determine the direction it will take in developing program services, and (2) incorporating citizen input into the decision-making process.

These two objectives arise from two bodies of literature that contribute to needs assessment. The first is social policy literature, which has sought to justify the services provided to citizens by suggesting that the services fulfill identifiable needs. The concept of needs as used by McKillip (1987) exemplifies this point of view: "Needs are value judgments that a target group has problems that can be solved" (p. 7). McKillip makes very clear his view that needs, and therefore decisions about them, are value laden, not objective.

The second body of literature, which is exemplified by the work of Summers (1987), stems from political science. Summers states:

> Citizen participation in decision making is the essence of needs assessment. It concerns grass-roots democracy and the importance of people being free and able to express their views on matters that affect their lives, families, and communities. Needs assessment is a social institution that integrates ideas from political theories of democracy with practices flowing from the mainstream of social science research. (p. 3)

He goes on to say that needs assessment "is a special case of citizen participation, and participation issues are essentially questions of value" (p. 3). The second objective of needs assessment, then, is how

RESEARCH UPDATE: How do you describe those you serve? The term you use to describe those you serve influences how you perceive your role and the professional paradigm you use. For example, if you view your service recipients as customers, you see them in an economic exchange model and you likely view your role as one of selling them a service. If you view them as clients, you likely see them has having some deficiency that your services will need to correct, as in a therapeutic model.

In a systematic random survey conducted by the authors, public park and recreation programmers in the state of Illinois were asked how they describe their service recipients. In the table below are the results of this survey. Overwhelmingly, they described them as participants.

This is an interesting choice in that the term "participant" implies more than any other that to experience leisure in a program, individuals must engage the interaction and participate in it. Participant is used throughout this chapter except in the section on marketing. Much of the marketing literature is from a business perspective, which uses the terms clients and customers.

Descriptors for Service Recipients
(Percentage of respondents indicating a descriptor was the one used in their agency.)

Descriptor	Frequency	Percentage Using the Descriptor
Participant	100	57.0%
Patron	24	13.0%
Customer	23	13.0%
Resident	10	5.6%
Client	4	2.3%
Other responses	6	3.4%

n of responses = 176

to best incorporate citizen input when making value judgments about what needs actually exist and which needs should be served.

Often, programmers feel unsure about the needs assessment step of the Program Development Cycle. They are uncertain about the appropriateness and adequacy of their needs assessment methods. Programmers have an especially difficult problem with needs assessment because of the multiplicity of leisure needs and the very personal nature of leisure participation preferences. Developing a better understanding of needs and assessment methods will help reduce some of the uncertainty about the process.

The literature has made clear several operational principles about needs assessment that will help programmers understand its limitations and its role.

First, the literature suggests that needs are not objective entities—they are value judgments. What programs are to be developed is always a matter of choice, not fact.

Second, any needs assessment will identify more needs than an agency can fulfill. Any needs assessment method must eventually lead to a decision about which competing needs will be met. These decisions are also value laden. Because of this, McKillip (1987) suggests that decisions among competing needs should be based on an analysis of the cost, impact, and feasibility of alternatives.

Third, because of the multiplicity of needs, needs analysis is not a maximizing strategy. That is, it will not lead to a final, objective determination about the one, clear course of action that programmers should follow. At best, it will help clear up some of the uncertainty about which programs should be developed.

Fourth, in actual practice, needs assessment is an ongoing process. Programmers must constantly assess needs and develop programs based on current information.

Fifth, needs assessments can fulfill three roles: (1) they can provide data that enable the agency to better understand the individuals who will be affected by the agency's actions; (2) they can assess patron response to new program proposals; and (3) they can help establish priorities among alternative courses of action (Summers, 1987).

Ultimately, the goal of needs assessment is to use participant input in identifying and documenting recreational needs that can be successfully met with leisure services developed by the agency. To systematically assess needs, programmers should understand both the definitional and methodological issues of needs assessment.

NEED CONCEPTS

Need is one of several constructs used to investigate motivation for participating in leisure (Mannell, 1999). In discussing leisure interest "finders," Witt and Groom (1979) point out that the literature often fails to distinguish between needs, wants, interests, demands, and other similar terms. Recreation professionals tend to use these terms interchangeably with little explanation of their meaning. Marketing literature (Kotler, 1980) offers a pragmatic approach to defining need and related concepts that will be used to give insight into leisure needs assessment.

NEED

A *need* is a state of deprivation arising out of the basic innate biological characteristics of humans. A need is not created by society, but exists apart from and prior to society. There is considerable evidence that humans have a need to participate in activities that are intrinsically rewarding, that stimulate arousal, and that are intrinsically motivating

Exhibit 9-1: Questions Contrasting Wants and Intentions

Wants

Listed below are many recreational activities. Some are activities that are currently offered by [the agency], and others are new activities that may be offered in the future. For each activity listed, indicate by checking the appropriate response whether you would participate in the activity if it were offered by [the agency] next year, and if so, whether you would pay for the cost of the activity program.

	Definitely No	Probably No	Unsure	Probably Yes	Definitely Yes
Baseball	( )	( )	( )	( )	( )
Cooking	( )	( )	( )	( )	( )
Cross-country skiing	( )	( )	( )	( )	( )
Scuba diving lessons	( )	( )	( )	( )	( )
Tennis Instructions	( )	( )	( )	( )	( )
Volleyball league	( )	( )	( )	( )	( )

Intentions

Following is a list of leisure activities that you may enjoy. For each activity, please tell us:

  1. If you participated in the activity in this past year and/or
  2. If you intend to participate in it this coming year.

For those activities in which you intend to participate next year, please tell us:

  3. The frequency with which you intend to participate in a typical month (if seasonal, when the activity is in season);
  4. The primary participants in the activity—that is, yourself alone, with family, or with friends;
  5. The location where you usually participate, (agency-owned facility or other supplier);
  6. The time(s) of the day or week you prefer to participate;
  7. The price at which you no longer can afford to participate; and
  8. Potential barriers, if any, to your participation.

[Note: Below are the items that need to be included on an instrument. Although they are laid out vertically in this exhibit, they should be displayed horizontally for each activity for which information is sought.]

Exhibit 9-1: (continued)

Baseball

1. Experienced this last year? Yes ( ) No ( )
2. Intend to participate this year? Yes ( ) (Go on to 3)
   No ( ) (Go on to next activity)
3. Expected frequency (in season) Daily ( )
   Several times per week ( )
   Several times per month ( )
   Once per month ( )
   Less often than once
   per month ( )

4. Primary participants (select one) Alone ( )
   With family ( )
   With friends ( )
5. Location (select one primary location) [Name of agency
   facility] ( )
   Competing facility
   or facilities if
   appropriate ( )
6. Preferred activity times (circle all that apply)

	Early Morning	Mid-Morning	Lunchtime	Early Afternoon	Mid Afternoon	Night
Monday	x	x	x	x	x	x
Tuesday	x	x	x	x	x	x
Wednesday	x	x	x	x	x	x
Thursday	x	x	x	x	x	x
Friday	x	x	x	x	x	x
Saturday	x	x	x	x	x	x
Sunday	x	x	x	x	x	x

7. Circle the number that represents the dollar amount at which you would no longer be able to afford to participate in this activity. Please use only one section depending on whether this activity is paid for on a per-participation basis or per-session basis.

7. a. Activities paid for on a per-participation basis:
   Could not afford to participate if there were a fee 1
   $1.00 per participation 2
   Over $1.00 but under $3.00 per participation 3

Exhibit 9-1: (continued)

Over $3.00 but under $5.00 per participation   4

Over $5.00 but under $7.50 per participation   5

Over $7.50 but under $10.00 per participation   6

Over $10.00 but under $15.00 per participation   7

Over $15.00 but under $25.00 per participation   8

Over $25.00 but under $40.00 per participation   9

Over $40.00 per participation   10

7. b. Activities paid for on a per-session basis:

Could not afford to participate if there were a fee   1

$5.00 per session   2

Over $5.00 but under $10.00 per session   3

Over $10.00 but under $15.00 per session   4

Over $15.00 but under $20.00 per session   5

Over $20.00 but under $25.00 per session   6

Over $25.00 but under $30.00 per session   7

Over $30.00 but under $50.00 per session   8

Over $50.00 but under $74.00 per session   9

Over $75.00 per session   10

8.   Potential barriers. Please check the barriers listed below that are most likely to keep you from participating in the activity. (Select no more than three)

Activity unavailable near my home   ( )

Lack of child care   ( )

Lack of transportation   ( )

Poor facility   ( )

Inconvenient hours of operation   ( )

Poor management of facility or program   ( )

Lack of program information   ( )

I am not skilled enough   ( )

I am uncomfortable with other users   ( )

Adapted from: The Leisure Needs Survey Instrument,
U.S. Navy Recreational Services Program.

Exercise 9-1: Developing Needs Assessment Questions

In class, discuss the different kinds of information you would have collected with the two types of responses to the needs assessment questions included in Exhibit 9.1. Which of these instruments would provide the most complete information for developing and designing a program? Which would be the most expensive to administer?

After the discussion, write needs assessment questions for the following three activities to be held at a public swimming pool:

Swimming lessons
Scuba lessons
Public swimming

Now exchange questions with a class member and critique each other's questions. Remember to try to determine a patron's intention to participate. The more specific you can be about the activity, time, place, and price, the more likely you are to obtain reliable information.

An interest is an awareness or feeling about what one would like to do or acquire.

(see, for example, Csikszentmihalyi, 1975; Ellis, 1973; Iso-Ahola, 1980, 1982; Neulinger, 1974). The need for experiences provided in leisure and recreation is innate; it does not have to be created by programmers through marketing, advertising, program design, or any other technique.

INTEREST

An *interest* is an awareness or feeling about what one would like to do or acquire. Interests are learned and are influenced by social forces. An individual's self-concept can also precipitate an interest in a specific activity.

WANT

A want is a culturally learned behavior pattern for satisfying specific needs.

A *want* is a culturally learned behavior pattern for satisfying specific needs. Individuals need food, but they learn to want a Big Mac, a steak, a taco, or a dish of sushi. Individuals need intrinsically rewarding and stimulating behavior, but they learn to want to participate in tennis, bowling, oil painting, or reading to satisfy the higher order, innate needs identified earlier. People have few needs, but many wants. Wants are constantly being altered by social forces, including family, friends, and social institutions such as churches, schools, and the business community. Furthermore, satisfying a want often leads to the creation of additional wants (Witt & Groom, 1979). Programmers can influence, manipulate, and satisfy wants.

INTENTION

Intention is the commitment to acquire specific satisfiers of wants under given market conditions. When someone intends to participate in a specific activity, he or she intends to do so at a given time, location, and price. Many people are interested in or want to scuba dive on a Caribbean island; considerably fewer intend to commit the necessary time and money to do so. For recreation program planning, it is essential to understand the number of individuals who actually intend to participate in a program under a defined market condition.

No needs have been discovered that are unique to leisure. Currently, the notion that leisure satisfies specific needs is thought to be a learned response to engage in specific activities (Mannell, 1999). Leisure needs assessment, then, is actually an attempt to determine the interests, wants, or intentions of potential participants. It is important when interpreting data from a needs assessment to know whether one actually has data that reveal interests, wants, or intentions. These three concepts imply varying strengths of motivation to participate in activities. Because each concept implies a different degree of motivation to participate, the patrons in each conceptual level will require varying promotional efforts to convince them to participate.

An individual who has an "interest" in an activity has the lowest level of motivation to participate. An individual who "wants" to get into a program has a stronger motivation and is therefore more likely to participate. An individual who "intends" to participate has made a strong commitment actually to participate in an activity and is likely to do so if given market conditions are met.

Practitioners have often been disappointed with the reliability of needs assessment data, because there has not been a significant correlation between what individuals indicate they intend to do and what they actually do. In many cases, this lack of reliability is caused by poor framing of the data collection questions; that is, they are not specific enough. Fishbein and Manfredo (1992) point out that although intention is a good predictor of specific behaviors, it is less accurate for predicting intention to reach goals or classes of behavior. For example, an individual's intention to participate in a company sponsored adult softball league that would be offered the next summer on Tuesday and Thursday evenings from 6:30 to 7:30 p.m. at a price of $100 per player could be predicted with a much greater degree of accuracy than that individual's intention to get more physically active (a general leisure participation goal) or to play in an adult sports league (a general class of behavior).

Unfortunately, many needs assessment instruments try simply to identify general interests or wants, rather than by considering specific market conditions about specific activities. Exhibit 9-1 on pages 155-157 presents examples of needs assessment questions that contrast the differences between wants and intentions. Questions about target intentions point out the additional detail needed if one is to assess an individual's intention to participate accurately and to gather sufficient data to actually develop a program that can be offered under a given set of market conditions.

Intention is the commitment to acquire specific satisfiers of wants under given market conditions.

Expressed needs are needs fulfilled through actual participation.

Complete Exercise 9-1 on page 158 to help you learn how to develop needs assessment questions.

NEEDS FROM A SOCIAL POLICY VIEWPOINT

Mercer (1973) has pointed out that, from a social policy standpoint, some types of needs are more debilitating than others. Therefore, resources are more urgently needed to alleviate these needs. Mercer has identified four types of needs: normative, felt, expressed, and comparative.

Normative needs are objective standards defined by various organizations and groups that are qualified to do so because of their training or position. The *Recreation, Park, and Open Space Standards and Guidelines* (Lancaster, 1983), published by the National Recreation and Park Association, is an example of such standards. Many communities develop their own park and open space standards in developing a park master plan.

When using normative standards, the need documented is the difference between what a community or neighborhood may have and what the normative standard suggests they should have. How much need exists in a community can be manipulated by supply, so that the gap between what is provided and what should be provided is narrowed, or by raising the standard, so that the gap between what is and what should be is widened.

Felt needs are perceptions about what an individual believes he or she would like to do. They are analogous to the wants, interests, and intentions identified earlier. Felt needs may be thought of as latent demands. That is, they are demands that could be turned into actual consumption. Felt needs are shaped by social forces that lead individuals to conclude that they have a need for specific services or facilities.

Expressed needs are needs fulfilled through actual participation. They are included as needs because, if the supply currently fulfilling the needs were terminated, they would immediately become felt needs again, demanding attention and resources.

Comparative needs are actual variations in services provided or variations in access to leisure opportunities experienced by different groups. Variations in leisure facilities and services provided to different neighborhoods are often a major point of contention in the delivery of community recreation services. It is also a concern in many other types of leisure service organizations. Two examples of comparative need problems in various agency settings are: (1) variations in the opportunities provided to persons on different work shifts in corporate recreation settings, and (2) variations in service access by personnel of different ranks in the military. Mercer (1973) suggests that although one may be able to document one of these four types of need for cohorts of individuals, from a social policy standpoint those most in need of additional services are those with a combination of needs. This conceptualization of a rank order of urgency to fulfill needs is especially useful when demand is too great for the limited resources or in retrenchment situations.

Felt needs are perceptions about what an individual believes he or she would like to do.

Normative needs are objective standards defined by organizations and groups that are qualified to do so because of their training or position.

Exhibit 9-2: Unscheduled Interview Agenda

1. Obtain the name and address of the participant.
2. Identify the specific program, facility, policy, or staff member about which the participant is commenting.
3. Ascertain if the participant is making a complaint, giving a compliment, or making a suggestion.
4. Make certain the participant identifies the specific issue he or she is concerned about.
5. Try to discover what resolution or outcome the participant would like to have.
6. Make note of all follow-up actions taken.

APPROACHES TO NEEDS ASSESSMENT

Programmers are often overly concerned about whether they are conducting needs assessments correctly. Because of their possibly ineffective needs assessment methods, they are concerned about overlooking a tremendous pool of unfulfilled needs. The inadequacy that many programmers feel stems from their not conducting a systematic random survey of the population on a routine basis. Often, this is not done for a variety of reasons, including a lack of skill or limited resources. In addition to surveys, however, several methods can be used to assess needs.

The National Park Service (n.d.) has defined needs assessment as gathering information directly from the public and analyzing it. Assessment involves placing that information into meaningful patterns that will lead to the development of leisure services that meet unfulfilled needs.

There are two methods for conducting community needs assessments: group approaches or surveys. Miller and Hustedde (1987) have identified nine methods of group approaches, including town meetings, public hearings, charrettes, futures conferences, the Delphi approach, nominal groups, jury, workshops, and consciousness-raising efforts. The reader interested in additional approaches should see Miller and Hustedde (1987).

The National Park Service (n.d.) has identified four approaches that are frequently used in conducting leisure needs assessments: citizen advisory committees, public meetings and workshops, unstructured inputs and structured exploratory interviews, and surveys. These four approaches will be explained below.

CITIZEN ADVISORY COMMITTEES

Citizen advisory committees are composed of community residents who are either appointed or elected to a committee whose responsibility is to advise the agency staff or board. Advisory groups can be very valuable in providing a communication link between the agency and its constituency.

Exhibit 9-3: Focus Group Interview Problem Statement and Agenda

Problem Statement:

To determine how single-parent families with children from 6 to 12 years of age make decisions about their children's participation in summer recreation programs.

Opening Narrative:

Welcome. Today we are going to discuss a topic I think you will find interesting and that you know a lot about—your children's summer recreation activities. We are interested in learning when and how decisions about summer recreation participation are made, who makes them, and what is important to you and your children about the activities selected.

Before we start, I have a couple of requests: first, that only one person speak at a time so that we can truly interact with each other; second, that you feel free to say exactly what you think—we want both positive and negative comments. Give us your true feelings.

Now, to get started, let's go around the table one at a time and have you tell us a little bit about yourself and your family. All of you are single parents—we would like to know how many children you have, their ages, their genders, and a little bit about them and each of you.

Focus Questions:

1. How would your children answer the following comment: I have to participate in this program because _____ . (Probe: What reason do they most frequently give about why they must be in a program?)

2. Who do your children most like to participate with in recreation activities? (Probe: Friends, siblings, schoolmates?)

3. How would you answer the following comment: I want my children in summer recreation programs because _____ . (Probe: What reasons do you give your friends, neighbors, or former spouses about why your children must be in a specific recreation program?)

4. In my home, _____ decides which recreation activities my children will select to participate in. (Probe: Is the decision made mostly by the children, the parent, jointly, or between the resident and nonresident parent?)

5. When do you normally make decisions about which summer recreation activities your children will be in? (Probe: How far in advance of summer do parents want to know what their children's schedules will be?)

6. How would your children answer this question: I wish I could _____ this summer. (Probe: Identify programs that children may want or programs that parents may want for them.)

7. I will not let my children be in a recreation program unless I am sure _____ (Probe: What must a program do or be before parents will allow their children to participate? Keep the discussion going on this until all fruitful information is obtained.)

Summers (1987) has pointed out that citizen advisory groups can be misused by both agencies and citizens. Agencies can mobilize citizen groups to support their own already formulated policies under the guise of citizen input. People often form citizen advisory groups to lobby for very narrow interests rather than to represent the general public interest. In this latter role, advisory groups can become formidable political forces that lobby to have scarce resources directed to their own activity interests. However, the most positive approach to the use of citizen advisory groups assumes that because of their knowledge and interest, they will consider all dimensions of an issue. These groups can provide programmers with valuable insight into the program needs of patrons.

PUBLIC MEETINGS AND WORKSHOPS

A public meeting is frequently used to solicit citizen input on policy development, planning issues, budget allocations, or leisure needs and preferences. In some instances, agencies are required to conduct such meetings to satisfy a grant or legislative requirement. In conducting a public meeting, the agency establishes two-way communication with its publics and facilitates dialogue by offering an outlet for expressing emotion about an issue. Often during a public meeting, a programmer can assess the strength of emotion accompanying an issue.

A workshop is a more organized public meeting during which people participate in small discussion groups with a focused agenda. Facilitating citizen input with an organized agenda will often lead to more productive meetings.

With either method, citizens self-select who will attend, and it is likely that those who do attend will have the strongest opinions either for or against an issue. Sometimes it is problematic determining how closely those opinions expressed at public meetings and workshops represent the views of the general population.

INTERVIEWS

An interview is a meeting in which information is obtained. Programmers can acquire needs assessment information from both unscheduled and scheduled interviews.

Unscheduled Interviews

While programmers are operating and supervising programs, they will have many opportunities to obtain information from current and prospective patrons. Unscheduled interviews include the many face-to-face unsolicited comments and telephone calls made by constituents to programmers. Programmers in an agency are accessible to the public. Thus, the public will come to you with information such as complaints, compliments, and suggestions.

These are valuable pieces of information, but they often require that the programmer be prepared to probe the comments immediately in order to discover all information that may be useful. In order to provide structure to these interviews and thereby obtain the most information possible, it is important to have a basic interview schedule prepared so the most critical pieces of information may be obtained. Exhibit 9-2 on page 161 shows a list of questions that may be used to provide structure to unscheduled interviews.

As with all unsolicited comments from self-selected individuals, it is important to ascertain how widespread a certain viewpoint is held throughout the population.

Focus Groups

Scheduled interviews are arranged and structured. They are conducted with an interview schedule and are given some direction by the interviewer. Several types of group interview techniques may be used, including nominal group interviews and focus group interviews. What follows is a general description of how to conduct a focus group interview for needs assessment purposes.

Although the use of systematic random surveys is widely recommended in recreation literature, their use as a needs assessment method has been questioned.

Focus group interviews can be used for one or more of the following:

- To develop hypotheses for further testing
- To provide information for structuring questionnaires
- To provide overall background information on programs
- To solicit patron impressions about new program concepts
- To stimulate new ideas about older programs
- To generate ideas for new programs
- To interpret previously obtained quantitative results

The focus group technique involves three distinct phases: preparing for the interview, conducting the interview, and analyzing the results.

Preparing for the Interview

Although it seems obvious, it is extremely important to prepare well before the actual face-to-face interview begins. Before good interview questions can be developed, one must have a thorough understanding of the problem being examined. Thorough preparation requires identifying a focused problem statement, developing questions that are logically deduced from the problem, and preparing topical areas that will be used to introduce the questions. Topical areas help the interviewer keep the interview moving smoothly in a logical fashion, thus providing coherence to the whole process.

The reader is cautioned against trying to develop a problem statement and questions that are too broad. The focus group interviewing technique is useful because it facilitates an in-depth examination of a problem and can lead to new insights into the problem. Covering too many topics in one session often precludes the in-depth examination of a problem or concept. Exhibit 9-3 on page 162 illustrates a focus group problem and an agenda.

The second part of preparing for the interview is to select the people to be interviewed. Because only a few individuals will be included in the interview, they must be selected carefully. The following points should be considered when selecting group members:

- It is important to keep the group small enough to facilitate open communication. Between 6 and 10 group members would be appropriate.
- The group should have both homogeneity and contrast (Wells, 1979). It is especially important to maintain homogeneity on factors that might otherwise inhibit open communication. For example, well-educated, middle-class individuals may inhibit the full participation of lower-class, less educated individuals in a focus group. In this case, it would be best to interview two groups, each made up of people with similar backgrounds. But some spark should also be provided through contrasts in the composition of the group. For example, in a focus group interview designed to examine the operation of an indoor tennis facility, it would be desirable to include both users of the agency's tennis facility and some users of a competitor's tennis facility. Groups, then, must be carefully constituted to ensure that there will be an open exchange of ideas and that the group is made up of members who can contribute to a thorough discussion of the idea, including its pros and cons.
- A decision about where to conduct the interview must be made. There are generally three choices: the agency's facilities, a neutral site, or the participant's facilities, such as someone's home.

Conducting the Interview

How the interview is conducted is critical to obtaining the information desired by the agency. The interview can be conducted in a directive or a nondirective style. In the nondirective style, the interviewer acts as a facilitator whose role is to introduce prearranged questions, get the group discussing them, and intervene only to keep the discussion fruitful. Ideally, the interviewer does not participate in the discussion, although this cannot always be avoided.

In the directive style, the interviewer provides much more structure and controls the flow of discussion. The interviewer generally introduces a topic and keeps the discussion going until the topic has been covered to the interviewer's satisfaction; a new topic is then introduced. With either style, the interviewer should elicit responses that are the true beliefs and feelings of the group members. The choice of style is influenced by the purpose of the interview, the content of the questions to be asked, and the members of the group.

Analyzing the Results

Analyses can range in detail and thoroughness from a brief impressionistic summary of the principal findings through a very detailed content analysis of tape recordings from the interview. In either case, results from an interview should be organized around the principal questions asked during the interview. Written results should reflect participant views, including the distribution of views, the strength of conviction, and new viewpoints elicited during the interview.

SURVEYS

Although the use of systematic random surveys is widely recommended in recreation literature, their use as a needs assessment method has been questioned. Heberlein (1976, cited in Johnson & Meiller, 1987) suggests that public involvement includes four major functions: informational, interactive, assurance, and ritualistic. The informational function includes getting information from the public. Surveys are excellent for gathering information but poor at giving information to the public.

Dillman (1987) has pointed out that the uniqueness of the survey is its ability to "tell the proportion in a population who have a certain attribute and the proportion who do not" (p. 192). This makes it a powerful tool for needs assessment. Dillman has also argued that it is possible to conduct scientifically valid surveys and meet the need for citizen involvement if the survey process is done appropriately. However, what it takes to conduct a needs assessment survey successfully has changed dramatically over the past decade because new survey methods and techniques have been developed.

A properly conducted survey is the method of choice to ensure the most representative view of all citizens. Technical information about how to conduct surveys is contained in Chapter Twenty-One—the chapter on evaluation. Implementing a needs assessment survey requires simultaneously coordinating many tasks; thus, many errors may be made. Readers interested in conducting a needs assessment survey are encouraged to read Dillman (1987, pp. 192–208) for a succinct briefing on how to avoid problems with nine tasks essential to implementing a survey.

There is some confusion among practicing programmers because survey methods are used for both needs assessment and for evaluation. Although the technology is the same, the focus of the questions is not. Program evaluation deals with the past and judges the worth of what was done. Needs analysis deals with the future and asks what should be done (McKillip, 1987, p. 29).

INTEGRATING THE FOUR APPROACHES

Each of these four approaches has strengths and weaknesses. No single approach can give a completely accurate picture of the needs in a community and provide the social action often needed to implement solutions. Although surveys are the method of choice, they are expensive and are usually not conducted annually in every organization. An agency should conduct one annually if possible, however. Certainly, a needs assessment survey should be conducted no less often than every three years.

The other three approaches are used to supplement the survey data and to provide focus to a survey when it is conducted. Survey data often do not provide sufficiently detailed information to make programmatic decisions, so one of the other approaches, such as a focus group, may be used to gather additional, focused information. In the latter case, exploratory methods may be used to discover issues or needs whose actual distribution in the population can only be assessed through a systematic random sample survey. The four methods identified, then, are used in a complementary manner to form a comprehensive needs assessment program for an agency.

NEEDS ASSESSMENT QUESTIONS

One can ask many different questions to determine wants that an agency can satisfy. Part of the uncertainty that programmers have about whether they are conducting an adequate needs analysis has to do with their lack of understanding of what actually constitutes needs assessment questions. The following are questions identified by the National Park Service (n.d.):

- What do its constituencies believe the agency should be doing? (Setting objectives)
- What needs and wants do citizens have? What are the characteristics of those who have a particular need (want)? How many are affected? What makes individuals decide to use or not use existing services? (Identifying target markets)
- How do potential target markets react to various service alternatives that could meet these needs (wants)? (Product development)
- What price should be charged? (Pricing)
- How can its availability be best communicated? (Promotion)
- At what time and locations should it be offered? (Distribution) (pp. 63–64)

A needs analysis is conducted whenever one seeks answers to these or similar questions in a systematic manner and analyzes the responses. The quality of the effort will depend on how pertinent the questions are, how the data are analyzed, and how representative the data are for the entire population. In conducting leisure service needs assessments, one can almost always identify a program need, develop the service to fulfill the need, have the program populated, and believe that needs are being fulfilled. However, programmers are concerned that an even greater need may not have been discovered. The only solution to this concern is to continue to do needs assessment and to revise program services as indicated by new information.

MARKETING LEISURE EXPERIENCES

Over the past thirty years, marketing techniques have been applied to the operation and management of leisure services. One of the first articles to advocate using marketing concepts to analyze leisure services was written by Crompton (1978). Crompton has continued to promote the usefulness of marketing principles as a major program management strategy for park and recreation services. Schultz, McAvoy, and Dustin (1988) have expressed concern about the adoption of business management strategies as the management paradigm for providing leisure services. Recent research has demonstrated that "agencies have not comprehensively integrated marketing techniques into programming efforts" (Tew, Havitz, & McCarville, 1999, p. 14).

> All individuals in a market desire to obtain a similar product or service that can fulfill a specific need or want.

> Any market will usually be made up of identifiable subgroups called market segments.

Exhibit 9-4: Common Descriptor Classes with Example Variable

Leisure Needs

Physical activity

Achievement

Social interaction

Geographic Area

Urban or rural location

Location of residence

Location of employment

Access to leisure locales

Sociodemographics

Education

Age or life cycle stage

Gender

Income

Employed unemployed

Family or marital status

Ethnicity

Behavioral Characteristics

Activity skill level

Usage rate

Loyalty to activity

Specialization in activity

Benefits sought

Leisure Interests

Socialization into a specific leisure
  activity

Sports and games

Outdoor recreation

Arts

Exercise activities

Travel, and so on

Synchrographics

Studying time as a variable that may
  define specific markets

Time of day

Day of week

Duration of program

Season of the year

Experiential Characteristics

Sensory experiences—feel, smell,
  see, hear, taste

Relational experiences—family,
  aspirational heroes

Action experiences—fantasy camps

Thinking experiences—concentration, surprise, intense emotional
  experiences

Adapted from: O'Sullivan, E. L. (1991). Marketing for parks, recreation, and leisure.
State College, PA: Venture.

Marketing is undergoing a revolution as marketers adjust to the experience economy. Schmitt (1999) has documented that marketing is moving from a focus on features and benefits (F & B marketing) to focusing on how products and services contribute to customer experiences and lifestyles. According to Schmitt (1999), experiential marketing differs from F & B marketing on four key characteristics. It focuses on customer experiences. Instead of focusing on product benefits and features, experiential marketing focuses on consumption situations, action vignettes wherein products are consumed. It is assumed that customers not only make purchasing decisions on rational grounds but on emotional ones as well. And finally, because of the eclectic nature of consumptions decisions, marketing research and tools must be eclectic. Marketing, then, has moved closer to methods used by programmers for many years. That is, it currently focuses much more on the experiences and the methods we have been using to create them.

Nevertheless, marketing literature contains a number of concepts and methods for program development and management that programmers can use. Although marketing techniques are used in programming, programmers possess the unique ability to design programs that provide maximal opportunities for the leisure experience. Programmers can do this because they have been educated in how humans experience leisure in social occasions and how these occasions can best be structured to maximize the opportunity to experience leisure. This unique professional ability does not stem from training in marketing. McCarville (1999) describes marketing as "a set of interrelated activities that focus on the client. The ultimate goal of this process is to discover an optimal fit between client preferences and agency capabilities, then to mobilize resources accordingly" (p. 415). A comprehensive marketing program can provide important information regarding programs that individuals desire, the price they are willing to pay, when and where they desire to participate, and how services may be promoted. Marketing activities require a focus on the clients, the clients' desires, and grouping clients with similar desires so that effective programs can be developed. To understand the contribution that marketing can make to leisure program development, one must understand some basic marketing concepts.

MARKETING AND EXCHANGES

First, what is marketing? The American Marketing Association (cited in Zikmund & d'Amico, 1993) states that "marketing is the process of planning and executing the conception, pricing, promotion, and distribution of ideas, goods, and services to create exchanges that will satisfy individual and organizational objectives" (p. 9). Kotler and Armstrong (1990) define marketing as "a social and managerial process by which individuals and groups obtain what they need and want through creating and exchanging products and value with others" (p. 3).

Crompton and Lamb (1986) state, "Marketing is a set of activities aimed at facilitating and expediting exchanges" (p. 16). Marketing is focused on meeting identified patron needs, including their logical extension through interests, wants, and intentions. In addition, all of

Market segments with whom the agency desires to have exchanges are termed target markets.

marketing is based on the notion that needs are met through exchange processes. Understanding the notion of exchange is critical to understanding marketing.

An exchange occurs when two or more parties satisfy their needs and wants through the interchange of something of value. In many cases, one of the items of value is money, although goodwill, satisfaction, and other intangibles are also valuable items that may be exchanged. Kotler and Andreasen (1987) identify four conditions that an exchange condition assumes:

1. There are at least two parties.
2. Each can offer something that the other perceives to be a benefit or benefits.
3. Each is capable of communication and delivery.
4. Each is free to accept or reject the offer. (p. 70)

This last point is the one that creates both a concern and a justification for using marketing concepts in administering municipal recreation and not-for-profit leisure services. Because municipal and not-for-profit providers have third-party funding sources to subsidize and keep the price of leisure services artificially low, how they incorporate patron desires into their programs becomes a major issue. These agencies have a monopoly on offering low-cost leisure opportunities, so patrons are less free to accept or reject them. Given this situation, these agencies can adopt one of three orientations or operating philosophies (Kotler & Andreasen, 1987). First, they can adopt a product orientation and offer what they believe is good for the public. Second, they can adopt a sales orientation and try to stimulate interest in the agency's existing services. Or third, they can adopt a customer orientation and try to develop services that meet identified patron needs and wants. This third option is a marketing orientation. The justification for using marketing techniques in agencies that have the financial resources to offer subsidized recreation is to incorporate, at the front end, patron input into the development of services. In addition, marketers are also admonished to practice "societal marketing," which advises them to consider not only individual needs and wants, but also the collective needs of society (Zikmund & d'Amico, 1993). Marketing provides a number of useful concepts and techniques for helping to accomplish this end.

A MARKET DEFINED

Kotler and Armstrong (1990) state, "A market is the set of actual and potential buyers of a product" (p. 7). Thus, they believe the programmer should be concerned with both current and potential buyers. On the other hand, Zikmund and d'Amico (1993) state that "A market is a group of potential customers for a particular product who are willing and able to spend money or exchange other resources to obtain the product" (p. 9). They believe one should focus on those who are ready and willing to purchase. All individuals in a market desire to obtain a similar product or service that can fulfill a specific need or want. This need or want may be an experience or contribution to a lifestyle they desire. A major chal-

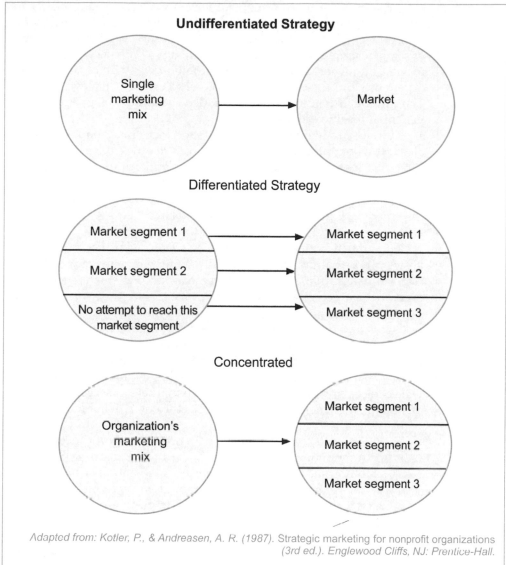

Undifferentiated Strategy

Single marketing mix → Market

Differentiated Strategy

Market segment 1 → Market segment 1

Market segment 2 → Market segment 2

No attempt to reach this market segment → Market segment 3

Concentrated

Organization's marketing mix →

Market segment 1

Market segment 2

Market segment 3

Adapted from: Kotler, P., & Andreasen, A. R. (1987). Strategic marketing for nonprofit organizations (3rd ed.). Englewood Cliffs, NJ: Prentice-Hall.

Figure 9-1: Alternate Target Marketing Strategies

lenge for all marketers is how to convince potential customers to actually become consumers of a specific product.

SEGMENTING MARKETS

Any market may be large or small, but it will usually be made up of identifiable subgroups called market segments. For example, fishermen make up a recreation market. This market can be segmented by subdividing all fishermen into two groups: saltwater or freshwater fishermen. The market could be further segmented into two groups: shore or boat fishermen. Further segmentation along any number of variables is possible. O'Sullivan (1991) has identified five classes of descriptor variables that may be used to segment leisure markets: leisure needs and interests, geographic characteristics, sociodemographics, behavioral area, and synchrographics. An adaptation of these, including examples of some descriptors, is displayed in Exhibit 9-4 on page 168. According to Shaw and Ivens (2005), "The new differentiators will be the customer experience and the emotions that the physical elements evoke" (p 17). Thus, in the fifth edition, we have added the additional category of Experiential Characteristics.

Markets are segmented to identify and focus the group of individuals with whom an agency may want to develop exchanges. Weinstein (1987) defines segmentation as "the process of partitioning markets into segments of potential customers with similar characteristics who are likely to exhibit similar purchase behavior" (p. 4). If the many variables identified in Exhibit 9-4 are used, markets can be segmented almost infinitely.

How much segmentation is enough? This is a difficult question to answer. In actual practice, segmentation must be managed to be effective. Weinstein (1987) identifies three reasons that this is true: (1) not everyone is a potential customer for every service the agency may develop; (2) an agency's service mix must be limited because of limited resources and economic efficiency; and (3) because the number of potential customers and the number of services available are limited, it is most efficient to match services with potential customers. No agency has the resources to meet all identified market segments; therefore, strategic choices must be made about which markets to serve. Market segmentation, then, helps agencies be more efficient in matching customers with services.

Differences in segments must have a practical significance that warrants separate marketing attention. Kotler and Armstrong (1990) suggest that four criteria must be met before segmentation is justified.

First, the segment must be measurable. One must be able to determine its size, the ability of the population to purchase the service, and other differences in market behavior that are unique to the market segment. This is why some recreation programmers reject marketing. Often, it is cheaper simply to offer a program and see if it succeeds than it is to confirm the existence of the market segment before offering the program. For example, one of the authors was once asked how to determine the market for weekend rentals of recreation equipment kits for picnics. Conducting a marketing survey for a community of 10,000 to determine the demand for the kits was more expensive than simply buying the equipment for five kits, publicizing the program, and adjusting from observed use. Because measuring many recreation markets is expensive, marketing is not the answer to every program development problem.

Second, the market must be accessible. It is possible to identify markets that need services but simply cannot be reached efficiently. In a city as large as Los Angeles, there may be a market of individuals who want to play Scottish bagpipes. Because the people are widely scattered, however, the critical number needed to make up a program may never materialize. The market cannot be readily accessed.

Third, a market segment must be substantial enough to warrant separate marketing attention. In commercial agencies, the test is whether or not a segment is large enough to be profitable. In not-for-profit operations, justifying serving identified market segments is more complicated. Two common tests are whether or not the segment is large enough to be served efficiently or whether is has a unique, demonstrable need that is part of the agency's service mission.

Fourth, the market segment must be actionable. Does the agency have the resources to treat the segment separately? Is the segment likely to respond to separate marketing attention, and is their unique characteristic likely to remain stable over time? In recreation, often many different market segments can be identified for a single facility. For example, in a public swimming pool there are children who want to play in the water, people who want to practice springboard diving, those who simply want to swim laps for an aerobic workout, those who want to snorkel or scuba dive, and so on. Some of these segments will be too small to justify separate treatment. In addition, some of these uses interfere with each other, therefore, the agency may not be able to offer service to every segment.

TARGET MARKETING

Once the total market is segmented, the agency may adopt different strategies to complete exchanges with the various segments identified. Some segments, for reasons outlined previously, will not be served. Market segments with whom the agency desires to have exchanges are termed target markets. Crompton and Lamb (1986) have defined a target market as follows: "A target market is a relatively homogeneous group of people or organizations that have relatively similar service preferences with whom the agency seeks to exchange" (p. 112).

The major reason for segmenting markets is to determine whether the market should be targeted as a whole, or whether specific segments should be handled differently. Marketers influence the target market through the marketing mix; that is, "the set of controllable marketing variables that the firm blends to produce the response desired in the target market" (Kotler & Armstrong, 1990, pp. 40–41). The four variables most frequently cited as being controllable by marketers are product, price, promotion, and place.

A different market mix is developed for each target market identified. One or more of the four market mix variables is altered for each target market identified. Product is a generic term used to describe the service, product, or facility the agency is developing, making, or constructing for the client. Many products could be developed. Changes in the product itself—that is, changes in the six key elements of a situated activity system—will obviously have a tremendous impact on the market mix. You will recall the discussion about developing leisure products that was included in Chapter Five.

The price at which a product is sold, including a zero price, will affect consumption. Pricing recreation services is dealt with in detail in Chapters Seventeen through Nineteen.

Promotional campaigns for the same leisure product can be designed differently for different target markets. For example, one could simply alter the promotion campaign to emphasize different benefits from the same service and distribute the different publicity campaigns to the different target markets. This could be done to promote a fitness facility to two different markets, one of which is most interested in opportunities to meet new friends and the other in keeping physically fit. The two groups could use the facility at the same time but would be attracted to it for different reasons. These differences would need to be incorporated into two different promotional campaigns. Information about developing promotional campaigns is included in Chapter Fourteen.

Place involves distribution of services, including the day, time, and location of service. Changing the place of a service will often change the market to whom the product will appeal. Information about scheduling leisure service products is included in Chapter Thirteen.

It is important to realize that developing different market mixes for each target market is more expensive than developing a single market mix for the entire market. For this reason, one should be sure that there are enough differences between market segments to justify developing separate market mixes.

TARGET MARKETING STRATEGIES

Kotler and Andreasen (1987) have identified three target marketing strategies: undifferentiated, differentiated, and concentrated. These three are illustrated in Figure 9-1 on page 171. The undifferentiated strategy assumes that the entire market will be handled as a single entity. Any existing market segments are not recognized, and a single market mix is developed. Or perhaps there are not enough differences between the market segments to warrant developing different market mixes. In this case, the undifferentiated strategy is justified. Often, however, this strategy is used for the wrong reason—the agency simply does not want to develop additional market mixes.

Using the differentiated strategy means that the agency will operate in two or more segments of the market and will design different mixes for each segment. It is assumed that better service will result from developing a unique mix for each target market. When using this strategy, it is important that each service have a unique position in the market. Kotler and Armstrong (1990) explain: "Market positioning is arranging for a product to occupy a clear, distinctive, and desirable place relative to competing products in the minds of target consumers" (p. 39). The service must possess this quality and the promotional campaign must communicate it to the target market for this strategy to fulfill its potential benefit. Generally, this method of operation will be more expensive, but it will result in deeper market penetration and more clients.

The concentrated target marketing strategy recognizes the existence of two or more market segments but devotes the agency's major marketing effort to only one. With this strategy, the agency simultaneously ignores some market segments while developing a market mix for one targeted segment. This strategy may be adopted when the agency does not have sufficient resources to service all identified markets, or when the agency wants to service market segments not currently being served by other providers. An example of the latter instance would be the development of a public golf course with inexpensive green fees in a community that has private country clubs with limited memberships and a commercial golf course with high green fees. The public sector would thus be target marketing golf to middle-and lower-income players who could not afford to play at the other two courses.

Public agencies and some not-for-profit agencies often have an ethical problem in applying the concentrated target marketing strategy. Which market segments may they ignore? Which should they try to serve? Often the temptation is to serve easily accessible markets, when in reality the public system should serve the most vulnerable clients. For example, Spigner and Havitz (1993), in discussing recreation opportunities for the unemployed, point out that the unemployed "are rarely singled out as a target market" (p. 52). The individuals who constitute these types of markets are often the most difficult to reach and therefore the most costly to serve.

COMPARING MARKETING AND PROGRAMMING

Marketing contributes to program development in several ways. The market mix is made up of price, promotion, place, and product. Changing any of these four variables alters the market that may be served. Of the four variables included in the market mix, product is the one for which programmers have unique expertise. They understand the leisure experience and how to structure leisure occasions. Thus, they are well prepared for marketing in the experience economy. Techniques and skills for accomplishing this are discussed elsewhere in this text.

The major contribution of marketing to recreation programming is in providing methods for identifying needs to develop into programs and knowledge about how to successfully exchange the services developed with target markets. Understanding the role of promotion, pricing, and place (distribution) in the consumption of leisure services are additional contributions of marketing techniques to recreation programming.

Some cautions about the misuse of marketing concepts are in order. Marketing technology provides excellent techniques for isolating market segments that are truly in need of social services. Although these techniques have been in use in recreation and leisure service agencies for over 30 years, they have generally been used to develop services for the average, middle-class constituent who can function in a market-driven, fee-for-service economy. Programs are rarely targeted for anyone other than the average person (Spigner & Havitz, 1993). Marketing technology has not been used to help public and not-for-profit agencies focus their efforts on markets that are specifically targeted by their mission statements—the implementation of societal marketing. The need to accomplish this makes marketing in public and not-for-profit agencies more complicated than in commercial and private agencies.

As target marketing techniques become more sophisticated, their summary effect is to provide the agency with the ability to manipulate the patron. Smith (1992) has stated, "Privacy in the 1990s includes not only the right to control personal information about oneself and how it is used, but also the right to be free of manipulation, whether in the marketplace or by the government" (p. 19). Thus, agencies whose missions include contributing to the public good must make certain that they are using these techniques ethically to further the legitimate interests of their patrons and community rather than catering to the sole interests of the agency.

Finally, although the conceptual constructs of marketing are engrossing and make logical sense, their successful implementation is dependent on a continuing stream of relevant data. McCarville (1999) states, "Clearly, a need for coordination exists around both the collection and dissemination of data" (p. 429). Few recreation agencies have allocated the resources to accomplish this. They often lack the personnel and infrastructure needed to routinely collect and analyze the data needed to support a comprehensive marketing campaign that would provide programmers with the data needed to develop market-based program services.

CONCLUSION

Developing successful programs requires the systematic collection of information from potential participants and other stakeholders for use in program development and operation. Three general methods for accomplishing this are: including stakeholders on advisory groups, using needs assessment techniques, and gathering strategic marketing information. Each method provides different types of information. They complement each other by providing comprehensive information about the leisure desires of the agency's constituents.

REFERENCES

Carpenter, G. M., & Howe, C. Z. (1985). *Programming leisure experiences.* New York: Prentice-Hall.

Csikszentmihalyi, M. (1975). *Beyond boredom and anxiety.* San Francisco: Jossey-Bass.

Crompton, J. L. (1978). Development of a taxonomy of a leisure services delivery system. *Journal of Leisure Research, 10*(3), 214–218.

Crompton, J. L., & Lamb, C. W. Jr. (1986). *Marketing government and social services.* New York: Wiley.

Dillman, D. (1987). Elements of Success. In D. E. Johnson, L. R. Meiller, L. C. Miller, & G. F. Summers (Eds.), *Needs assessment, theory and methods* (pp. 188–209). Ames, IA: Iowa State University Press.

Ellis, M. J. (1973, April). *Why people play.* Englewood Cliffs, NJ: Prentice-Hall.

Fishbein, M., & Manfredo, M. J. (1992). A theory of behavior change. In M. J. Manfredo (Ed.), *Influencing human behavior: Theory and applications in recreation, tourism, and natural resources management* (pp. 29–50). Champaign, IL: Sagamore.

Herberlien, T. A. (1976). Principles of public involvement. Department of Rural Sociology Staff Paper Series in Rural and Community

Development, University of Wisconsin–Madison. Cited in D. E. Johnson, & L. R. Meiller (1987). Community Level Surveys. In D. E. Johnson, L. R. Meiller, L. C. Miller, & G. F. Summers (Eds.), *Needs assessment, theory and methods* (pp. 126-141). Ames, IA: Iowa State University Press.

Iso-Ahola, S. E. (1980). *The social psychology of leisure and recreation.* Dubuque, IA: Wm. C. Brown.

Iso-Ahola, S. E. (1982, February). Intrinsic motivation: An overlooked basis for evaluation. *Parks & Recreation, 32, 33, 58.*

Johnson, D. E., & Meiller, L. R. (1987). Community level surveys. In D. E. Johnson, L. R. Meiller, L. C. Miller, & G. F. Summers (Eds.). *Needs assessment, theory and methods* (pp.126–141). Ames, IA: Iowa State University Press.

Knowles, M. S. (1970). *The modern practice of adult education.* New York: The Association Press.

Kotler, P. (1980). *Marketing management* (4th ed.). Englewood Cliffs, NJ: Prentice-Hall.

Kotler, P., & Andreasen, A. R. (1987). *Strategic marketing for nonprofit organizations* (3rd ed.). Englewood Cliffs, NJ: Prentice-Hall.

Kotler, P., & Armstrong, G. (1990). *Marketing: An introduction* (3rd ed.). Englewood Cliffs, NJ: Prentice-Hall.

Lancaster, R. A. (Ed). (1983). *Recreation, park, and open space standards and guidelines.* Alexandria, VA: National Recreation and Park Association.

Mannell, R. C. (1999). Leisure experience and satisfaction. In E. L. Jackson & T. L. Burton (Eds.), *Leisure studies: prospects for the twenty-first century* (pp. 235-251). State College, PA: Venture.

McCarville, R. (1999). Marketing public recreation services. In E. L. Jackson & T. L. Burton (Eds.), *Leisure studies: Prospects for the twenty-first century* (pp. 415–433). State College, PA: Venture Publishing, Inc.

McKillip, J. (1987). *Need analysis: Tools for the human services and education.* Beverly Hills, CA: Sage.

Mercer, D. (1973). The concept of recreational need. *Journal of Leisure Research, 5*(1), 37–50.

Miller, L. C., & Hustedde, R. J. (1987). Group approaches. In D. E. Johnson, L. R. Meiller, L. C. Miller, & G. F. Summers (Eds.), *Needs assessment, theory and methods* (pp. 3-19). Ames, IA: Iowa State University Press.

National Park Service. (n.d.). *Marketing parks and recreation.* State College, PA: Venture.

Neulinger, J. (1974). *The psychology of leisure.* Springfield, IL: Charles C. Thomas.

O'Sullivan, E. L. (1991). *Marketing for parks, recreation, and leisure.* State College, PA: Venture.

Schmitt, B. H., (1999). *Experiential marketing.* New York: Free Press.

Schultz, J. H., McAvoy, L. H., & Dustin, D. L. (1988, January). What are we in business for? *Parks & Recreation,* 52–54.

Shaw, C., & Ivens, J., (2005). *Building great customer experiences.* New York: Plagrave Macmillan.

Smith, R. E. (1992). Target marketing: Turning birds of a feather into sitting ducks. *National Forum, 72*(1), 18–21.

Spigner, C., & Havitz, M. E. (1993, November). Societal marketing or social justice: A dialogue on access to recreation for the unemployed. *Parks & Recreation,* 51-57.

Summers, G. F. (1987). Democratic governance. In D. E. Johnson, L. R. Meiller, L. C. Miller, & G. F. Summers (Eds.), *Needs assessment, theory and methods* (pp. 3–19). Ames, IA: Iowa State University Press.

Tew, C. P. F. J., Havitz, M. E., & McCarville, R. E. (1999). The role of marketing in municipal recreation programming decisions: A challenge to conventional wisdom. *Journal of Park and Recreation Administration, 17*(1), 1–20.

Weinstein, A. (1987). *Market segmentation: Using demographics, psychographics, and other segmentation techniques to uncover and exploit new markets.* Chicago: Probus.

Wells, W. D. (1979). Group interviewing. In J. B. Higginbotham, & K. K. Cox (Eds.), *Focus group interviews* (pp. 2–12). Chicago: American Marketing Association. (Reprinted from Ferber, R. [1974]), *Handbook of marketing research.* New York: McGraw-Hill.)

Witt, P. A., & Groom, R. (1979). Dangers and problems associated with current approaches to developing leisure interest finders. *Therapeutic Recreation Journal, 8*(1), 19–30.

Zikmund, W. G., & d'Amico, M. (1993). *Marketing* (4th ed.). St. Paul, MN: West.

Fitquest Bike Giveaway
Photo courtesy of Westerville Parks and Recreation Department, Westerville, OH
Photo by Jody Stowers

Writing Program Design Goals

STEP 4: PROGRAM GOALS

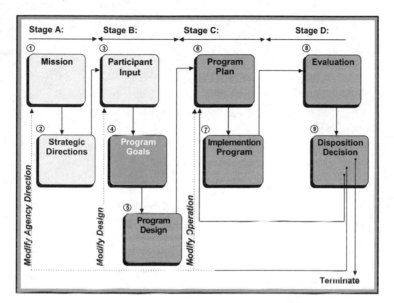

10

KEY TERMS

Program Design Goals
Program Design Standards
Terminal Performance Objectives
BBP Target Issues
BBP Activity Components

Program design goals are the final stratum of goals in the hierarchy of goals and objectives. They evolve from planning and management goals that were developed earlier in the cycle. These were explained in Chapters Six and Eight. For an example of the entire hierarchy, see Figure 10-1 on page 182. In this figure, the mission statement is included in Box A. It establishes the overall direction of the agency, as was discussed in Chapter Seven. Three- to five-year planning goals are included in Box B. As was discussed in Chapter Eight, they are used to further define the programmatic direction of the agency. One-year, management by objective-type objectives are included in Box C. These were also discussed in Chapter Eight. At this point, program planning and budget development are integrated and resources are actually committed to the development of a specific program. Program design goals are included in Box D. Their functions are to provide definition to a program and provide direction to design, staging, and implementation decisions. They are discussed in this chapter.

Program design goals describe in detail what is supposed to happen to people as a result of their participation. That is, they describe the experience the designer intends to produce across all points of contact (Shaw and Ivens, 2005) so its occurrence can be imaged. Writing them requires a shift in the

Program design goals must describe the service in detail by articulating what is supposed to happen to people as a result of their participation...

Figure 10-1: An Example of Networked Goals and Objectives

Box A

Mission: To provide comprehensive year-round opportunities for recreation and use of physical resources that are accessible and respond to the articulated needs and desires of all residents of the city of Knoxville, with an emphasis on educating citizens on the value of learning and practicing lifetime leisure skills and appreciations, and serving as a catalyst and facilitator for the provision of recreation programs by other organizations in the community.

Box B

1 to 8 Goals: To enhance the quality of life for all citizens of Knoxville through the provision of public recreation services.
1. To establish a senior citizens program.
2. To establish an athletic facility reservation system.
3. To establish a cultural arts division.

Box C

1. To operate a cultural arts fair during the spring of 2004.
2. To offer an arts instructional program for adults with at least five different media during fall (October and November) 2004.
3. To operate a concert in the park series during September 2004.
4. To operate a summer cultural arts workshop for children, with three different media, during summer of 2004.
    a. To offer a children's drama class during the summer of 2004, with at least 15 enrollments.
    b. To offer an oil painting class during the summer of 2004.
    c. To offer guitar for beginners during the summer of 2004.

Box D

1. By the end of the class, students will be able to play at least three songs with three different chords.
2. By the end of the class, students will be able to tune his or her guitar.
3. At the end of the program, 90% of the students will be able to identify the parts of the guitar correctly.
    a. When requested, participants will correctly identify five of the following parts of the guitar on the first inquiry.
        i. Neck
        ii. Body
        iii. Sound Hole
        iv. Strings
        v. Tuning Keys
        vi. Frets

Exhibit 10-1: Program Design Goals–Concert in the Park Series

- To provide a series of concerts featuring live music at no change to the public
- To stage the concerts in an easily accessible downtown park
- To feature the natural setting of the park as part of staging the experience
- To feature a band that will play a variety of musical styles
- To create a festive, picnic atmosphere at each concert
- To create an atmosphere conducive to family relational building

focus of goal development from "what staff will do" to "what will happen to individuals in the leisure experience." They should be rich in descriptive detail about all of the outcomes to be produced, including emotional as well as more traditional outcomes. Precise and descriptive design goals will facilitate designing and staging the experience intended.

Program design goals are developed with varying levels of specificity. They should define the program design problem; that is, a program needs to be designed that will facilitate the experiences outlined in the design goals. Exhibit 10-1 includes a series of program design goals for a concert in the park series. You will recall that this is one of the one-year objectives for the goal of establishing a Cultural Arts Division for the City of Knoxville, Tennessee. This goal is included in Box B of Figure 10-1. Design goals, in this case, serve as a framework around which the program is designed. Decisions about what to include or exclude from a program are guided by the goals specified.

These goals are not exhaustive; complete details will be provided in the program design and the program plan. These goals do, however, give form and direction to the program. They provide a basic outline of the experience(s) that will result from participating in the program. In this case, it is assumed that patron needs assessment data were incorporated into the goals. Patrons may have expressed a desire for quality, live entertainment, and a preference to have events in their downtown area. Now complete Exercise 10-1 on page 184.

Programmers are cautioned that needs assessments only provide enough information for a partial list of design goals. Programmers must often complete the design goals with additional data from their organizational environment, clientele, and previous professional experience. For example, an assessment may make apparent the need for a program that will serve mothers with preschool children during the morning

hours, giving them a noncompetitive activity that allows the mothers
to socialize. This need is obviously not a program, but it could serve as
a partial list of program design goals. The programmer would need to
add more goals and then design a leisure program to solve the original
design problem.

Another example of design goals is provided in Exhibit 10-2. Basically, these goals outline an Easter egg hunt, designed so that each child
can find an egg and search without competition from parents or other
children, but in a way that will permit parents to observe their own
children. Opportunities to visit the Easter Bunny will also be provided.
Each specific experience the program designer believes is critical to the
overall experiencing of the program is outlined as a goal. Furthermore,
it is critical that each experiential vignette across all points of contact
during the experience be specified (Shaw & Ivens, 2005). Collectively,
these goals define the program design problem.

Design problems frequently involve developing programs for a specific facility. For example, unused time at a bowling alley, recreation
center, swimming pool, or ice rink may need to be filled with a program
service. In these instances, it is the organizational need to fill a facility
that becomes the primary impetus for developing a program. Patron
input from a needs assessment is then added to the design problem, and
a program is developed to meet articulated client needs and to fulfill
the organizational need of facility use. Now complete Exercise 10-2 on
page 186.

PROGRAM DESIGN STANDARDS

Program design is often dictated by the program standards used
in an agency. In this case, an agency develops a list of goals and objectives for a specific type of program, and the standards provide a ge-

Exhibit 10-2: Program Design Goals–Easter Egg Hunt

Key experiences to be staged:

- To facilitate each child finding an Easter egg
- To provide opportunities for children to visit the Easter Bunny
- To keep parents from hunting eggs
- To help parents enjoy seeing their children hunt Easter eggs

Exhibit 10-3: Ten Elements of a Theme Program

A theme is an underlying, dominant, or recognizable concept. Programmers generally do an excellent job of developing themes for major holidays and events like Christmas, Easter, or Independence Day. To add experiential depth to programs, this concept needs to be carried through in other programs. In a military recreation operation, a program that includes at least six of the ten elements will meet the standard of a theme program.

1. Activities (active games)
2. Refreshments (food and beverages)
3. Decorations or props
4. Entertainment (live)
5. Audiovisuals (films/slides/videotapes)
6. Costumes
7. Lighting (special room arrangement)
8. Prizes
9. Music (canned, for atmosphere)
10. Gimmicks (giveaways, mystery or special guests, special effects, animals, etc.)

From: H. Rice, Director V Corps Recreation Centers, 1986.

neric design. This is similar to the process discussed in Chapter Eight on Program Management Standards, except in this case it is applied to designing specific types of programs and the outcomes expected from participating in them. An example of program standards for "theme programs" used by the U.S. Army V Corps is presented in Exhibit 10-3.

Exercise 10-2: Program Design Goals

Prepare design goals for an Independence Day theme party at a nursing home. Be sure to list the experiences you want to create. When finished, discuss the following questions:
- How might patron input be solicited and incorporated into design goals?
- Are the essential experiential elements of this program apparent from the list?
- Is the list explicit enough to guide the design of the program?
- Does the list make apparent the unique experience that will be offered in this program?

Theme programs are a specific form of program service that military recreation employees who work in the Army V Corps Recreation Centers are required to develop. By their standards, a theme program is one that includes at least six of the ten elements of a theme program. Obviously, each program element is developed around a single theme.

The goal in this instance is to develop a theme program. The ten elements serve as pre-designated design objectives. If six of the ten elements are incorporated into the program's design, a theme program will have been produced. The design of a theme program in this agency is thus guided by program standards. Incorporating patron desires into the final design will increase the probability of developing a successful program. Exhibit 10-4 on page 188 shows an example of program design goals developed with this concept. Now complete Exercise 10-3 on page 189.

TERMINAL PERFORMANCE OBJECTIVES

The most specific type of program design statement is the terminal performance objective, which states an observable behavior to be performed by the participant. As the name implies, these objectives are always the last strata of a hierarchy of goals and objectives, and they need to be written differently than goals and objectives discussed previously. A terminal performance objective must include: (1) a condition under which the performance will be demonstrated, (2) the performance or observable behavior that will be performed, and (3) an objective criterion that will measure successful accomplishment of the objective. Once these are written, a program is designed that will facilitate the behaviors desired. Exhibit 10-5 on page 189 presents examples of terminal performance objectives for a baseball clinic.

The condition specified in Exhibit 10-5 on page 189, "when tested at the end of the clinic," shows when the participants are expected to exhibit the behavior. For the first objective, the observable behavior is an exam score and the criterion is a score of 70 percent or more correct answers. An implicit assumption of this process is that the abilities demonstrated resulted from the participant's involvement in the program designed and operated by the programmer.

It is important to recognize that the subject in this list of objectives is different from the subject in the goals and objectives developed previously. In this list, the subject is the participant in the program. Instead of implying that staff will accomplish them, this series of objectives clearly indicates what the participants themselves will accomplish.

Another example of this technique is shown in the goals and objectives included in Box D of Figure 10-1. Specifically, objective #3, "At the end of the program, each student will be able to correctly identify the parts of the guitar," is operationalized with the sample performance objective #1 under it, "When requested, participants will correctly identify five of the following parts of the guitar on the first inquiry: neck, body, sound hole, strings, tuning keys, and frets." Collectively, the three performance objectives included in Box D give direction to the design of the guitar class. They, too, are written so that they can be measured and their attainment thereby verified.

Terminal performance objectives that are well written are essential to good program design for programs providing instruction or therapy. They are also essential to implementing outcome-based programming.

PUTTING OUTCOME-BASED PROGRAMMING (BBP) INTO ACTION

In this section, we illustrate how the various concepts found in this and earlier chapters combine to implement an outcome-based approach such as Benefits-Based Programming. Merry Milers, a senior citizen walking program developed by the Miamisburg, Ohio, Department of Parks and Recreation, will be used to illustrate these concepts. The purpose of this program was to encourage active and healthy lifestyles for seniors by offering a walking program. Let's reexamine the BBP Model (see Figure 4-3 on page 59). An example of how Phase 1, target issues, may be developed is given in Exhibit 10-6 on page 191. Examples of the community issue, the target goal, and the protective factors goal statements for the Merry Milers program are listed in this exhibit as well.

Phase 2 of the BBP model, activity components, requires the programmer to develop several subcomponents. One of these is writing performance objectives, as discussed in the previous section of this chapter. Exhibit 10-7 on page 191 offers several examples of performance objectives for the Merry Milers program. Note that each objective contains the three necessary parts—condition, performance, and criterion—thus making them observable and verifiable.

The terminal performance objectives included in Exhibit 10-7 will measure and document the successful implementation of the Merry Milers program. Although more may be accomplished, these are key outcomes that will be used to judge the worth of the program.

Exhibit 10-4: A Caribbean Christmas Theme Program

(Note: research at the library how Christmas is celebrated in the Caribbean islands, and incorporate those elements.)

Program Element #1: Activities
a. Limbo contest
b. Seashell hunt
c. Straw hat decorating
d. Salsa or Caribbean dancing

Program Element #2: Refreshments
a. Fresh fruits (tropical)
b. Fruit cocktail bowl with shredded coconut
c. Other recipes researched in library or from family members of Caribbean origin

Program Element #3: Decorations or Props
a. Hanging suns (large colorful swatches of fabric stapled to walls in
   interesting patterns)
b. Palm trees, banana trees (potted)
c. Large seashells made of papier-mâché

Program Element #4: Entertainment
a. Steel band
b. Caribbean music group

Program Element #5: Audiovisuals
a. Movies (travelogues) of the Caribbean islands
b. Slides of scenes from the Caribbean islands
c. Recordings of Caribbean drums playing

Program Element #6: Costumes
a. White shirts open to the navel with colorful cummerbunds for men
b. Colorful sundresses for women

Program Element #7: Lighting
a. Colored spotlights with bright colors: red, orange, yellow, and so on illuminating the
room

Program Element #9: Music (canned)
a. Steel drum music
b. Have a limbo expert perform

Adapted from an original program concept by Darmstadt Recreation Center Staff.

Exhibit 10-5: Performance Objectives for a Baseball Clinic

When tested at the end of the clinic:

- Participants will be able to correctly answer 70 percent or more of written questions on baseball rules.
- Participants will be able to correctly answer 70 percent or more of written questions on baseball strategy.
- Participants' batting averages will have increased by .050 or more.
- Seventy percent or more of the participants will indicate that their skill at playing their chosen position will have increased significantly.

Exercise 10-3: Developing Program Standards

Develop programming standards for one-day workshops in an agency. When finished, discuss the following questions:

- How will patron input be solicited and Incorporated into the final program design?
- Does the description give the workshop a unique programming format in the agency?
- Do your workshop programming goals give enough guidance and direction to programmers who wish to develop workshops?

The next subcomponent of Phase 2 is identifying specific daily activities and procedures that will facilitate the achievement of the target goals. Thus, the program should be animated through the design of a series of animation frames that will ensure that each performance objective is accomplished. The performance objective, "When tested, participants will be able to correctly answer 70 percent or more of written questions on the dangers of physical inactivity," might lead to a frame in which participants would view a video on the subject matter. This could be followed by a frame in which they actively take part in discussing the video, role playing, or completing a brief survey that profiles their own levels of physical activity. As discussed in this chapter, the key point here is that the program is animated through the development of a series of frames that are designed to ensure accomplishment of program objectives.

The next subcomponent of Phase 2 is to process the daily activities, in which staff and participants discuss their perceptions about how well the target goals are being achieved. Once this discussion has occurred, staff will need to determine the extent to which the objectives were achieved and keep written notes to use in documenting program process and accomplishments (see Figure 4-7 on page 64 for a suggested form for documenting program accomplishments). The final subcomponent of Phase 2, Activity Components, is to monitor the achievement of activity objectives and engage in formative evaluation of the implementation processes. If changes need to be made before the next activity session, they should be made now.

In the next phase of the BBP model, Phase 3, Benefit Outcomes, the achievement of target goals leading to increased resiliency among participants is evaluated and summarized. (How goal and objective evaluations are implemented is discussed in Chapters Twenty and Twenty-One.) The final phase, Phase 4, Benefits-Based Awareness, involves communicating BBP successes to the general public, funding sources, and stakeholders in the form of newsletters, promotional materials, news releases, and others media. The reader will learn how to develop these skills in Chapter Fourteen, Techniques for Program Promotion.

CONCLUSION

To design a program, the programmer must specify the actual interventions that will be staged to implement the program and create the leisure experience intended. At this point, it is important to develop clear, specific, and measurable program design goals that describe the experience to be created or the terminal performance objectives to be attained. These specify what patrons will be able to do or will experience as a result of their participation. Thorough work at this point will expedite the program design process.

ADDITIONAL READING

Gronlund, N. E. (1970). *Stating behavioral objectives for classroom instruction*. New York: Macmillan.

REFERENCES

Management Learning Laboratories. (1985). *Assessment of the Management Function of the Knoxville Bureau of Recreation, Knoxville, Tennessee: Report 1, Review of Existing Organizational Structure*. Champaign, IL: Management Learning Laboratories.

Pine B. J., II, & Gilmore, J. H. (2005). *Field guide for the experience economy*. Aurora, OH: Strategic Horizions, LLP.

Shaw, C., & Ivens, J. (2005). *Building great customer experiences*. New York: Plagrave Macmillan.

Exhibit 10-6: Phase 1—Target Issues

The Issue

The major problem being addressed in this Benefits-Based Program is inactivity among senior citizens in the city of Miamisburg, Ohio. It is assumed that this issue was initially raised by local stakeholders (i.e., Miamisburg government officials, local physicians, senior citizen service providers, and local leisure service agencies, such as a park and recreation department).

The Target Goal

In order to purposefully address the issue of senior citizen inactivity, a Benefits-Based Walking Program will be developed to encourage active and healthy lifestyles among seniors.

Protective Factors Goal Statements

The following goals outline the specific protective factors that will be developed by the senior citizen participants during the Merry Milers walking program:

- Senior citizens will be knowledgeable of local walking resources, namely, walking trails, local parks, indoor tracks, shopping malls.
- Senior citizens will develop the perceived competence to complete all aspects of a daily walking program, namely, completing a warm-up and cool-down, walking at their target heart rate, wearing the proper attire, and so on.
- Through participation in the walking program, seniors will develop a positive attitude toward the future that is based on active and healthy lifestyles.

Exhibit 10-7: Phase 2—Activity Components

The following performance objectives identify observable outcomes for daily activities:

- When requested to do so, participants will be able to analyze their walking workout correctly, based on three pulse readings taken during their workout.
- When tested at the end of the program, participants will have improved their cardiovascular fitness levels as evidenced by a decrease in their post-test score over their pre-test score on the Rockport Fitness walking test. (This is a time test for a given distance and thus a lower score is a better score.)
- When completing their daily activity report, participants' responses will include descriptions of at least three personal benefits obtained from the Merry Milers program.
- When tested, participants will be able to correctly answer 70 percent or more of written questions on the dangers of physical inactivity and community resources available for exercise walking.

Wildlands Workshop
Photo courtesy of Westerville Parks and Recreation Department, Westerville, OH
Photo by Jody Stowers

Program Design

11

STEP 5 : PROGRAM DESIGN

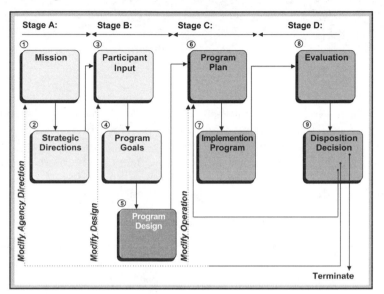

Program Design
Design Goals
Design
    Components
Design Tactics
Imagined
    Interactions
Multiple
    Forecasts
Visualization
Vignette

Program design is a transitional step that plans the details of how a program will actually be staged to facilitate a leisure experience for participants. It is implemented as the final step in Stage 2 of the Program Development Cycle. In this step, the programmer uses data collected in Stages 1 and 2, including the agency's philosophy and goals, marketing, and needs assessment information. This data and other background data should indicate the need to develop a specific program and program's content, for example, a Spring Arts Festival. This data is combined and a program design is prepared.

The programmer must stage a situated activity system that will animate a program to move it through time and orchestrate its flow (Edginton, Hanson, & Edginton, 1992) by altering the pattern of attention demanded from participants so that there is variety in the content and intensity of consciousness demanded. Staging the design prepared in this step results in a managed experience pattern. Evidence for this phenomenon is provided by Hull, Stewart, and Yi (1992), who, while discussing a hiking experience, noted that "a recreation experience is dynamic: It fluctuates over the course of the engagement. Moods change. Scenic beauty varies. The degree of absorption in one's activity fluctuates" (p. 249). Furthermore, they document that these experience patterns not only vary over the du-

Implementing Outcome-Based Programming

In this chapter, we assume that the first step of outcome-based programming, program *inputs*, have already been determined. Inputs refer to the kinds of resources that will be needed for a program, including equipment, staff, facilities, money, etc. The next step in outcome-based programming is to determine the *activities* that will be used in the program. Programmers can use the projective imaging techniques described in this chapter to visualize their activities before they occur, and uncover potential problems and solve them before the program is implemented.

ration of the experience, but that subsets of participants have different experiences. Thus, the same program can provide different individuals with different experiences. They speculate that recreation experience patterns may be influenced by the management of the recreation site. Program design, then, is a process that plans the staging of a program to facilitate this notion of a managed experience pattern.

PROGRAM DESIGN DEFINED

The program-mer must plan a situ-ated activity system that will animate a program to move it through time and orches-trate its flow...

Program design is planning the step-by-step action scenarios and configu-rations of the six key elements of a situated activity system that will stage the program and guide participants through the social interactions necessary to fa-cilitate the leisure experience intended by the designer. It requires a technique that enables the programmer to anticipate and predict social interaction and to vicariously experience a model of the program. The technique should also facilitate easy iterations for redesign.

How this is accomplished by programmers is neither specified nor discussed in the literature. Our own experiences at programming and our interviews with numerous programmers have convinced us that imaging is a primary technique that is used. A systematic method for using it to design the staging of program services is explained in the following pages.

A PROGRAM DESIGN MODEL

Figure 11-1 is a diagram of the program design model. There are three major components to the model, including design goals, design components, and design tactics. In the first component, the programmer must specify the design goals, namely, the program outcomes, i.e. the experiences and/or benefit outcomes that will result from participation in the program. At a minimum, a program is to provide a leisure experi-ence for participants. Remember, from Chapter Two, that this requires the program be designed to provide perceptions of freedom, to be in-trinsically satisfying, and to provide opportunities for positive affect, as well as be relaxing, fun, and enjoyable (Kleiber, Caldwell, & Shaw, 1992; Kleiber, Larson, & Csikszentmihalyi, 1986).

◀ 194 **Recreation Programming: Designing Leisure Experiences** ▶

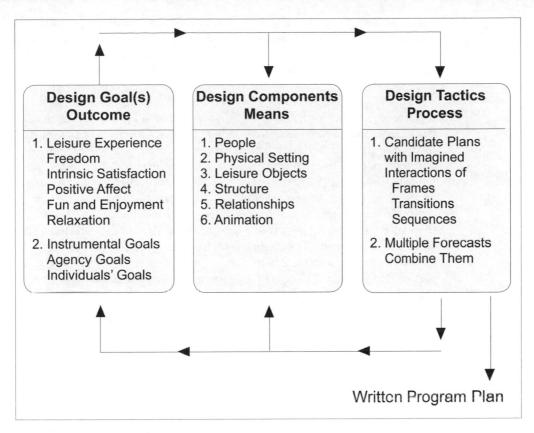

Design Goal(s) Outcome	Design Components Means	Design Tactics Process
1. Leisure Experience Freedom Intrinsic Satisfaction Positive Affect Fun and Enjoyment Relaxation 2. Instrumental Goals Agency Goals Individuals' Goals	1. People 2. Physical Setting 3. Leisure Objects 4. Structure 5. Relationships 6. Animation	1. Candidate Plans with Imagined Interactions of Frames Transitions Sequences 2. Multiple Forecasts Combine Them

Written Program Plan

Figure 11-1: Program Design Model

There can be two additional sources of goals: the agency and the participants. The agency may have specific social goals that it attempts to achieve through leisure programs. These are derived from the three- to five-year program management goals and the one-year management by objective (MBO) goals (see Chapter Eight). For example, a corporate recreation operation may try to build esprit de corps among its employees in all programs offered.

The outcomes desired by patrons that are deduced from needs assessment data (see Chapter Nine) are yet a third possible source of program design goals. These can only be incorporated as design goals if the patrons' desires are known and sufficient consensus about them exists. In the first component, then, program design goals need to be specified (see Chapter Six) and the aim of the design becomes their realization. *(Additional material about how to write program design goals was included in Chapter Ten.)*

The second design component includes the six key elements of a situated activity system that were discussed in Chapter Three. They are the major elements that may be manipulated to stage occasions of social interaction and affect outcomes. Planning their manipulation is the process of program design. Staging and delivering events designed in this way provides participant's access to the leisure experiences or benefits intended by the designer. The final element of these six, animation, involves determining how the program will move through time, and how changes in the other five elements will occur as a program progresses through time. In this component, the five elements are altered through planned animation of social interaction to facilitate the leisure experience.

Finally, the third component requires the programmer to use a technique to develop the design intended. Because leisure programs occur in real time, a major problem in leisure program design is finding a technique that can simulate this passage of time in the design process and thus permit the programmer to experiment with and model alternate stagings of a program. Practitioners in many fields can use techniques that permit real-time rehearsals. For example, musicians practice their musical scores, actors rehearse their scripts, and athletes practice their plays. However, leisure services are usually staged and delivered simultaneously and thus cannot be rehearsed in real time. Using projective imagery can simulate this time dimension in the design process and provide a technique that facilitates experimentation with different stagings of a program at the speed of thought and at almost no cost.

The goal of the process is to determine the specific actions that need to be implemented to reach the design goals specified.

TECHNIQUES FOR IMPLEMENTING PROGRAM DESIGN

Several concepts and techniques need to be mastered to implement the design process that is illustrated in Figure 11-1 on page 195. The goal of the process is to determine the specific actions and venue alterations that need to be implemented when the program is staged to reach the design goals specified. These actions are termed *design tactics*, the actions that must be implemented to stage the animation of a program; that is, to actually operate it. "Tactics are specific actions that are intended to facilitate implementation of a plan and to produce progress toward their goal," according to Beach (1990, p. 8). As Shaw and Ivens (2005) have pointed out, because participant's impressions are formed throughout a program, it is important to plan thoroughly "...across all moments of customer contact" (p. 38). Design tactics are developed through *imagined interactions*, "a type of instrumental thought process as well as a type of simulation heuristic" (Honeycutt, 1991, p. 122).

The notion of imagined interactions stems from symbolic interaction theory discussed earlier in the book (see Chapter Two). Mead (1934) identifies the ability of humans to carry on an internalized conversation with themselves as a distinguishing feature of human intelligence. The notion that we are self-reflexive indicates we are capable of becoming objects in our own minds, and thereby taking the role of others in an effort to understand how they see us. This internal dialogue can be focused on imagined interactions with others. Edwards, Honeycutt, and Zagacki (1988) indicate, "This type of mental activity is important, because one may consciously take the role of others, imagining how they might respond to one's messages within particular situations, and thus one can imagine and test the consequences of alternative messages prior to communication" (p. 24). They conclude that "imagined interactions are one mechanism allowing individuals to plan and to measure social action. Imagined interactions allow for the rehearsal, and perhaps discovery, of situation-dependent behaviors. Individuals may use imagined interactions to search for or practice behaviors relevant to anticipated conversations," according to Edwards, et al. (p. 41).

Using projective imagery, the programmer simulates the possible social interactions of a program in his or her mind and experiments with various configurations of the situating elements of program staging. With these images, the programmer rehearses and models alternate stagings of the program's operation, thereby simulating and projecting different outcomes with different configurations.

Analogy with a previous sequence of events or with imagined future events is the major underlying representational system that should be used. This is supported by Kaufmann's (1988) work on the use of mental imagery in problem solving. He states, "In imagery we try to imagine what will happen under actual or hypothetical perceptual conditions (rather than inferring it through logical transformations)" (p. 234). The images are heuristic and thus created to experiment with "what if" questions about various combinations of the six key elements of a situated activity system that could be used. Their selection is also volitional (self-directed) and one thereby uses directed consciousness to select different combinations of elements for experimentation.

Using visualization, the programmer develops candidate plans, alternate design tactics that could be used to stage program implementation. Each candidate plan should receive conscious attention and be developed until it is a feasible solution to the design problem, i.e., it will facilitate the experiences and/or benefits intended from participating. To achieve this, one must imagine *multiple forecasts* of candidate plans

Once several candidate plans are developed, they compete with each other for adoption as the final solution.

so that alternate stagings of a program may be developed and considered. Techniques for pushing the formulation of multiple forecasts are discussed in Chapter Twelve on creativity and innovation.

Once several candidate plans are developed, they compete with each other for adoption as the final solution. In addition, they may be altered, with various parts of individual candidate plans combined into a final plan.

PROJECTIVE IMAGING TECHNIQUES

Forecasting and modeling candidate plans is accomplished through *visualization* of imagined interactions. In your mind's eye, you visualize the actual operation of the program; that is, how the interaction scenarios of a program might be staged. This involves more than sight and can include all of the senses (Green, 1976). It may also produce feelings (Penfield, 1961, cited in Green, 1976). Thus, you vicariously experience the sense of a program as though you are there, going through it step-by-step, and feeling the emotion of participating. Now try Exercise 11-1.

You must learn a variety of skills to use visualization successfully. The first is to discover how you personally organize visualizing. Individuals tend to routinize this behavior and organize them in only one way. Therefore, we must consciously force ourselves to visualize a pro-

During internal visualization, one tries to actually experience the program.

Exercise 11-2: Visual Imaging from Different Perspectives (Rossman & Schlatter ©2001)

Description of Visual Imaging Perspectives	Directions: Use this instrument to record comments about any changes you'd make as a result of the vicarious rehearsals you've made of your program.
Entire Program Use external imaging to visualize the entire operation of a program.	Entire Program – COMMENTS:
Participant's Perspective Use internal imaging to experiencing the program from the participant's perspective.	Participant's Perspective – COMMENTS:
Perspective of Others Use internal imaging to experience the program from the perspective of each of the other participants who may be in the program, i.e. parents, spectators, referees, and so on.	Perspective of Others – COMMENTS:
Entire Program Use external imaging and visualize the entire program from the program manager's perspective.	Entire Program – COMMENTS:
Comprehensive Visualization Use internal and external imaging to visualize the program from all perspectives.	Comprehensive Visualization – COMMENTS:

gram differently. Following are several techniques for accomplishing this.

Any visualization will occur from one of two perspectives: external or internal (Weinberg, 1988). During *external visualization*, you become an object to yourself. For example, you may observe yourself participating as the leader of an event. It is analogous to watching a videotape of yourself leading the event. The goal is to experiment with various leadership styles and strategies in order to forecast the optimal style for the event. During *internal visualization*, you attempt actually to be at a program and to experience it vicariously from beginning to end. The goal is to understand how the program will affect a participant; that is, what it is like to participate in this program. You normally assume one of these two perspectives when imaging and must consciously convert to the other to thoroughly use visualization to design a program.

You may also force yourself to change your physical *viewpoint* of the program. What will it look like from an aerial view? What if you reversed the sequential order of the program? You might take a side view of it or an under- the-ground view. What will it look like to a child who is 36 inches tall? Attempt to see the program from a different geographical location or physical position.

Each frame represents a single episode of experience.

It is also useful to change the *social role* you are using to visualize the interactions of the program. Changing from leader to participant is one such change. But you must also internally visualize the program from the roles of other program participants, such as parents, spectators, the program manager, referees, and those in other similar roles. It is important to be thorough in this step so that all possible difficulties and problems can be predicted and dealt with in the design of the program rather than during its operation. Now try Exercise 11-2 on page 199.

USING PROJECTIVE IMAGING TO ANIMATE THE PROGRAM DESIGN

A useful icon to use while experimenting with candidate plans is the vignette of a cartoon strip (Ableson, 1976). As illustrated in Figure 11-2, visualize that your program is a series of frames and transitions between frames that occur in a temporal sequence (Goffman, 1974). Each frame is an interactional episode made up of a single configuration of the six key situating elements of program production. The length of time that a frame will exist is the amount of time the elements in the frame will occupy the conscious attention of program participants. To carry through with the theatrical metaphor used earlier, consider each frame a scene that must be staged appropriately to accomplish the program's design goals. Film producers often use a similar technique called *story boarding*, wherein each important scene of a film is framed for staging. Each frame, then, represents a single episode, and a program is composed of numerous episodes that occur in temporal order.

The spaces between frames are *transitions* from one frame to another, times when the six key situating elements of program design are being reconfigured and the conscious attention of participants is shifting from one element in a frame to another. An additional design con-

SEQUENCE: Temporal Order

Frame 1	T1	Frame 2	T2	Frame 3	T3
People Physical Setting Leisure Objects Structure Relationships Animation		People Physical Setting Leisure Objects Structure Relationships Animation		People Physical Setting Leisure Objects Structure Relationships Animation	

Frame: a single configuration of the six program elements
T = Transition: a reconfiguration of the six program elements

Figure 11-2: Planning Frames

sideration is that of identifying the intervention(s) that must occur to transition participants from one frame to the next

For example, how does one move patrons from one exhibit to the next in a museum? This can be accomplished with arrow signs, through instructions included on an audiotape tour, with an employee guiding the tour, or through a physical layout that creates a natural progression through the exhibit.

The icons of a cartoon strip or story boarding are useful for graphically depicting a temporal sequence of experience frames. Using these techniques, the programmer may rewrite the experience in each frame or change their temporal order at will. Each candidate plan that is visualized is a rewritten vignette. Animation of the overall experience is created because of the following designed changes:

- the key situating elements in each frame are changed,
- the temporal order of frames is rearranged, and
- interventions for essential transitions are directed.

This succession of changes, and the need for patrons to consciously attend to and interpret them, produces interaction and thereby animates a program.

For an example of how focus on different elements can be changed from frame to frame to create animation, let's visualize the three frames in Figure 11-2. Let us assume we are going to program the dedication of a new recreation facility, complete with a tour and buffet dinner. Participation is by invitation only. Imagine that in the first frame, the primary focus is on the interactions between the people as they arrive. Renewing acquaintances and meeting new people is the first experiential sequence of this program that must be staged. The interactions in this frame could be facilitated with "ice breaker" social recreation activities, or the interaction could be allowed to occur without intervention. The relational history of the group, one of the six key situating elements, would certainly need to be considered in determining the type and extent of intervention to use.

In Frame 2, the focus of attention is on the new facility. Thus, the physical place is the key element in Frame 2. There are many staging options for altering the place. It could be decorated, illuminated, or treated in some other special manner during this frame to highlight it and focus further attention on it. How individuals will be moved from the opening frame to the facility tour is a transition design problem to solve, as is how they will be moved through the tour itself. For example, will they be placed in small groups and be given a guided tour? Or will they be allowed to do a self-guided walk-through? Will you stage this tour with real live action in the facility; i.e. participants actually using the building?

In the third frame, food, a social object, will be the main focus; a secondary focus will be on social interaction as the meal is consumed. Moving the participants to the meal location after the tour, queuing them in the buffet line, and seating them at an appropriate table are transition design problems that also must be resolved.

In this example, a different situating element became the focus in each frame: interacting people, the physical facility, and finally, leisure objects. In actual operation, this program would probably have additional frames for dedication speeches, ribbon cutting, and so on. At a minimum, the programmer must develop a well thought out frame for accomplishing each design goal.

A second method of creating animation is to change the temporal order of the frames. In the current example, the frames could be reordered by allowing the second frame to be the meal and the third frame the facility tour. In any program, attention must be given to the temporal order of frames so the overall flow of the event—that is, its impact on attention and emotion—are carefully orchestrated to achieve the desired effect. In this program, one could assert that the facility tour should be the final frame used to showcase the new facility, rather than ending the event with the meal. Reordering frames in this manner changes the flow of a program and the overall experience.

The candidate plan that best solves the original design problem is implemented.

A third possible intervention strategy involves orchestrating the transitions between frames in a variety of ways. Transitions need to be designed so that they contribute to the overall experience desired. For example, at Disneyland, queues for rides, which are a transition, are staged to place the patron in a mood that contributes to the overall theme of the ride itself. In the dedication program being used as an example, how participants are to be moved either to or from the building tour is an essential transition design problem.

FIVE PREPLANNED FORECASTS

The number of visualizations that are possible can be overwhelming. However, experience with program operations can provide us with a useful guide for getting started. Below are five preplanned visualization forecasts to use in formulating candidate plans for each program.

1. Use external imaging to visualize the entire operation of a program.

2. Use internal imaging to experience the program from the participant's perspective.

3. Use internal imaging to experience the program from the perspective of each of the other participants who may be in the program, for example, spectators, parents, referees, and so on.

4. Use external imaging and again visualize the entire operation of the reconfigured program from the program manager's perspective.

5. Use external and internal imaging to visualize the final program with imagined interactions, changing roles from observer to participant, and give special attention to evaluating how the program operation, as currently configured, addresses the design goals developed earlier.

CRITERIA FOR EVALUATING CANDIDATE PLANS

How does one determine which candidate plan to adopt, or which to alter and combine into the design tactics to be implemented? How well a candidate plan solves the design problem (specified by the design goals) is the primary criteria. How well the candidate plan facilitates a leisure experience for the participant is the first consideration. Thus, the candidate plan that facilitates perceived freedom by creating choices; that facilitates intrinsic satisfaction; that provides opportunities for positive affect; and that makes the program fun, relaxing, and entertaining will be adopted. Second, the candidate plans that best contribute to accomplishing specific patron, agency, or community goals will also be adopted.

CONCLUSION

Participation in a program, then, can be thought of as a sequence of experiences. These experiences consist of interactions in frames in which conscious attention is given to various configurations of the six key elements of a situated activity system. Program design must be conducted from this knowledge base—programming involves understanding and intervening in social interaction by using the six situating elements to stage each frame, to reorder frames, and to design key transitions between frames. Visualization techniques can be used as a method for the programmer to simulate the interactions of a program. These are used in the design process to develop and experiment with a variety of candidate plans that are eventually combined into a single set of design tactics that solve the design problem.

The design process seemingly results in a program that is linear in its implementation and perhaps imposing on the participant. However, the designer must remain cognizant of the emergent, interpretive nature of the leisure experience. Each frame designed should be a situated activity system that allows participants volitional action in interpreting and directing the outcome of the interaction. Here is where staging experiences departs from the theatrical metaphor: actors perform as directed, but in a leisure program, one must allow for people to perform with their own interpretations of the program's script. Designing and staging programs to allow for this freedom to interpret and respond is the programmer's continuing challenge.

REFERENCES

Ableson, R. P. (1976). Script processing in attitude formations and decision making. In J. S. Carrol & J. W. Payne (Eds.), *Cognition and Social Behavior*. Hillsdale, NJ: Erlbaum.

Beach, L. R. (1990). *Image theory: Decision making in personal and organizational contexts*. New York: John Wiley & Sons.

Edginton, C. R., Hanson, C. J., & Edginton, S. R. (1992). *Leisure programming: Concepts, trends, and professional practice* (2nd ed.). Dubuque, IA: Wm. C. Brown Communications.

Edwards, R., Honeycutt, J. M., & Zagacki, K. S. (1988, Winter). Imagined interaction as an element of social cognition. *Western Journal of Speech Communication, 52*, 23–45.

Goffman, E. (1974). *Frame analysis: An essay on the organization of experience*. New York: Harper Colophon Books.

Green, H. (1976). *Mind and image: An essay on art and architecture*. Lexington: University of Kentucky Press.

Honeycutt, J. M. (1991). Imagined interactions, imagery, and mindfulness/mindlessness. In R. G. Kuzendorf (Ed.), *Mental imagery* (pp. 121–128). New York: Plenum Press.

Hull, R. B., IV., Stewart, W. P., & Yi, Y. K. (1992). Experience patterns: Capturing the dynamic nature of a leisure experience. *Journal of Leisure Research, 24*, 240–252.

Kaufmann, G. (1988). Mental imagery and problem solving. In M. Denis, J. Engelkamp, & J. T. E. Richardson (Eds.), *Cognitive and neuropsychological approaches to mental imagery* (pp. 231–239). Dordrecht, the Netherlands: Martinus Nijhoff.

Kleiber, D., Caldwell, L., & Shaw, S. (1992, October). Leisure meaning in adolescence. Paper presented at the 1992 Symposium on Leisure Research, Cincinnati, OH.

Kleiber, D., Larson, R., & Csikszentmihalyi, M. (1986). The experience of leisure in adolescence. *Journal of Leisure Research, 18*, 169–176.

Mead, G. H. (1934). *Mind, self, and society*. Chicago: University of Chicago Press.

Rossman, J. R., & Schlatter, B. E. (2001, October). Improve your programs through visual imaging! Paper presented at the meeting at the National Recreation and Park Association, Denver, CO.

Shaw, C., & Ivens, J. (2005), *Building great customer experiences* (rev. ed.). New York: Palgrave Macmillan.

Weinberg, R. S. (1988). *The mental advantage: Developing your psychological skills in tennis*. Champaign, IL: Leisure Press.

Sign Language Tennis
Photo courtesy of City of Aurora, Colorado, Department of Library, Recreation, & Cultural Services

Creative Programming

STEP 5 : PROGRAM DESIGN

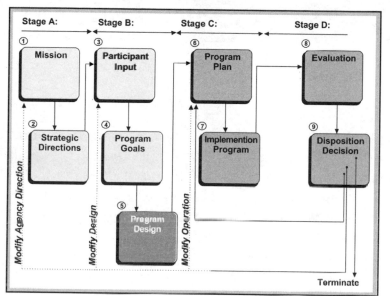

KEY TERMS

Creative
Programming
Applied Creativity
Innovation
Diagram of the
Creative Pro-
gram Design
Process
Problem
Definition
Generation of
Approaches
Exploration/
Interpretation

Throughout industry, the search for creative products and services, and innovative methods for implementing them, is underway. We are constantly barraged with new problems that cannot be solved with current approaches. Many organizations have responded by creating "idea centers" where employees from throughout the organization are sent to create and innovate (Ward, 1985). Programmers, too, must create new program services and develop innovative ways of operating them.

Creative programming is different from program planning. In the latter, the programmer examines existing, alternate solutions to a problem and then selects the best solution. This methodology stems from problem-solving literature that identifies the following steps: problem definition, identification of alternatives, evaluation of alternatives, implementation of the alternative selected, and finally, evaluation of the solution implemented. Creative programmers not only synthesize the facts available and identify existing, alternate solutions; they also consciously create additional programmatic solutions for the identified design problem. Furthermore, they develop innovative procedures for program implementation. Thus, creativity may be applied both during program design and while developing the implementation plan

...creativity refers to the ability to overcome problems by approaching them in novel ways...

Implementing Outcome-Based Programming

The creativity portion of programming is assigned to the *activity* step of outcome-based programming. As one writes performance objectives and the accompanying daily activities for those objectives, creativity techniques may be employed. Because of the iterative nature of creativity, programmers should feel free to reconsider their plans several times before selecting the best alternative for the program.

RESEARCH UPDATE: Where do new program ideas come from? Recent research by the authors indicates that creativity sessions are one of the top three sources for new program ideas.

Top 5 Sources for New Programs
1. Other agency brochures
2. Citizen suggestions
3. Creativity sessions
4. Needs assessments
5. Popular media

UNDERSTANDING APPLIED CREATIVITY

Are you a creative person? Can you find creative solutions to programming problems? Can you develop innovative implementation procedures? In all likelihood you can, if you put forth enough effort with the techniques outlined in this chapter.

What is creativity? Although many definitions of it exist, there is little consensus about its definition. On the one hand, it refers to that rare gift of genius and insight that enables a person to unlock great mysteries of the universe. This cannot be taught. On the other hand, creativity also refers to the ability to overcome problems by approaching them in novel ways and by systematically developing innovative solutions to them. According to Tudor Richard (as cited in Howard, 1985), the opposite of this type of creativity is "stuckness," habitual thinking that generates the same solutions to problems. Creativity training will not produce a Michelangelo, but it does help one escape from "stuckness" and develop more novel solutions to programming problems.

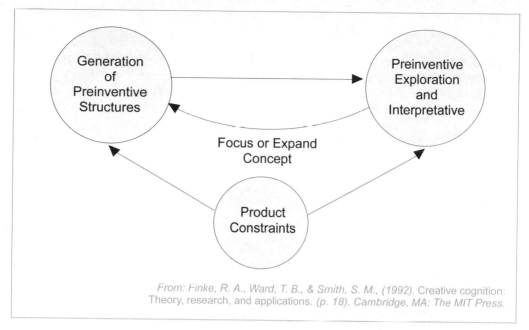

From: Finke, R. A., Ward, T. B., & Smith, S. M., (1992). Creative cognition: Theory, research, and applications. (p. 18). Cambridge, MA: The MIT Press.

Figure 12-1: The Geneplore Model

Von Oech (1990) suggests that to be creative, one must first have a broad base of knowledge about a subject. This knowledge base does not guarantee creativity, but is a prerequisite to it. Secondly, by using techniques that manipulate this knowledge and experience, one is opened to new ideas and thoughts about the subject. He calls getting unstuck "opening our mental locks" that keep us from seeing things differently.

Finke, Ward, and Smith (1992) have developed a model of creativity based on their research. It is called the Geneplore Model, illustrated in Figure 12-1. Creativity is modeled as an iteration between generating preinventive structures with special properties. This promotes creativity by reinterpreting their meaning in a new context. This iterative process occurs within the constraints of the program being developed. They conclude that creativity is the result of not one but several mental processes that lead to creative insight and discovery (Finke et al. 1992). Applied creativity, then, requires the development of a kit-bag of techniques.

Although the search for the origins of creativity and the mental processes that give rise to it continues, programmers operate in the present, and thus must develop innovative programs for people to enjoy tomorrow. A pragmatic definition of creativity for use in organizations efforts is offered by Ackoff and Vergara (1981):

> We define creativity in problem solving and planning as the ability of a subject in a choice situation to modify self-imposed constraints so as to enable him to select courses of action or produce outcomes that he or she would not otherwise select or

RESEARCH UPDATE: USE OF VISUALIZATION FOR NEW PROGRAM DEVELOPMENT. Recent research conducted by the authors indicates that visualization is used by more experienced programmers for developing new programs.

Use of Visualization for Developing New Programs

Females	68.8%
Males	57.7%
Experienced programmers (8+ yrs)	71.4%
Less experienced (<8 yrs)	55.4%
Certified	66.7%
Not certified	60.9%

produce, and are more efficient for or valuable to him or her than any he or she would otherwise have chosen. (p. 9)

The processes and techniques used to develop creative programs, then, must first provide the means to unlearn, and second, to see things in a new way. Specifically, they must prevent us from imposing our default responses to identified problems—the blocks to innovation. These are a result of our training or our routinized responses to the same or similar problems. Once we have removed our default blocks, we need techniques to facilitate the generation of novel ideas. In this case, novel means an idea we would not normally have developed given our previous assumptions and methods of operation. These may seem like modest goals, but in many cases, our thinking and methods of operating have become so routinized that we do not realize how stuck we actually are!

A change in any one element will result in a new program...

CREATIVITY IN DEVELOPING PROGRAMS

Several unique factors of recreation programs are relevant to the use of creativity. First is the unique problem-solving mode faced by recreation programmers. There are few widely recognized and accepted protocols for the operation of leisure programs. Step by step implementation procedures for specific programs are not included in the literature of the field. Thus, the creative problem-solving situation faced by the programmer is one in which few established procedures allow for computational transformations based on rule-governed interferences, such as deductive or inductive reasoning (Kaufmann, 1988). Engineering is a discipline in which computational transformations would likely be used, but recreation programming is not.

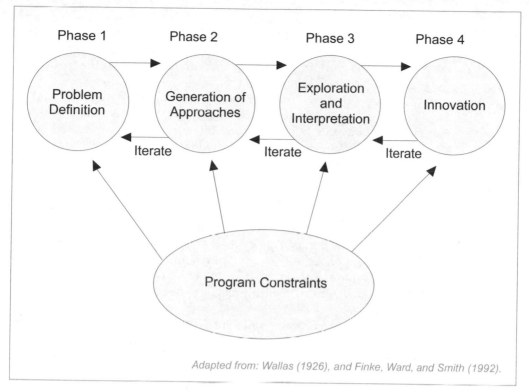

Adapted from: Wallas (1926), and Finke, Ward, and Smith (1992).

Figure 12-2: Creative Program Design Process

The programming problem to be solved, then, is most likely a novel, complex, and ambiguous one because of the many different approaches that may work if placed in the correct context. Solving the kinds of problems faced by recreation programmers is more likely to be accomplished by using an analogical technique—simulated mental models of what might happen—rather than inferring what will happen through computational transformations. The mental imagery techniques outlined in the previous chapter are an example of an analogical technique.

Second, you will remember from Chapter Three that there are six key elements in a situated activity system, and that a change in any one of them will result in a different program. The effort to create a new program does not necessarily require beginning completely anew. A change in any one element will result in a new program; thus, our goal in being creative is to change at least one element in a way that will make a difference.

Finally, a program is new if it has not been previously experienced by its patron group. So "new" does not necessarily mean it is new to you or your staff; rather, it means it is new to its patron group.

Having a good definition of the problem or well-developed program design goals facilitates the creative process.

CREATIVE PROGRAM DESIGN PROCESS

Is there a method to creativity? How does one organize efforts to systematically approach creativity? Wallas (1926) identified four stages of the creative process: (1) preparation, (2) incubation, (3) illumination, and (4) verification. In the first edition of this book, these stages were presented as a linear model of creativity. Based on the work of Finke et al. (1992), the model has been revised, and the work of these authors as well as the work of Wallas has been used to develop the model presented in Figure 12-2 on page 211.

The model is not linear; rather, it assumes that creativity and innovation occur as the cumulative result of activity conducted in four phases: problem definition, generation of approaches, exploration and interpretation, and innovation. Individuals iterate between the phases as insights become apparent. Having a good definition of the problem or well-developed program design goals facilitates the creative process. Thus, prior to implementing techniques that facilitate the generation of novel approaches, one must frame the problem appropriately and thereby prepare to solve the right problem. What is commonly called creativity is the iterative process that occurs between the generation of approaches phase and an exploration and interpretation of their applicability phase. The cumulative effort between these two phases is harnessed to produce novel approaches for solving the program design problem.

The first three phases—problem definition, idea generation, and interpretation of the ideas—should lead to creative, novel ideas. However, these must be transformed into something that is tangible and useful. This is innovation—verifying the applicability of the novel ideas generated to solve the program design problem and developing methods to implement them.

The entire process is constrained by the known limitations of the program. These could include constraints or predefinitions of any of the six situating elements (Chapter Three). For example, the programmer may be attempting to develop an innovative program for the use of an older, existing recreation center. Ideally in this case, he or she will have total creative freedom beyond the constraining fact that an existing facility must be used.

FOUR PHASES OF THE CREATIVE PROCESS

PHASE 1. PROBLEM DEFINITION

The major goal during this phase is to develop a statement of the problem; that is, the difference between the way things are and the way we believe they ought to be or desire them to be. The initial effort is to make certain the real problem is understood by asking a series of focusing questions. What is known? What is unknown? What are the assumptions underlying the problem? What if we make different assumptions? These and other similar questions should be asked. Additional focus will result from data about the program that are gathered from a variety of sources. These could include a completed needs assessment, a market study, observed incongruities in current operations, observations of successful or unsuccessful program operations, or other similar sources.

Once the data are gathered, they must be analyzed. To completely analyze the problem, it is necessary to explicate the problem complete-

Every act of creation is first of all an act of destruction. (Picasso) ly by breaking it down into its parts and determining the relationship among parts and all parts to the whole. Time spent in this step is well invested, for it is unlikely that the programmer will develop a good solution to a problem that is not well understood.

Many techniques can be used to further one's understanding of a problem. One of the key efforts is to "unlearn" what we already "know"—to remove those mental blocks that keep us from seeing things in a new way (Von Oech, 1990). Pablo Picasso once said, "Every act of creation is first of all an act of destruction."

To facilitate this, we must use techniques that force us to look at things in a different way by changing the question, using different words to ask the same question, or denying there is a problem in the first place. You might use these techniques to see if the answers give you insight into the problem.

Try questioning the basic assumptions of your organization by playing "Fools and the Rules" (Von Oech, 1990), in which "You take your holiest sacred cow and sacrifice it on the alter of foolishness" (p. 148). The idea is to use humor to make fun of agency products, rules, or policies and to expose their basic assumptions and possible flaws. Here is an example of this technique given to an author by Julia Dunn (personal communications, 1991):

Rule: We will have state of the art programs.

Fool: *Who needs state of the art programs? They create state of the art problems. Why not let someone else be the innovator and we'll copy what they've done. It would be cheaper.*

Redefining the problem can often trigger a solution. Consider the following example.

One of the authors was once involved in deciding what was to be done with a piece of playground equipment at a park-school site. A rather large number of children had fallen from the two slides on a large, integrated wooden play unit. The local school principal and a P.T.A. committee had decided that the slides were the problem and thus needed to be removed. The author was asked to meet with them to discuss the problem. Before the meeting, however, children actually using the equipment were observed.

From these observations, it was apparent that the problem was the placement of the two slides and the large number of children who wanted to play on them. The slides were placed so that the children could slide down one and immediately get in line to slide down the second one. Going down the second slide put the children in a position to get in line to use the first slide again. Thus, the two slides were actually being used as one, and there were simply too many children to be accommodated by this arrangement.

After the analysis, the problem was redefined as having insufficient slides and incorrect slide placement. A two-fold solution was proposed: (1) move one slide so that the two could not be used in a circular manner, and (2) add a third slide, thereby increasing the number of opportunities to slide. The solution was innovative compared with removing

The best problem statements are those that are written with the fewest restrictions possible.

Exhibit 12-1: Divergent Thinking Techniques

Brainstorming is one of the most widely known and widely used divergent thinking techniques. It is organized ideation by groups whose goal is to generate as many ideas regarding a design problem as possible within a given time limit. Ideas are generated in an atmosphere of "suspended judgment," that is, the goodness or bad-ness of any idea is suspended during idea generation. Brainstorming sessions are conducted with the belief that generating a large quantity of ideas will produce good ideas for problem solutions.

To conduct a brainstorming session, the leader should clearly define the problem to the group before starting the session. It is best if the individuals making up the group have diverse backgrounds so that idea generation will not be stifled by "group-think." When the session begins, group members are allowed to say anything that comes to mind as a possible solution to the identified problem. The group leader records all ideas as they are given. Everyone is encouraged to piggyback on a previous idea by adding to it, combining it with others, and so forth. During brainstorming sessions, the following four principles should be followed:

- Suspended judgment. To encourage as many ideas as possible, critical evalua-tion of their feasibility and worth are temporarily suspended.
- Encourage quantity. The more ideas that are generated, the more likely you are to get the one that will solve the problem.
- Piggy-Back. Encourage individuals to cross-fertilize, add to, innovate from, or combine with the ideas already generated.
- Encourage wild ideas. Encourage people to reveal their wildest ideas and not prejudge their feasibility or acceptability by the group.

Brainwriting is a modification of brainstorming; participants write down their ideas rather than give them orally. Participants do not identify their own papers. After a given time, papers are exchanged and each person is to modify, combine, or in some way build on the work of the previous writer. The exchange of papers continues until all apparent possibilities are exhausted.

This technique works better than brainstorming for some groups. This is especially true for groups that may have some dominant members, or groups in which un-equals, in terms of job position, may be working together.

the slides, and it was developed primarily by analyzing and restating the problem. This solution has worked for over 20 years.

The final effort in this phase is to develop a statement of the problem. How detailed this statement will be depends on the known constraints of the program being developed. The best problem state-ments are those that have emergent properties (Finke et al., 1992). They are written with the fewest restrictions possible and thus enhance, rath-er than inhibit, the generation of novel approaches. The problem state-ment should have clear implications for the key needs to be addressed and the key program elements to be manipulated. Consider the following two problems statements:

1. To develop a one-week special event to serve as the finale of a summer sports camp for boys and girls 8 to 12 years old.
2. To develop a program for working mothers with children 1 to 3 years of age to provide them with quality interaction time with their children.

The second example leaves the most room for creative discovery because less is specified in the problem statement. The constraints imposed by a specific program will partly determine how restrictive a problem statement must be. Too often, however, more is included than is necessary and creativity is inhibited.

PHASE 2. GENERATE APPROACHES

The major goal during this phase is to generate novel approaches. Some of the key creative efforts are: to be impractical and irrational, to be playful, to suspend judgment to facilitate a free flow of imagination, and to relax and spend time (Von Oech, 1990). There is some disagreement about how one's time is best spent in this phase. There is a trade-off between using techniques whose purpose is to force the generation of many ideas and those that focus efforts on producing a few good ideas. One theory suggests that if you generate enough ideas, you will surely include one good enough to solve your problem. However, a second school of thought suggests that you should be more contemplative, mull over ideas, and use critical judgment in order to generate a few good ideas. Buffington (1987) suggests that the best problem solvers "creatively worry and carry a problem around with them even while doing other tasks" (p. 121). Their effort is to produce quality over quantity. After all, you only need the one good idea that will solve your problem. You must develop the style that works for you.

Miller (1988) has identified two methods of thinking—linear and intuitive—either of which may lead to the generation of good approaches. Linear thinking helps us "organize information in ways that give us new 'entry points' for solving problems" (p. 116). Through the use of logical, incremental, sequential thinking, one is led to look for novel solutions. In contrast to this, intuitive techniques provide the means to make inferential insights that facilitate a conceptual leap to a whole solution.

Each programmer needs to develop a variety of techniques that will facilitate the discovery of approaches one would normally not have considered. We will provide you with some techniques that have worked for us. However, you need to go to the sources referenced at the end of this chapter to identify techniques that work for you, because the correct technique is a matter of personal style and the type of problem being addressed.

The use of matrix analysis (Miller, 1988) is an excellent example of linear thinking. The Programmer's Evaluation Cube (Exhibit 7-4 on page 118) is a three-dimensional matrix that can show the program-

Programmers need to develop a variety of techniques that will facilitate the discovery of new approaches.

Creative worrying—setting aside a period of time for the mind to completely wander.

12

mer, through logical extension, where to look for new program ideas. By cross tabulating life cycle stages, program formats, and activity types, one can document existing services and concurrently identify voids to be filled with new services.

Brainstorming is a common technique used in this phase to generate a large number of ideas. It is divergent thinking that is characterized by five distinct skills: (1) fluency—the ability to generate a large number of solutions; (2) flexibility—the ability to use many different approaches or strategies in solving a problem, and a willingness to change directions; (3) originality—the ability to produce clever, unique, and unusual solutions; (4) elaboration—the ability to expand, develop, particularize, and embellish ideas; and (5) irrationality—the ability to allow the right, irrational, creative side of the brain to dominate one's thinking. All divergent thinking techniques attempt to systematize the ability to accomplish these skills. However, realizing what we are attempting to accomplish enhances our ability to get the job done. See Exhibit 12-1 on page 214 for explanations of two divergent thinking techniques.

Rather than employing techniques that force us to innovate, to get unstuck, to get out of our routine, and to come up with the next logical extension, some of us succeed by engaging in the "creative worrying" identified earlier. One consciously sets aside a period of time for the mind to wander completely and to be free of the conceptual discipline imposed by analytical and linear thinking techniques.

Paul MacCready, who developed the Gossamer Albatross, the first human powered airplane to successfully cross the English Channel, was aware of how others were attempting to solve the problem by building a very small aircraft, barely capable of carrying a pilot. He sat the problem aside and went on vacation. While observing birds in flight, particularly birds soaring, it occurred to him that the solution was to make the plane large rather than small, so there would be enough wing surface to provide the lift needed to get the craft airborne. Super-light plastics provided the material needed to build a large, but still lightweight, aircraft. Once airborne, the craft was more of a glider than an aircraft. Yet technically, it was a man powered aircraft. Waiting, contemplating, and reinterpreting seemingly incongruent data are also successful strategies for developing novel approaches.

Analogies are examples of intuitive thinking. They require us to find a correspondence between dissimilar things by thinking in a way that makes the familiar strange and the strange familiar. Reconciling these incongruities produces insights into novel associations. For example, Von Oech (1990) recommends imagining how others would solve your problem. What analogies might result if Superman rather than you were going to develop the program? How might a surgeon, an airline pilot, or an army tank commander approach your program? What questions would they ask; what assumptions would they make; what tools, equipment, and places would they use; or what processes would they employ?

An analogy one of the authors has successfully used is to ask students to compare (identify the similarities and differences between) operating a recreation program and giving a stand-up comedy routine.

Some of their answers were:

They both play to an audience.
They have their ups and downs.
They must be novel to sustain interest.
Both a depend on a good leader.
Either can fail!
A good plan or script is essential for success in either.

A continuing effort throughout this phase is to keep focused on the correct problem. It is recommended that you continually define and redefine the problem based on new insights gained through your efforts in Phase 2. This process helps focus the unconscious thought process on the critical issues needed to successfully solve the problem. By doing this, the unconscious thinking will be sharpened and kept on target. The check may reveal some insight or unifying direction that will provide the adaptations or innovations needed to unify the direction of further thoughts. Often one needs to keep redefining the problem until a more suitable problem statement is developed. Complete Exercise 12-1 to obtain additional insight into how to redefine problem statements.

PHASE 3. EXPLORATION AND INTERPRETATION

The primary goal in this phase is to synthesize the approaches generated in Phase 2 into an acceptable solution. This is accomplished by exploring and interpreting the feasibility of the ideas generated in the previous phase for solving the programming problem. This, too, can be difficult. Sometimes we cannot recognize a solution even though it is before us, because we simply have not discovered the cognitive structure that will allow the pieces to come together as a solution. The creative efforts in this phase require rearranging ideas to make seemingly diverse elements converge. Various types of analogies and projective imagery (discussed in Chapter Eleven) are useful techniques for completing this phase.

Another method is to use several different analogical positions to shift the context of an experience in order to test the applicability of approaches. Try each of the following four analogies.

1. *Personal Analogy.* Place yourself at the center of the program, and identify how each novel approach would contribute to your leisure experience in a program. What are the paradoxes, the problems, or the conflicts? How might they be combined and resolved?

2. *Direct Analogy.* Draw a direct comparison to another event. How would the novel approaches you have developed be used in a trip to the moon? How would they be used to stage an arts festival or the Olympics? How would they be used in the NCAA Final Four tournament or the Super Bowl?

3. *Symbolic Analogy.* Try to find the symbolic essence of the approaches. For example, when one of the authors lived in Texas, the state celebrated its sesquicentennial. Since these events occur so infrequently, it isn't certain what events are appropriate for celebrating a sesquicentennial. The essence of the event, though, seemed to be to celebrate patriotism and political liberty. Most community celebrations included events similar to those normally operated on the Fourth of July. There were symbolic similarities between the two events.

4. *Fantasy Analogy.* In this case, you may go beyond objective reality into fantasy. What would the program be like if it were operated for the Flintstone family? What would a Star Wars production of your program be like?

You need to accept that there may be more than one right answer to your program problem.

You may also expand the conceptual space used to frame the program problem. For example, instead of conceptualizing a citywide annual softball tournament, think that you are planning a national or international tournament. If you think of a larger, more encompassing event, new contexts and viewpoints may emerge.

After you have given this your best effort, get dissatisfied with everything. Change it all to see what happens! Osborn's (1963) manipulative verbs can be applied to help accomplish this. Ask the following: What if I adapt, modify, magnify, minify, substitute, rearrange, reverse, or combine the concepts? Applying these verbs will rearrange, combine, and recombine your approaches to help investigate their feasibility.

When do you stop? Von Oech (1990) offers important advice about this. You need to accept that there may be more than one right answer. Much of our education and training is organized around finding the correct answer to a question, as if there is only one! Because of this, he recommends finding the second right answer. Thus, the effort continues until one finds a second solution that is the approximate equivalent of the first right answer. If you find one that is better, you keep going, of course!

PHASE 4. INNOVATION

The primary goal during this phase is to be innovative and shape the proposed solution into a feasible program. One must first verify that one's final proposal truly solves the program design problem. Then one must screen the program to determine its feasibility for implementation. Discoveries during this phase may require some redesign of the program or development of a new method of operation.

Simonds (1961) has designed five preplanned scenarios that can be used to verify the conceptual harmony of the final design. This harmony results from the integration of all working relationships, functions, and elements so that each complements the other and the overall design. During this process, one will often again use projective imagery to vicariously experience the program and to model its operation.

Simonds's five scenarios are: (1) outward and inward plan progression, (2) expansion and contraction of the plan concept, (3) satellite plan verification, (4) integral planning, and (5) proving the plan.

In examining the outward and inward progression of a design, one must consider the effect of each design element from the innermost point of its generation to its final outcome. Conversely, one must make certain that each design element included in the final design is a logical conclusion of the outermost components and implications of the overall design. For example, in outward progression, the designer would need to examine the effect on the participant's overall experience of waiting in line for 30 minutes before an event. What effect would this have on the participant's overall leisure experience? It is well documented that standing in line creates anxiety. This type of anxiety would interfere with a leisure experience, so some other method of queuing would need to be developed in order to meet the design goal.

In inward progression, one needs to consider the outermost components of the design and logically progress into the most minute details of the design to make certain that they are consistent. For example, if a programmer had advertised a noncompetitive volleyball tournament, but then staged it in a gym with a center arena, spectator seating surrounding a center court, and a public address system announcing the score after each point, the operational details of the event would be inconsistent with the overall design concept. Although these are extreme examples, failure to verify the details of a plan in this thorough, detailed manner often leads to operations that are inconsistent with original design goals.

In expansion and contraction of the plan, the designer expands the areas of consideration to the farthest extensional aspects of the plan and contracts each part down to its most trivial detail. In doing this, the designer is attempting to develop a worst-case and best-case scenario of actual program operation in order to anticipate and plan for the most probable events. Consider the role of weather in the design of an outdoor program. If the possibility of good weather is extended to rainy

In expansion and contraction of the plan, attempt to develop a worst-case and best-case scenario of actual program operation.

Exercise 12-2: Let's Get Creative!

Directions: Read the following problem statement and work through the creative design process model.
Answer the questions as you go. **Use a PENCIL!**

Problem Definition	Generation of Approaches
Write problem statement here:	Brainwrite a list of ideas. Suspend judgment, be impractical and irrational, be playful, etc.

→

Generation of Approaches

1.
2.
3.
4.
5.
6.
7.
8.
9.
10.

What don't we know about the problem statement?

1.
2.
3.

What do we know about the problem statement?

1.
2.
3.

Given the above list, do you want to redefine the problem statement? (circle one)

Yes (if yes, rewrite below)   No

New statement:

Rules and Fools:
Rule:

Fool 1:

Fool 2:

Fool 3:

Exercise 12-2: (continued)

Exploration and Interpretation

→

Test out your favorite approach from the following four perspectives:

Personal analogy (imagine yourself doing the event)
1. What's fun about it?
2. What's potentially bothersome? _____

Direct analogy (compare this to another event)
1. Name other event _____
2. Would this be **more** or **less** fun (circle one)? Why? _____
3. Would this idea be **more** or **less** challenging? Why?

Symbolic analogy
1. Name the symbolic elements in your idea. _____

2. Name a program with similar symbolic elements.

3. Which idea is better? Why? _____

Fantasy analogy
1. Choose two fantasy populations.

2. Is one of these a possible theme for your idea or not? Why?

Given these explorations, do you want to select another idea or stick with the one you've chosen? If you switch, erase the above and start again.

Innovation

Which idea do you want to consider given your progress through this creative design model?

Now go to the Program Screening Instrument at the end of Chapter 12 and work through the form with your idea.

Evaluation of this learning exercise:
1. How has this exercise helped you develop your creative skills?

_____

2. Which part(s) was/were most helpful regarding your ability to be creative?

_____

Program Characteristic	Score			
	4	3	2	1
	Excellent	Good	Fair	Poor
1 Provides Benefits to Target Patrons				
2 Is Significantly Different from Other Programs				
3 Can Be Produced Economically				
4 Can Be Marketed Economically				
5 Fits In with Rec. Dept. Image				
6 Rec. Dept. Personnel Have The Needed Skills to Produce and Promote It				
7 Rec. Dept. Personnel Have Time Needed to Produce and Promote It				
8 Adequate Facilities Are Available				
9 Contributes to Agency Mission				
10 Material Resources Are Readily Available				

Subtotals

Total Score   [   ]   Programs scoring 28 or more points are innovative and feasible

Adapted from a form used by the U.S. Navy Recreational Services Unit.

Figure 12-3: Program Screening Instrument

weather, how does this affect program design? Will it alter the equipment used, the location, or the date, or will it require that the program be called off? What if too many or too few participants show up? Does this need to be known in advance? What are the implications of either of these scenarios? If this expansion and contraction technique is applied thoroughly, it should raise many questions that need to be planned for during the design process.

In using the satellite plan verification scenario, one examines the relationship of each part of the plan to the whole plan. Each element of the plan design must be in harmony with the whole design concept. In leisure program design, consideration must be given to the wholeness of a program, including aspects such as the procedure for registration, as well as cleanup procedures, the location and timing of refreshments, and so on. To be thorough, the programmer should examine the choices made for each of the six elements of a situated activity system discussed in Chapter Three to make certain that each contributes appropriately and complementarily to solving the identified design problem.

Integral planning puts further order and conceptual harmony into the program design with a final check of the key program frames, the key activating elements that are assumed to be central to each frame, the key transitions planned, and the appropriateness of their sequential order. Some frames and transitions and some of the situating elements are more critical to accomplishing the design goals than others. This is the final opportunity to take steps to assure that these key design features are incorporated into the design and the operational plan (which will be discussed in Chapter Thirteen) to maximize the probability that the experience intended will occur.

As one example, let us look again at the Easter Egg Hunt discussed previously. Although there were many considerations, two key design frames were an integral part of this event. First, each child needed to find an Easter egg, and secondly, parents needed to be able to watch their children hunt but be kept from helping them. Once these key design frames were identified, all other design elements considered for inclusion were evaluated by the degree to which they would maximize the probability of these two elements occurring. In integral planning, then, one attempts to make certain that the elements integral to accomplishing the overall design goals are included in the design.

Finally, Simonds (1961) suggests proving the plan to determine if the design created does indeed correspond to the original design concept. The designer must aim to make the final solution an accurate reflection of the original problem statement. An easy mistake to make when manipulating elements is to invent new needs, to inflate the importance of one, or to deemphasize another. Once again, the test for this is to vicariously experience the program step by step as if actually participating in it, seeing it, and touching it. Through projective imagery, programmers must imagine themselves not as designers, but as participants—an older participant, a younger participant, or even a participant from another race or socioeconomic background.

Throughout the verification process, the programmer must be faithful to the original programming problem. If the design does not solve the original problem, you have not succeeded. Accomplishing the origi-

Creativity is an iterative process used to identify novel approaches to programs and innovative methods of operating them.

nal design goal involves correlating established and prioritized relationships of the major determinants (design elements, goals, objectives, and so forth) with the whole. The detailed scenarios just discussed will direct the designer in successfully searching for all relationships and interactions among the six situating elements of program production. Now try Exercise 12-2 on pages 220-221.

The final effort in this phase is to screen programs to make certain it is feasible to implement them and that they are truly innovative; that is, sufficiently different from current offerings. Figure 12-3 on page 223 is an instrument for conducting this screening. Each of the components on the instrument is scored and then the scores are summed. Programs that score a total of 28 points or more are considered to be feasible to implement and innovative enough to be worth the effort.

CONCLUSION

Creativity is an iterative process used to identify novel approaches to programs and innovative methods for operating them. It is used to create alternative solutions for programming problems and should be a routine part of the program design and planning steps of the Program Development Cycle.

There are four distinct phases of the creative process, with identifiable techniques in each to facilitate one's efforts. Throughout the process, one must continuously return to the problem itself to make certain it is correctly defined, and that the assumptions one has made about the constraints are valid. In many cases, the selection of techniques used to facilitate one's effort is a matter of personal choice and style. Thus, the programmer must develop a kit-bag of techniques that may be applied until one that works in a given situation is identified.

Creative program design is hard work and requires the application of many diverse skills. However, if the techniques and processes presented in this chapter are thoroughly applied to identified program design problems, programmers will be able to develop innovative programs for their constituents. Good luck!

REFERENCES

Ackoff, R. L., & Vergara, E. (1981). Creativity in problem solving and planning: A review. *European Journal of Operational Research,* (7), 1-13.

Buffington, P. W. (1987, February). *Sky: Delta Airlines Inflight Magazine.* Miami, FL: Halsey.

Finke, R. A., Ward, T. B., & Smith, S. M. (1992). *Creative cognition: Theory, research, and applications.* Cambridge, MA: The MIT Press.

Howard, N. A. (1985, March). How to generate bright new ideas. *Success,* p. 54.

Kaufmann, G. (1988). Mental imagery and problem solving. In M. Denis, J. Engelkamp, & J. T. E. Richardson (Eds.), *Cognitive and neuropsychological approaches to mental imagery* (pp. 231–239). Dordrecht, the Netherlands: Martinus Nijhoff.

Miller, W. C. (1988). Techniques for stimulating new ideas: A matter of fluency. In R. L. Kuhn (Ed.), *Handbook for creative innovative managers*, New York: McGraw Hill.

Osborn, A. F. (1963). *Applied imagination*. New York: Scribner & Sons.

Simonds, J. O. (1961). *Landscape architecture*. New York: McGraw-Hill.

Von Oech, R. (1990). *A whack on the side of the head: How can you be more creative?* New York: Warner Books.

Wallas, G. (1926). *The art of thought*. New York: Harcourt, Brace.

Ward, B. (1985, June). Centers of Imagination. *Sky: Delta Airlines Inflight Magazine*. Miami, FL: Halsey.

ADDITIONAL READINGS

12

Alexander, C. (1970, March). Changes in form. *Architectural Design*, 122–125.

Broadbent, G. H. (1966). Creativity. In S. A. Gregory (Ed.), *The design method*. London: Butterworths.

Gordon, W. J. (1961). *Synectics: The development of creative capacity*. New York: Harper and Brothers.

Howard, N. A., Hoffer, W., Ingber, D., Raudsepp, E., Niemark, J., & Johnson, H. (1985, March). Creativity: A special report. *Success*, 54–61.

Jones, J. C. (1980). *Design methods: Seeds of human futures*. New York: Wiley.

Smith, E. T. (1985, September 30). Are you creative? *Business Week*, 80–84.

Weisberg, R. W. (1986). *Genius and other myths*. New York: W. H. Freeman.

Stage C: Operational Strategies

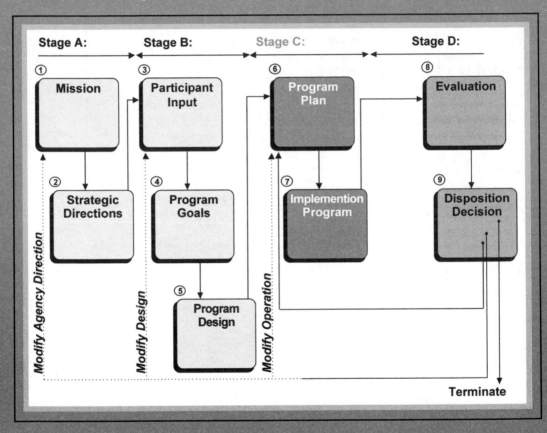

Stage A: Stage B: Stage C: Stage D:

① Mission

③ Participant Input

⑥ Program Plan

⑧ Evaluation

② Strategic Directions

④ Program Goals

⑦ Implemention Program

⑨ Disposition Decision

⑤ Program Design

Modify Agency Direction

Modify Design

Modify Operation

Terminate

Part IV
Operational Strategies

In Part IV—Stage C, Operational Strategies, the program design that has been developed for a targeted population is written so that it may be shared with all who will help implement the program. When the plan is prepared, the realities and limitations of agency resources must be dealt with and the program design altered to fit the resources. During this stage, all of the preparations for staging the program are completed and the program is implemented.

Chapter Thirteen explains how to write a program plan. The next six chapters all deal with staging the program. You will recall from previous discussions that this is the step where programmers spend the majority of their effort. Thus, the need for multiple chapters to explain the many tasks needed to stage a program. Spending time on this step is easy to justify because it involves completing tasks that have an obvious, direct relationship with producing program services. However, programmers must guard against allowing this step to dominate their time to the exclusion of other steps in the cycle.

Furthermore, there is a tendency to believe that all program failures are traceable to inadequate implementation. Inadequate implementation could be the cause of failure, but there are also other possible explanations. For example, failure could be traceable to an inadequate analysis of needs and the consequent development of a program service for which there is simply no demand. The programmer is cautioned, then, that spending too much time on program implementation and too little time on the other steps of the Program Development Cycle can create problems for the programming agency.

Chapter Fourteen includes the techniques normally used in recreation agencies to promote program services. How to queue and register individuals is covered in Chapter Fifteen. Staffing and supervising program services are discussed in Chapter Sixteen. Issues involved in developing an agency's program pricing policy is the subject of Chapter Seventeen. Methods for determining program costs are outlined in Chapter Eighteen, and how to establish a price for a program is developed in Chapter Nineteen.

Healthy Cities Tutoring Program
Photo courtesy of City of San Carlos Parks and Recreation Department, San Carlos, CA

Preparing the Program Plan

STEP 6 : PROGRAM PLAN

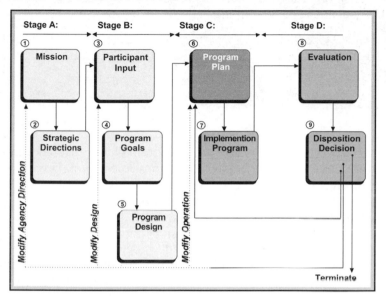

KEY TERMS

**Program Plan
Management Plan
Flow Chart
Animation Plan
Program
  Scheduling
Facility
  Scheduling**

In most instances, programmers will be unable to produce a program single-handedly. To produce a program as the designer intends, one must communicate details of the design to other staff members who will help implement it. Through a written program plan, programmers communicate the role of each person involved in producing a program. Clearly communication through the program plan is therefore necessary for successful implementation.

The written program plan is analogous to the architect's blueprint or the project manager's network diagram. Through a blueprint, an architect communicates to various trades people their roles and functions in completing a structure as designed by the architect. Project managers in many professional areas, such as construction planning, movie production, and political campaigns, plan to execute projects with a written plan that outlines all of the activities to be accomplished and the development of a timeline for their completion.

Once the program design is well thought out and clear in the programmer's mind (this is accomplished with the techniques covered in Chapters Ten, Eleven, and Twelve), a written program plan is prepared. Although one might believe that the program is well designed and clear, actually writing down the plan in detail often exposes design flaws that must

*To produce a
program as
the designer
intends, one
must commu-
nicate details
of the design
to other staff
members who
will help
implement it.*

This chapter addresses the *activities/processes* portion of outcome-based program-ming. The corresponding component in the Benefits-Based Programming model is *daily activities and procedures*. To implement BBP, programmers should develop their daily activities and procedures by addressing the topics in the *operations details of the program plan* section of this chapter with guidance from the *programming principles* outlined in Figure 4-2. In designing the daily activities and procedures for a program, the programmer is considering and defining the six elements of the situated activity system which includes animating the program.

be corrected. One benefit of writing a program plan is that flaws can be discovered and corrected before actual implementation. Even though the planning step is illustrated as separate from the design step, one will often iterate between the two as the plan is written and the need for redesign becomes apparent.

Successful programs are operated or experienced four times. First, they are vicariously experienced by the designer during the design step. Second, in writing the program plan, the designer must again vicarious-ly experience the program and develop the interaction scenarios nec-essary for animating. Third, the program is actually operated. Fourth, in evaluating the program, the designer relives it vicariously through regressive imagery, and the program is modeled with proposed modifi-cations using projective imagery.

The written plan is a working document that is subject to ongoing revision. It is written to serve one or more of the following purposes:

- to provide a record of information about the current status of the program,
- to provide a record of the resources used to operate the pro-gram, or
- to provide a reference for use during future operations of the program. (Adapted from Kliem, 1986).

THE PROGRAM PLAN

The following is a brief explanation of what is involved in each of the steps numbered in the program plan outline presented in Exhibit 13-1.

PROGRAM TITLE

This section should include the name of the program, the sponsor-ing agency, and a brief, introductory descriptive paragraph indicating the who, what, when, where, why, and how of the program. After read-

Exhibit 13-1: The Program Plan

1. Program Title
2. Agency Mission and Programming Philosophy
3. Need for the Program
4. Design Goals of the Program
5. Operation Details:
   a. Venue Arrangements
   b. Special Arrangements
   c. Inclusion Plan
   d. Equipment, Supplies, and Material Needs
   e. Promotion Plan
   f. Budget and Pricing Information
   g. Registration Plan
   h. Staffing and Staff Orientation Plan
   i. Management Plan
   j. Cancellation Plan
   k. Set-Up
   l. Risk Management Plan
   m. Animation Plan
   n. Program Wrap-Up
6. Program Evaluation
7. Disposition Decision Plan

Note: The authors are grateful to J.C. Crossley and L. Jamieson (1997) for some of the concepts and ideas that are included in this exhibit.

ing this paragraph, the reader should have basic familiarity with the leisure experience that the program is to create.

AGENCY MISSION AND PROGRAMMING PHILOSOPHY

A statement of the agency's mission and its programming philosophy should be included in the plan to make it apparent why the agency is involved in producing this program.

NEED FOR THE PROGRAM

A statement of the need for this program should be included. It should answer the question: Why is this program needed, and how was this need determined?

DESIGN GOALS OF THE PROGRAM

Specific statements about what this program is supposed to accomplish should be written. The design goals should specify what leisure experiences the program is supposed to create and the participant outcomes expected. If the programmer is using the Benefits-Based Programming model, the benefits intended for participants should be specified. The design goals also serve to guide resource allocation. A rationale for how these goals are consistent with the agency's goals and objectives should also be included.

OPERATION DETAILS

The operational details included in this section should form a detailed set of instructions about how the program is to be implemented and operated. There is always a question of how much detail to include. Unfortunately, programmers too often provide so little detail that only someone who has previously observed the program being operated could actually use the "details" to reproduce the program. At the very minimum, one must provide enough details so that another professional programmer from a different agency could reproduce the program. Generally, if there is any doubt about the need to include additional detail or description, include it.

VENUE ARRANGEMENTS

Venues are locales used to stage leisure experiences and include buildings, special facilities, and park areas. Examples of frequently used program areas are recreation centers, gymnasiums, theatres, or parklands; playgrounds or athletic fields; or water resources such as a swimming pool, lake, or beach. Any unique facility attributes needed for the program should be noted.

How arrangements may be made to obtain the venue needed should be specified in the plan. In many cases, the programmer may be using agency venues, in which case the program will need to be placed on the schedule for the venue. In some cases, venues owned by other agencies may be needed. At the very least, the programmer is likely to need to schedule the venue. In other cases, a reservation may need to be secured, a deposit made, or a contract obtained.

Maps that indicate the location of the venue and diagrams of the areas and facilities should also be included in the plan.

SPECIAL ARRANGEMENTS

Some programs require special arrangements with agencies or businesses outside of the recreation agency. It is advantageous to make such arrangements or reservations early in the planning process to ensure availability. Contractual agreements are commonly used when making provisions for transportation, entertainment, and concessions. Other arrangements may require the procurement of camping permits, insurance, and special maintenance services.

> *One must provide enough operational details so that another programmer could reproduce the program.*

> *Venues are locales used to stage leisure experiences and include buildings, special facilities, and park areas.*

INCLUSION PLAN

Individuals with disabilities have the right to participate in programs with the general population. Recent research has demonstrated that communities are increasing the number of inclusive options for individuals with disabilities (Devine & Kotowski, 1999). Agencies are required to provide reasonable accommodation in all programs for those with disabilities. In a recent survey, agencies ranked the lack of funding for providing these opportunities, constraints on staff due to a lack of adequate support resources, the lack of an adequately trained staff, and negative staff attitudes as the four highest limitations that prevented them from implementing inclusive services (Devine & Kotowski, 1999).

Accommodations that reduce the barriers to participation may be provided in many different ways, depending on the disability of the individual desiring to participate and the type of program service being offered. The types of accommodation most frequently provided by agencies include pool lifts, the relocation of classes to accessible facilities, the provision of adaptive equipment, the provision of sign interpreters, and the development of inclusion plans (reported by 50 percent or more of the agencies in a recent survey conducted by Devine & Kotowski, 1999). Until the specific disabilities of individuals who wish to participate are identified, it is difficult to develop this part of the plan. However, in advance of such requests, programmers must help develop the following: a sensitivity to providing inclusive services in the agency and community, the policy infrastructure needed to support inclusion services, adequate funding to support these services, and the resources likely to be needed to provide inclusive services. The concept of inclusiveness is discussed here to alert the programmer to this possible contingency that may need to be dealt with in planning any program service.

EQUIPMENT, SUPPLIES, AND MATERIAL NEEDS

A list of equipment, supplies, and materials needed to operate the program should be included in the plan. Equipment is a nonconsumable product used to participate in leisure; thus, it includes items that can be used more than once—usually for several operations of a program. Equipment covers everything from tents and basketballs to lifeguard rescue buoys. Supplies are the items used in program operations that are consumed, such as chalk, paper, paint, writing implements, clay, food, paper cups, and coffee filters. Materials are those items that are used to construct something of a permanent nature, such as cement or lumber. Any special supply or material needs should be noted and their availability and source indicated. Supplies and materials that may need to be acquired through a bidding process or that take some lead time to obtain should be identified.

PROMOTION PLAN

In this section, the target market for the program and the plan for how the program will be promoted to this market is explicated. Details about the types of promotional materials, their distribution, and the

13

...communities are increasing the number of inclusive options for individuals with disabilities...

timeline for implementing the promotion plan should be included. How to develop promotional materials is discussed in Chapter Fourteen.

BUDGET AND PRICING INFORMATION

The budget for the program, including revenues, income projections, expenses, and how the price for participation was determined, should be included. How to budget and price programs is discussed in Chapters Eighteen and Nineteen.

REGISTRATION PLAN

If registration is required, how it will be done should be detailed in this section. When registration will occur, who will conduct it, where it will occur, and how it will be conducted should all be specified. If there are any special registration requirements for this program, they should be specified. For example, only individuals who hold American Camping Association certification as Campcrafters may be permitted to register for a wilderness camping program. How to conduct registration is discussed in detail in Chapter Fifteen.

STAFFING AND STAFF ORIENTATION PLAN

The number and qualifications of the staff needed to operate the program should be specified. How the staff is to be hired, oriented, and trained should also be specified. Staffing is discussed in Chapter Sixteen. Similarly, if volunteers are necessary for the program, a plan should be developed for their recruitment, training, and supervision.

MANAGEMENT PLAN

If an employee is unable to lead or supervise a workshop, class, or another scheduled event, contingency plans should always be in place.

Programs are rarely implemented by a single individual. Program operation most often requires the coordinated effort of many individuals. Program implementation is most analogous to project management. According to Moder, Phillips, and Davis (1983), "A project is a set of tasks or activities related to the achievement of some planned objective, normally where the objective is unique or nonrepetitive" (p. 3). A project is not repeated in an identical manner, as is the case in product production. Flow charts identify the activities needed to complete a project and to schedule their completion in an acceptable time span, given a finite set of resources. How this is accomplished in programming is discussed later in this chapter under the heading, "Management Plan."

CANCELLATION PLAN

A plan detailing what will happen if the program is cancelled should also be included. Many alternatives could be considered, but contingencies need to be specified. Cancellations are often due to weather, but can also be due to illness or some other unforeseen incident. If an employee is unable to lead or supervise a workshop, class, or another scheduled event, contingency plans should always be in place that specify possible substitutes so that the program does not have to be cancelled. However, some programs require the presence of employees who possess special qualifications or certifications, such as a lifeguard. In this type of situation, where customer safety is at stake and there are no qualified substitutes, cancellation is the safest option.

For outdoor events, there could be an alternative indoor location. Often, there is simply an alternate date for outdoor programs that are cancelled because of unfavorable weather. If weather conditions are unsettled, the programmer should delay making a decision to cancel a program until the last moment possible. If bad weather clears shortly before the scheduled starting time, patrons will appear and expect service. To avoid bad public relations, the program staff must be ready to operate the event or be at the event location to redirect patrons to an alternate place or date. The major point here is that the programmer must cancel an event and manage its cancellation—events will not cancel themselves.

For events for which a fee was paid, it is best to let patrons know how their fee will be refunded at the time of cancellation. Failure to inform patrons about refunds at the cancellation of an event will lead to many individual inquiries.

SET-UP

Detailed plans for program set-up should be specified. It is essential that a venue be set- up and ready for operations when patrons arrive. However, depending on the program and venue, set-up can be time-consuming and may involve many individuals. Therefore, programmers should allow plenty of lead-time and, if needed, allow for plenty of assistance to complete program set-up.

Set-up may involve creating a specific atmosphere in a particular location, such as decorating a gymnasium with a tropical theme for a teen dance. It may also involve collecting equipment and supplies for a program, such as a day hike. For special events, programmers may need to request set-up assistance from the maintenance staff through the use of a work request form. Although these vary from agency to agency, work request forms generally contain the same information. The person completing the form fills in the date and time of the event and provides a detailed description and diagram of the work to be done. It is important to provide explicit details. If set-up arrangements are critical to the success of a program, it is best for the programmer to be present during set-up.

If set-up arrangements are critical to the success of a program, it is best for the programmer to be present during set-up.

RISK MANAGEMENT PLAN

Although many recreation and leisure services agencies employ risk management coordinators to manage the overall safety and well-being of participants and agency personnel, there is also a general expectation that people must assume some risks in recreation participation. Risk management coordinators work with board members, administrators, programmers, and leaders in preparing risk management plans.

Programmers should address the following risk management components in their plans: reporting and record keeping, facilities inspection and hazard abatement procedures, participant safety briefing and preparation, staff supervision, and emergency procedures (Kraus &

Exhibit 13-2: Incorporating Risk Management Components into the Program Plan

Below are examples of how programmers might address risk management components.

Reporting and Record Keeping—Programmers should make sure that:
- Participants or parents/guardians have read and signed all required forms, including waivers, releases, and assumption of risk.
- Program leaders know where to find and are capable of completing and filing all risk management forms, including accident and incident reports.

Facilities Inspections and Hazard Abatement—Programmers should make sure that:
- Appropriate staff inspect all required equipment and facilities before each session.
- Broken equipment is identified and either repaired or removed immediately.
- Routine maintenance procedures on the program area are completed in a timely fashion.

Participant Safety Briefing—Programmers should make sure that:
- Appropriate participant behavioral expectations regarding the program and equipment usage are established and enforced.
- Participants are informed of behavioral expectations.

Staff Supervision—Programmers should make sure that:
- Programs have adequate staff/participant ratios.
- Staff understand sexual harassment laws.
- Staff know their supervisory responsibilities pursuant to the program.

Emergency Procedures—Programmers should make sure that:
- Emergency procedures are clearly posted.
- Program leaders know what to do in case of an emergency.
- If appropriate, participants know what to do in case of an emergency.

Note: The authors are grateful to R.G. Kraus and J.E. Curtis (2000) for some of the concepts and ideas that are included in this exhibit.

Exhibit 13-3: Checklist for Implementation of a Summer Day Camp Program

Major Function	Task	Time Required to Complete (Weeks)	Deadline
Program Design	Design program	2	1/15
Site Selection	Select sites	2	1/30
Staffing	Prepare position announcements	2	2/28
	Announce staff positions	1	4/1
	Prepare staff manual	6	3/30
	Interview applicants	2	4/21
Promotion	Plan promotional flyer	2	2/1
	Send flyer to printer	1	3/1
	Distribute flyers	1	3/30
	Submit news release	1	5/15
Equipment, Supplies, and Materials	Research suppliers	1	3/1
	Order equipment, supplies, and materials	1	3/15
	Monitor equipment, supplies, and materials (reorder if needed)	3	4/15
	Deliver to sites	1	6/18
Registration	Plan registration process	2	4/30
	Program registration	1	5/15
	Assign campers	1	5/30
Staff Training	Staff training	1	6/18
Program Operation	Summer Neighborhood Day Camp Program	8	8/13
Evaluation	Plan evaluation methods	1	5/15
	Collect evaluation data	1	8/13
	Evaluation report	1	8/20

Exhibit 13-4: Flow Chart for Summer Day Camp Program

Program Design   • 1/15—Design program

Site Selection   • 1/30—Select sites

Staffing   • 2/28—Prepare position announcements

                             • 4/1—Announce staff positions

                  • 3/30—Prepare staff manual

                       • 4/21—Interview applicants

Promotion   • 2/1—Plan promotional flyer

                  • 3/1—Send flyer to printer

                  • 3/30—Distribute flyers

                       • 5/15—Submit News Release

	Jan	Feb	Mar	Apr	May	Jun	Jul	Aug

Equipment,   • 3/1—Research suppliers

 Supplies, and   •3/15—Place order

 Materials   • 4/15—Monitor order

                      • 6/18—Deliver to sites

Registration   • 4/30—Plan registration process

                   • 5/15—Conduct program registration

                   • 5/30—Assign campers

Staff Training   • 6/18—Conduct staff training

Program Operation   • 8/13—Camp

Evaluation   • 5/15—Plan evaluation methods

                      • 8/13—Collect data

                   • 8/20—Prepare
                         evaluation report

Curtis, 2000). To see examples of how programmers might cover each of these components, see Exhibit 13-2 on page 236.

ANIMATION PLAN

A description of the key animation frames, transitions, and scenarios should be included in the written program plan. How this is dealt with in a recreation program plan is included in a later section of this chapter.

PROGRAM WRAP-UP

In this step, programmers make sure equipment is returned and venues are returned to their pre-event state. Thank you letters, a post-event news release, and other follow-up correspondence may also be prepared and sent. This step may also include the distribution of awards, trophies, and/or certificates.

PROGRAM EVALUATION PLAN

The specific instruments and techniques for evaluating the program should be outlined. Techniques and instruments for conducting program evaluation are included in Chapters Twenty and Twenty-One.

DISPOSITION DECISION PLAN

The plan should include a basis on which the future of the program will be determined. How this is accomplished is detailed in Chapter Twenty-Two.

THE MANAGEMENT PLAN

Once the program has been conceptualized and designed, it is necessary to develop a management plan that outlines how the event will be implemented. The Flow Chart Method (FCM) (Murphy & Howard, 1977) has been discussed in the recreation programming literature as an effective method for managing the implementation of recreation programs. The method provides a specific technique for identifying, sequentially ordering, and prioritizing the tasks that must be completed to implement a program.

FLOW CHART METHOD

The FCM provides an elementary network diagram (Murphy & Howard, 1977; Russell, 1982) that can be used to manage a program.

According to Kliem (1986), "A network diagram is a graphic representation of a series of activities and events depicting the various aspects of a project and the order in which these activities and events must occur" (p. 35). Used properly, the FCM will help reduce the possibility of careless mistakes or omissions in the program planning process. The FCM has been identified by Russell (1982) as the most useful to her as a practitioner. It is a management technique that will serve the needs of most recreation programs.

An explanation of the steps that must be completed to implement the FCM for a Summer Day Camp program follow. How they would be organized into a checklist is illustrated in Exhibit 13-3 on page 237. How they would be placed on a flow chart is illustrated in Exhibit 13-4 on page 238.

DEVELOPING THE CHECKLIST

1. Divide the program into its major functions. These major functions generally include staff, facilities, promotion, program design, registration, and so on.

2. Analyze each major function independently by generating a list of necessary tasks or activities that must be addressed. It is not required in this step to place the tasks in any particular order. A list of the staff functions could include updating the staff manual, recruiting, interviewing, hiring, conducting orientation, and evaluating.

3. Prioritize each activity within the major functions by projecting the amount of time required to complete the task and establishing a deadline for that task (Exhibit 13-3). For example, for the staff function, the task of interviewing applicants will take two weeks to complete, and the deadline for that activity has been determined as April 21 of the current year.

Exhibit 13-5: Animation Plan for Balloon Ascension

Program Design Goals

- To provide a non-skill-based balloon flying contest on the morning of the Fourth of July.
- To provide an event that will attract family units and foster parent–child interaction.

Schedule

The Balloon Ascension is scheduled for 11:00 a.m. Staff should report at 6:00 a.m. to begin filling balloons with helium. Gates will open at 10:00 a.m. Most patrons will begin arriving at 10:30 a.m. Taped patriotic music will begin at 10:00. The event will be completed by 11:30 a.m.

Staff Orientation

Patrons who attend the Balloon Ascension will most likely be family units, so there will be many parents with small children. There will also be unaccompanied children from about 12 to 15 years of age. Since this is primarily a family event, there are usually few discipline problems. Patrons come fully expecting to be able to help their children launch their balloons in a pleasant, enjoyable atmosphere. Your job is to help them in a low-key, courteous manner to obtain a card and a balloon, tie the card to the balloon, and be in the appropriate area to launch their balloon on time.

Because we have a large number of staff members at this event in order to personalize leader–patron contact, we will not use the P.A. system except to help create an upbeat atmosphere with taped patriotic music and to announce the final instructions and countdown to launch. You will give directions and encourage interactions by speaking to small groups of individuals and keeping them informed about what must occur.

The day will probably be very hot. You may become easily irritated with patrons who may not understand instructions or procedures. It is very likely that you will have to explain the same point over and over. Be sure you know how the event will operate and be prepared to answer questions. Patrons' pleasure at the event will depend on your courteous treatment of them. It will require effort to remain pleasant, but all staff members are expected to do so.

(continued on p. 242)

Exhibit 13-5: (continued)

Scenario of Frames and Transitions (with Key Elements)

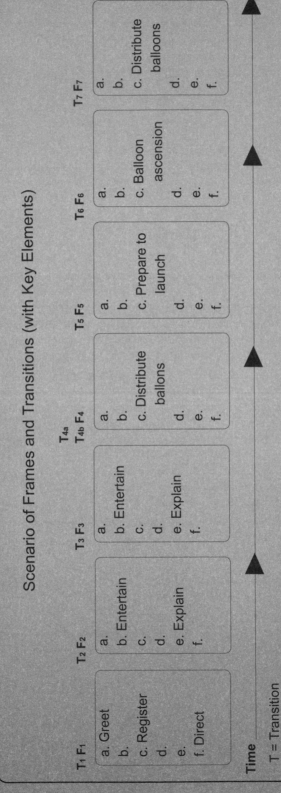

T_1 F_1	T_2 F_2	T_3 F_3	T_{4a} T_{4b} F_4	T_5 F_5	T_6 F_6	T_7 F_7
a. Greet	a.	a.	a.	a.	a.	a.
b.	b. Entertain	b. Entertain	b.	b.	b.	b.
c. Register	c.	c.	c. Distribute	c. Prepare to	c. Balloon	c. Distribute
d.	d.	d.	ballons	launch	ascension	balloons
e.	e. Explain	e. Explain	d.	d.	d.	d.
f. Direct	f.	f.	e.	e.	e.	e.
			f.	f.	f.	f.

Time

T = Transition

F = Frames (a = People; b = Physical Setting; c = Leisure Objects; d = Rules; e = Relationships; f = Animation)

An explanation of each transition and frame is given on the following pages.

Exhibit 13-5: (continued)

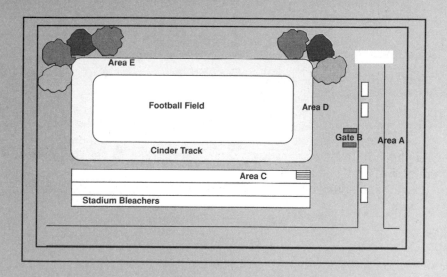

Animation of Program Production Elements

T1   Patrons are directed to the tables in Area A by staff assigned to this area.

F1

a.   Patrons are greeted at the tables by staff.

b.

c.   Postcards are completed for each participant.

d.

e.   Staff will make an effort to address family units.

f.   People are directed to Gate B.

T2   At Gate B patrons are directed to be seated in Area C.

F2[a]   For those in Area C:

a.   Families are seated together and are advised by staff in the area that at approximately 10:45 they will proceed to the track and be given their balloon, which must be tied securely to the card.

b.   The U.S. flag will be flying from the flagpole, and the whole area decorated with red, white, and blue banners and streamers.

c.   Patriotic music will be played and flyers announcing the remainder of the community-sponsored Fourth of July events will be distributed.

d.   Emphasize that everyone will launch their balloons at the same time, on signal after a countdown.

e.   Encourage parents to help make certain that balloons are tied securely to cards.

f.

Exhibit 13-5: (continued)

T3   At approximately 10:45, Gate B is closed and patrons arriving from Area A are queued outside Gate B.

F3   For those queued in Area B:

a.   Staff will reassure the families in line that they will be admitted and that there are sufficient balloons for all.

b.

c.   Patriotic music will be played and flyers announcing the remainder of the community-sponsored Fourth of July events will be distributed.

d.   Emphasize that everyone will launch their balloons at the same time, on signal after a countdown.

e.   Encourage parents to help make certain that balloons are tied securely to cards.

f.

T4[a]   Staff will move patrons seated in Area C, row by row, to Area D.

T4[b]   Once all of the patrons in Area C have been moved through Area D to Area E, Gate B will be opened and those in the queue outside Gate B will be moved through Area D to Area E. This may occur sooner if the queue out side Gate B gets too long and the staff in Area D seem to have the capacity to handle more patrons.

F4.   At Area D:

a.   Staff will greet families when possible. Helium-filled balloons will be distrib-uted to all participants with cards—only one per participant.

b.

c.   Getting balloons and tying cards to balloons are the focus of attention. Patri-otic music continues.

d.   Emphasize that everyone will launch their balloons at the same time, on signal after a countdown.

e.   Encourage parents to help make certain that balloons are tied securely to cards.

f.   Everyone must be moved through Area D and onto Area E.

T5.   It is very important that staff effectively and courteously move the first patrons from Area D to the end of Area E, or there will not be room for all patrons. This will be accomplished by individual requests from staff mem-bers, not by P.A. announcements.

F5.   At Area E:

a.   Parents prepare their children to launch their balloons.

b.   Staff should keep patrons on the track and off the grass infield.

c.   Getting balloons to launch is the primary focus of this frame.

Exhibit 13-5: (continued)

d.   Staff should encourage patrons to hold onto the balloon until the signal to launch is given.

e.   Encourage parents to help their children with the activity.

f.

T6.   After all of the balloons are distributed and people are assembled in Area E, the P.A. announcer will stop the patriotic music and give people final instructions about the event. They will then give a countdown, and at the end of the countdown an air horn will sound. This is the signal to launch.

F6.   At Area F—after the launch:

a.   Parents and their children will stand and watch the balloons fly away for about 3–5 minutes after launch.

b.   Staff should keep patrons on the track and off the grass infield.

c.   Watching the balloons ascend is the primary focus of this frame.

d.

e.

f.

T7   As balloons fly out of sight and the patrons get ready to leave, they should be directed to Gate B. Staff should attempt to keep them on the track during this process. At Area D, each child will receive a balloon to take home. It is important for staff to assure parents that there are enough balloons for everyone so there is not a rush to Gate B.

F7   At Area D and Gate B

a.   Staff and patron interaction is fostered by giving each child a balloon as everyone leaves. Flyers announcing the rest of the community Fourth of July events are also made available.

b.

c.   Patriotic music begins again. Getting a balloon to take home is a key in this frame.

d.

e.

f.

DEVELOPING THE FLOW CHART

4. The final step is to chart all of the activities on a flow chart (Exhibit 13-4). The flow chart should be as long as the time estimates indicated in the previous step. For example, if it were determined that a total of six months would be needed to adequately plan, implement, and evaluate a special event, then approximately six months should be allotted in the flow chart. Lastly, each activity on the flow chart should include a completion date. Murphy and Howard (1977) state that "The placement of all these activities on the time line (or flow chart) is the most difficult and time-consuming, but also the most important, step in the application of FCM" (p. 200).

Once the flow chart has been established, it serves as a guide that can be used to map the progress of the plan. Programmers can estimate the impact of proposed or necessary changes on the program. Finally, the flow chart makes an excellent record of work accomplished and a good guideline for use in the next operation of the program. Now complete Exercise 13-1 on page 239.

ANIMATION PLAN

Through the animation plan, the program designer shares with other staff members the frames of interactions, the transitions, and the sequences that will be used to create a specific experience for patrons. The animation plan is analogous to the playwright's script or the sport coach's playbook. Each of these documents communicates to a number of different individuals their roles in producing a scenario of actions called a play. Actors, stage technicians, the director, and others all take direction from the playwright's script in order to produce the play as it was designed and written. The players in different sport positions take direction from a coach's playbook about the scenario of actions that must occur for a play to be executed.

In a similar way, the animation plan for a leisure program describes step by step, frame by frame, how patrons will move through the program experience. A thorough understanding of the intended leisure experience and its facilitation is crucial for preparing the animation plan.

This plan contains many cause-and-effect predictions by the program's designer. The designer assumes that if X happens, patrons will respond in a predictable manner. For example, if there are identifiable places to form lines, the designer assumes patrons will queue in the designated area. All animation plans are predictions based on knowledge of the patrons to be served; this information comes from data acquired through research or previous experiences with similar patrons.

Exhibit 13-5 on pages 241-245 contains an animation plan for a Fourth of July Balloon Ascension. The plan details what is to happen to patrons and how staff members are to interact with them. How detailed an animation plan depends on the complexity and size of the event. The plan should be sufficiently detailed so that staff members understand the total program and their role in facilitating the leisure experience. Complete Exercise 13-2 on page 240 and prepare an animation plan.

Technology in League Scheduling

Using computer software, programmers are able to:

- Create and manage numerous sports leagues.
- Add, edit, or delete schedules.
- Provide for tournament design, such as round robin and single, double, and consolation elimination.
- Provide teams and officials with schedules and statistics.
- Process fees and other payments.
- Link sports officials with scheduling.

SCHEDULING PROGRAMS

Developing a comprehensive schedule of programs in an agency is an important task. Appropriate scheduling is necessary to maximize attendance and patron satisfaction. Four elements must be considered simultaneously in scheduling program services—balance, impact, location, and timing.

BALANCE

A program schedule needs to be balanced along two dimensions. First, it is wise to avoid simultaneously scheduling similar activities that may appeal to the same target group of patrons. To avoid overlap, one must be familiar with all of the agency's program services and with programs being offered by other providers in a given service area. Second, scheduling a balanced variety of activity types at a given time will maximize the attendance at all activities. For example, at a given time, it would be best to have an art, drama, individual sport, team sport, and fitness activity scheduled, rather than five team sport activities.

IMPACT

In developing a schedule, one should understand how different activities scheduled in close proximity to each other will affect patron enjoyment. For example, scheduling a Valentine Dance for teenagers and a Valentine Dance for senior citizens at the same time in different rooms of the same facility would not be a good idea. Each group would adversely affect the enjoyment of the other because of incompatible age groups, loud noise, incompatible activity requirements for the same space, and similar problems.

LOCATION

The location of a program will affect attendance. Individuals seek out programs that are accessible. Access promotes use; therefore, it is

Exercise 13-3: Scheduling

Use a calendar for the month of December in the current year. Develop a program schedule for December for two facilities.

The first facility is a private health club with a swimming pool, weight room, running track, 16 racquetball courts, a snack bar, and a nursery. The facility is usually open from 6:00 a.m. through 12:00 midnight Monday through Saturday, and from 9:00 a.m. through 12:00 midnight on Sunday. Membership in the health club consists of mostly families with school-age children.

The second facility is a recreation center on a military base. The facility includes a game room with a pool table and a table tennis table; a hall for banquets, dances, card-playing and so forth, complete with a catering kitchen; a snack bar with video games; and a TV lounge. Eighty percent of the base population will be on leave beginning December 20th. Those remaining after that will be mostly young singles. The commander wants the recreation center open and operating every day of the month.

Discuss the following:
* What data do you need to collect first?
* What are the most obvious dates for scheduling special programs?

wise to schedule programs at locations that are accessible to the target population.

TIMING

The time when a program is offered will partly account for attendance at the program. When scheduling a time for a program, programmers should know the personal schedules of typical target patrons. Any program is competing for all other available uses of patrons' time, so the programmer needs to know the time use habits of patrons to make wise decisions about when to hold a program.

Information about program balance is developed from acceptable practice in the profession. Offering a balanced program is generally recommended, although documented local interest and past participation history would justify offering an unbalanced set of program offerings. Information about how to avoid adverse effects is derived through a thorough understanding of, and previous experience with, an event.

In scheduling the location and timing of events, the programmer has two choices. First, market research data or needs analysis data should include questions that will enable the programming staff to determine when individuals are available and where they are located. Obviously,

Exhibit 13-6. Recreation Center Schedule

Upper-Level Room

Time	M	T	W	TH	F	SA	SU
8:00							
9:00							
10:00							
11:00							
12:00							
1:00							
2:00							
3:00							
4:00							
5:00							
6:00							
7:00							
8:00							
9:00							
10:00							
11:00							

Lower-Level Room

Time	M	T	W	TH	F	SA	SU
8:00							
9:00							
10:00							
11:00							
12:00							
1:00							
2:00							
3:00							
4:00							
5:00							
6:00							
7:00							
8:00							
9:00							
10:00							
11:00							

Exhibit 13-7: Racketball Court Scheduling Matrix

Day:						Date:			
Court	1	2	3	4	5	6	7	8
Time								
6:00 a.m.								
7:00 a.m.								
8:00 a.m.								
9:00 a.m.								
10:00 a.m.								
11:00 a.m.								
12:00 p.m.								
1:00 p.m.								
2:00 p.m.								
3:00 p.m.								
4:00 p.m.								
5:00 p.m.								
6:00 p.m.								
7:00 p.m.								
8:00 p.m.								
9:00 p.m.								
10:00 p.m.								
11:00 p.m.								

scheduling programs that are available when patrons can participate in them and that are close to their residences is the best option. Second, facilities are not always available at the appropriate time or patrons' schedules are unknown. In these instances, the programmer will need to develop a program schedule based on availability or past practice with the target population.

SCHEDULING CYCLES

The time frame used to cycle program changes and periods of operation will vary from agency to agency. Community customs and accepted practice will most often determine the cycle used. The usual program scheduling cycles are explained on the following pages.

ANNUAL

The first step in developing an annual schedule is to obtain a calendar with lots of space to make entries for each day. Scan the calendar and mark the days on which obvious programming events fall. Christmas, Easter, Independence Day, Jewish holidays, Memorial Day, Thanksgiving, and so on, are examples of days when special programs will most likely be operated. Additionally, identify any special days or seasons for which local custom would dictate the need for a special program. For example, flower festivals during the spring or fall are popular in many communities; Cinco de Mayo Day (May 5th) is the day individuals of Mexican descent celebrate their victory in the battle of Puebla; and Juneteenth (June 19) is the day many African-Americans in Texas celebrate the implementation of the Emancipation Proclamation. Additional programming ideas may be obtained from Chase's Calendar of Events (www.chases.com), a day-by-day directory of special days, weeks, and months.

It is also important to block out programming seasons. Many public park and recreation systems organize their program offerings around winter, spring, summer, and fall. The specific dates on which these seasons start and end need to be specified. There are other time periods around which program seasons can be scheduled, including every two weeks, every four weeks, monthly, every six weeks, bimonthly, and so on. Once operating seasons for the year are identified, specific program services that will fill each season can be specified.

It is equally important to identify dates that must be avoided. Local custom will dictate these dates. For example, in many communities Wednesday night is church night. Because of this, schools and public recreation departments avoid scheduling events on Wednesday nights.

In scheduling a facility, one must not ignore the need for facility maintenance, custodial care, and set-up and tear-down time.

OTHER SCHEDULING CYCLES

As suggested above, many agencies schedule their programming cycles according to the seasons of the year. This arrangement usually makes good sense because many recreational activities are dictated by the weather.

Some recreation operations can run only seasonally. For example, marinas, ski resorts, outdoor ice-skating rinks, golf courses in many parts of the country, waterparks, etc. are usually seasonal operations. In these cases, the first step in developing a program schedule will be to specify when the operation will open and when it will close.

In some settings, scheduling cycles will be dictated by other events. In employee recreation, for example, production schedules will sometimes influence how workers' time is organized and therefore when patrons will be available for programs. On some military training bases, recreation scheduling seasons conform closely to the training schedule. If service personnel are rotated in and out of a base after completing a ten-week training course, then the recreation department's programming cycles will need to be coordinated with this schedule.

In a similar manner, different agencies schedule program services with other cycling frames, including monthly, weekly, daily, or hourly scheduling. Regardless of the time frame, the general method of scheduling is similar. Try developing schedules by completing Exercise 13-3 on page 248.

FACILITY SCHEDULING

Scheduling a facility is one of the easiest tasks programmers complete. However, an ineffective scheduling system leads to double-booking, with much patron displeasure and bad public relations for the agency. To schedule competently requires a good scheduling system and constant attention to implementing the operational details of the system.

The most foolproof system is to create a scheduling matrix appropriate for the facility. Each facility, and each hour that it may potentially be scheduled, must be included on the matrix. By creating such a matrix, one has created blank spaces that represent the potential hours available for programs. Exhibit 13-6 on page 249 shows such a matrix for a small neighborhood recreation center with two rooms.

When the specific facility is scheduled, the name of the individual, group, or program that will occupy the space is written onto the schedule in the appropriate place. In this way, each space can be scheduled only once. To avoid confusion, there should be only one scheduling matrix. All methods, even computerized scheduling programs, use this simple, basic procedure.

How, then, can scheduling go wrong? Inattention to detail is the most frequent error. Busy staff members may give out a reservation but fail to write it on the master schedule. This error often results in double-booking. It is obviously important to have a system that is designed so that each space available can be scheduled only once. Normally, recreation operations do not overbook facilities for which they take reservations.

The most detailed scheduling matrix that is usually used in recreation operations is a facility schedule. Exhibit 13-7 on page 250 is an example of a scheduling matrix for a racquetball club. Properly scheduling such a facility requires a schedule for each day of operation, with an hourly schedule for each court in the facility. Other facility schedules can be developed using a similar system.

In scheduling a facility, one must not ignore the need for facility maintenance, custodial care, and set-up and tear-down time. An attractive, clean, well-maintained facility contributes to patron satisfaction. However, to accommodate the level of maintenance and custodial care desired, an appropriate amount of time must be included in the schedule for these operations. For additional information and exercises regarding schedules and scheduling, visit our web site at www.recreationprogramming.com.

CONCLUSION

The written program plan is used to share the operational details of what must occur so that patrons can have the leisure experience intended by the program designer. Writing the plan requires that the designer clarify design and operational details. A written program plan should contain enough detail so that the program can be duplicated by another programmer.

A management plan provides organizational details for the many activities that must be accomplished to implement a program. Management planning identifies all activities that must be completed to implement a program and places them in the order in which they need to occur. The FCM is the most frequently used technique for implementing recreation services.

A unique component of a recreation program plan is the animation plan. In this plan, the scenario of interactions—including the contents of each frame, the transitions, and their sequence—that must occur for patrons to have the leisure experience intended by the designer are explicated.

To maximize attendance and make efficient use of facilities, there needs to be an overall design in the scheduling of recreation program services. The programmer may use a variety of time frames for scheduling programs. Documented patron preferences are the best data to use in scheduling. Facility scheduling can be accomplished by developing a scheduling matrix appropriate for the facility being scheduled.

REFERENCES

Crossley, J. C., & Jamieson, L. (1997). *Introduction to commercial and entrepreneurial recreation* (Rev. ed.). Champaign, IL: Sagamore.

Devine, M. A., & Kotowski, L. (1999). Inclusive leisure services: Results of a national survey of park and recreation departments. *Journal of Park and Recreation Administration, 17*(4), 56–72.

Kliem, R. L. (1986). *The secrets of successful project management.* New York: Wiley.

Kraus, R. G., & Curtis, J. E. (2000). *Creative management in recreation, parks, and leisure services* (6th ed.). Boston, MA: McGraw-Hill.

Moder, J. J., Phillips, C. R., & Davis, E. W. (1983). *Project management with CPM, PERT, and precedence diagramming* (3rd ed.). New York: Van Nostrand Reinhold.

Murphy, J., & Howard, D. (1977). *Delivery of community leisure services: A holistic approach.* Philadelphia: Lea & Febiger.

Russell, R. V. (1982). *Planning programs in recreation.* St. Louis: C. V. Mosby.

Pennington Balloon Championships
Photo courtesy of Recreation and Park Commission for the Parish of East Baton Rouge, LA

Techniques for
Program Promotion

STEP 7 : IMPLEMENTATION

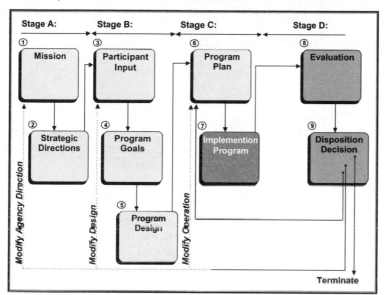

14

KEY TERMS

Promotion
Communication
Persuasion
Channel
Brochure Copy
News Release
Flyer
Electronic
    Communication

Howard and Crompton (1980) define promotion as "basically communication that seeks to inform, persuade, or remind members of a potential client group of an agency's programs and services" (p. 448). To this list, Crompton and Lamb (1986) add "to educate." Kotler and Andreasen (1987) suggest that "any communication process involves a message sender and a message receiver (a target audience)" (p. 506). To truly communicate in promoting program services, the programmer must be concerned not only with the form and content of the message to be sent, but also must understand the educational and cultural background of those who are intended to receive the message.

Promotion will be more successful if it is accompanied by services that have been developed within a marketing framework (Russell & Verrill, 1986). A good promotional campaign will not sustain participation in services that are not well designed and based on identified participants' wants. Only one of the four primary marketing elements—promotion—must also be supported with a product that is well designed, delivered at the right time and place, and made available at the appropriate price.

An agency's promotional campaign, then, will involve fulfilling one or more of the following functions: to inform, to

The benefits of participating in outcome-based programs should be the central focus of all advertising and promoting of the program. The benefits participants may anticipate from participating should be clearly communicated. Furthermore, once a program is completed and the benefits obtained have been documented, their achievement should be the focus of follow-up publicity to the general public and key stakeholders. You will recall that this activity is key to repositioning the agency as a provider of important services that make a difference in the community.

An agency's promotional campaign, then, will involve fulfilling one or more of the following functions: to inform, to educate, to persuade, or to remind.

educate, to persuade, or to remind. There is some disagreement about which of these functions is most appropriate for a leisure service agency to use in attempting to attract participants. Which strategies will dominate an agency's promotional campaign depends on the type of leisure service organization that is offering the program.

PERSUASION

Persuasion is a different activity than the other three forms of promotion because its articulated goal is to bring about a change in attitude or behavior (Manfredo & Bright, 1991). Persuasive communication theory suggests that individuals are persuaded with either central or peripheral methods (Ajzen, 1992). The central method assumes participants exercise a high degree of information processing through rational behavior that involves a thorough examination and evaluation of the ideas and information presented, which results in selecting the best alternative from all that are possible.

The peripheral method assumes that participants are not thorough at processing information because of a lack of interest, ability, or time. In this instance, persuasion is achieved with factors tangential to the content of the message, for example, the credibility of the presenter or the communication channel.

Most practitioners today recommend using advertising strategies that simultaneously account for both methods (Manfredo, Bright, & Haas, 1992) because the likely case is that participants use both methods for processing information about leisure participation. For example, one may carefully decide to begin participating in an exercise program and be persuaded to do so with information provided from several sources, which shows a high degree of rational processing. However, once the decision to participate is made, little time may be spent in selecting a health club to join. In fact, the decision may be based on an advertised testimonial from a local professional athlete featured in health club's advertisement, a decision which shows a low degree of information processing.

The persuasiveness of any form of communication will be affected by the following: comprehension of the advertisement, effects of prior knowledge, involvement with the topic, repetition of the message, credibility of the source, and attitudes toward the advertisement (Manfredo et al., 1992). Current information about persuasive communication is too voluminous to reiterate here. However, several myths that persist must be dispelled. First, too much material is written at a reading level above the ability of the intended recipients; and consequently, they cannot comprehend it. The programmer must know the target market very well to correct this.

Second, information acquired from direct experience has the most salience and will therefore be the most difficult to alter. Inexperienced or infrequent participants of a given activity will be easier to influence than experienced, frequent users. This is also why it is critical to make certain the agency is ready to provide a service effectively and efficiently prior to launching it. The knowledge and image that accompany a bad experience with an agency's service, acquired from direct experience, is very difficult to alter.

Third, continued repetition of an advertisement does not increase the recipient's favorableness toward the advertisement in a linear fashion. There is usually an initial increase in favorableness, followed by a point of diminishing returns when it declines. The dynamics of this variation depend on a number of factors, including the type of advertisement, the complexity of it, and the attitude of the recipient about the advertisement itself (Manfredo et al., 1992).

Persuasion is usually accomplished through advertising, which is not neutral. It is at least mildly aggressive in attempting to persuade someone to purchase the sponsor's product or service (Russell & Verrill, 1986). Commercial recreation operations often use an aggressive advertising campaign to attract customers to use their services instead of the services of another supplier; that is, they try to increase their market share.

Persuasive promotion brings about a change in attitude or behavior.

COMMUNICATION CHANNELS

The type of promotion used should be selected to bring the agency's services to the attention of the intended audience, thereby channeling the promotional campaign to its target market. Kotler and Andreasen (1987) explain that "a channel is a conduit for bringing together a marketer and a target customer at some place and time for the purpose of facilitating a transaction" (p. 473). Leisure service agencies normally use at least two channels to promote their program services.

One channel is aimed at the general public. Because of concern about equity of access, municipal leisure service agencies in particular must inform participants about available services, thus allowing general access to program services. Although commercial recreation operations may conduct a promotional campaign directed at the general public, equal access to program information, in these cases, is a marketing rather than an equity decision.

A second channel is a more targeted effort directed to the target market for the service. The purpose of this second channel is to inform and remind the individuals who are most likely to participate in the program. Targeting a promotional campaign is considered more cost effective because it places information about a program in the hands of the individuals most likely to purchase or use the service.

The usual medium for the channel directed to the general public is an agency publication that includes all of the agency's services for a given period. These publications educate the public about the agency, its services, and its facilities. Often, this type of publication is mailed to all residents of a community, or it is distributed as an insert in a community newspaper. Additionally, news releases may be sent to a local newspaper. The usual medium for the more targeted effort is an in-house-produced, single-page flyer that is distributed at recreation centers, the agency's main office, neighborhood locations, and perhaps mailed to previous participants of the same or similar programs.

To effectively promote program services, programmers need to be proficient at writing copy that describes their programs and services to include in a general agency publication. They must also be proficient at preparing public service news releases for the local press and be able to produce single-page flyers to promote a program. Techniques for producing each of these will be discussed below.

WRITING BROCHURE COPY

Writing copy that will effectively promote a program is challenging. Unfortunately, many agencies do no more than simply inform participants about their services, because information copy is the easiest to write. Copy written to simply inform participants does not need to include any more than the basic five Ws and the H used by reporters to ensure the completeness of a story; that is, who, what, when, where, why, and how (Ryan & Tankard, 1977).

Well-written copy also tries to capture the expectations of the target market and conveys how the program will provide benefits by meeting these expectations (Leffel, 1983). Consider the two pieces of copy for a men's weight-training class contained in Exhibit 14-1. One piece of copy was taken from a seasonal brochure published by a municipal recreation department. The other was taken from a publication of a commercial recreation operation. (Both sets of copy have been altered to protect the identities of the agencies.) Can you guess which is from the commercial agency? Which one captures the interest of the reader? Which one communicates the benefits to be derived from participation? Does either of them overstate what one could reasonably expect to accomplish in a few hours of instruction? What else do you notice about the copy?

Writing creative copy is an art. It is therefore difficult to offer cookbook solutions about how to write good copy. Following are nine guidelines for preparing creative copy that Foster (1990, 29–31) offers:

1. Clarity—simple, clear sentences and words are preferred.
2. Details—providing detail creates familiarity with a program.
3. Use the senses—using references to the senses keeps a reader's interest and humanizes the content of the copy.
4. Use personal experiences—use both your own and those of your satisfied customers to create interest and association with a program and its benefits.
5. Use conversational speech—reading dialogue creates a sense of "being there" and sharing in an experience.

Well-written copy also tries to capture the expectations of the target market and conveys how the program will provide benefit by meeting these expectations.

Exhibit 14-1: Sample Promotional Copy

Copy Example 1

Weights for Men

Learn how to use the Universal weight machines under the guidance of a knowledgeable instructor. No black sole athletic shoes. Instructor: Jim Smith. Class: Z4756. Day: T/TH. Time: 7:30–8:30. Length: 8 wks. Start: 10/09. Fee: $20.

Copy Example 2

Weight Training for Men

There is nothing more appealing than a toned body. Weight training is an effective way to achieve the kind of physique you've always wanted—but thought was impossible! In the comfortable setting of Fairmount Gym, you will be thoroughly introduced to free weights and machines. An individual program for your specific needs and goals will be designed for you. You will develop a clear understanding of the anatomy of your body and your diet and nutrition in relation to weight training.

Coach and instructor for North Community College, Bill Smith is a physical educator who has coached and taught weight training for 15 years. In 1982 he coached the N.C.C. weight-training team to the state championship. Fairmount Gym, Tues. April 4, 11, 18, 25, 7:30–9:00. Course Fee: $40.

6. Opposition—contrasting long with short sentences, fast with slow pace of reading, and so on, creates interest.
7. General versus detail—anchor detail (usually unknown information) to more general information that is more likely known.
8. Repeat—repeat and repeat words, phrases, and details that are strong and add support to one's point when repeated.
9. Parallel construction of sentences and phrases—this is a more sophisticated form of repetition that can be used for additional emphasis.

Writing concise, informative, and interesting copy for a promotional brochure requires practice. Complete Exercise 14-1 on page 260 and see how many ways you can write up the same program.

PREPARING NEWS RELEASES

Writing news releases requires preparing longer copy than that for promotional brochures or flyers. Space in newspapers for items actually considered news is free to the sponsoring agency. However, when news

Exercise 14-1: Writing Brochure Copy

Write at least four different pieces of brochure copy for the following program: a pastry baking class. In one, emphasize the setting in which the program will occur. In the second, emphasize the opportunity for sociability that the program will present. In the third, emphasize the opportunity for personal achievement that the program will present. Write one more with an emphasis of your own choosing.

Program Facts

Who: Program participants and the instructor, Helen Cork, head pastry chef for the Farmint Hotel, Clarksberry bake-off winner for 2010, and state fair bake-off winner for 2011.

What: Holiday pastry baking class, including cookies, fruit cakes, and ethnic breads.

When: One night per week, 6:30–9:30 p.m. for the six weeks before Christmas.

Where: In the test kitchen of the Farmint Hotel.

Why: To become better at baking, to prepare excellent holiday baked goods, to make Christmas presents for family, friends, and others.

How: Sign up by November 1, 2012, at the Recreation Department office; class fee is $45, including all supplies.

releases are submitted, the writer is competing for a limited amount of space with other organizations seeking publicity. To increase the probability that a news release will be published, the programmer should know and meet the newspaper's deadlines and prepare well-written copy.

Many newspapers will rewrite a news release submitted by a programmer. Expect your wonderfully written copy to be rewritten. Newspaper editors know that the same news release has probably been submitted to several different outlets, and they do not want the same copy to appear in their own paper. Many smaller papers do not have sufficient staff to rewrite news releases, so the copy you have prepared will most likely appear verbatim. In fact, well-written copy that requires little or no rewrite will probably be given priority and published because of tight production schedules. News organizations live by the clock. If you do not meet their deadlines, the materials submitted will not be published, no matter how well written or important they are.

Preparing a news release involves writing copy in a specific style and preparing the copy according to standard newswriting conventions. All news stories should be brief but accurate. They should have a good lead and use the inverted pyramid form of writing. The lead is the first paragraph or two of a story that immediately lets the reader know what the story is about. Ryan and Tankard (1977) suggest that "good, straight news leads quickly satisfy a reader's need and desire for information, and attract a reader to the rest of the story" (p. 101).

The inverted pyramid form of writing requires that the most important pieces of information be placed at the beginning of a story. The assumption is that the reader may stop reading at any point. The story should therefore be written so that the reader has the pertinent facts immediately and each succeeding paragraph contains progressively less important information.

Formatting a news story is also important. A newsroom is a busy place, and a great deal of copy crosses an editor's desk each day. Each story should therefore have a slug, which is placed in the top left corner of each page of the story. The slug should include the writer's name, address, e-mail address, and phone number; the title of the story; a release date for the story; and the approximate number of words. All news releases should be double-spaced to allow room for the editor's proofing marks and corrections. If the story is longer than one page, the bottom of each page, except for the last page, should end with "more." The end of the story is signified by "end." Exhibit 14-2 on page 262 contains a sample news release for a balloon flying contest. After reading the news release, complete Exercise 14-2 on page 263.

It is important to be selective in the types of materials submitted to newspapers. Not everything done in the agency is newsworthy. The programmer is most likely to have material published if it meets one or more of the following news values (Ryan & Tankard, 1977).

- News events that involve local events with local people. Almost all news releases by not-for-profit recreation agencies meet this requirement.
- News releases that are timely. For example, an announcement of a Turkey Trot race has a high likelihood of being included in a series of articles about Thanksgiving.
- News releases that involve prominent individuals or institutions. When the mayor of a local community joins a fitness program at a local Boys and Girls Club, an event that would not normally be newsworthy becomes so.
- Stories involving a large number of people and that have human interest are newsworthy. Tot swimming programs always generate fascinating copy and excellent pictures for a news story.
- Stories that involve novel happenings are almost always newsworthy. Agencies that have zoos have an almost unlimited supply of novel, interesting stories.

Successfully obtaining space in newspapers requires that the programmer selectively submit newsworthy items, that they be well written in a journalistic style, and that they be written in the conventional journalistic format. Some newspapers have policies about distributing space to local agencies and organizations. It is therefore important that

News organizations live by the clock. If you do not meet their deadlines, the materials submitted will not be published, no matter how well written or important they are.

Exhibit 14-2: Sample News Release

NEWS RELEASE

Anytown Park and Recreation Department

Fred Bloom

Recreation Supervisor

(xxx) 565-2651

30th Annual Fourth of July Balloon Fly

Release any time after June 20, 2010

Approximately 220 words

30th Annual Fourth of July Balloon Fly

Silver balloons will be used when Anytown Park and Recreation Department conducts its 30th annual Fourth of July Balloon Flying Contest. The Balloon Fly will take place at Veterans Park, 5th and Locust, at 11:00 a.m. Registration will begin at 10:00 a.m. There is no charge, and all children through 16 years of age may participate.

Last year, the winning balloon flew over 300 miles to eastern Arizona. The farthest any balloon has ever flown over the past 24 years is 500 miles. In 1976, a balloon flew the 500 miles to western New Mexico in about 12 hours.

The silver balloons being used this year to celebrate the 30th anniversary of the event are several mills thicker than the balloons usually used. The extra thickness will allow the balloons to remain airborne longer and thus fly farther. According to Sid Kinder, Assistant Director of the Park and Recreation Department, "We expect to set a new record this year."

Usually about 1,500 balloons are released each year. Mr. Kinder said, "This event is very popular with families. We want everyone to know that all children are welcome and every one of them will get a balloon to release." In case of rain, the event will be held at the same time and place on the following Saturday morning, July 8, 2010.

the programming agency understand what it most needs to do to get published in the local paper. A frank discussion with the news editor about the most essential pieces of information needed to get into the paper is often necessary so that the agency's allocation is used wisely.

PREPARING FLYERS

FLYER PRODUCTION

Almost all agencies use in-house-produced flyers to promote their program services. The quality of these flyers varies among and within

agencies. The quality of a program flyer produced to promote a service
often depends directly on how much revenue a program produces.

Regardless of the agency, it is highly likely that programmers will
need to be skilled in producing single-page promotion flyers. To produce them, the programmer will need to do the design, art work, layout,
and copywriting, and should understand how the flyer will be reproduced. Furthermore, the programmer may even need to actually reproduce the flyer.

FLYER DESIGN

Nelson (1981) states that "designing means creative action that fulfills its purpose" (p. 112). When designing a flyer, programmers should
remember its purpose. In most instances, the purpose will be to inform,
educate, remind, or in some cases, persuade individuals to participate
in a program. The design should include attractive art work, good layout, well-written copy with complete information, and good quality
production. Unfortunately, many flyers produced in-house are often
of poor quality and give participants a bad image of the agency and
its programs. Taking some effort at producing well-designed flyers is a
good investment in the agency's overall promotion campaign.

Flyer design results in a paste-up of the flyer. A paste-up is simply
a black and white original from which the flyer is actually printed. It is
called a paste-up because the final composition is often made up of copy
and artwork that are pasted to a piece of white cardboard or paper. The
paste-up is then either copied on a copying machine or reproduced with
any number of printing methods.

All copy, however, begins as black and white copy. To obtain color,
one may print on colored paper, print with colored ink on white paper,
or print with colored ink on colored paper. A flyer is most often printed
on 20-pound paper, but a heavier paper will produce a more substantial
flyer. Obtaining more than one color of printing on a flyer requires a

more complicated paste-up and printing process. This usually requires professional help, which increases production costs considerably. Therefore, multiple color printing is seldom done unless one is preparing a flyer for a major program.

ARTWORK

When a flyer is being prepared, the artwork will often be selected or created first. The illustration becomes the central theme around which the remainder of the flyer is developed. In all cases, it is important that the artwork contribute to the purpose of the flyer and that it not simply be appended to it to "make it look good." Artwork included in a flyer should be a part of the overall message.

Obtaining good-looking artwork on in-house-produced flyers can be a problem unless the programmer is artistic or has access to a staff artist. Many agencies use stock art (or clip art), which is a published series of black and white line drawings of many sizes and of many different subjects. There are several publishers of stock art. It can be purchased at most art supply or graphic art stores. The use of stock art produces copy that is far superior to amateur drawings.

Several personal computer programs on the market can simplify the process of developing good artwork and flyer copy. Print Master and Gem Draw are two popular programs that are IBM compatible. Microsoft Word, PageMaker, and MacDraw are equally popular for Apple products. With a word-processing system and an art program, a programmer can easily produce attractive flyer copy in a very short time. Exhibit 14-3 is an example of a flyer produced by pasting up copy and producing illustrations with a word-processing system.

LAYOUT

The layout gives visual form to the arrangement of graphic illustration and copy. According to Wills (1965), during layout these two elements are arranged and adapted to each other to produce the flyer. Nelson (1981) suggests that illustration and copy need to be laid out with the following in mind: balance, proportion, sequence, unity, and emphasis.

FORMAL AND INFORMAL BALANCE

The flyer should be at rest with itself, leaving the reader with an overall pleasing visual image. Balance can be achieved by using formal or informal balance. In formal balance, everything that is done on one half of the flyer is repeated on the other half. Formal balance is achieved with symmetry.

Informal balance is asymmetrical. An asymmetrical layout that is balanced is a more difficult undertaking for someone who is inexperienced at layout. The objective is still an overall pleasing visual image, but it is more difficult to achieve. Informal balance is achieved by rearranging the various design elements in different ways until an overall visual balance is achieved. Neither copy nor illustrations should be pasted in place until the desired balance is obtained.

Blues Style Guitar Class!

Description: Learn to Play Blues Style Guitar with ease. Learn the fundamental 12-bar blues, turnarounds and endings, and how to improvise in our 10-week program. Basic blues chord progressions will be taught, as well as fingerpicking techniques for the right hand.

For Whom: Adult students (16 years or older) who are playing at the intermediate guitar playing level. This means that the student can change chords smoothly and can demonstrate several strumming patterns. Students must provide their own guitar and music stand.

When: Thursdays, 7:30-9:00 pm, from January 26 to March 30, 2008 at the New Town Recreation Center, Room 10.

Your Instructor: Andy Young, who trained and studied blues style guitar under Artie Traum in New York City, instructs all classes. With more than 25 years of teaching experience, Andy believes that guitar playing helps people discover their creative and imaginative talents.

Cost: $80 for 10 lessons

How to Register: You can register online at http://www.newtown.org or by completing a form from the Spring 2008 Program Brochure. Send, fax, or bring your registration form to New Town Recreation Center, 4th and Vine, New Town, NE, 38520, Phone: 493-569-8539, FAX: 493-569-8530.

Accommodations: If you will need a special accommodation, please contact the event sponsor at 498-2249.

Sponsored by Newtown Parks and Recreation Department

PROPORTION OF ELEMENTS

Proportion is the relationship of sizes of the various design elements to each other and to the overall flyer. For example, what is the proportion of illustration to copy? What is the proportion of the title lettering to the rest of the flyer? What is the proportion of "white space," that is, the ratio of space left blank to the space printed with copy or illustrations? Ideally, the flyer should have enough white space to look uncluttered.

To achieve the most pleasing overall look, one should avoid arranging spaces with obvious mathematical relationships. Dividing a flyer into halves or quadrants is less interesting than other ways of dividing space. Unequal divisions of space result in the most interesting flyers.

SEQUENCE OF PRESENTATION

Layout gives visual form to the arrangement of graphic illustration and copy.

The layout will determine how the reader progresses through the flyer while reading it. The material should present both the copy and the illustrations in a logical sequence that leads the reader through the flyer to a conclusion or final point. In Western civilization, individuals naturally progress through written material by reading from left to right and from top to bottom. Layout should be arranged to accommodate this habit.

To add interest, however, one can redirect how the eye will move through a flyer by taking advantage of other likely sequences of eye movement. Nelson (1981) has suggested that "the eye moves naturally, too, from big elements to little elements, from black elements to lighter elements, from color to noncolor, from unusual shapes to usual shapes" (p. 119). With either type of sequence, the goal should be to enable the eye to progress smoothly through the contents of the flyer.

UNITY OF CONTENT

The illustrations, copy, and overall look of a flyer should make a harmonious presentation. It should make a single statement to the reader and not create visual or rhetorical dissonance. An example of visual dissonance would be the inclusion of photographs and line drawing on the same flyer. Using two different styles of type—for example, Old English and Western—on the same flyer would create visual dissonance. Undesirable rhetorical dissonance would be created by using different verb tenses in different sections of the copy on a single flyer, or by writing in a different person in various sections of the copy.

The relationship of elements should be so strong that after one is removed, all others need to be repositioned.

EMPHASIS

Certain things on the flyer should be emphasized: the headline, artwork, or copy. If there are several pieces of artwork, one of them should dominate. If there are several copy blocks, one of them should receive primary emphasis. When nothing on a flyer is emphasized, everything and nothing stands out! When laying out a flyer, one should take control of what will be emphasized, make certain it is the dominant feature, and make certain nothing else upstages it.

Nelson (1981) suggests that the best test of good layout is to remove one element. The relationship of elements should be so strong that after one is removed, all others need to be repositioned. If this is not the case, the original layout was not properly designed.

WRITING COPY

Copy writing for flyers is similar to copy produced for the general circulation brochure. But brochure copy will normally be written in paragraph form and clustered together, whereas flyer copy may be split apart and dispersed throughout the flyer. It is important, therefore, not to simply split apart the sentences of the copy used for the brochure and display them on the flyer. Normally, one needs to expand brochure copy into complete, logical passages that can then be distributed throughout the flyer and intermingled with artwork and other illustrations.

PRODUCTION METHODS

14

Many agencies use copying machines for producing a small number of flyers. These machines can often accommodate colored paper. Many agencies also use some type of offset printing. In any case, you will need to produce good, clean, camera-ready copy. This means that the paste-up you present for reproduction will need to have good contrast between the black copy and the white background. There should be no extraneous pencil marks or smudges on the paste-up. What you present for reproduction is what you get! Printing will not cover up sloppy paste-up work, bad layout, or poorly written copy.

Although an agency's promotional campaign may involve more than what has been discussed above, in most cases programmers will be expected to write clear, concise copy describing their programs. This copy will be included in agency brochures, news releases, and flyers. Promoting a program, then, is one of the first processes in implementing a program. The promotional campaign for any program must be started well in advance of registration for the program. Well-written and well-designed promotional materials that are not made available to the target market on a timely basis will be of little benefit in promoting programs.

Technology for Promotion

Using computer software, programmers are able to:
- Design program brochures and flyers.
- Create logos and letterhead.
- Produce a website.
- Write a newsletter.
- Create art images for all of the above.

INNOVATIVE PROMOTIONAL TECHNOLOGIES

Like many other industries, the leisure service industry has begun to embrace technological advances in the area of program promotion.

In this section, we will describe how technology can enhance program promotion through use of the World Wide Web, e-mail, specialty publication, tourism offices, and cable-TV public access programs. The authors are grateful to Slottag (1999) for some of the information included in this section.

WORLD WIDE WEB

The idea for the World Wide Web began in Switzerland in 1989 at the CERN (translated from French as the European Particle Physics Laboratory). Researcher Tim Berners-Lee wanted to create an efficient and easy environment for information-sharing among geographically separated research teams. Two years later, the Web arrived. The Web is generally used for graphic design of information, dissemination of research, browsing and ordering of products, client and customer support, and display of creative arts (December & Randall, 1994).

Although many leisure service agencies and businesses already have websites, even more are in the process of getting online. Exhibit 14-4 is the MetroParks home page (http://www.neo.rr.com/MetroParks). By browsing websites, customers can learn about agency programs and services, see images of venues, and even see products for sale. Websites, if designed well, are excellent promotional tools. They must also be maintained with up-to-date information so that they are a ready source of information. A question agencies will have to answer in website design is who will do it. Many agencies find that it is more efficient to contract out the service because of the amount of time consumed by web design and maintenance.

ELECTRONIC MAIL (E-MAIL)

Electronic mail (e-mail) messages are transmitted from one computer to another. The low cost of e-mail makes it an appealing communication tool. For example, it generally costs the same to send an e-mail message overseas as it does to a colleague in the next office. A common use of e-mail is for agencies to send news releases to editors. E-mail is also used to contact people. Websites, business cards, and agency letterhead often post an e-mail address so that the public can contact the agency about questions they might have. An innovative use of e-mail that is on the rise is the use of listservs. Listservs are established for a group of persons who are interested in a particular topic, for example, competitive tennis. The tennis players can use the listserv as a discussion forum or to inform players of upcoming events and activities. Assuming the responsibility for developing and maintaining leisure interest listservs is a modern extension of the traditional role agencies have assumed for nurturing leisure interest groups.

SPECIALTY PUBLICATIONS

Newspapers, magazines, and newsletters targeted to niche markets, such as senior citizens and special interest groups, are excellent places to promote programs and activities. Writing copy for these publications may require more preparation because the article will need to focus

Exhibit 14-4:

specifically on the target market, as opposed to a generic population. With modern production software, these publications may be produced efficiently, and an agency can publish niche publications more effectively.

TOURISM OFFICES AND CHAMBERS OF COMMERCE

Opportunities exist for leisure service agencies and businesses to display promotional items at tourism offices and the local Chamber of Commerce. It is also possible to post events and programs on the web calendars of these organizations, as well as to establish links between these organizations and leisure service agencies.

CABLE-TV PUBLIC ACCESS PROGRAMS

Some agencies may choose to seek airtime on cable-TV public access programs. Depending on the cable company, the on-camera presentation may be produced by either the agency or the cable company itself. It is best to publicize the channel and the show time to attract as many viewers as possible.

The most important point to be made about these promotional technologies is that programmers need to hone their writing skills, because now more than ever before, agencies and their program promotions are being examined by citizens through multiple conduits. A site on the Web, in particular, makes your agency public to the world.

CONCLUSION

Developing the material for a promotional campaign is an early step in program implementation. Standard methods of promotion include an agency brochure, news releases, individual program flyers, and a website. In most agencies, programmers do much of the copy writing and other promotional work themselves, with the exception of website design. To be effective, promotional materials must be well written and the promotional campaign executed in a timely manner.

REFERENCES

Arnold, E. (1982). *101 memos for reporters.* Chicago: Lawrence Ragan Communications.

Ajzen, I. (1992). Persuasive communication theory in social psychology: A historical perspective. In M. J. Manfredo (Ed.), *Influencing human behavior: Theory and application in recreation, tourism, and natural resource management* (pp. 1–28). Champaign, IL: Sagamore.

Crompton, J. L., & Lamb, C. W., Jr. (1986). *Marketing government and social services.* New York: Wiley.

December, J., & Randall, N. (1994). *The world wide web unleashed.* Indianapolis, IN: Sams.

Foster, K. (1990). *How to create newspaper ads.* Manhattan, KS: Learning Resources Network.

Howard, D. R., & Crompton, J. L. (1980). *Financing, managing, and marketing recreation and park resources.* Dubuque, IA: Wm. C. Brown.

Kotler, P., & Andreasen, A. R. (1987). *Strategic marketing for nonprofit organizations* (3rd ed.). Englewood Cliffs, NJ: Prentice-Hall.

Leffel, L. G. (1983). *Designing brochures for results.* Manhattan, KS: Learning Resources Network.

Manfredo, M. J., & Bright, A. D. (1991). A model for assessing the effects of communication on recreationists. *Journal of Leisure Research, 23,* 1–20.

Manfredo, M. J., Bright, A. D., & Haas, G. E. (1992). Research in tourism advertising. In M. J. Manfredo (Ed.), *Influencing human behavior: Theory and applications in recreation, tourism, and natural resource management.* Champaign, IL: Sagamore.

Nelson, R. P. (1981). *The design of advertising* (4th ed). Dubuque, IA: Wm. C. Brown.

Russell, T., & Verrill, G. (1986). *Otto Kleppner's advertising procedure* (9th ed.). Englewood Cliffs, NJ: Prentice-Hall.

Ryan, M., & Tankard, J. W., Jr. (1977). *Basic news reporting.* Palo Alto, CA: Mayfield.

Slottag, R. (1999). Embracing the age of niche marketing. *Illinois Parks and Recreation, 30*(4), 43–44.

Wills, F. H. (1965). *Fundamentals of layout for newspaper and magazine advertising, for page design of publications, and for brochures.* New York: Dover.

Silver Splash
Photo courtesy of City of Aurora, Colorado, Department of Library, Recreation, & Cultural Services

Registration Procedures

STEP 7 : IMPLEMENTATION

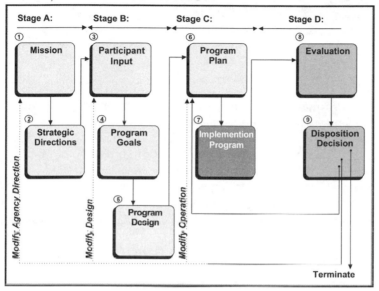

Registering individuals involves developing a list of persons qualified to be in a specific program. It is an inconvenient process for both staff and participants and therefore should not be undertaken unless such a list is necessary. Most frequently, registration is conducted for programs that require a fee for participating, but it is also useful for purposes other than documenting who has paid for a service. Registering participants is necessary in the following four cases:

1. *Participants must pay a fee to be in the program.* These programs require registration because only those who have paid the fee are allowed to be in the program.

2. *The number of spaces in a program is limited.* If a program has a limited capacity, it is wise to have people register even if a fee is not being charged. Participants thus secure one of a limited number of spaces by their position in a queue or some other qualifying method.

For example, Oak Park, Illinois, annually operated Easter Egg Hunts, which were designed to handle 200 children. It was estimated that approximately 2,000 children would want to hunt eggs. To accommodate the estimated demand, 10 hunts were operated during the day, with 200 children per hunt. Although each hunt was free, children were required to obtain a ticket to a specific hunt. In this way, queuing was arranged

Implementing Outcome-Based Programming

Agencies using outcome-based programming often display their benefits-based theme on their promotional and registration materials. For example, the letterhead and logo on the registration form might include a list of benefits that participants can derive from agency programs. The more central the outcome-based programming theme is in your promotional and registration form, etc., the more your constituents will know and look forward to the positive outcomes to be derived from your programs.

Registration is conducted for programs that require a fee for participating, but it is also useful for purposes other than documenting who has paid for a service.

beforehand to determine who could be admitted to each hunt. In this case, being "qualified" simply meant that a person had obtained one of a limited number of tickets for a particular hunt.

Spaces in a program may also be limited because of the carrying capacity of the facility. In outdoor recreation, often the number of participants permitted into some wilderness areas is restricted because of the physical limits of the ecological systems, or because the perception of an area as a wilderness would be impaired with too many people in the area. Sometimes, then, it is necessary to limit participation in order to maintain the leisure experience that the agency is trying to offer. Thus, individuals need to register to obtain one of the limited spaces available.

3. *Places in the program are expensive to provide.* Because of this, it is necessary to know the number who will participate. In some events, it is also necessary to know how many people are going to attend so that proper arrangements can be made. Dances with sit-down seating, parties or events involving a caterer, and so forth, are examples of such events. In these programs, some type of invitation with a R.S.V.P. system or other registration system is often used to enable the programmer to have a reasonable estimate of the number who will attend.

4. *Some special qualifying procedure for admission to a program is required.* Some programs are open only to those with special qualifications. In these cases, a list of those qualified must be developed. In sports, for example, tryouts are often necessary to place players into leagues or programs appropriate for their skill levels. In outdoor adventure programming, one often must make certain that individuals have the requisite skills. For example, participants may be required to demonstrate a level of swimming proficiency before being permitted to participate in a canoe trip.

...registration should be conducted to maximize convenience for patrons rather than for staff.

Sometimes, the special qualification may simply be that the participant has provided the agency with certain information. Some recreation centers require all participants to register during their first visit to the center. Registration is free, but people must register and provide their name, address, phone, and the name of someone to contact in case of emergency. The City of Santa Clara, California, Parks and Recreation Department uses this system at its Youth Activity Center. Exhibit 15-1 displays a copy of the registration card used. After the card is

Exhibit 15-1: Registration Card

dBASE _____   Residency _____   Picture _____

CITY OF SANTA CLARA
PARKS and RECREATION DEPARTMENT
RESIDENT YOUTH CARD

PARTICIPANT _____
               Last Name   First Name

The undersigned, in consideration of participation in this activity, agrees to indemnify and hold the City of Santa Clara harmless, and release the City of Santa Clara from any and all liability for any injury which may be suffered by the above named individual arising out of, or in any way connected with, participation in any activity the above named individual is registered in.

PARENT SIGNATURE _____   DATE _____

| | | | | | | | | | | | | | |
Day Pass

PARTICIPANT INFORMATION

NAME (Print) _____ PHONE _____

ADDRESS _____ CITY _____ ZIP _____

DATE OF BIRTH _____ AGE _____ SCHOOL _____

FATHER'S NAME _____ WORK PHONE _____
MOTHER'S NAME _____ WORK PHONE _____

In case of emergency, contact:
1 _____ PHONE _____ RELATIONSHIP _____
2 _____ PHONE _____ RELATIONSHIP _____
PREVIOUS INJURIES, ALLERGIES, MEDICAL CONDITIONS: _____

| | | | | | | | | | | | | | |
Photo Retake

completed, the child is issued a picture identification card. Registration and the first card are free, but there is a charge for replacement cards. Registrations for drop-in day use, which includes paying an admission fee and signing a liability release waiver, are also being used more frequently.

Registration, then, is often a necessary part of program implementation. When registration is undertaken, it should be conducted to maximize convenience for participants rather than for staff. The timing and location of the registration should be convenient for participants.

There are trade-offs between participant convenience and having a manageable, well-organized registration with adequate cash collection procedures. One of the most convenient registration methods is to have participants register with the program leader at the first class meeting. Although this method may maximize convenience, having cash collection occurring in many locations makes it very difficult to follow adequate cash control procedures. Following are six registration methods that could be implemented; each is characterized by specific advantages and disadvantages.

REGISTRATION METHODS

CENTRAL LOCATION METHOD—WALK-IN

In the central location method, all registration for many different programs takes place at a central location, such as a recreation center, school building, or other facility. Parking should be adequate for the number of people anticipated, queuing should be well organized, and staff members conducting the registration should be well oriented and trained to answer participants' questions. Registration workers should provide correct information. If a question cannot be answered correctly when first asked, the best solution is to have the employee call the participant once the correct information has been obtained. It can be damaging to the agency if questions are answered incorrectly.

In a very large operation, it is often wise to specialize operations and have a station-to-station method of completing registration. It is especially important to centralize cash collections so that the money collected is accounted for in the proper accounts. Centralized registration has the following advantages and disadvantages:

Advantages:

- All registration is accomplished at one time and in one place.
- Centralized registrations are easiest to advertise and supervise.
- A centrally located staff member can serve participants better by answering questions about all of the agency's programs from one well-publicized location.
- The central location method also makes possible centralized cash collections and excellent cash control. This minimizes the opportunity for embezzlement and makes it easier to supervise the posting of cash received to the proper accounts.

In the central location method, all registration for many different programs takes place at a central location...

Disadvantages:

- Participants do not see the actual program meeting place or meet the actual program staff. These meetings often raise people's level of anticipation about participating in a program. These interactions can also lead to additional registrations from people who initially may not have been aware of a particular program, did not realize what a program involved, or for some other reason did not choose initially to register for a program.
- Attracting all registrants to one location can mean long lines with accompanying frustrations if the registration procedures and queues are not well planned and managed.
- Registration fee accounts may be mixed up if good accounting procedures are not in place.

PROGRAM LOCATION METHOD—WALK-IN

In the program location method, registration takes place at the program site, such as a swimming pool, tennis court, or playground. This method has the following advantages and disadvantages:

Advantages:

- Registrants become familiar with the program site.
- Registration affords a good opportunity for participants to meet and interact with program staff.

These first two advantages are important features when registering young children. This method gives them an opportunity to become familiar with the setting and the staff of the program before being left "alone."

- There is no delay in registering while waiting for people who are registering for other programs. These delays often occur in the central location method of registration.

Disadvantages:

- This method requires considerable travel time and standing in more than one queue for participants who may be registering for several different programs.
- Decentralized registration is more difficult to supervise.
- Problems associated with cash collection and cash control are increased when registration occurs in several locations.

MAIL-IN METHOD

In the mail-in method of registration, participants complete a registration form and mail it, along with any payment required, to the agency. This method is a centralized system that is accessible to people throughout the community. It has the following advantages and disadvantages:

In the program location method, registration takes place at the program site...

In the mail-in method, patrons complete a registration form and mail it, along with any payment required, to the agency.

Advantages:

- This method is convenient because it requires very little of a participant's time.
- The mail-in method allows for the greatest flexibility in scheduling staff to process registrations.
- Because the payment accepted with mail-in registration is something other than cash, the need to supervise cash collections is eliminated.

Disadvantages:

- This method allows no interaction between agency staff and participants.
- To receive answers to questions, participants must place a phone call to the agency.
- Participants do not see the location of the program until the first session.
- If the agency accepts credit card payments, a return receipt will need to be mailed.

TELEPHONE METHOD

With this method, participants simply telephone the agency to register for a program. Usually, all calls are directed to a central location. This method has the following advantages and disadvantages:

Advantages:

- Staff members can keep accurate, up-to-date records of the registration status of each program; that is, the number of spaces filled and open at any given time.
- The agency is relieved of the burden of managing a physical queue. If demand for registration is heavy, however, some method of queuing phone calls needs to be implemented. It is possible to obtain electronic equipment that will mechanically answer and queue phone calls.

Disadvantages:

- There is no face-to-face interaction between participants and the program staff.
- The participants do not see the program location until the program begins.
- If a fee is involved in registering for the program, collection is often a problem unless the agency accepts credit card payment for fees.
- If the agency accepts credit card payments, a return receipt will need to be mailed.
- When the fee is not paid at the time of registration, registrants may not appear when the program begins.

In the telephone method, patrons simply telephone the agency to register.

In the FAX-in method, patrons complete the registration form, but must supply their credit card information.

FAX-IN METHOD

In the fax-in method of registration, participants complete the registration form, the same as in the mail-in method, but must supply their credit card information on the fax form. The completed registration form is then faxed to the agency's facsimile machine. This method has the following advantages and disadvantages:

Advantages:

- This is a very convenient method for participants who may FAX their registration at any time.
- Because the facsimile machine may receive messages at any time of the day, it expands the time the agency is "open" to receive registrations with no increase in staffing costs.
- The agency does not need to manage a queue, and because the facsimile machine can receive only one transmission at a time, there is an order of receipt of registrations.

Disadvantages:

- There is no interaction between participants and staff, and thus no opportunity to answer questions or give out additional information about the program.
- The program participants do not see the program location until the first class session.
- If a fee is charged for the program, the agency must use credit cards or bill the participant. In either case, this method usually requires the agency to mail something to the participant, either a bill or a credit card receipt.

WEB-BASED METHOD

In the web-based method of registration, participants with access to the Internet may complete their registration on-line, including having their registration confirmed and a receipt provided to print out at their computer. This asynchronous method is unique compared to the other methods because registrants are not limited to open hours of operation. They can register 24 hours a day, seven days a week. It has the following advantages and disadvantages:

Advantages:

- This method is convenient because participants can register whenever they desire.
- Participants receive automatic confirmation of registration.
- This form of registration is easy for persons who are familiar with computers.

Disadvantages:

- Web-based registration serves a small proportion of the constituency, although this will change as more people gain access to the Internet.

In the web-based method, patrons with access to the Internet may complete their registration online.

- Poorly designed websites can result in poor public relations.
- Currently, this method is expensive. The agency must either purchase costly computer programs or hire highly skilled Internet specialists. Many agencies do not have the funds to offer this service.

COMBINATION OF METHODS

The agency may decide to permit participants to register using two or more of the methods outlined above. Typically, the central location or program methods are combined with the mail-in, telephone, or fax methods. Sunnyvale Parks and Recreation Department, Sunnyvale, California, has created a centralized registration center that accepts walk-in, mail-in, phone-in, and fax-in registrations in one location, thus enabling them to coordinate all registrations from one location. Using a combination of methods offers the following advantages and disadvantages:

Advantages:

- Participants have the greatest flexibility and opportunity in completing their registration.
- In making registration convenient, the agency maximizes its chances of fully enrolling its programs.

Disadvantages:

- When registration is accepted in several locations, lists can be confused and programs over-enrolled unless registration is carefully coordinated. Using remote computer terminals with a centralized database for maintaining program rosters is one solution. The allocation of a given number of spaces in each program to each registration location is another solution. In this case, staff members at any one location may accept only a given number of registrants unless additional spaces are approved by a central coordinator.
- Participants may be confused about which registration method they are to use when several methods are available.

Keep registration forms simple to complete while obtaining as much information as possible for use in marketing.

It is important to indicate how registrations will be queued when a combination of methods is used. For example, does a participant who has phoned to register receive priority over someone who may be standing in a queue in the outer office? How are mail-in registrations queued compared with walk-in and faxed registrations? What happens with mail-in registrations that are received before or after a deadline?

THE REGISTRATION FORM

Dobmeyer (1986) believes the registration form should be placed inside the last page of the catalog or brochure. This placement allows the prime space in the front of the publication to be used to promote programs. Participants reach the form when they are most likely ready to complete it. When this is done, messages should appear throughout the brochure informing participants about the location of the registration form, for example, "For registration information, please see page XX."

In addition, using the last page usually means the returned registration form will also include the mailing label, which will contain information that can be used for marketing purposes.

The City of Kettering, Ohio, places their registration form in the center of their brochure. It is included in a center pull-out that is printed on clay-coated paper inserted among the rest of the pages that are printed on recycled newsprint. This seems to be an equally effective placement because the recipient of the brochure is almost forced to open to the center section first because of the stiffness of the paper relative to the stiffness of the remainder of the brochure. Increased numbers of agencies put their brochures and registration forms on the World Wide Web for their participants. How this is accomplished will be discussed in an upcoming section about Computerizing Registration.

WHAT TO INCLUDE?

One is often faced with two mutually exclusive objectives in designing the registration form itself: keeping it simple to complete, and obtaining as much information as possible for use in marketing. Current practice is to keep it simple and easy to register for a program. To facilitate this, design registration forms that request only information that is needed and easily supplied by the participants. Exhibit 15-2 on page 282 is a sample registration form that includes the following:

- today's date,
- the registrant's name, address, day and evening phone,
- the program(s) the participant wants to register for,
- the fee for each program,
- to whom the check should be written,
- what to expect after he or she registers (e.g., will the participant receive a confirmation or should the person consider himself or herself registered unless he or she is notified differently),
- a liability release form,
- information about the method of payment, and
- instructions about where to send the registration.

Depending on the type of agency involved, some of this information may be omitted or may be handled differently. In a club, such as a YWCA or a commercial club that has an existing membership list, participants may not need to supply more than the enrollments desired and their names and membership numbers. In these cases, treating them like members, people who are well known to the agency, and thus voiding the need to supply information again, enhances the relationship. Club members may not even be required to make payment to register—they may simply be billed every thirty days for their club activities.

To maintain the illusion that the form is easy to complete, it should be kept as small as possible. This can be difficult in some situations. For example, in public agencies, the brochure is often mailed to a household and the registration form must be large enough to accommodate a family that is likely to have multiple registrants in multiple programs. The inclusion of credit card information and a release of liability also increases the size and reduces the ease of completing a registration form.

Exhibit 15-2: Sample Registration Form

Name _____   Date _____

Address (Include Apt # if applicable) _____

City _____   State_____   Zip _____

Day phone _____   Evening phone _____

Please provide the name and phone number of a local person to contact in case of an emergency if there is no answer at the above number.

Name _____   Phone (   ) _____

Each adult participant must sign below. In addition, the signature of a parent or legal guardian is required for youth participants (under 18 years of age).

I, the undersigned or parent/guardian of the individual named below, do hereby agree to allow the individual named herein to participate in the aforementioned activity, and I further agree to indemnify and hold harmless the City of Sunnyvale and its employees, officers, and agents from and against any and all liability, save and except for the sole negligence of the City or its employees, resulting in injury associated with that individual's participation in this activity. I/we agree to allow use of my/our photograph for program publicity. I/we have read and agree to the registration and program policies.*

    Check the appropriate box(es) and sign.

____ **Participant (18 or over)**   ____ **Parent**   ____ **Legal Guardian**

Signature/date _____

Signature/date _____

Signature/date _____

Participant's Name	Birth-date (If under 18)	Sex	Class No.	Class Title	Fee
1					
2					
3					
4					
5					
6					
7					

Total Fees _____

Make checks payable to: Anytown USA

Participants are automatically enrolled in the activity unless notified otherwise by [the agency].

NOTE: NO CONFIRMATION WILL BE MAILED

FOR OFFICE USE ONLY		
Fees accurate	Refund Due	Notes
Clerk	Date Processed	

*Taken from the Sunnyvale, California, Parks and Recreation Department's GUIDE, Fall 1993. This release is used for illustration purposes only. No warranty is given regarding the legal appropriateness of this statement for the reader's use, and the reader is cautioned to not copy this statement. Any such statement should be developed and approved by the agency's legal counsel.

Exhibit 15-3: Liability Release Form

Release of Liability and Assumption of Risk Agreement

In CONSIDERATION of the acceptance of the application for entry into the classes or activities listed on the Registration Form on the reverse side of this agreement, I hereby WAIVE, RELEASE, and DISCHARGE any and all claims for damages for death, personal injury, or property damage which I may have, or which may hereafter accrue to me as a result of my participation in said classes or activities. This release is intended to discharge in advance the City of Santa Clara, City Council, its officers, agents, and employees, the Santa Clara Unified School District and the School Board, its officers, agents, and employees from and against any and all liability arising out of or connected with my participation in said classes or activities, even though that liability may arise out of NEGLIGENCE or CARELESSNESS on the part of the persons on entities mentioned above.

I HAVE READ THE DESCRIPTION IN THIS CATALOG OF EACH CLASS OR ACTIVITY FOR WHICH I HAVE REGISTERED, AND I AM AWARE THAT THESE CLASSES OR ACTIVITIES SUBJECT ME TO PHYSICAL RISKS AND DANGERS. NEVERTHELESS, I VOLUNTARILY AGREE TO ASSUME ANY AND ALL RISKS OF INJURY OR DEATH, AND TO RELEASE, DISCHARGE, AND HOLD HARMLESS ALL OF THE ENTITIES OR PERSONS MENTIONED ABOVE WHO, THROUGH NEGLIGENCE OR CARELESSNESS, MIGHT OTHERWISE BE LIABLE TO ME OR MY HEIRS, PERSONAL REPRESENTATIVES, NEXT OF KIN, SPOUSE, OR ASSIGNS.

It is understood and agreed that this waiver, release, and assumption of risk is to be binding on my HEIRS, PERSONAL REPRESENTATIVES, NEXT OF KIN, SPOUSE, and ASSIGNS.

I have carefully READ this Agreement and fully UNDERSTAND its contents. All participants in the classes or activities, including minors 13–17 year of age, must sign this Agreement.

Date: _____

ADULT PARTICIPANTS SIGN BELOW

Signature: _____ Print Name: _____

Signature: _____ Print Name: _____

PARTICIPANTS, AGES 13–17, SIGN BELOW

Signature: _____ Print Name: _____

Signature: _____ Print Name: _____

TO BE COMPLETED BY PARENT OR GUARDIAN OF MINORS

I have fully read this Agreement and fully understand its contents. Furthermore, the significance of this release of liability and assumption of risk agreement has been EXPLAINED TO THE MINOR.

Signature of parent or guardian: _____ Date: _____

Print Name: _____

Address: _____

Please indicate whether you are signing as:

Parent ____ Guardian ____

Note: Taken from the Santa Clara Recreation Activities Guide, Fall 1993, Santa Clara Parks and Recreation Department, Santa Clara, California. This release is used for illustration purposes only. No warranty is given regarding the legal appropriateness of this statement for the reader's use, and the reader is cautioned not to copy this statement. Any such statement should be developed and approved by the agency's legal counsel.

LIABILITY RELEASE FORM

Because the law regards anyone registered in an agency's program as an invitee (Peterson & Hronek, 1992), the agency is held to the highest legal standard of care in operating its programs. Thus, the completion of liability release forms as a part of registration is becoming increasingly common. The release form included in Exhibit 15-3 on page 283 is found on the reverse side of the registration form used by the City of Santa Clara, California, and thus is a physical part of it. The degree of risk a participant is asked to waive in advance of participation will vary between agencies. For example, compare the release in Exhibit 15-3, used by the City of Santa Clara, with the one used by the City of Sunnyvale, included in Exhibit 15-2. Although Sunnyvale accepts negligence in its release, Santa Clara asks participants to release it from negligence.

DISTRIBUTION

The obvious key to distributing the advertising brochure is to get it to the market for the program. Depending on the agency involved, this can include different groups of individuals. For example, governmental agencies, because of their responsibility to all citizens in a community, try to distribute the brochure to all citizens. Many will use the bulk mail method utilizing the "Postal Participant, Local" addressing method. With this method, the agency must presort the brochures and mail carriers will leave one in each mailbox on their route. However, the post office allows between two to five days to deliver this type of mail; therefore, citizens in various parts of town will receive them at different times—up to five days apart. This can create problems with the timing of registration and equity of access.

Mailing the brochure with a pay-per-piece method will assure that participants receive the brochure at almost the same time. Organizations with members that accept registrations from both members and non-members usually mail a brochure to their members and then use different conduits for distributing additional brochures. Tracking the returns from various distribution locations is an important marketing effort, and the agency should use some type of method for coding the brochures used in each distribution conduit so those that are most effective can be identified.

TIMING OF REGISTRATION

Ideally, registration should be possible when the participant receives the brochure. However, this can become a major issue if everyone does not receive the brochure at the same time. Thus, many agencies indicate a starting date for accepting registrations. In addition, in many municipal operations and some YMCAs and YWCAs, residents or members are given a priority registration period. Clearly communicating the date at which each group (e.g., residents, non-residents, members, or the general public) may begin registering is important.

FEES

In registering for a program, participants are making a commitment to participate, which is intensified when they are required to pay a fee at the time of registration. The policy in most agencies is that the participant is not registered until the fee is paid. The fee for each program should be specified, and the form should make it easy for the participant to total his or her fees. However, because of the use of line-item accounting practices, some governmental agencies require a separate check for each program so that the fee for any class that is closed may be returned. Alternatives to this method include accepting one check and informing the participant that any refunds could take up to 30 to 60 days, or providing them with a voucher that can be used for a future enrollment. Any of these alternatives are less desirable for the participant than returning his or her money.

How differential pricing is handled is important. If club members or community residents receive a lower price than non-members or non-residents, this should be stated. How this is communicated can both enhance it as a benefit and reduce its adverse impact. For example, one community states the price for participating and then states the discounted price for residents. This method clearly presents the price difference as a benefit to residents and a penalty to no one.

CREDIT CARDS

The problem of credit cards must also be dealt with during registration. It is assumed that credit card use will increase sales volume. However, allowing individuals to use credit cards costs the agency three to five percent of total sales, which must be paid to a credit card company for collecting fees. In many municipal government operations, there is resistance to using credit cards because most municipal fees are mandatory and it makes no sense to give away three to five percent of the fees. However, fees for recreation and leisure services are not mandatory, and most practitioners agree that using credit cards to pay for services will most likely increase sales volume.

CANCELLATIONS AND REFUNDS

Most agencies have a minimum number of participants before a program is operated. You will need to make certain this operational procedure is part of the information provided in the advertising brochure. Additionally, you will need to make certain participants know the procedures you will follow in handling their registration for a class that does not reach minimum enrollment. Agencies should give full refunds for classes that are canceled.

Likewise, make certain participants know what will be done with their registration if the class is full when their registration arrives. Some agencies place them on a waiting list until the class begins. If this is the case, the participant needs to be notified about what is occurring. For example, if you have already told participants they are registered unless they hear differently, they will need to be notified they are not registered, but instead have been placed on a waiting list. Clear, on-

15

...make certain patrons know the procedures you will follow in handling their registration for a class that does not reach minimum enrollment.

...make certain participants know what will be done with their registration if the class is full when their registration arrives.

going communication needs to be implemented to maintain customer confidence and satisfaction.

The agency's policy regarding the cancellation of one's space in a non-fee program should also be made known. No-shows can be an especially difficult problem when spaces in a program are limited, demand is high, and no fee is charged for the program. Some restaurants keep lists of people who make reservations and then do not show up. After a certain number of no-show incidents, reservations are no longer accepted from offending individuals.

Another solution is to charge a refundable reservation fee at the time of registration and return the fee to those who attend. Forfeit fees in athletic leagues are a good example of this technique, which could be implemented more frequently in other programs to solve the problem of no-shows. In one case, a refundable one dollar fee was charged those registering for a downhill slalom ski course. In a previous year, many individuals had registered and then did not run the course, even though staff members were waiting in freezing temperatures at the end of the course. When the refundable fee policy was implemented, almost all who registered actually participated in the slalom run. With this technique, only those who do not participate actually pay. In essence, they are charged a penalty for denying someone else the opportunity or for putting an unreasonable burden on the agency.

TRANSFERS

Some agencies will allow those already registered to transfer their registration to another class with available space prior to the beginning of a program. When using this option, be certain to state the terms of the offer; for example, that this may be done up to one week prior to the start of the program.

GUARANTEES

Another feature being offered in some agencies is a guarantee of satisfaction with their programs. If a customer is dissatisfied, they may receive a voucher for another program or a full refund. Often, some activities, such as golf fees or athletic league fees for teams, are exempted from this policy.

COMPUTERIZING REGISTRATION

Several software packages are currently available to computerize the registration process. It is most likely that during your career you will be managing computerized registrations, so you need to learn about them.

Before purchasing software, it is advisable to determine whether services such as touch tone registration and membership cards will be needed. Consulting groups can provide valuable advice to agencies by helping them ask the right questions about their computer registration needs. Attending trade shows and conference exhibitions provides hands-on experience to get the feel for how a program works. The Internet can be used to search for "recreation software." By e-mailing for more information, interested agencies can receive demo disks or links

Case 15-1: A Realistic View of Program Registration via the Internet

Elmhurst Park District, Elmhurst, IL

Elmhurst Park District (EPD) has one of the most advanced systems for program registration in the state of Illinois. Information systems specialists Steve Dittemore and Mike Smith explain that registration via the Internet generally evolves within an agency in one of four ways. The most basic approach is to post the program brochure on the Internet for browsing purposes. Potential participants will still need to register for programs by the more traditional methods, such as walk-in, mail-in, phone, and so on. EPD used this approach in 1995 in their earliest experiences with the Internet.

The second approach builds on the first with the addition of a registration option via e-mail message. This approach is not fully automated because a staff member still needs to call the interested party back to complete the registration process. Many recreation and park departments and districts are beginning to use this technology for registration.

The third approach, which is the one used currently by EPD, is substantially more involved than the others. In the public sector, the availability of funds is lower when compared to profit-oriented businesses. Such funding limits the degree to which agencies can acquire computer hardware, software, Internet access, and the like. Although potential participants may enjoy the convenience of registration over the Internet, they are also wary of using their credit card for payment. To address this problem, EPD formed an Internet Club. Interested persons sign up in the traditional manner (mail-in, walk-in, etc.) by providing such general information as their name, age, address, phone number, e-mail address, credit card name and number, and other family members' names and ages. A signed waiver is also required.

At this point, the Internet Club member enters a private, secure website that permits one to browse the brochure and register for programs. Through a series of mouse clicks and menus, the registration information and credit card number is sent to a park district staff member. The system is not foolproof, however. A staff member must complete the registration by checking things such as credit card expiration dates and age restrictions. Once the registration is complete, the Internet Club member receives a confirmation via e-mail. Currently, only a handful of people use the Internet to register for EPD's programs. However, Smith and Dittemore speculate that it is only a matter of time before agencies begin to hire full-time information specialists to manage similar systems.

The final approach to Internet registration is a fully-automated registration program that does not require humans to complete the process. Unfortunately, few public agencies can afford this expensive technology. As technology improves and costs come down, however, more agencies will use fully automated registration systems.

to the company website to become familiar with products. Some of the most popular software systems used to automate registration are: RecWare by Sierra Digital Inc.; Escom Software Services, Ltd.; Get Physical!; and Vermont Systems Inc. (The reader will find links to the websites for these and other vendors on the book website, www.recreationprogramming.com).

Technology in Program Registration

Using computer software, programmers are able to:

- Monitor class rosters and waiting lists.
- Maintain accident report records and liability waivers.
- Use mail merge functions to target specific populations or for previous customers.
- Track age and ability restrictions, instructors, and resident/non-resident restrictions.
- Process payments, refunds, transfers, and cancellations.

How well a registration is operated will send a message to patrons about the quality of the agency and its programs.

Software programs can perform a multitude of tasks. Programs that are currently available allow participants to register via the Internet, produce registration lists, keep track of enrollment numbers, produce lists of under-enrolled classes, maintain waiting lists for over-enrolled classes, and track sales, expenses, and net revenue. Additionally, they will permit the generation of many analytical marketing reports, allowing the tracking of a wide range of sociodemographic variables that can be cross-tabulated to facilitate target marketing to specified groups. A client database can be created to store everything from names, addresses, and phone numbers, to e-mail addresses, dietary needs, and emergency contact information for each client. Thus, registration data can support the agency's marketing effort with current registrants. Remember, however, that non-users are not included in this database.

Moving to an automated registration system can be a daunting task at first, but the software is designed to simplify the registration process. Taking the time necessary to properly train staff who will use the system will minimize any problems that might occur during program registration. Case 15-1 on page 287 includes an account of how one agency, the Elmhurst Park District, in Elmhurst, Illinois, determined how they could best implement electronic registration.

OPERATING REGISTRATION

How well a registration is operated will send a message to participants about the quality of the agency and its programs. The brochure is the first contact with the participant; registration is usually the second, and is also the first participant-initiated contact. Good customer service is essential at this stage of the service encounter in order to keep the participant satisfied. Following are some suggestions for operating a well-organized registration.

REGISTRATION CONSIDERATIONS

• Provide enough staff to handle the anticipated number of registrants. Supervisory staff should keep track of how long it takes individuals to register and make adjustments as needed so that registrations can be completed in a reasonable time.

• Schedule registration at a time consistent with local customs. Early mornings, evenings, or other time slots when participants are available should all be scheduled.

• Completely orient and train staff before registration:

    a. Emphasize the need to be courteous to participants.

    b. Try to have established objective methods for handling potential points of disagreement. For example, if registrants must show that they are residents of the community, determine in advance how this point is to be established. Must the participant have a driver's license with an appropriate address or a voter registration card? Do not leave it up to the registration staff to improvise methods for verifying age, height, weight, skill level, residency, and so forth.

    c. Fully inform registration personnel about program details, waiting lists, fee payment policies and methods, refund procedures, non-resident registration policies, and the like.

    d. Have details about each program available for the registration staff. Agencies often become too lax and do not require that contract leaders completely inform the agency about program details. Remember, in the eyes of the public, this is the agency's program, and the public expects agency personnel to know the details of its operation.

• Establish well-defined and well-organized queues.

• Provide simple and clear registration forms. Try to arrange for individuals to have completed as much of the registration form as possible before receiving the attention of registration personnel.

• Carefully instruct cashiers how to accept payment and properly record and account for each type of program fee.

• Provide additional, well-oriented staff for agency telephones immediately before, during, and shortly after the registration period.

• Provide adequate pens and space for writing at the registration location. Now complete Exercise 15-1 on page 290.

QUEUING PROCEDURES

Queuing is simply standing in line waiting for a turn to be served. There is an old story about the British: When two or more British people get together, the first thing they must determine is how the queue will be organized. Often, we do not think of managing a queue until it has gotten out of control.

That queues can get out of control and become a major problem was made clear by the poorly conceived queuing system at a "Who" rock concert in Cincinnati, Ohio, on December 3, 1979. Only a limited number of reserved seats were sold by the Riverfront Coliseum management. Approximately 80 percent were unreserved "festival seating" (Stuart, 1979). Instead of taking care of the order in which to serve people at the point of sale, the management let the audience scramble for desirable seats the night of the concert. Because of the group's popularity, the audience began gathering for the 8:00 p.m. concert in mid-afternoon. It was the usual practice for the coliseum to open its doors two hours before a concert. On this evening, however, the "Who" were late

Queuing is simply standing in line waiting for a turn to be served.

If a person is willing to invest large amounts of time and suffering standing in a line—there should be an appropriate reward...

in setting up their equipment, so the doors did not open until about 7:00 p.m. In addition, all of the doors around the coliseum did not open at the same time. The crowd at the end of the coliseum that was delayed in opening became unruly and charged the doors for admission. In the ensuing melee, eleven young people were trampled and killed (Thomas, 1979). Poorly conceived queuing, then, can create major problems.

There is evidence that standing in a queue can be an anxiety-producing experience (Mann, 1973). Traditionally, leisure programmers have ignored queues and assumed that the program began when the participants entered the facility itself or came into the program. Programmers did not worry about the queue.

Standing in a queue may be the participant's first self-initiated contact with a program. Successfully managing queues requires that the programmer adequately deal with the first two laws of service delivery (Maister, 1985): (1) satisfaction equals perception minus expectations, and (2) it is hard to play catch-up ball. The participants' satisfaction will depend on both their level of expectation and their perception of actual performance. As long as their perception of performance equals or exceeds their expectations, they will be satisfied. However, if it does not, they will be dissatisfied and it will be difficult to ameliorate this dissatisfaction with your performance in operating the program. There is evidence that queues for concerts, movies, sporting events, and other leisure events are perceived as occasions for socializing (Mann, 1973), so participants usually arrive expecting to have a positive, satisfying experience. The key is to operate registrations in a satisfactory manner so that you do not begin a program in a deficit condition of participant dissatisfaction.

To better manage queues, it helps to understand the sociological principles that underlie the behavior of people in queues. Mann (1973) points out that queues are governed by the "rule of distributive justice," which was first outlined by Homans (1961). According to Mann, the rule as applied to queuing suggests that if a person is willing to invest large amounts of time and suffering in an activity—that is, standing in a line—there should be an appropriate reward—that is, preferential treatment. If individuals in a queue are to believe the queue is fair, they must perceive "a direct correspondence between inputs (time spent waiting) and outcome (preferential service)" (p. 48). Violating this principle creates stress and anxiety.

Four sources of stress and anxiety are associated with being in queues. First, there is the problem of queue jumping. This practice is a breach of distributive justice and a threat to the social order of a queue. Second, individuals are responsible for guarding their own territory. People in the queue are expected to remain vigilant and protect the queue position directly in front of them from queue jumpers. Their stress level is elevated when someone does jump the queue directly in front of them. When this happens, the individual bears the responsibility of dealing with the queue jumper and protecting the position. Third, one must make sure of being in the right queue for the service desired. When there are several queues for different services, poorly identified queues are a source of anxiety and stress. Finally, there is the problem of how long one will have to wait before receiving service. Not knowing how long the wait will be is also stress producing.

If the stress and anxiety of queuing are reduced, queuing will be eliminated as a possible source of participant dissatisfaction with the event. Furthermore, a well-managed queue can contribute to the overall satisfaction with a leisure experience. Program implementation begins with the queue. The burden of managing it rests with the recreation staff. How the queue is to be operated, then, needs to be well planned.

FOUR TYPES OF QUEUES

The first step in managing stress-free, enjoyable queues is to define them with barriers or other physical guides and to reduce the possibility of queue jumping. Four types of queues can be established (Mann, 1973): (1) a single line with a single service, (2) multiple lines with multiple services, (3) a single line with multiple services, and (4) station-to-station services. In the United States, the single line with a single service and multiple lines with multiple services queue types seem to be the most popular. These two types work well if the service being provided to each participant is similar in the amount of time it will take to deliver. However, the multiple line with multiple service approach can be terribly stress producing. Because of the differential service needs of each participant, some lines move much more rapidly or slowly than others. The solution is the single line with multiple service approach. This

15

approach seems to be gaining popularity in the United States, partly because it better implements the rule of distributive justice. It is the method of choice for large registrations in which participants may be registering for one or more programs and for themselves, a whole family, or a group of people.

The station-to-station method of queuing is effective when a series of steps must be undertaken to complete a transaction. This method essentially links together various combinations of the first three methods. One must make certain that no unacceptable, stress-producing bottlenecks occur in this type of queue.

Several other procedures can also be implemented to ensure stress-free, enjoyable queues:

1. *Register the order of arrival, using a recognized system.* A take-a-number or similar system determines the order of service and eliminates the need for a physical queue and its associated problems.

2. *Improve the speed of service.* This can be done by having more service stations or reducing the burden of completing the transaction. For example, do participants have to place their name, address, and phone number on a separate card for each program they enter? Must they write a check for each separate program? Eliminating repetitious actions will help speed service and require no additional personnel.

3. *Assure the certainty of service.* If participants know there are enough services to meet their needs, much of the stress will be alleviated. Guaranteeing this will not always be possible. However, if queue managers know that the service is adequate, they should let the participants know that their waiting is not in vain. A corollary to this is to let queuers know as soon as possible when they cannot expect service so that they can stop investing their time.

4. *Start service for participants while they are in line.* An in-process wait seems shorter than a pre-process wait (Maister, 1985), so one should create the perception that service has started as soon as possible. For example, one could distribute registration forms, instructions about the event, instructions about the queue, brochures about other events, and so on. Station-to-station queues often create this perception, because individuals move through a series of encounters that provide some service at each step.

5. *Post the time required in the queue.* Keep queuers informed about how soon they can expect service. The Disney organization does an excellent job of informing participants about the waiting time before they can gain access to an attraction. For example, they post signs in many queues that state, "Approximate Waiting Time is 30 Minutes." A pizza restaurant in Champaign, Illinois, posts a sign in its queue, informing participants that "From this point, you will be eating pizza in approximately 10 minutes." Providing this information creates reasonable expectations for queuers about how long it will take in the queue before receiving service. This step helps avoid unreasonable expectations, complaints, and unnecessary anxiety.

6. *Have the queue move forward toward the point of service.* When designing the queue, make certain that queuers are actually moving toward the point of service or at least have the illusion of progressing toward it. This builds anticipation and relieves anxiety.

Giveaways should be well managed and offer sufficient service to all.

Exercise 15-2: Ensuring Stress-free, Enjoyable Queues

Directions: As a class, provide real-life examples of the seven ways to create stress-free, enjoyable queues.

Ways to create stress-free, enjoyable queues	Recreation Example	Other Example
1. Register the order of arrival using a recognized system.		
2. Improve the speed of service (multiple stations, room to complete forms).		
3. Assure the certainty of service.		
4. Start service for patrons while they are in line.		
5. Post time required in the queue.		
6. Have the queue move forward toward the point of service.		
7. Make the queue fun.		

7. *Make the queue fun. Standing in a queue can be incorporated into the leisure event itself.* This is a desirable goal and can both decrease stress and make queuing part of the whole experience. For example, at Disneyland the queue area for each attraction is thematically developed as part of the attraction and is designed to build excitement for the forthcoming experience. When one author was a faculty member at the University of Illinois, the football team received a bid to play in the Liberty Bowl in Memphis, Tennessee. The local Liberty Bowl committee treated queuers waiting for tickets to hot coffee, donuts, and entertainment from a pep band. Their efforts certainly turned a boring queue into an enjoyable event that helped build excitement for the Liberty Bowl itself. Implementing similar activities can help make queues a positive component of the event. Now try Exercise 15-2.

GIVEAWAYS

Giveaways should be well managed and offer sufficient service to all. Public agencies should not be a part of giveaways when service for

If giveaways are not handled properly, they can be a detriment to an event rather than a positive contribution.

all who desire it is inadequate, or if the event is not properly organized and operated. Sponsors who wish to participate in giveaways at public agency events should be required to provide enough service for all and to follow queuing guidelines developed by the agency to ensure an orderly and fair queue.

While employed in a public agency, one author was once involved with a group of puppeteers who performed in a park one Sunday afternoon. Their performance was excellent. Some 150 to 200 children were seated on the lawn in front of the stage watching the performance. Parents were standing in a semicircle behind the children. At the end of the performance, a cast member came onto the stage with a box of candy suckers and announced that the children in the audience would be treated to a sucker. All of the children immediately stood up and began pressing forward. Many were very small and were getting crushed against the stage. Children who had already received a sucker could not leave the scene because they were trapped against the stage by the children still trying to press forward. The worst that happened was that some parents were anxious and upset, and some children were crying and frightened. Two points about this event need to be made. First, the puppet performance was excellent and there was no need to add a sucker giveaway to the event. Second, the way the giveaway was handled damaged what was, up to that point, an excellent event.

If giveaways are not handled properly, they can be a detriment to an event rather than a positive contribution. Giveaways that do not have sufficient service for all also create problems. People who are not served usually feel that the queue was unfair and are disappointed. An agency suffers adverse publicity when it allows incomplete or poorly managed giveaways to occur under its auspices.

> *Queues must be managed to maximize their positive contribution to partipant satisfaction with a program.*

PRE-QUEUES AND NO QUEUES

Two final issues to be discussed are pre-queues and no queues. Despite well-developed agency plans for queues, participants will often take matters into their own hands and begin pre-queues before the start of the official agency queue. One needs to anticipate this possibility and be prepared to deal with it. One must decide if the order established by the pre-queue will be recognized and how it will be recognized. No matter how well one plans, an uncomfortable interface always occurs when the time comes to make the transition between the pre-queue and the official queue. Some agencies have therefore stopped using a queue for determining the order of admission to events and now use a system of random drawing for admission positions. The N.C.A.A. has done this for "Final Four" public tickets. The demand is simply too great and queue management too much of a hassle to do otherwise. A number of college campuses have also implemented such a system for admission to rock concerts and other high-demand events.

Some people object to a random draw system because it totally eliminates the rule of distributive justice. All who enter the drawing have an equal chance of being admitted to the event. Without a queue, those who strongly desire admission do not have the opportunity to invest their time in a queue and receive the appropriate reward (preferential treatment).

How the queue is managed sends messages to participants about the quality of the program. It is usually the first face-to-face contact the agency has with the participant. Queuing needs to be considered as part of the program and should be dealt with during the implementation stage. It needs to be managed to maximize its positive contribution to participant satisfaction with a program.

CONCLUSION

Implementation includes efficiently registering participants at a location and time that is convenient for them. There are a variety of registration methods, each with its own advantages and disadvantages. Understanding queuing behavior is essential to properly managing queues. Queues that are fairly and efficiently managed at registration and at program locations contribute to participant satisfaction with services.

REFERENCES

Dobmeyer, E. (1986). *Registration techniques*. Manhattan, KS: Learning Resources Network.

Homans, G. C. (1961). *Social behavior: Its elementary forms*. New York: Harcourt.

Hronek, B. R., & Spengler, J. O. (1997). *Legal liability in recreation and sports*. Champaign, IL: Sagamore.

Maister, D. H. (1985). The psychology of waiting in lines. In J. A. Czepiel, M. R. Solomon, & C. F. Surprenant (Eds.), *The service encounter* (pp. 176–183). Lexington, MA: Lexington Books, D. C. Heath.

Mann, L. (1973). Learning to live with lines. In J. Helmer & N. A. Edginton (Eds.), *Urbanmen: The psychology of urban survival* (pp. 42–61). New York: Macmillan.

Peterson, J. A., & Hronek, B. B. (1992). *Risk management: For park, recreation, and leisure services* (2nd ed.). Champaign, IL: Sagamore.

Stuart, R. (1979, December 5). Cincinnati officials order inquiry into concert crush that killed 11. *New York Times*, p. 1, D21.

Thomas, R. M., Jr. (1979, December 4). 11 killed and 8 badly hurt in crush before rock concert in Cincinnati. *New York Times*, pp. 1, 13.

DOCUMENTS WITH LIMITED CIRCULATION

Documents and brochures from the following agencies were cited in this chapter.

City of Kettering Parks, Recreation, and Cultural Arts Department, 3600 Shroyer Rd., Kettering, OH 45429

Recreation and Community Services Department, 1 West Campbell Ave. #C31, Campbell, CA 95008

Santa Clara Parks and Recreation Department, 1500 Warburton Ave., Santa Clara, CA 95050

Sunnyvale Parks and Recreation Department, P.O. Box 3707, Sunnyvale, CA 94088-3707

Plant Westerville Watch Us Bloom!
Photo courtesy of Westerville Parks and Recreation Department, Westerville, OH
Photo by Jody Stowers

Staffing and Supervising Program Operations

STEP 7 : IMPLEMENTATION

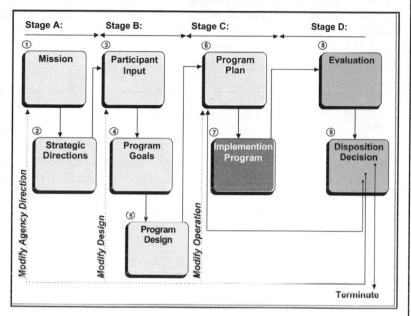

16

Staffing recreation services involves recruiting, selecting, orienting, training, deploying, supervising, appraising, compensating, and contracting staff. In this chapter, the essential elements of the process are outlined, and personnel management problems and techniques associated with supervising program operations are outlined.

Most recreation agencies have well-developed, written policies for the management of full-time personnel in the agency. Unfortunately, this is not always true for part-time and seasonal employees, even though leisure service agencies typically employ a large number of such people to operate their many recreation facilities and programs.

Programmers are usually the first-line, full-time employees in a recreation agency. According to Sterle and Duncan (1977), the two primary roles of program supervisors are program development and development of leadership personnel. In many agencies, face-to-face delivery of the recreation service is accomplished solely by the part-time and seasonal workers. This is the case in many commercial recreation operations such as water parks, tennis facilities, and amusement parks. This is also true in municipalities, not-for-profit organizations, church recreation, and other organizations that operate recreation services.

Implementing Outcome-Based Programming

If you are using outcome-based programming for the first time, it may be necessary to train staff in its use. If the agency staffs its first-line leadership positions with seasonal or part-time employees, these individuals may not have the background knowledge to implement outcome-based programming techniques. Thus, it is likely that the programmer will need to provide this type of employee with both training and close supervision in order to successfully implement and operate programs with this approach.

When outcome-based programming is being used to offer programs for at-risk populations, indigenous leaders with a positive pre-existing reputation and networks in the neighborhood may be the best choice for staffing the program. However, it is likely that these individuals will also need training and supervision in the techniques of this approach.

Staffing recreation services involves recruiting, selecting, orienting, training, deploying, supervising, appraising, compensating, and contracting staff.

McKinney and Chandler (1991) suggest that this practice has become popular because it increases staffing flexibility and lowers labor costs. With part-time workers, programmers can match the number of staff to their needs on a seasonal basis. In addition, because the interest in many recreation activities is cyclical, programmers can also hire staff who can lead and teach the activities currently being demanded with no commitment to their future employment.

However, problems are created by this practice. First, part-time staff are less loyal to the organization and its programs (McKinney & Chandler, 1991) and thus may not promote the long-term interests of the organization by building customer loyalty. Participants rarely know if an employee is part-time or full-time, so the organization as a whole is judged by the performance of part-time as well as full-time employees. Second, there is a higher rate of employee turnover among part-time and seasonal workers. This results in a need to recruit and train new employees frequently. Both of the preceding problems lead to a third problem: the need for close supervision of their work performance.

Programmers will not be able to personally deliver all of the recreation services under their direction. As a successful professional football coach once said, "It does not matter how much I know about how to play football. What matters is how much the players on the field know about playing football." He was implying that he had a tremendous role in teaching and preparing the players to play the game. The same is true for the delivery of recreation services. Research suggests that seasonal employees are more happy and motivated when supervisory practices create a work environment that is challenging and provides employees the skills needed to perform at the level desired (Henderson & Bialeschki, 1993). Thus, operating successful programs will often depend on how well the programmer can recruit, train, deploy, and supervise all part-time and seasonal staff.

Exhibit 16-1: Recreation Leader Job Analysis

1. Information Input. Where and how does the worker get the information used in performing the job?

   Examples:
   - Uses policy manuals.
   - Takes verbal direction.
   - Uses leadership instruction manuals.

2. Mental Process. What reasoning, decision-making, and information-processing activities are involved in performing the job?

   Examples:
   - Makes decisions about safe playground practices.
   - Makes decisions while leading activities.
   - Maintains order and discipline on the playground.

3. Work Output. What physical activities does the worker perform, and what tools or devices does he or she use?

   Examples:
   - Leads games and other recreation activities.
   - Must set-up and take-down recreation equipment.
   - Must be able to drive a van

4. Relationships with Other Persons. What relationships with other people are required in performing the job?

   Examples:
   - Instructs and leads activities.
   - Must relate to all playground users.
   - Needs to work cooperatively with other workers.

5. Job Context. In what physical or social context is the work performed?

   Examples:
   - Works out-of-doors.
   - Works in a fun, social atmosphere.
   - Works in constant interaction with participants.

6. Other Characteristics. What activities, conditions, or characteristics other than those already described are relevant to the job?

   Examples:
   - Must work unusual hours.
   - Often works without constant, direct supervision.
   - Must be able to enforce rules tactfully.

Adapted from: McCormick E. J., Shaw, J. D., & DeNisi, A. S., (1979). Use of PAQ for establishing the job component validity of tests. Journal of Applied Psychology 64(1), 51–56.

JOB ANALYSIS

Staffing begins with an understanding of the agency's goals and objectives. Staff members who can fulfill the agency's goals and objectives and deliver program services consistent with the agency's programming philosophy need to be hired. In most instances, organized recreation services are people-to-people services involving face-to-face interactions between participants and staff members in a leadership, instructor, or customer service role. It is essential, therefore, that qualified and well-trained staff members be placed in these roles. The first step in acquiring an adequate staff is to complete a job analysis.

Mathis and Jackson (1982) define job analysis as "a systematic investigation of the tasks, duties, and responsibilities of a job, and the necessary knowledge, skills, and abilities someone needs to perform the job adequately" (p. 143). A job analysis contains all of the information necessary to develop and administer the job, including a detailed statement of work behaviors and other information relevant to the job. A job description, orientation and training needs, and information for employee appraisal are all derived from the data in a job analysis.

An outline of information to include in a job analysis is provided by the Position Analysis Questionnaire (PAQ), developed by McCormick, Shaw, and De Nisi (1979). The PAQ identifies six job dimensions that characterize most jobs. In analyzing a job, one should use these six dimensions as a checklist for determining what is required to perform the job. The six dimensions and examples of work statements that might be characteristic of a recreation leader's job are contained in Exhibit 16-1 on page 299.

A job analysis is a thorough study of the principal components of a job, including the necessary knowledge, skills, and abilities plus other unusual facts about or requirements for doing the job. Each job in an agency requires different knowledge, skills, and abilities. Knowledge is a body of information one must possess that is directly applied to the performance of the job. For example, knowledge about water chemistry would be required for a pool operator. Skill is the possession of a demonstrable competence to perform a learned psychomotor act. Skill in water rescue techniques would be required for a lifeguard. An ability is a current competence to perform a behavior that can be observed or that results in an observable product. An ability to develop and write a weekly playground program plan would be required of a playground leader. Obviously, one must have a clear concept about the job and its functions before an accurate and thorough job analysis can be prepared.

Although an agency may have a personnel department, preparing statements of the principal components of a position is often assigned to the program supervisor requesting the position. Therefore, programmers should fully understand and be able to articulate the knowledge, skills, and abilities necessary to perform a job. Incumbents in a similar position in another agency are good sources of information about what is required to do a specific job.

JOB DESCRIPTION

Job analysis data are used to write a job description, which is a summary of the duties and responsibilities of the job. The job description is

A job analysis contains all of the information necessary to develop and administer the job...

...programmers should be able to articulate the knowledge, skills, and abilities necessary to perform a job.

Exhibit 16-2: General Outline of a Job Description

Function Statement
 A general statement of the responsibilities of the position.

Supervision
 A statement specifying to whom the employee is responsible.

Domains
 Statements outlining the major areas of responsibility of the employee.

Task Statements
 A list of work behaviors that distinguish the position.

Worker Traits
 A list of the knowledge, skills, and abilities that are essential for the position.

Desired Education Experience
 A statement of the education, training, and/experience required or desired for the position.

Special Requirements
 A list of any special knowledge, certifications, or other specific requirements for the job.

not as detailed as the job analysis, but it must be representative of the principal components of the job and give an applicant a good indication of what the major responsibilities include and what qualifications one must possess. Exhibit 16-2 includes a general outline of a job description.

Exhibit 16-3 on page 302 is a sample job description for a playground leader; it was developed using the outline in Exhibit 16-2. Notice that the job description outlines the nature of the position, the requirements for employment, the nature of the work to be performed, the type of supervision to be performed, and special requirements needed. The personnel department in an agency will usually have a specific outline for job descriptions that are to be used in the agency. However, any outline is likely to include components similar to those in this example. Exhibit 16-4 on page 303 is a sample job description for a front desk attendant in a health or racquet club. Compare these two descriptions to see how the jobs differ. After the two descriptions have been compared, complete Exercise 16-1 on page 304.

Recruitment involves obtaining a pool of candidates who are qualified to assume the agency's positions.

Exhibit 16-3: Job Description: Playground Leader

Basic Function and Responsibility

Under general supervision and direction, playground leaders plan and operate recreation programs at assigned locations. Leaders are also responsible for supervision, safety, and light maintenance of play areas.

Supervision

Playground leaders are responsible to the recreation supervisor of their geographic region.

Must be able to function independently with only periodic supervision.

Domains

Plans and operates playground recreation program.

Is responsible for the safe operation of playground and play area.

Task Statements

Plans weekly recreation program.

Promotes program to area participants.

Leads and operates programs.

Supervises play apparatus area and general playground.

Recognizes and removes safety hazards from playground.

Worker Traits

Knowledge of recreation program activity planning.

Knowledge of game rules.

Knowledge of developmental abilities and activities.

Ability to deal tactfully and effectively with children and adults when enforcing rules and regulations in a recreation setting.

Ability to recognize safety hazards.

Desired Education and Experience

Completion of college-level courses in recreational leadership is required (or desired).

Previous experience in leading recreation activities and/or working with children is desirable.

Specialized knowledge of specific recreation activities is desirable.

Special Requirements

Must possess a valid vehicle operator's license.

Applicants with certification in first-aid will be given priority.

Exhibit 16-4: Job Description: Front Desk Attendant

Basic Function and Responsibility

Under general supervision and direction, front desk attendants oversee the operation and smooth functioning of the club, including greeting participants, explaining rules and policies, taking reservations, making sales, and other duties as assigned.

Supervision

Front desk attendants are supervised by the management personnel on duty.

Domains

Public relations.

Operate facility.

Sales.

Task Statements

Greets participants by name and issues equipment.

Makes reservations for equipment and facilities.

Makes sales of equipment and club services.

Explains club rules and policies.

Checks in users and assigns court space or equipment.

Worker Traits

Knowledge of club policies and rules.

Knowledge of game rules and techniques.

Knowledge of club equipment and facilities.

Skill in learning and remembering club members by name.

Ability to deal tactfully and effectively in enforcing club rules and policies.

Ability to explain and interpret club policies.

Ability to make sales.

Desired Education Experience

Completion of college-level courses in recreational leadership or appropriate physical education courses is required (or desired).

Previous experience in the operation of recreation facilities or hospitality facilities is desirable.

Specialized knowledge of specific club activities is desirable.

Special Requirements

Applicants with certification in first-aid will be given priority.

RECRUITMENT

Recreation agencies recruit a large pool of part-time and seasonal employees to meet their needs throughout the year. When an agency employs a large number of part-time workers, turnover is often heavy. Because of this, recruitment, orientation, and training are constantly going on in the agency.

Recruitment involves obtaining a pool of candidates who are qualified to assume the agency's positions. Ray and Grossman (1980) observe that "managers often fall into the trap of assuming that the right employees will come along as summer approaches" (p. 98). Recruitment should be done before the actual need for employees' services. The idea is to have a pool of qualified applicants who are ready to assume agency positions when they need to be filled. Agencies recruit from both within and outside their organization.

INTERNAL RECRUITMENT

Internal recruitment methods, such as promotion and transfer, can be strong motivators for employees.

Internal recruitment is an important source of employees for an organization. If overused, it can lead to charges that employment practices in the agency are "closed" and "you need to know someone" in the organization to get a job there. If true, these practices can lead to legal problems for the agency. Even if they are not true, the belief that they are will eventually diminish the number of applicants, and the agency's ability to attract a sufficiently large pool of qualified applicants will be hampered.

External recruitment involves an organized effort to attract employees from sources outside the organization.

Despite these problems, internal recruitment is still an important source of employees, and it is implemented in several different ways. The promotion or transfer of existing employees is one method of internal recruitment. Promotion and transfer to more desirable or higher paying jobs is a strong motivator for employees. It is also more cost effective for the agency to use employees who have been oriented and are already familiar with policies and operational procedures than to train new employees again. Internal promotion and transfer can be initiated by the supervisor or requested by part-time and seasonal employees to whom a list of current openings has been distributed.

Agency recruitment is also accomplished by using current and former employees to recruit new employees (Mathis & Jackson, 1982). This method can be used only in conjunction with a widely distributed, open announcement of available positions to the public at large. However, current and former employees are often part of a community network of individuals who have the requisite knowledge, skills, and abilities to be good recreation workers. The potential usefulness of this network should not be overlooked.

A final internal recruitment method is to examine previous applicants for positions currently available in the agency. Technically this is not an internal recruitment method, but it does make good use of resources invested previously in obtaining a pool of applicants. If the agency has a sufficiently large pool of good applicants, there will always be some on file when needed. A general practice of most programmers is to keep a file of such applicants indexed by their ability to lead or instruct specific recreation activities.

EXTERNAL RECRUITMENT

External recruitment involves an organized effort to attract employees from sources outside the organization. A mandatory part of external recruitment is announcing the availability of positions to the general public. This should be done through the local print and broadcast media and through issuing and posting job announcements. In addition, external recruitment involves an organized and focused effort to make the availability of positions known to individuals who are likely to be qualified; that is, to target recruitment efforts. Recruiting in high schools for summer leaders is one example. Recruiting in junior college and senior college recreation, physical education, and hospitality curricula is another targeted recruitment source for seasonal and part-time employees. Still other sources might be church youth groups, recreation clubs or hobby groups, and other recreation agencies. External recruitment, then, uses announcements to the general public and a targeted recruitment effort focused on specific groups of individuals who are likely to possess the knowledge, skills, and abilities to be good recreation employees.

SELECTION

It is frequently the case that applicants in the pool are eliminated from further consideration because they do not meet basic expectations of the position. These could include an unfavorable background check, an unacceptable result from a drug test, or failure to meet the basic bona fide occupational qualifications (BFOQs) of the position. Once this process is completed, the programmer must select the applicants who will actually be hired. Selection techniques usually involve either a test, an interview, or both. In any case, the criteria on which selection is made must be valid indicators of the qualifications actually needed to perform the job. The focus of legislation passed in recent years has been

...the criteria on which selection is made must be valid indicators of the qualifications actually needed to perform the job.

The goals of an orientation are to create an initial favorable impression of the agency for the employees, to help them adjust to the demands of their job, and to enhance their acceptance in the agency.

16

to make certain that job selection is made on BFOQs. Selection must be based on criteria that actually relate to the performance of the job. This same legislation has also identified a number of criteria that may not be used, including race, color, religion, gender, age, or national origin. Race and color are never exceptions, and age is an exception only if it can be demonstrated that it is a BFOQ.

Culkin and Kirsch (1986) recommend that employers "exercise caution in taking advantage of these permissible exceptions" (p. 13). The burden for demonstrating the validity of any criterion used in selecting employees for a job clearly rests with the employer. Demonstrating validity is necessary even for part-time and seasonal employees.

ORIENTATION

All new employees, including those who are part-time and seasonal, should receive an orientation to the agency. The goals of an orientation are to create an initial favorable impression of the agency for the employees, to help them adjust to the demands of their job, and to enhance their acceptance in the agency. For many of the young people hired to staff part-time and seasonal recreation jobs, the job will be their first work experience. They often need special help in adjusting to simply having a job, in addition to needing help with the specific responsibilities of the job itself.

The orientation should include three types of information (Mathis & Jackson, 1982). First, the nature of the organization should be outlined. The orientation should answer the following questions for new employees: Who are they working for? What is this organization trying to accomplish? What is their role in helping the organization accomplish its goals?

Second, the nature of a typical workday should be outlined. What can employees expect their workday to be like on this job? What is a typical order of events in a workday? What kinds of tasks will they do in a typical day? From the orientation, the employees should have a good idea of what to expect from a typical workday.

Finally, the work rules, policies, procedures, and special skills needed to perform their role in the agency should be covered. Often, work rules, personnel policies, and procedures that apply to all of the agency's employees will be covered at a general orientation session conducted by the personnel department.

However, the task of covering job-specific policies, procedures, and special skills needed to perform the job will be the responsibility of the programmer. How much training is needed before assigning a new employee to work is a matter of agency practice. For example, the Disney organization requires every employee to complete Traditions I, a one-day orientation session. Part-time and seasonal ticket takers must also complete an additional four days of training before an actual duty assignment (Pope, 1987).

Although this level of preassignment training is desirable, most agencies simply cannot afford it. Part-time and seasonal employees often do not need to know every detail of agency operation, only the essential information to get started on the job and keep themselves and

...an orientation program should also include a time for the new employees to meet and ask questions about what they may not have thoroughly understood the first time.

Training is the process whereby employees acquire the knowledge, skills, abilities, concepts, and attitudes they need to fulfill the responsibilities of their positions in the agency.

the agency from having problems. For example, each new employee must receive an orientation regarding emergency procedures before an actual assignment. This is a must, and failure to do so could cause undue harm to participants and place the agency in a litigious situation. Many part-time and seasonal employees are given an orientation and some training, and are then placed in a position where they are closely supervised and given on-the-job training.

New employees should not be subjected to information overload during the orientation. All of the information covered will be very familiar to the programmer and totally new to the employee. Because of this, an orientation program should also include, within one to two weeks of the original orientation, a time for the new employees to meet and ask questions about what they may not have thoroughly understood the first time.

TRAINING

Training is the process whereby employees acquire the knowledge, skills, abilities, concepts, and attitudes they need to fulfill the responsibilities of their positions in the agency. The amount and content of training depends on job responsibilities and how much of the required knowledge, skills, abilities, concepts, and attitudes employees already possess.

Part-time and seasonal employees often have fewer skills and need more training than full-time employees in order to fulfill their job responsibilities in the manner desired by the agency. The Disney organization is firmly committed to thoroughly training part-time and seasonal workers (Pope, 1987). They never allow workers to learn on the job, but make certain that they thoroughly know a job before a duty assignment. Part-time and seasonal employees often need instruction in how to operate specialized pieces of equipment and apparatus. Training in leadership skills, recreation planning, and game rules are also often needed as well.

Peters and Waterman (1982) point out in their book *In Search of Excellence* that a major difference between a production and a service organization is that in the latter, the product is manufactured and delivered simultaneously. A supervisor in a leisure service organization must therefore provide employees with excellent, thorough training, followed up with close, on-going supervision (McKinney & Chandler, 1991).

One aspect of training is to make certain that staff members have the activity skills necessary for the specific program they have been hired to lead, direct, or supervise. In training part-time and seasonal recreation employees, it is especially important to convey the type of recreation service the agency desires to offer and good customer service practices, for example, how they should treat participants in face-to-face interactions. The recreation experience a participant has is in large part dependent on interactions with recreation workers. However, training in the appropriate face-to-face demeanor and how to interact to obtain compliance with policies and rules are only part of the training that part-time and seasonal recreation workers usually need.

16

Appraisal involves evaluating how well employees are performing their responsibilities.

Informal appraisal is conducted whenever the supervisor believes it is necessary.

Formal appraisals are the supervisor's written impressions and observations.

Exhibit 16-5: Training Outline for Area Supervisors

As part of your ongoing duties, you will be assigned the responsibility to supervise park areas and facilities. This is one of the most difficult assignments you will have. When you supervise an area, your responsibility is to protect the facility, to protect the programs in operation at the facility so that participants can have the experience they desired from participation, and finally, to protect the drop-in participants of the facility. Following are ten duties you must perform in order to fulfill the supervisor's role:

Enforcement 1–5

1. You must actively work at supervising. Supervising time is not your break—supervision cannot be accomplished from the employee lounge or office window.

2. You should circulate around the grounds or building and let your physical presence be known. Make certain all participants know there is a supervisor on duty—someone who is in charge of the facility. Make certain to wear your uniform so that you are easily identified.

3. Supervisors should protect organized programs in operation at the facility from harassment by other users (especially drop-in users) of the facility.

4. You must handle any trouble or problems that may erupt in the area. You must be aware of locations where trouble is likely to happen and become familiar with the participants likely to cause trouble.

5. You should get at problems likely to occur in the area aggressively. Try to anticipate problems and head them off.

Good Customer Service Practices 6–10

6. Talk to participants and encourage them to participate in organized programs. Know the answers to their questions. To do this, you must be familiar with all of the services available from the agency.

7. Give the job your own personal touch. Make your area of responsibility a place you would like your own children, brothers and sisters, or friends to attend.

8. Try to get "pick-up" activities started. Always have a few activities to suggest to participants who seem to have run out of things to do.

9. Accept people as they are. Blacks and whites, long-hairs and baldies, young people and old people should all receive the same courteous treatment from you. Every user is a VIP and should be treated with courtesy and respect.

10. Use the magic mirror of your smile. Handle people with a smile and in a courteous manner.

Exercise 16-2: Using an Employee Appraisal Instrument

In class, use the employee appraisal instrument included in Exhibit 16-6 to develop an appraisal instrument for the job outlined in the job description in Exhibit 16-4. When finished, discuss the following questions:
- Does the appraisal instrument include all of the major responsibilities?
- Will the employee and supervisor clearly understand the items that are to be observed and evaluated during the appraisal?

They will likely need training in the specific skills of their position. Exhibit 16-5 gives an outline of a training program for staff members who will be responsible for supervising a recreation area or building. The program instructs employees in what is expected of them and exactly what the supervision of an area or facility involves. It defines the role and function of the task and prepares individuals to fill the role. How to implement good customer service is also pointed out.

Training and retraining are important and time-consuming tasks for programmers. The types of training that are needed become obvious as programmers observe staff operate programs and facilities. A general rule is that if the programmer wants something accomplished a specific way, instructions for performing the procedure must be included in the training process. A well-trained staff is an essential ingredient to a successful program and well worth the time invested.

APPRAISAL

Appraisal involves evaluating how well employees are performing their responsibilities. The information acquired in appraisals is used to determine compensation, placement of employees (transfer or promotion), and training needs (Mathis & Jackson, 1982). An appraisal is most often used to determine eligibility for a raise, but one should not overlook using it to identify employees who are qualified to assume different responsibilities in the agency and to determine training needs.

There are two types of appraisals: informal and formal. Informal appraisal is conducted whenever the supervisor believes it is necessary. The day-to-day personal interactions of the supervisor with employees will give employees feedback about how well the supervisor believes they are performing. The supervisor's reactions and comments about an employee's work are communicated during site visits, over coffee, and in similar settings, thus providing informal evaluative feedback to the employee.

The agency should also have a formal appraisal system during which the supervisor's impressions and observations of the employee's performance become a matter of written record. Four decisions need to be made before implementing a formal appraisal system.

Exhibit 16-6: Employee Appraisal Instrument—Employee Performance Evaluation Report

Employee's Name: Appraisal Date:

Department: Job Title:

Employment Date:

Appraisal Period: From: To:

Reason for Review: ( )Mid-Probation   ( )Probation   ( )Annual   ( )End of Season

Factors Considered in Ratings and Comments	% Weight Value	1 Unsatis-factory	4 Satis-factory	7 Above Average	10 Excep-tional	Factor Total
1. Plans weekly recreation program.	——	( )	( )	( )	( )	——
2. Promotes program to area patrons.	——	( )	( )	( )	( )	——
3. Leads and operates programs.	——	( )	( )	( )	( )	——
4. Supervises play apparatus area and general playground.	——	( )	( )	( )	( )	——
5. Recognizes and re-moves safety hazards from playground.	——	( )	( )	( )	( )	——
6. Demonstrates knowledge of recreation program activity planning.	——	( )	( )	( )	( )	——
7. Demonstrates knowledge of game rules.	——	( )	( )	( )	( )	——
8. Demonstrates knowledge of developmental abilities of children.	——	( )	( )	( )	( )	——
9. Demonstrates skill in face-to-face leadership of games and activities.	——	( )	( )	( )	( )	——
10. Demonstrates ability to deal tactfully and effectively in enforcing rules and regulations with children and adults in a recreation setting.	——	( )	( )	( )	( )	——
11. Demonstrates ability to recognize safety hazards.	——	( )	( )	( )	( )	——

                                                     Adjective Rating

              100%   (Total of all factors)

Exhibit 16-6: (continued)

Additional Comments and Plans for Improvement:

Comments/Reactions of Employee Regarding Evaluation:

Reviewer's Comments:

Rater:_____ Date:_____ Reviewer:_____ Date:_____
Employee:_____ Date:_____ Dept. Head:_____ Date:_____

Note: Signature of employee does not mean agreement or disagreement with rating, but indicates that the evaluation has been reviewed.

Adjective Rating Equivalents
1.00–2.99 = Unsatisfactory
3.00–5.99 = Satisfactory
6.00–8.99 = Above average
9.00–10.00 = Exceptional

Instructions
1. Prepare this rating carefully and with sound judgment.
2. Be sure to rate each criterion separately and do not apply a generalized view of the overall employee performance.
3. Comments are encouraged and are required for any factor rated Exceptional or Unsatisfactory.
4. Use additional sheets of paper if necessary to record comments or a plan of action.

Adapted from a form used in Plano, Texas.

WHO WILL CONDUCT THE APPRAISAL?

Recreation programmers are almost always designated as the ones responsible for appraising the performance of the part-time and seasonal staff members under their supervision. However, a senior-level, seasonal staff member may be asked for input. For example, a public school teacher who is hired to direct a summer day camp may have significant input in to the appraisal of younger, less experienced camp counselors. Although the programmer may have the final responsibility for appraising part-time and seasonal employees, it is important to obtain input from employees who are qualified to make such judgments and who are in a better position to have firsthand information about an employee's performance.

It is also common practice in recreation operations to obtain input from participants about the performance of employees. Participant ratings are often obtained at facility operations and after program operations. These data should also play some role in the overall appraisal of the employee.

A popular method of appraisal is an all-purpose rating scale that uses the duties and responsibilities outlined in the job description as the evaluation criteria.

HOW WILL APPRAISAL DATA BE COLLECTED?

Several methods can be used to collect appraisal data (Culkin & Kirsch, 1986; Mathis & Jackson, 1982). Programmers in most instances will be required to use an employee appraisal instrument that already exists in the agency. The instrument should be examined before the appraisal period. This is necessary so that supervisors know what employee behaviors they should be observing and can take note of specific behaviors during their on-site observations. It is also important to explain the appraisal system and instrument to employees before they begin work. Employees should understand the criteria on which they will be evaluated, who will do the evaluation, and how it will be used in determining raises and personnel actions.

A popular method of appraisal in organizations with many different positions is an all-purpose rating scale that uses the duties and responsibilities outlined in the job description as the evaluation criteria. An example of an all-purpose rating scale applied to the job description for a playground leader (Exhibit 16-3) is contained in Exhibit 16-6 on pages 310-311. With this method, each position in the agency is rated in the same manner, but the appraisal criteria in each case are those required by the job. Now complete Exercise 16-2 on page 309.

It is also important for the programmer to record critical incidents of employee performance. Critical incidents are highly favorable and highly unfavorable actions in an employee's performance (Mathis & Jackson, 1982). When a critical incident occurs, the programmer writes it down. These documentation notes are used as the basis for comments recorded on the formal review instrument.

If the incident is unfavorable enough to cause an unsatisfactory performance rating, it is recommended that a consultation review with the employee be held within 24 hours of the incident. During this consultation, the written documentation should be shared and discussed with the employee. The employee should be asked to sign off on the incident report, acknowledging that he or she has been counseled about the incident. The employee should also have the opportunity to make a written comment on the report. In this way, personnel incidents are thoroughly documented and become a part of the employee's record. This procedure is also recommended for exceptional performance. In either case, the procedure creates a written record that can be used to justify any personnel action required, including promotions, demotions, raises, denial of a raise, dismissal, transfer, or recommendation for training.

WHEN WILL APPRAISAL OCCUR?

Frequent and timely feedback is essential if the employee appraisal system is to fulfill a redirecting function in the agency. With full-time employees, the normal practice is to conduct an appraisal midway through the probationary period and another at the end. At the end of the probationary period, a decision is made either to place the employee on permanent status or to dismiss him or her. Once an employee is on permanent status, then performance is usually appraised either semi-annually or annually.

> Employees on permanent status are usually appraised either semi-annually or annually.

> The appraisal interview should be conducted immediately after each performance appraisal.

In many organizations, part-time and seasonal employees are never given permanent status, although they are usually appraised when their responsibilities will end. For example, the performance of all summer employees would be appraised at the end of the summer program. A performance appraisal usually determines whether they will be hired for the next operation of the program. In some agencies, part-time employees who work more than a specified number of hours per week (more than 20 hours, for example) are treated the same as full-time employees.

HOW SHOULD THE PERFORMANCE APPRAISAL INTERVIEW BE CONDUCTED?

The appraisal interview should be conducted immediately after each performance appraisal. These interviews provide an opportunity to communicate directly with employees about their strengths and weaknesses.

Employees usually approach an appraisal interview with a great deal of concern. It is useful for both the supervisor and the employee to remember that the worth of the employee as a human being is not being judged here, but the worth of the employee's job performance for a specified period of time is being judged. The appraisal interview is also an important opportunity to set an agenda with the employees for retraining or reorganizing how they will conduct their work. This is a primary time for counseling employees on how to do the work and to discover weaknesses that may need to be corrected through additional training.

There are three types of employee compensation: pay, incentives, and benefits.

COMPENSATION

There are three types of employee compensation: pay, incentives, and benefits (Mathis & Jackson, 1982). Pay refers to the direct wage or salary that the employee receives. Incentives refer to commissions or bonuses for exceptional performance. These are rarely given in recreation positions except in some private health clubs where a commission may be paid on the volume of memberships or services and products sold by an employee. Benefits include medical insurance, retirement, workmen's compensation, and other benefits given by the agency. Most full-time recreation employees receive pay and benefits for their positions. Part-time and seasonal employees usually receive pay and minimal benefits. The compensation of this latter group is the focus of this section.

Often, wages for part-time and seasonal employees are purposely kept low to keep agency operating costs low. As stated earlier, many recreation agencies operate with a large number of part-time and seasonal employees. A low wage structure for these employees enables many recreation businesses to remain profitable. Thus, there is usually pressure in an agency to keep part-time and seasonal wages low.

Programmers usually bear the direct adverse effect of this strategy because they are forced to operate program services with low-wage, untrained employees whom they must train extensively and supervise

One benefit that part-time and seasonal workers in recreation operations often receive is the opportunity to use the employer's facilities free of charge.

closely. Even though wages are low, programmers are well advised to develop a merit-based compensation plan. It is important to have a sufficiently attractive incentive pay structure so that one can retain the employees already trained, thereby avoiding having to constantly retrain new employees.

The usual practice in incentive plans is to make all raises merit based and to require that employees spend a certain amount of time in a specific pay grade before being eligible for a raise. For example, an employee earning the minimum wage may have to complete 1,000 hours (about six months at 40 hours per week) before being eligible to be considered for a raise. The raise is not automatic after 1,000 hours, however. The employee still must have a favorable or exceptional merit review and must spend the requisite time at the beginning pay rate. The performance appraisal will then determine how well the employee is performing the responsibilities of the position and his or her eligibility for a raise in pay.

Part-time wages paid by the agency must be competitive with prevailing rates for similar part-time work in the area. The availability of part-time workers will partly determine the prevailing rate. Agencies can control how selective they can be in hiring by where they position themselves in the local part-time wage market. Obviously, offering wages on the high end of what generally prevails in the community will assure the agency first choice of available workers.

Part-time and seasonal employees rarely receive any benefits other than those required by law. Employers are usually required to pay Social Security and workers' compensation insurance on every employee. One benefit that part-time and seasonal workers in recreation operations often receive is the opportunity to use the employer's facilities free of charge. For example, employees at a water park may be admitted to the park on their day off. These types of benefits, which are low cost to the agency, should be used and promoted as part of the compensation package. Sometimes they also can provide a sufficient incremental advantage to enable the agency to attract better part-time and seasonal employees.

CONTRACTING FOR PERSONNEL SERVICES

It is becoming common practice for agencies to contract for the services of individuals rather than place them in the agency's employ. For example, athletic league officials are contracted for a per-game fee to officiate athletic contests. Or a person may be contracted to teach a tennis class consisting of 16 one-hour lessons. The instructor is given a flat rate or a percentage of the revenue and is not placed in the employ of the agency. As a result, these individuals do not receive any benefits from the agency. Contractors are supposed to pay their own Social Security, income tax, and workers' compensation.

This practice is controversial. Using a contract arrangement definitely reduces direct costs for the agency because the agency does not have to pay benefits and the practice eliminates their exposure to the requirements of a number of employment laws (Moiseichik, Hunt, & Macchiarelli, 1992). However, maintaining control of the quality of contract services is sometimes difficult. The individual under contract is not an

One requirement of operating a service industry is the need for close, ongoing supervision.

Exhibit 16-7: Contract for Individual Services

Mesa Parks and Recreation
Contract for Individual Services

Date: _____

It is agreed by and between Mesa Parks and Recreation of Mesa, Arizona, hereinafter referred to as "City," and _____, hereinafter referred to as
"Second Party," as follows:

That Second Party agrees to perform for the City the service or services described
below, and the City agrees to pay the Second Party for such services as provided
below.

1. Person who will provide service:

       Name: _____ Soc.Sec. No.: _____
       Address: _____
       City: _____ Zip: _____
       Phone (Day): _____ Phone (Evening): _____

2. Services to be performed:
       a. _____
       b. _____
       c. _____
       d. _____
       e. _____
       f. _____
       g. _____

3. Services to be conducted for the following period:

    a. Beginning _____ and continuing through _____

    b. Hours:_____ Days/Frequency:_____

4. Place or places where services will be provided:

    _____

    _____

    _____

    _____

5. The City shall pay _____ per hour/activity (circle one) for services rendered and
   no deductions shall be subtracted therefrom. The Second Party does not participate in any fringe benefits of the City, nor does the City provide liability insurance
   for the Second Party.

Exhibit 16-7: (continued)

6. The Second Party is performing the above services and is acting as an independent contractor and is not an employee of the City of Mesa.

_____   _____
        Second Party   Date

Approved and execution witnessed by:

_____   _____
     Immediate Supervisor   City of Mesa

_____   By: Parks and Recreation Director
      Section Supervisor

Source: Mesa Parks, Recreation, and Cultural Division, Mesa, Arizona. No warranty is given regarding the legal appropriateness of this statement for the reader's use. The reader is cautioned to not copy this statement, because any such statement should be developed and approved by the agency's legal counsel.

employee and thus not subject to direct supervision and control. Any irregularities in performance or delivery of service are contract violations rather than personnel matters. Compliance with a contract can be enforced, but it is a more cumbersome and less direct process.

The Internal Revenue Service reviews this practice carefully since their studies have revealed that many employers "are misclassifying employees as independent contractors to avoid paying employment taxes" (Moiseichik et al., 1992, p. 63). The major group of employees who have been investigated thus far are athletic league officials. At least two city recreation departments had been required to pay back taxes that would have been due if the workers were correctly classified as employees.

Making certain both the contract and the contractual relationship reflect the following features will increase the likelihood that a worker will be accepted as a contractor (adapted from Moiseichik et al., 1992). Agency supervisors must not control the detail and manner of how work is performed by a contractor and they must not directly supervise the performance of their work. Contractors should not be subject to the agency's personnel policies and cannot be hired, fired, or disciplined under them. They are not paid through the agency's payroll system, there are no payroll deductions from their contract price, and they are paid a lump sum for the completed project or on the amount of items completed, for example, the number of games officiated. Furthermore, they supply all of their own equipment and materials; they are free to provide their services to other agencies; they are obviously in business for themselves as evidenced by a business letterhead, address, and

Exhibit 16-8: On-Site Visit Quality Service Activities

Dimension	Activities
Reliability	Confirm scheduled service is being operated as advertised and intended by the agency.
	Make adjustments necessary to bring service up to quality standards if warranted.
Tangibles	Confirm cleanliness of facility and equipment.
	Check safety of equipment and operational practices.
	Confirm the neatness of the appearance of personnel.
Responsiveness	Initiate contact with patrons to confirm your willingness to help them and provide prompt service or to resolve their problems.
Assurance	Present a demeanor of confidence and courtesy.
	Make certain you and your on-site staff know the answers to questions and willingly provide them to patrons.
Empathy	Present a caring, empathetic demeanor.
	Make certain on-site personnel have sufficient authority to make reasonable exceptions to policies and rules so that service can be customized to meet patron needs.

In all cases, the visiting programmer must exhibit these behaviors and confirm that on-site personnel are also exhibiting them.

Adapted from: Berry, L. L., & Parasuraman, A. (1991). Marketing Services: Competing through quality. New York: The Free Press.

phone; there is a definite term to the contract period; and their work is not scheduled by the agency.

Because of the potential tax liability of these arrangements, it is important to have a well-written contractual arrangement with these individuals. Exhibit 16-7 is a Contract for Individual Services used by the Mesa, Arizona Parks, Recreation, and Cultural Division. The terminology in this contract focuses on the service provided rather than the person, because there are some questions about whether or not there can be a "contract employee." An agency can, however, contract for the services of an individual or a group.

SUPERVISING OPERATIONS

One of the unique requirements of operating a service industry is the need for close, ongoing supervision. "The nature of leisure services is that once the service has been delivered, it cannot be recalled," according to Edginton and Edginton (1993, p. 42). Thus, quality must be assured at the time of delivery, and on-site observation and supervision of services is a key method for accomplishing this.

There are three objectives to accomplish during these visits. First, the programmer needs to verify that a program is actually being conducted. Usually, many details must be coordinated before a program can actually occur. If any one of these details is not completed, the program may not occur, or it will occur with problems. If one is using a contract employee to deliver the service, on-site verification of operation is a necessary part of a performance audit to assure contract compliance.

A second objective of these visits is to observe program operations to make certain they are being delivered as intended by the agency and at the level of quality desired by the agency. During a visit, one may face any of several operational problems, including program cancellation, poor staff performance, unsafe conduct of a program, or inadequate facility preparation. Interactions that will occur with participants at this time are what McCarville (1993) terms "key encounters." Failure to reconcile these irritations to the participant's satisfaction may result in the agency losing its patronage.

Berry and Parasuraman (1991) indicate that there are five general dimensions that influence a customer's assessment of service quality: reliability, tangibles, responsiveness, assurance, and empathy (p. 16). On-site visits provide an opportunity for demonstrating the agency's commitment to quality service. Exhibit 16-8 on page 317 contains specific activities to accomplish during these visits that address each of these dimensions.

The third objective of the visits is to observe on-site leadership staff and to gather data to use in appraising staff performance. On-site visitations are important to staff members conducting programs because programmers can give verbal directions to staff to make any necessary corrections in operations. Programmers can also give immediate feedback about the quality of work being done. Observations of how well part-time staff members are functioning will also reveal any need for additional training. Remember, however, that contractors are not subject to this type of supervisory direction.

On-site supervision of recreation and leisure services can accomplish several important program management functions. It is time consuming and often occurs at odd hours, but it is an essential part of the programmer's job.

CONCLUSION

Staff members who actually operate program services are often part-time or seasonal employees. They must be recruited, oriented, trained, and supervised. Because recreation is very often a people-to-people service, a well-trained and well-supervised staff is essential to successful program delivery. Conducting on-site supervision of service delivery is a necessary quality control function that the programmer must perform.

REFERENCES

Berry, L. L., & Parasuraman, A. (1991). *Marketing services: Competing through quality.* New York: The Free Press.

Culkin, D. F., & Kirsch, S. L. (1986). *Managing human resources in recreation services.* New York: Macmillan.

Edginton, C. R., & Edginton, S. R. (1993). Total quality program planning. *Journal of Physical Education, Recreation, and Dance, 64*(8), 40–42, 47.

Henderson, K. A., & Bialeschki, M. D. (1993). Optimal work experiences as "flow": Implications for seasonal staff. *Journal of Park and Recreation Administration, 11*(1), 37–48.

Mathis, R. L., & Jackson, J. H. (1982). *Personnel: Contemporary perspectives and applications* (3rd ed.). St. Paul, MN: West.

McCarville, R. E. (1993). Keys to quality leisure programming. *Journal of Physical Education, Recreation, and Dance, 64*(8), 34–36, 46–47.

McCormick, E. J., Shaw, J. D., & DeNisi, A. S. (1979). Use of PAQ for establishing the job component validity of tests. *Journal of Applied Psychology, 64*(1), 51–56.

McKinney, W. R., & Chandler, C. L. (1991). A comparative assessment of duties between full-time and part-time recreation leaders. *Journal of Park and Recreation Administration, 9*(1), 13–29.

Moiseichik, M., Hunt, S., & Macchiarelli, D. (1992). Recreation sports officials: Contractors or employees? *Journal of Park and Recreation Administration, 10*(1), 62–70.

Peters, T. J., & Waterman, R. H., Jr. (1982). *In search of excellence: Lessons from America's best run companies.* New York: Harper & Row.

Pope, N. W. (1987). Mickey Mouse marketing. In J. L. Crompton (Ed.), *Doing more with less in parks and recreation services* (pp. 168–176). State College, PA: Venture.

Ray, M. B., & Grossman, A. H. (1980). Recruiting and selecting professional personnel. In A. H. Grossman (Ed.), *Personnel management in recreation and leisure services* (pp. 89–116). South Plainfield, NJ: Groupwork Today.

Sterle, D. E., & Duncan, M. R. (1977). *Supervision of leisure services.* San Diego, CA: Campanile Press.

16

Men's Basketball League
Photo courtesy of Blacktown Leisure Centre, Stanhope, Australia

Developing a Program Pricing Philosophy

STEP 7 : IMPLEMENTATION

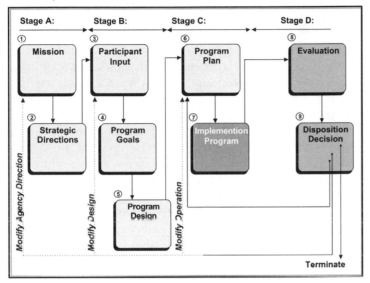

KEY TERMS

**Program
Management
Accounting
System (PMAS)
Management
Accounting
Comprehensive
Pricing Policy
Service Category
System
Public Programs
Merit Programs
Private Programs**

Pricing is one of the "four p's" of marketing. A marketing approach to programming requires that programmers be concerned with the costs of services and how to generate the revenue to pay for them, as well as designing and producing program services. Although commercial agencies have always had to charge prices appropriate to ensure the survival of the agency, more recently public and not-for-profit agencies have also become concerned with pricing issues. Today, at least one in three dollars in public recreation budgets is from fees and charges, and this percentage is increasing in many communities as tax income fails to provide the financial base to provide the quantity or quality of programs desired (Brademas & Readnour, 1989). Howard (1988) has stated, "The real issue facing recreation managers today is no longer the question of 'should we charge,' but rather one of 'how much?'" (p. 1).

Although the issue of establishing a price seems, at first glance, a simple matter, the prices charged in commercial, public, or not-for-profit agencies have many implications. Charging for services can accomplish a variety of policy objectives for an agency. Howard and Crompton (1980) have identified six objectives of pricing: the efficient use of all financial resources, fairness or equitableness, providing maximal opportunity for participation, rationing, developing positive user attitudes,

Today, at least one in three dollars in public recreation budgets is from fees and charges, and this percentage is increasing in many communities...

and commercial sector encouragement (p. 419). A key point is that the price set for services will determine who may or may not participate in an activity. Participants who cannot afford the price charged are excluded from participation. Therefore, the price established for services in any type of agency must be affordable by the intended target market, or the program will not reach its intended audience.

Pricing also determines the amount of revenue an agency will receive, and thus, enables the agency to recover some or all of its costs of production. The financial goals of the agency will determine the contribution that the price charged will make to overall agency revenue. For example, in a commercial agency, fees and charges are the sole source of revenue. Thus, they must be set to recover all of the costs of production, plus contribute to the agency's overhead costs and profit margin. In many not-for-profit and governmental agencies, the revenue from fees and charges represents a secondary funding source that is usually used to accomplish one of two ends—expanding the quantity of services offered or enhancing their quality.

To better manage program pricing practices, agencies need to implement a Program Management Accounting System. In this chapter and in Chapters Eighteen and Nineteen, such a system is outlined. Management accounting is an accepted field of accounting that is distinctly different from financial accounting (Anthony & Welsch, 1981). The purpose of financial accounting is to prepare information for reporting the financial performance of the organization to parties outside the organization. To ensure that each organization's report is comparable to the reports of other organizations, financial accounting reports are prepared according to strict, "generally accepted accounting principles and unified by the basic equation, Assets = Liabilities + Owner's equity" (Anthony & Welsch, 1981, pp. 9–10).

In contrast to financial accounting, management accounting information is prepared for three different purposes, each of which is governed by a different set of principles. A management accounting system prepares information for internal use by managers (Horngren, 1970). The information can be prepared for the following three purposes: (1) full cost accounting, which is used to determine the full cost of producing a good or service in an agency; (2) differential accounting, which is used to examine fiscal differences between alternate courses of managerial action; and (3) responsibility accounting, which is used to account for the financial performance of sub-units in an organization. These sub-units are called responsibility centers. They are areas of operational responsibility such as individual programs or work groups that produce programs whose financial performance is isolated so that the costs and revenues associated with them can be matched and observed. To implement the recommended program management accounting system, both full cost and responsibility accounting must be used.

Although a management accounting system requires preparing additional accounting data beyond those needed for the financial accounting system, the management accounting system uses financial accounting information as its database. It is a reinterpretation of the same information so that programmers can use it in fulfilling their responsibility to manage the organization's resources to achieve the goals and

To better manage program pricing practices, agencies need to implement a Program Management Accounting System.

Exhibit 17-1: Program Management Accounting System (PMAS)

1. The agency needs to develop a comprehensive policy to guide its pricing decisions (covered in Chapter Seventeen).
2. Operational units in the agency need to be identified as either line or service units (covered in Chapter Eighteen).
3. Line-item object-classification budgets that match revenues with expenses needed to operate a program should be prepared for each of the line units identified in step two (covered in Chapter Eighteen).
4. With appropriate methods of cost allocation, service unit costs need to be allocated to line units (covered in Chapter Eighteen).
5. An analysis of cost, volume, and profit is used to calculate the full cost of service production (covered in Chapter Nineteen).
6. A price for an individual service is established using the conjoint implications of two data sets—the principles from the agency's comprehensive pricing policy and the production cost data developed in the cost-volume-profit analysis (covered in Chapter Nineteen).

objectives of the organization (Horngren, 1970). The system also provides the data necessary to implement a procedure for systematically developing appropriate fees for programs and services.

Implementing and using a Program Management Accounting System (PMAS) in an agency can be accomplished in six steps (see Exhibit 17-1). Some agencies may already have completed some of these steps. It is important to realize that this system may have to be implemented in phases over a period of several years.

In this chapter and in Chapters Eighteen and Nineteen, the way each of these steps can be accomplished is outlined. In most of the examples, a public recreation system is used as the model. This type of agency was selected because it is the most complex type of agency in which prices need to be established. Even though a public system is used as the example, the general principles outlined can be used in any leisure service agency.

DEVELOPING A COMPREHENSIVE GUIDE TO PRICING DECISIONS—STEP 1 PMAS

Howard and Crompton (1980) suggest that there are two major pricing strategies—cost-based pricing and pricing not directly based on cost. Many agencies establish prices that are not directly based on cost. Going-rate pricing and demand-oriented pricing are two such methods. In going-rate pricing, the agency bases the price for a service on the price other providers are charging for similar services. In demand-oriented pricing, the agency bases the price on "what the traffic will bear." With this latter method, the agency is trying to charge all it can get or whatever the participants are most likely to pay for a service. The price established with both of these techniques is not based on how much it actually costs the agency to provide the service; the price can be above, below, or equal to agency production costs.

Although these two methods are widely used, they are not recommended because they lack precision in revealing where agency resources are being used to subsidize services. The program management accounting system being outlined is a cost-based pricing method. It assumes that knowing the full cost of service production is a prerequisite for establishing fair prices for agency services and for guiding the allocation of agency subsidies.

An agency's pricing philosophy is determined by its role in society, the funding available to fulfill this role, and the types of services offered by the agency. For example, the role of a commercial agency is to market goods and services in a manner that is socially responsible and that maximizes profits. Their only source of funding is through earned income that is generated from the sale of goods and services. To fulfill their role in society, they must set prices that recover all production costs and contribute sufficient profit to give owners a fair return on their investment. In contrast to this, public and not-for-profit agencies generally have third-party funding in the form of tax or fund-raising income that can be used in one of two ways. It may be used to pay for services in full, thus making them available at a zero price to the consumer, or it may be used to partly pay the costs for many services and concurrently require the user to pay part of the costs, thus providing subsidized services.

The program management accounting system assumes that knowing the full cost of service production is a prerequisite for establishing fair prices for agency services and for guiding the allocation of agency subsidies.

As a profession, we believe that having access to ongoing opportunities for enjoyable, fun, or peak experiences enhances the quality of life. Each provider has specific responsibilities in creating access to these opportunities. Not-for-profit organizations usually have a specific group or program they are interested in promoting. Thus, their concern is more focused and less comprehensive. Economic efficiency and consumer demand generally establish the target markets for commercial recreation enterprises. The result is that they, too, usually have a narrow range of products and a small, carefully defined target market. However, the public system is responsible for ensuring equal access to leisure opportunities (Wicks, 1987); thus, it has a more comprehensive responsibility and has public funds for use in fulfilling this social welfare function. Although it is true that participation in leisure is beneficial to the individual and to society, it does not necessarily follow that each public leisure program is of immeasurable benefit (Ellerbrock, 1982). Furthermore, the system cannot meet all demand for service from tax revenues. Sorting out who to charge and how much to charge them, and who to subsidize and how much to subsidize them, are the major philosophical issues to be resolved in an agency's pricing policy.

PRICING PUBLIC RECREATION: CURRENT ISSUES

Local public park and recreation systems in the United States have frequently found themselves in a financial dilemma while implementing fees and charges for services. Ironically, public systems that have implemented fees have often done so in a piecemeal or rushed way and have alienated participants because of a poorly conceptualized fee and charge system. Yet public systems that have not implemented fees and charges often lack adequate resources to operate comprehensive recreation services, and they, too, have alienated participants because of incomplete services. The issue is not one of deciding whether or not to charge: to have a comprehensive community recreation system, fees and charges must be implemented to supplement tax-generated revenue. Rather, the issue is one of determining how to use fees fairly to recover the costs of providing service, and how to use tax revenue to provide subsidized services. Wicks (1986) has demonstrated that citizens hold definite yet different views regarding the services and the clients who should have priority in receiving subsidized services. In the future, agencies with a heterogeneous population will very likely need to administer a differential pricing scheme for the same services for different population cohorts. When implementing a fee and charge system, then, agencies must remain sensitive to constituent views and desires regarding the distribution of tax dollars and the subsidization of various programs and client groups.

The egalitarian social philosophy that characterized the recreation movement through the first decade of the twentieth century was predicated on two assumptions that today seem rather naive, or at least outdated. First was the assumption that recreation services were good for people, and that providing more services led to accomplishing more good. Although this may be true, the political and economic resource base supporting ever-expanding services was eventually exhausted. Second was the assumption that all recreation programs were of equal value and in the public interest. Although public recreation officials may be able to do many useful things with other people's money, this does not mean they have the right to tax people to meet all identified recreation needs. The increasing diversification of program interests, the demand for program sophistication, and a diminishing willingness to pay with public dollars for services that seem to provide private benefits, have led taxpayers to rebel against supporting public services, including public recreation.

Furthermore, public agencies have undertaken a diverse set of operations, which requires that they implement different pricing strategies. Soderberg (1988) points out that some agencies operate facilities that are intended to be revenue producing and must compete with other similar for-profit agencies in their service area. The operation of athletic stadiums, arenas, raceways, and other similar spectator event sites are examples of revenue-producing operations. The operation of regional tourist attractions, which are most frequently attended by tourists from out of town as opposed to community residents, is another example of an operation that needs a different pricing strategy.

Community dissatisfaction with public recreation, which has resulted in a withdrawal of political and financial support, has occurred not because the public questions the contribution that recreation can make to human existence, but because the public questions whether society as a whole should pay for providing recreation opportunities. The issue is: Who benefits and who pays? Although a significant number of agencies have instituted fees and charges, in many cases this revenue has only broadened the resource base for continuing to provide all things to all people. However, current financial management techniques used in agencies do not keep adequate track of financial activity to truly match revenue with expenses (Howard & Selin, 1987). Consequently, managers are unable to achieve congruence between pricing practices and the agency's social welfare philosophy and policies. Correcting this problem begins with the development of a new philosophy concerning the role and function of recreation services, with particular focus on who benefits and who pays. There is also a need to develop policies to implement the philosophy and the financial management techniques that will enable agencies to achieve congruence between fiscal practice and agency policy.

THE SERVICE CATEGORY SYSTEM PHILOSOPHY

A philosophy regarding fees and charges should provide a base for differentiating services on the basis of who benefits and who should pay for the service.

A philosophy regarding fees and charges should provide a base for differentiating services on the basis of who benefits and who should pay for the service. Economists have differentiated goods in the economy in this manner and have designated three different types of goods: public, merit, and private (Howard & Crompton, 1980). Programs offered by an agency can also be put into these three categories. Adopting a philosophy that acknowledges these three levels of goods shifts the social welfare philosophy of the public recreation agency away from the notion that all services are of equal value and should be provided for everyone. This egalitarian philosophy is replaced with one that provides a basis for sorting out costs and benefits derived from various program services, and provides a rationale for who should pay. In this conceptualization, each type of program has specific characteristics that imply who should pay for it. To develop a comprehensive fee and charge policy, agencies need to establish three categories for pricing programs that parallel these three types of economic goods; that is, public, merit, and private programs. Each category has features that distinguish it from the other categories. These features are outlined below.

PUBLIC PROGRAMS

Public programs are the basic programs supported totally by tax dollars and are available to patrons free of charge.

Public programs are the basic programs supported totally by tax dollars and are available to participants free of charge. Theoretically, these programs are equally available to all. However, it is operationally not possible to make services equally available. For example, a park cannot be placed equidistant from all participants. Operationally, a public program is beneficial to all, even though only some will actually use the program. Its provision is clearly in the "public interest" (Friedmann, 1973). Because the public at large derives benefit from these programs, it is assumed that their cost will be paid through public financing. Public programs, then, are available with no fee to users—they are completely subsidized services.

Ideally, the public recreation movement would like all services to be in this category. However, the diverse demands for programs almost always exceed a community's ability to pay for them totally. It should be the goal of public agencies to use public tax dollars to provide a core set of free recreation programs for all citizens. Usually public programs include provision for park areas or facilities, and low-organization events such as drop-in activities, special events, single-time block instructional workshops, and the like. Public programs usually do not require specialized leadership, the use of expensive equipment or facilities, or other high-cost components. What is to be included in this category varies from community to community, depending on the resources available and the community's willingness to support public recreation.

In not-for-profit organizations, the services that would be offered at no cost to the user are those that directly accomplish the stated social purpose of the agency. For example, scouting would not charge for the basic weekly meeting. Nor would a Boys and Girls Club charge a daily admission fee to its after-school program in a low-income neighborhood. A corporate recreation program may not charge for use of the basic fitness facility because its purpose is to keep company health care costs low. A commercial facility may offer such a service as a "loss leader"; that is, an activity priced below cost to attract a specific target market to enhance profitability in some other way. Examples of this would be teaching introductory racquetball lessons at a loss to attract new customers, or operating the nursery at such a facility at a loss to obtain customers during the usually low volume day time.

MERIT PROGRAMS

Merit programs are partly subsidized with tax dollars, but also have user fees attached to help recover some of their production costs. In not-for-profit or commercial agencies, the source of these subsidy dollars is different, but the basic concept is the same. In not-for-profit agencies, the subsidy comes from third-party funding from fund-raising or donations. In commercial agencies, the funding source is profits from other activities. In this case, the price charged would recover part of the costs of production.

The benefits from merit programs can be partly attributed to public interest and private individual gain. For example, one could argue that a summer recreation program directly benefits each child who participates and also, to some extent, benefits the public at large. Partitioning out the proportion of individual and private benefits accrued from "merit goods" is obviously problematic. However, the key element of the merit good concept is that some benefit accrues to both public and private interests. Thus, it is assumed that these goods will be jointly paid for with both individual and public funds. There are widely differing philosophies about the appropriate groups to subsidize and the percentage of a subsidy they should receive. Operationally, merit programs are services that are partially subsidized for any reason.

PRIVATE PROGRAMS

Private programs are paid for entirely by the participants. It is assumed that the benefit from private goods or private programs is received exclusively by the individuals using the program—not by the general public. In a free society, people may use their own personal resources to purchase any goods or services they believe will benefit them, including recreation services. Because the decisions are private and the benefit derived is private, it is assumed that the individual will pay the full cost of acquiring these services. These programs are the principle type offered by commercial agencies.

17

> *Merit programs are partly subsidized with tax dollars, but also have user fees attached to help recover some of their production costs.*

> *Private programs are paid for entirely by the participants.*

SUMMARY

Collectively, it is through the public and merit programs that the social purposes of governmental and not-for-profit agencies are fulfilled. Market positioning and targeting may be accomplished by commercial agencies using these types of pricing philosophies. Public programs are the basic free system—they are completely subsidized free services directed to accomplish the mission of the agency. Merit programs are partly subsidized services.

In allocating resources to merit programs, the agency is further defining who it wants to subsidize with tax dollars and other nonuser-generated sources of revenue. It is important to recognize that, with limited resources, an agency probably cannot have all the public and merit programs for which demand can be documented. Decisions for allocating resources between these two types of services are policy-level decisions that should be made by a policy-level board.

POLICY IMPLEMENTATION

Implementing the service category system in an agency is time consuming and involves iterations among the philosophical and policy concepts presented above, the accounting database of the agency, the local political process, and the limitations imposed by local resources. If agencies fail to distinguish adequately among these three levels of service and continue to act as if everything provided by the agency is in the public interest, agencies will have a further erosion in the quality of services they offer. In implementing this system, one should first determine what the publicly provided programs in a community should and can be in view of the public resource limitations of the community. If all nonpublic sources of funding were cut, what programs could the community support and what would it choose to support?

Second, programs, services, and facilities that are truly private and self-sustaining need to be identified and the true costs of providing them recovered from the users. Continuing to subsidize programs in public recreation systems because of inadequate policies and poor accounting procedures should not continue. Frequently, agencies have programs they designate as "self-sustaining," but often the accounting procedures in the agency are so inadequate that only direct costs can be identified and recovered (Howard & Selin, 1987). Indirect or overhead costs cannot be identified and continue to be subsidized with public tax dollars. This practice makes self-sustaining programs merit rather than private programs and siphons away resources from program areas that the agency, from a social policy standpoint, may prefer to subsidize.

Finally, agencies will need to develop policy guidelines for how to subsidize the merit programs to be offered to constituents. Decisions about whom to subsidize can be made around many variables, such as participant characteristics, program types, and geographic service areas. An agency may be required by law or charter to subsidize certain groups. Typically, communities choose to subsidize youth, teenagers, senior citizens, disabled citizens, and other vulnerable groups who do not have the personal resources to acquire needed services. Other communities choose to subsidize certain specific types of program services.

Exhibit 17-2: Categories of Park District Service

	Basic Public	Extra Public	Private	Enterprise
Definition	Services provided by the District available to all people	Additional services provided by District: an embellishment of a basic service	Private business offers this service within the District boundaries	Services that are designed to meet the ENDS policies and provide surplus funds
Who Benefits?	All ages levels in the District benefit either directly or indirectly	Individual participant benefits most: all members of the community benefit somewhat	Some community members benefit: users who participate benefit	Some community members benefit: users who participate benefit
Who Pays?	The community pays through taxes: no user charges	Partially subsidized by taxes: individual users pay all direct and some indirect costs	No tax subsidy: users pay full OPERATIONAL costs, both direct and indirect	No tax subsidy: users pay at least CAPITAL and OPERATIONAL cost (direct and indirect)
Feasibility for Exclusion	Not feasible to exclude or limit individuals from service or benefit	Feasible and desirable to exclude or limit individuals	Feasible and desirable to exclude or limit individuals	Feasible and desirable to exclude or limit individuals
Examples	Celebration of the arts Winter sports Baseball fields Outdoor tennis	Adult softball Summer day camps Lighted ball fields Lighted tennis	Aerobics Karate Extended day care	Golf course Courts plus Pro shops Refreshment stands

Notes
1. Not-for-profit organizations are not considered private businesses.
2. Director is to use discretion in setting fees until 1994 to phase in appropriate fee increases for recreation programs in each category.
3. Indirect costs = all out-of-pocket costs associated with a program: namely, wages, FICA, retirement, contractual services, continuing education, program printing and postage, athletic field electric and maintenance, and tournament fees, internal and external.
4. Indirect Costs = all out-of-pocket costs, plus administrative and supervisory wages, office support staff, utilities, general postage, promotional and marketing, advertising, and registration costs. All of these are expressed by applying a 15 percent factor to the total of direct costs.
5. Recreation programs or facilities can be offered even if a private entrepreneur already offers a similar service within the community, provided the benefit appears to be great enough. Other services may thereby be subsidized and the tax burden relieved.

Source: Elmhurst Park District, Elmhurst, IL.

For example, the U.S. Navy will not charge for any physical fitness activity because of the priority and importance of fitness activities to their mission—combat readiness. Subsidizing program costs with tax dollars should occur only in those program services that are wholly or partly in the public interest.

Before subsidization decisions can be made, the social welfare functions of a local recreation system must be well conceptualized. Many programs currently operated by public systems are truly merit goods that are presented as public or private goods. Agencies need to realize that subsidies are instruments through which the social welfare function of public recreation is carried out; therefore, comprehensive policies should be formulated to ensure that the subsidies are being used to achieve the results desired.

At the local level, developing policies to implement the proposed social welfare function of local recreation systems requires a serious review of the agency's facilities, services, and functions. The overall goal of policy development should be to preserve the public recreation system first by identifying the goods offered. Those that are truly public should be funded totally through public financing. The second goal is to identify the private goods being offered and to make certain that they are not actually merit goods receiving inappropriate public subsidy. The final goal is to further develop the social welfare function of public recreation. This is done by giving clearer direction to the subsidization of merit goods so that a community's social welfare desires are realized.

An example of how one community accomplished this is provided in Exhibit 17-2 on page 329, the pricing policy adopted by the Elmhurst Park District Board of Commissioners, Elmhurst, Illinois. In this policy, an additional category has been created. The "basic public" category equates with the public category just discussed. The "extra public" category equates to the merit services previously discussed. The "enterprise" category equates with the public category and requires recovery of all operational and capital costs so there is no public subsidy. The "private" category requires recovery of all operational costs but does not require the recovery of capital costs. Based on the examples provided, this "enterprise" category includes activities requiring expensive, dedicated facilities, whereas the "private" category includes programs that typically use more general, multiple-use facilities. Although this categorization uses some different terminology from that used in the book, the basic principles outlined in this policy will need to be dealt with in any agency that is attempting to develop a pricing philosophy.

Implementing these policies in any agency will require an accounting methodology and budgeting procedure that provides the data needed to allow congruence between fiscal practice and policy. The program management accounting system outlined in the next two chapters is such a system.

CONCLUSION

Systematically determining prices for an agency's programs is an important program management function. The price charged for a service often determines which participants will have access to the service.

Issues relevant to pricing decisions were discussed. A pricing philosophy that sorts out costs and benefits and serves as a basis for a differential pricing scheme was outlined. In addition, a step-by-step procedure for implementing a program management accounting system was provided.

REFERENCES

Anthony, R. N., & Welsch, G. A. (1981). *Fundamentals of management accounting.* Homewood, IL: R. D. Irwin.

Brademas, D. J., & Readnour, J. K. (1989). Status of fees and charges in public leisure service agencies. *Journal of Park and Recreation Administration, 7*(4), 42–55.

Ellerbrock, M. (1982, January). Some straight talk on user fees. *Parks and Recreation, 17,* 59–62.

Friedmann, J. (1973). The public interest and community participation: Toward a reconstruction of public philosophy. *Journal of the American Institute of Planners, 39*(1), 2–12.

Horngren, C. T. (1970). *Accounting for management control: An introduction* (2nd ed.). New York: Prentice-Hall.

Howard, D. (1988). Pricing public parks and recreation. In G. G. Lamke & D. L. Dustin (Eds.), *User fees for public recreation? A question of equity* (pp. 1–9). San Diego, CA: San Diego State University, Institute for Leisure Behavior.

Howard, D. R., & Crompton, J. L. (1980). *Financing, managing, and marketing recreation and park resources.* Dubuque, IA: W. C. Brown.

Howard, D. R., & Selin, S. W. (1987). A method for establishing consumer price tolerance levels for pubic recreation services *Journal of Park and Recreation Administration, 5*(3), 48–64.

Soderberg, P. (1988). Implementing a fee program. In G. G. Lamke & D. L. Dustin (Eds.), *User fees for public recreation? A question of equity* (pp. 1–9). San Diego, CA: San Diego State University, Institute for Leisure Behavior.

Wicks, B. E. (1986, October). The equitable allocation of publicly provided recreation and park services: Citizens' perceptions of equity. Paper presented at the 1986 Leisure Research Symposium, Anaheim, CA.

Wicks, B. E. (1987). The allocation of recreation and park resources: The court's intervention. *Journal of Park and Recreation Administration, 5*(3), 1–9.

ADDITIONAL READINGS

Crompton, J. L. (1982). Psychological dimensions of pricing leisure services. *Recreation Research Review, 9*(3), 12–20.

Crompton, J. L. (1984). How to establish a price for park and recreation services. *Trends, 21*(4), 12–21.

Manning, R., & Barker, S. (1981, September). Discrimination through user fees: Fact or fiction? *Parks & Recreation, 16,* 70–79.

Hiking at Middlefork
Photo courtesy of Lake County Forest Preserves, Libertyville, IL

Determining Program Costs

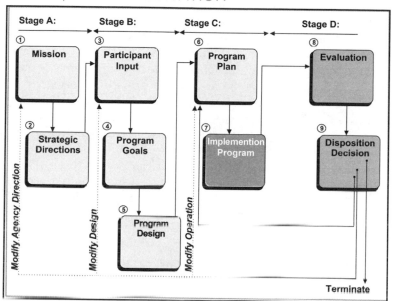

KEY TERMS

Line Units
Service Units
Line-item
    Budgets
Cost
Price
Cost Objective
Direct Costs
Indirect Costs
Cost Allocation
Cost Allocation
    Methods

An important part of implementing the program management accounting system is determining the cost of program production. In this chapter, three additional steps necessary for determining costs will be discussed.

ESTABLISHING LINE AND SERVICE UNITS—STEP 2 PMAS

The second step in implementing a program management accounting system is to classify all sub-units as performing either line or service functions. Managers have a good deal of discretion in defining what constitutes a unit. In any case, a unit should be headed by a manager who is responsible for its output. In most cases, the output will serve either a line or a staff purpose. However, the classification of units for cost purposes does not always dovetail neatly with the arrangement of units and personnel as defined by the organizational chart. Because of this, some activities of a unit may indeed be line functions and others may be service functions. Although it is possible to separate line from service costs in an individual unit, it is best to separate the line and service functions into their own units for cost analysis.

The second step in implementing a program management accounting system is to classify all sub-units as performing either line or service functions.

Line units are those units that are directly involved in the production and delivery of the organization's services and products. For example, recreation center staff members are directly involved in producing and supervising recreation services. Their work group and its costs of operation would therefore be classified as a line unit.

Service units provide services to other units and to the organization as a whole. They are not involved in producing the primary product or service of the organization. In a recreation and park department, the finance office would not be involved in directly producing recreation services and would therefore be classified as a service unit. Office clerical staff would also be classified as service personnel because they are not involved in the direct production and delivery of recreation services.

How an operational unit should be classified is less clear in some instances. One difficult unit in a park and recreation agency is the park department. Some of its activities involve providing service to other units, for example, cleaning recreation centers and lining ball diamonds. Other activities of a park department clearly result in the direct delivery of recreation services. Having well-maintained and beautiful parks for passive recreation is clearly a direct service.

Understanding what is to be done eventually with these data is the best guideline in making these classifications. This whole procedure is predicated on the notion that the agency exists to deliver or produce some product. (Product here is used in the generic sense to include programs, parks, facilities, and other services produced by a park and recreation agency.) The reason for the agency's existence is outlined in its mission statement and in its long-range and short-range goals and objectives. In the current example, a park and recreation agency exists to deliver recreation and leisure services.

It is further assumed that all of the agency's resources are used to accomplish its mission. The final goal of the program management accounting system is to account for all of the agency's expenditures through its line units, since these units are directly engaged in accomplishing the agency's mission and in delivering its services. It is assumed that service units exist to serve line units. From the viewpoint of the organization as a whole, there is no need to have service units except to enable line units to accomplish their missions. When the missions of all individual line units are summed collectively, they are the mission of the organization as a whole. Therefore, in classifying units as line or service units, the manager must make certain that all of the legitimate service outputs of the agency are in line units so that the expenses of all outputs can be determined.

If providing parks for informal recreational enjoyment is a legitimate service output of the agency, then a portion of the park department's expenditures should be classified as a line unit output that provides the informal recreation program. The final objective in implementing this process is to determine as accurately as possible the full cost of producing each unit of agency output; that is, each program, park, facility, or other service amenity. A classification decision that provides more accurate information regarding the full cost of each agency output is the correct and desirable decision.

The third step in this process is to prepare line-item object-classification budgets for all units, both line and service, identified in the second step.

Classifying operational units as line or service units is an important step in this whole process. Because the manager will eventually be forced to write off all service unit costs to the line units they serve, it is foolish to try to bury costs and hide the true costs of production. The process is designed to reveal the true costs of production so that accurate decisions about pricing and subsidization can be made. Classification decisions that cause inaccuracies in the true cost of any one product will appear elsewhere and drive up the cost of some other product. All costs incurred by the agency will eventually need to be accounted for.

PREPARING LINE-ITEM BUDGETS—STEP 3 PMAS

The third step in this process is to prepare line-item object-classification budgets for all units, both line and service, identified in the second step. This step is not as formidable as it might seem. Most agencies already have a line-item object-classification budget. If the agency uses a program budgeting procedure (Deppe, 1983), which assembles the budget from the lowest administrative level to the top, these budgets already exist. They are the source of revenue and expenditure information from which agency budgets have been prepared.

It is not the purpose of this section to demonstrate how to develop a line-item object-classification budget. Readers interested in this topic should see Deppe (1983), Edginton and Williams (1978), or Rodney and Toalson (1981) for a complete explanation of this process. The purpose of this section is to make clear the need to match revenues with expenses in budget preparation, and to explain why service unit budgets do not have a revenue side.

Although general budgeting convention is to display revenues before expenses, in actual budget preparation, one usually calculates expenses first, then identifies the amount and source of revenues that will support the activity. Using this principle of matching all expenses with the revenues requires all staff members to be concerned with the source of revenues for supporting their activities. This technique forces one to consider the number of dollars it will take to support an activity. It also forces one to identify the source of revenue for supporting each activity. In this latter instance, one begins at the time of budget preparation to observe where the revenue support for an activity is originating.

Line units will have both an expenditure and a revenue side to their budgets. However, service units will have only an expenditure side. Because service units exist only to support line units, service unit budgets do not have a revenue side. Their only source of revenue is from providing services to line units. Only line unit budgets, then, actually have a revenue side. The costs of service units must be allocated to line units.

ALLOCATING COSTS IN THE AGENCY—STEP 4 PMAS

The fourth step in implementing the program management accounting system is to allocate all service unit costs to line unit budgets. The technique for accomplishing this is cost allocation. Before cost allocation is discussed, however, it is necessary to define and differentiate terms.

The fourth step in implementing the program management accounting system is to allocate all service unit costs to line unit budgets.

COST

One must first distinguish between cost and price. "Cost is a measurement, in monetary terms, of the amount of resources used for some purpose," according to Anthony & Welsch (1981, p. 10). Full cost is the total cost; that is, all of the resources used by the agency in developing a specific program. Cost includes all dollars the agency uses in producing a program, regardless of the source of those dollars. Dollars acquired through taxation, fees, donations, and the like are all expended as costs to a specific program when they are used to produce the program. The agency's costs for developing and offering a program are all of the resources used to produce the program. If an agency's resources were not used to produce program A, then those same resources could be used to produce program B or program C. Producing any program causes the agency to incur a cost whether or not the agency recovers any of these costs through fees or third-party payments.

PRICE

Price is the dollar amount the agency charges participants to participate in a specific program. The price that participants must pay is a cost to the participants; that is, it is a resource they must give up to participate in the agency's program. In some cases, such as a fully subsidized public program, there is zero cost to the participant. The price the agency charges to participate should be established through the conjoint implications of the full cost of production and the agency's fee and charge policy. Pricing is looked at in more detail in the discussions accompanying steps five and six of the program management accounting system in Chapter Nineteen.

COST OBJECTIVE

A cost objective is any activity for which a separate measurement of cost is desired. The functions performed by line and service units are cost objectives. In the program management accounting system, service unit costs are handled as cost objectives in order to identify the full costs of their operation. Then, through one or more of the methods outlined in this section, the costs of service units are allocated to line units so that the full costs of line unit operations can be identified.

The goal in implementing cost allocation is to determine, as accurately as possible, the cost of providing a program or group of programs; in other words, the full cost of the cost objective. One must understand two types of costs in order to accurately classify and allocate them to cost objectives. All costs may be classified as direct or indirect costs.

DIRECT COSTS

Direct costs are those that can be traced to a specific cost objective. They are therefore assigned to a specific cost objective as direct costs. For example, a direct cost of providing a swimming pool is the cost of chlorine. Chlorine is purchased only because the agency operates a swimming pool; this is the only use for chlorine in the agency. If the

Direct costs are those that can be traced to a specific cost objective.

Indirect costs are those that the agency incurs regardless of whether or not it operates a specific program.

Exhibit 18-1. Cost Structure of a Program

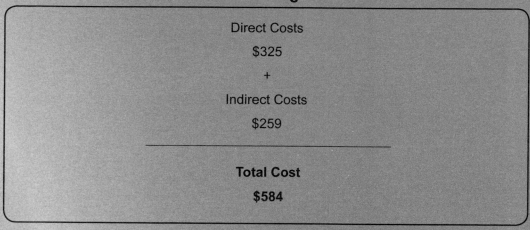

Direct Costs

$325

+

Indirect Costs

$259

_____

Total Cost

$584

agency no longer operated a swimming pool, it would no longer need chlorine. Chlorine, then, is a direct cost to the operation of a swimming pool. The cost of the chlorine would be assigned as a direct cost to the swimming pool operation in determining the full cost of its operation.

INDIRECT COSTS

Indirect costs are those that the agency incurs regardless of whether or not it operates a specific program. They are created by two or more cost objectives and are therefore not traceable to a single cost objective. For example, the cost of an office typewriter is an indirect cost to all program services and facilities. The agency will have a typewriter regardless of whether or not it operates any one specific program. Even so, this cost must be absorbed by all programs and services. The agency must give up resources to acquire the typewriter, and these foregone resources must be accounted for within the budgets of all the services provided. Indirect costs are often called "burden" or "overhead" costs.

According to Anthony and Welsch (1981), "The full cost of a cost objective is the sum of (1) its direct costs, plus (2) a fair share of its indirect costs" (p. 51). Through the accumulation of these costs, it is possible to determine the full cost of a specific cost objective. Exhibit 18-1 illustrates the structure of the cost of any single cost objective. The full cost of any cost objective, then, is the sum of its direct and indirect, or overhead, costs.

COST ALLOCATION

Cost allocation is the process of identifying and assigning costs to various cost objectives. In the current case, the indirect costs of service units will be allocated as costs to line units. Other kinds of indirect costs may need to be allocated to various cost objectives as well. The principles that follow will apply to either case. In implementing cost allocation, the programmer is faced with a number of decisions regarding how costs can or should be allocated. Three principles should be used to guide these decisions:

1. Implementing cost allocation is an attempt to assign indirect costs to line cost objectives in a fair and equitable manner. The goal is to reflect the full costs of service production.
2. The method of cost allocation selected should accurately reflect how much of an indirect cost a specific cost objective actually uses or consumes. Again, try to reflect reality.

Both of these principles affect the eventual accuracy and usefulness of the data to be developed. Because many cost allocation decisions need to be made, and because managers have a good deal of discretion in making them, management can do so in a manner that will influence the full cost of various programs. However, since all costs must eventually be accounted for in line operations, decisions initially favorable to the costs of one specific unit are almost always detrimental to those of some other unit. Pursuing accuracy as the guiding principle is not only the best policy, but it often must be resorted to in order to make everything reconcile properly.

3. In any cost allocation method, there is a tradeoff between accuracy and cost. For example, it may be possible to achieve perfect accuracy of actual costs, but only at a very high cost of time and effort. Each of the methods outlined below provides various combinations of ease of implementation and degree of accuracy. One needs to try to achieve as much accuracy as possible within the limits of reasonable effort. Remaining consistent over a period of time in how costs are allocated is as important as perfect accuracy because consistency ensures reliability of data from one reporting period to another. One can begin with easily obtainable but less accurate cost allocation data in the initial stages of implementing a program management accounting system. These figures can then be replaced at a later time with more accurate cost data as they are researched and developed.

COST ALLOCATION METHODS

EQUAL SHARE OF INDIRECT EXPENSES

In this method, each functional line unit receives an equal share of indirect expenses. For example, the salary of the Director of Parks and Recreation may be shared equally by the parks and the recreation divisions. Because there are two divisions, each is assigned one half of the director's salary. Obviously, if there were three line units, each would assume one third of the salary. With this method, each unit assumes an

In the Equal Share of Indirect Expenses method, each functional line unit receives an equal share of indirect expenses.

Exhibit 18-2: Budget Percentage Method of Cost Allocation

Parks Budget:	$150,000	33%
Recreation Budget:	$300,000	67%
Total:	$450,000	100%

equal share of the indirect expense to be allocated. This is the easiest method to implement, but it may also be the least accurate.

With this method, no effort is made to base the indirect costs to be assumed by a unit on actual costs used by the unit. This method may often be appropriate, however. One could argue that the director's main responsibility is to maintain the organization's external relationships and provide overall direction to the agency. From this perspective, the time the director may spend with any one unit in a given time period is irrelevant to assigning the director's salary cost. The director's function- al accomplishments are equally essential to both the park and the rec- reation units, so they must share equally in the cost of having a director on staff. There can be many of these kinds of cases in organizations. It is often not practical to try to assign costs on a more sophisticated basis. Spending time and resources to achieve increased accuracy of cost al- location in these instances is nonproductive.

PERCENTAGE OF BUDGET

With this method, each line unit is assigned a percentage of indirect costs that equals its percentage of some overall budget figure. Again, let us use the director's salary of $90,000 as an example of an indirect cost to be allocated to the park and the recreation units. Exhibit 18-2 displays the percentage of the overall budget assigned to each of these two line units.

In this case, $30,000, or 33 percent, of the director's salary cost would be allocated to the park department budget; the remaining $60,000, or 67 percent, would be allocated to the recreation department budget.

In allocating costs with the percentage of budget method, one is as- suming that the actual use of the cost to be allocated is accurately char- acterized by the percentage of the overall budget each of the individual line units currently consumes. Although this method is easy to imple- ment, the accuracy of the data generated is contingent on the validity of the assumption outlined above. In the case of the director's salary, one could argue that the director's time is spent in proportion to the size of each line unit's relative size in the organization. Allocating the

In the Percentage of Budget method, each line unit is as- signed a percentage of indirect cost that equals its percentage of some overall budget figure.

In the Time Budget Study method, the time a service unit spends on each cost objective is studied.

Exhibit 18-3: Measurement Study Method of Cost Allocation

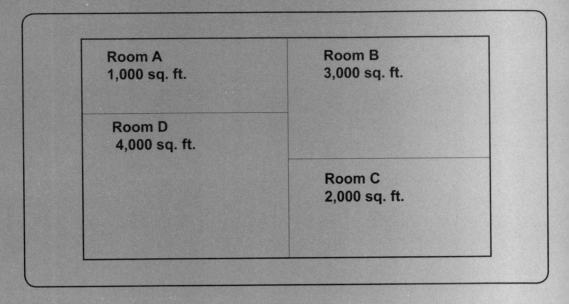

Room A **1,000 sq. ft.**	**Room B** **3,000 sq. ft.**
Room D **4,000 sq. ft.**	**Room C** **2,000 sq. ft.**

director's salary with a method based on the relative size of each line unit is justifiable in this type of situation. Whether these assumptions for allocation are valid is usually best determined by on-site managers who are close enough to the situation to know how time is spent.

TIME BUDGET STUDY

Determining how individuals or units actually spend their work time through a time budget study provides the most accurate data on which to allocate costs. With this method, the time a service unit spends on each cost objective is studied. The percentage of time is then used as the database for allocating the indirect costs of the service unit to line units. The actual allocation of costs is similar to the percentage of budget method, except that more accurate data are being used to develop the percentage figures for allocating the costs.

This is a very accurate method. However, conducting the study is itself a costly and time-consuming process. Because of this, one must make certain that the data to be developed are important enough to warrant the research effort. Once time budget figures are developed, agencies usually continue to use the percentages generated in the initial study unless drastic alterations in work assignments or practices warrant altering the percentages. Time budget figures should be verified periodically on a three- to five-year staggered rotation schedule. In this way, agencies do not have to conduct these time-consuming and costly studies each budget period. The percentages are of course altered if there is any apparent change in operational practices.

In the Cost Tracking System, the actual use of an item by a cost objective is tracked, and the actual cost of the item is charged back to the unit using it.

COST-TRACKING SYSTEM

With this method, the actual use of an item by a cost objective is tracked, and the actual cost of the item is charged back to the unit using it. This method is needed particularly where materials in addition to time are being used to complete a job. Tracking only time, which is the case in a time budget study, will often fail to give an accurate enough cost estimate of the true costs to be allocated from a service unit to a line unit. In park operations, for example, time (labor) and materials are often needed to complete a job, so cost tracking the materials is also necessary.

Cost tracking is often used to account for costs in an individual budget year. That is, the actual costs used are assigned to the various units who used them. These cost-tracking data, accumulated over time, can be used during the budget preparation process to estimate the percentage of costs that will be allocated from various service units to line units.

SPACE OR MEASUREMENT STUDIES

This method of cost allocation is used in instances where one can determine the appropriate proportion of cost to allocate to a specific cost objective by measuring the relative proportion of overall costs that is being used by each cost objective. For example, the building shown in Exhibit 18-3 contains 10,000 square feet of space. This space is divided into four rooms: room A with 1,000 square feet, room B with 3,000 square feet, room C with 2,000 square feet, and room D with 4,000 square feet. In implementing this method of cost allocation, one calculates the respective proportion of the overall space each room accounts for. Thus, room A contains 10 percent of the total building space, room B 30 percent, and so on.

In allocating building operating expenses, such as electricity, water and sewer charges, gas or heating bills, and maintenance expenses, one can simply allocate a percentage of total costs to each room in proportion to the percentage of overall building space that each room actually represents. Thus, room A would be allocated 10 percent of these charges, room B 30 percent, and so on.

Although the building diagrammed in Exhibit 18-3 does not include any common areas, such as hallways, a foyer, or restrooms, most buildings do contain this type of space. Usually expenses of the common areas are allocated to the space represented by the usable rooms in a building. In the current example, then, the proportion of costs allocated to each room would not change, because the amount of usable space in the building would still be 10,000 square feet.

This method is useful in situations where one can accurately determine the proportion of costs to be allocated. Allocating costs for a fertilizing program in parks, maintenance in a building, and other similar instances, are best handled in this manner.

In step four of the program management accounting system, then, the cost allocation decisions that are made enable one to allocate the indirect cost from service units to line operations. This procedure is necessary in order to allocate the indirect, or overhead, costs of service units to the direct costs of the line operating units that actually deliver services and thereby produce the agency's service output.

CONCLUSION

To determine program costs, three additional steps of the program management accounting system must be implemented. All operational units must be designated as either line or service units. Line-item object-classification budgets must be prepared for each operational unit. Indirect costs must be allocated to their cost objectives. Several methods of cost allocation appropriate for use in leisure service agencies were discussed. The program management accounting system recognizes program services as the line output of the agency and requires that all costs be reported in relation to their contribution to the development of program services.

REFERENCES

Anthony, R. N., & Welsch, G. A. (1981). *Fundamentals of management accounting*. Homewood, IL: R. D. Irwin.

Deppe, T. R. (1983). *Management strategies in financing parks and recreation*. New York: Wiley.

Edginton, C. R., & Williams, J. G. (1978). *Productive management of leisure service organizations*. New York: Wiley.

Rodney, L. S., & Toalson, R. F. (1981). *Administration of recreation, parks, and leisure services*. New York: Wiley.

Mural Painting in Cal Heights
Photo courtesy of Long Beach Parks, Recreation, and Marine Department, Long Beach, CA

Pricing Program Services

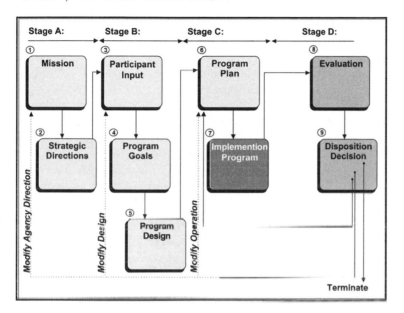

19

KEY TERMS

**Cost Volume
  Profit Analysis**
Variable Costs
Fixed Costs
**Changing Fixed
  Costs**
Tabling Cost Data
**Graphing Cost
  Data**
Break-Even Point
Revenue
Revenue Line
Profit
Loss
Cost Recovery
**Resistance to
  Prices**
**Establishing a
  Price**

In this chapter, the final two steps of the PMAS are explained. The fifth step is to isolate specific programs and calculate the actual costs of providing an individual service. This is accomplished with cost-volume-profit analysis, which is also called break-even analysis or contribution margin theory. The same technique has various names because of different emphases in using the technique. The implications of this will become apparent later in this section.

COST-VOLUME-PROFIT ANALYSIS—STEP 5 PMAS

Cost-volume-profit analysis of a specific activity or segment of an enterprise permits a complete financial analysis of the expected financial results of an activity. This analysis enables the programmer to match the revenue with the expenses for an activity and to simultaneously account for changes in volume (participation level) and changes in production costs. The data generated by using cost-volume-profit analysis inform the manager about the actual costs of providing specific services. With this information, it is then possible to make cost-based decisions regarding the price to be charged for specific services.

CLASSIFYING COSTS

To implement cost-volume-profit analysis, the programmer begins by examining the expenses or costs associated with a specific activity. To use this analysis, costs of a program must be classified as variable, fixed, or changing fixed.

VARIABLE COSTS

Cost-vol-ume-profit analysis of a specific activity or segment of an enterprise permits a complete financial analysis of the expected financial results of an activity.

Variable costs are those that change directly and proportionately with changes in volume. A variable cost is one that changes by the same amount of money with the addition of each new participant or some other unit of volume (see Endnote 1, p. 359). The cost of an instruction book to be used in a class is an example of a variable cost. The agency would need to purchase a book for each participant and would need as many books as there are participants in the class. If the book costs $12, $12 in variable costs would be added to the program for each partici-pant who enrolls. Some programs will have several variable costs. Let us assume that the book is to be purchased for a synchronized swim program. A swim cap and nose clip also need to be purchased for each participant. These three items come to $20 in variable costs for the syn-chronized swim program, so for each participant added to this pro-gram, the agency would incur $20 in variable costs.

FIXED COSTS

Fixed costs are those that do not change with changes in volume (that is, the number of participants). These costs are fixed because they remain the same for the duration of a program, regardless of the num-ber of participants. There are both direct and indirect fixed costs. In the previous chapter, direct and indirect costs were defined and explained. This is where this work is applied. It is important to remember that the direct–indirect classification deals with the relationship of a cost to a cost objective, and the fixed–variable classification deals with the behavior of a cost in relation to changes in volume. It is therefore possible to have costs that are classified as direct fixed costs or indirect fixed costs.

An example of a direct fixed cost would be the cost of renting a swimming pool for the program discussed above. This cost would be directly related to the specific cost objective, the synchronized swim program. It would also remain the same regardless of the number of participants in a program. Whether one or 30 people participate, the rental fee would remain the same. It is therefore a fixed cost. It is prob-ably apparent that the notion of a fixed cost has limitations. That is, the notion of a cost remaining the same is only true within certain param-eters. The swimming pool does have a limited swimmer capacity and can accommodate only a limited number of participants, for example, 100. These parameters are known as the *relevant range*.

An example of an indirect fixed cost is a proportion of some over-head cost that may be allocated to a specific cost objective or program. The synchronized swim program may be required to absorb some overhead increment of allocated cost, such as a share of office and ad-ministrative expenses, utilities, and advertising or marketing costs. The agency must incur these costs, but they are not directly traceable to a specific cost objective or program. They are fixed because they do not increase with each new participant added to a program.

CHANGING FIXED COSTS

Changing fixed costs are those that change in the same direction, but not proportionately, with changes in volume or the number of participants. These costs do not change in the same amount for each participant added. Most often, they are costs that change after certain numbers of participants are added. In the synchronized swim program, a lifeguard would be hired to guard a class of 25. The lifeguard's wage would be a direct fixed cost to this program. A second lifeguard would be needed when the program enrollment exceeded 25 participants. It would therefore be necessary to hire a second lifeguard when the 26th person entered the class. From the 26th through the 50th participant, the agency would have the additional cost of a second lifeguard. The cost of the second lifeguard is therefore a changing fixed cost.

Because the cost of the second lifeguard does not go up with each participant added, it is not a variable cost. Because it is not a cost that is fixed over the relevant range of this program—that is, 100 participants (which is determined in this case by the capacity of the pool)—it is not a fixed cost. It is therefore a changing fixed cost. It changes in the relevant range of the program, but remains fixed from the first through the 25th, and again from the 26th through the 50th swimmer.

PRESENTING COST DATA

Analytical information about cost-volume-profit analysis can be provided in two ways: by tabling the data, or by placing them in a graph. Each of these methods has unique ways of revealing important information regarding cost behavior.

TABLING COST DATA

To illustrate this technique, the synchronized swim program cited earlier will be developed further. Following are a set of facts regarding the program:

1. The Delaware Recreation Center has a pool, which can be rented for $50/hour. The pool can accommodate 100 swimmers. The rental fee also includes the use of the new stereo system with underwater speakers.
2. The synchronized swim coach to be hired will make $12 per contact hour.
3. The lifeguard to be hired will make $10/hour and can supervise 25 swimmers.
4. A second lifeguard must be hired at $10/hour if there are between 26-50 swimmers.
5. Each participant will use an instructional book costing $12, a swim cap costing $5, and a nose clip costing $3.

Cost Items	Actual Cost
Fixed Costs	
Direct Fixed Costs	
Synchronized Swim Coach	
30 hours X $12/hour	$360
Lifeguard	
30 hours X 10/hour	300
Rent	
30 hours X 50/hour	1500
Indirect Fixed Costs	
Overhead	100
Program Supervisor	
9 hours X 15/hour	135
Changing Fixed Costs	
Second Lifeguard (from 26th to 50th swimmer)	
30 hours X 10/hour	300
Total Fixed Costs	$2695
Variable Costs	
Book	12
Swim cap	3
Nose clip	5
Total Variable Costs/Person	$20

Table 19-1: Synchronized Swim Cost Data

6. Each program in the aquatics division must absorb $100 in overhead expenses for administrative and supervisory wages, advertising, and marketing of the aquatics program, and office expenses for handling registration.

7. The program supervisor estimates she will spend nine hours of her time on this program for hiring, training, and supervision of the synchronized swim coach and lifeguard(s). The program director makes $15/hour.

8. The program will operate for ten weeks, one night per week, for three hours each night. There is an enrollment limit of 50 swimmers for the program.

The first step in analyzing these data is to classify each cost and determine any additional facts needed to solve the problem. The only fact needed is that there will be 30 hours of instruction time (three hours per

Cost Items	Number of Participants					
	10	20	26	30	40	50
Direct Fixed Costs						
Swim Coach	360	360	360	360	360	360
Lifeguard	300	300	300	300	300	300
Rent	1500	1500	1500	1500	1500	1500
Indirect Fixed Costs						
Overhead	**100**	**100**	**100**	**100**	**100**	**100**
Program Director	**135**	**135**	**135**	**135**	**135**	**135**
Changing Fixed Costs						
2nd Lifeguard			**300**	**300**	**300**	**300**
Total Fixed Costs	**2395**	**2395**	**2695**	**2695**	**2695**	**2695**
Variable Costs						
$20/swimmer	**200**	**400**	**520**	**600**	**800**	**1000**
Total Costs	**2595**	**2795**	**3215**	**3295**	**3495**	**3695**
Cost/Participant	260	140	124	110	88	74

Table 19-2: Synchronized Swim Program Cost-Volume-Profit Table

night x one night per week x 10 weeks = 30 hours). The data from these facts are displayed in Table 19-1.

These data can then be placed in a cost-volume-profit table, Table 19-2. This table shows the various volumes of participation as column headings. Choosing the levels of participation to include in such a table is somewhat arbitrary. But in this case, 50 is included as the largest level of volume because it is the maximum capacity of the program. Twenty-six is included because it represents a breaking point at which the changing fixed cost of a second lifeguard is introduced.

A volume level of ten participants is also included. An agency's operational policies and the program supervisor's previous experience with volume levels will dictate choices of volume levels to include. For example, the agency may not operate an adult program with fewer than ten participants. In this case, ten represents the lowest level of activity that would be used in a table and also the lower limit of the relevant range. Rows in the table show various cost items and different cost summaries at the volume levels specified in the columns.

The cost per participant, which is the final row in Table 19-2, is also known as the break-even point. At each volume specified, the cost-per-participant dollar amount represents the price that each participant must be charged if the agency is to recover all of its costs associated with producing the program. With these data, it is possible to determine how much it costs the agency to produce a specific service. How this break-even point is used in setting a price for a specific service is discussed in step six.

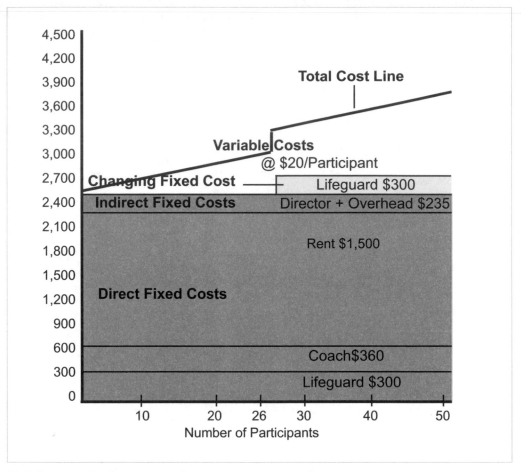

Exhibit 19-1: Graphed Cost Volume Profit Analysis Data

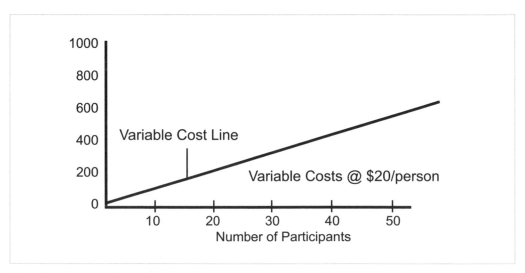

Exhibit 19-2: Graphing Variable Costs

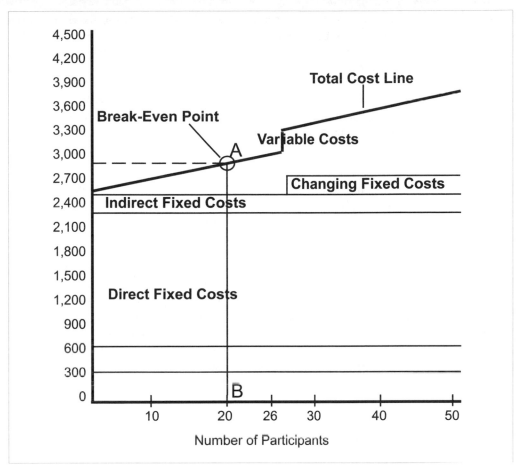

Exhibit 19-3: Graphing the Break-Even Point

GRAPHING COST DATA

These data can also be placed in a graph, which makes it possible to visually observe the behavior of each cost component. The data from the synchronized swim program in Table 19-2 are graphed in Exhibit 19-1.

Graphed data enable the programmer to observe clearly the effect of each cost component. Direct and indirect fixed costs remain constant through the relevant range and are therefore represented by a line that is parallel to the volume line—fixed costs do not increase with increases in volume. Changing fixed costs are represented by a line that is also parallel to the volume line, but that is entered on the graph in a stepped-up fashion to represent the incremental increase in fixed costs that are characteristic of fixed costs. Variable costs are represented by a sloped line, the steepness of which will vary depending on the amount of variable costs per person. A large amount of variable costs per person will result in a steep line, whereas a small amount of variable costs per person will result in a less steep line.

Graphing the cost data makes it possible to visually observe the behavior of each cost component.

The total cost line summarizes the fixed, changing fixed, and variable costs. This line often coincides with the variable cost line on the finished graph, but only because the variable cost component is added above the fixed cost line, which was already drawn. The variable cost component of total costs can be graphed separately, as is done in Exhibit 19-2 on page 350. The total cost line, then, coincides with the variable cost line on a total cost graph only because fixed and variable costs have been summarized on the graph.

GRAPHING THE BREAK-EVEN POINT

Once the variable costs have been added to the fixed costs and graphed, the break-even point at each level of participation can be determined from the graph as well as from the tabled data. As demonstrated in Exhibit 19-3 on page 351, the break-even point is determined by drawing the vertical line A-B directly above any participation level. In this example, line A-B has been drawn above 20 participants, but lines can be drawn at any participation level. The break-even point is the point at which similarly drawn lines intersect the total cost line. In Exhibit 19-3, the break-even point for 20 participants is $2,795. In this case, one would need to charge each participant $140 ($2,795 divided by 20 participants) to break even. The advantage of the graph over the tabled data is that the programmer can observe the steepness of the total cost line and quickly see the break-even point at any level of participation.

APPLYING THE REVENUE LINE

Once the total cost graph is completed, one can draw revenue lines that represent various levels of revenue. Exhibit 19-4 is a total cost graph of the synchronized swim program with the revenue line A-B added to it. Line A-B illustrates the effect of revenue at $150 per person. It is possible and advisable to draw additional revenue lines that estimate the effect of different pricing levels within the parameters of the current cost structure. The point at which line A-B crosses the total cost line is also a break-even point; that is, the point at which revenue equals the cost of producing the program. With this method, we can observe the effect of various prices on the minimum participation level needed to break even. With the previous method, we can observe the effect of various participation levels on the price we will need to charge to break even. Once the total cost graph is completed, either approach can be used to determine a minimum price or minimum participation level. When one is determined, the other is also determined. However, the one that will take precedence in determining price and participation level is a matter of circumstances.

In Exhibit 19-4, the break-even point occurs somewhere between the 18th and 19th participant. With 18 participants, revenue is $2,700 ($150 X 18) and costs are $2,755 ($2,395 in fixed costs + 18 X $20 per person in variable costs). With 18 participants, costs still exceed revenue by $55. With 19 participants, revenue is $2,850 ($150 X 19) and costs are $2,775 ($2,395 in fixed costs + 19 X $20 per person in variable costs). With 19 participants, revenue exceeds costs by $75.

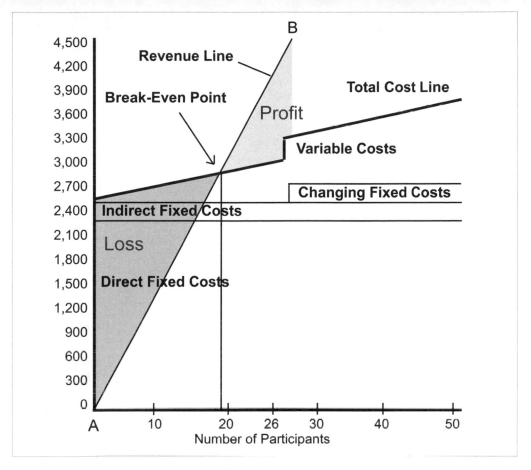

Exhibit 19-4: Plotting the Revenue Line

When revenue estimates are used to determine participation levels, the break-even point will seldom occur with a whole unit of participation. Because it is not possible to have part of a person in a program, the break-even point is established at the next highest volume level. This practice also ensures that the agency does not incur a loss. In this case, the break-even point with revenue at $150 per person is 19 persons.

In Exhibit 19-4, the area above the break-even point shaded with the vertical lines represents profit for the agency. The area below the break-even point shaded with dots represents a loss to the agency. Volume above the break-even point on the graph will result in a profit or retained income for the agency; that is, income in excess of production costs. Volume levels below the break-even point will result in a loss, which will need to be compensated for with increased fees, through subsidization with tax dollars, with third-party donations, or with profits from other activities.

This latter situation often occurs in a commercial recreation operation in which one activity is used as a "loss leader" to draw customers into a facility or program. For example, the nursery at a tennis club may operate at a loss, but be subsidized by profits from increased court usage due to the nursery being available.

In actual practice, once accurate costs for program production have been determined, the programmer usually determines a price, estimates a reasonable volume level expected, and estimates total revenue to be earned. If the estimated total revenue is not sufficient to cover costs, then the programmer must subsidize the cost of the program, try to reduce costs to match revenues, increase prices, or not operate the program. If the program is operated and revenue from participants does not cover the production costs, then the program is being subsidized by the agency. There has been a tendency in public recreation to simply hide these costs; however, the program management accounting system will not allow this to happen. Managers using this system are required to identify all costs and to match them with revenues.

Cost-volume-profit analysis enables the programmer to isolate specific activities in order to match costs with revenues generated. With this technique, it is possible to determine accurately the full cost of producing services, and then to use this information to determine a price.

ESTABLISHING A PRICE—STEP 6 PMAS

The sixth and final step in implementing the program management accounting system is to determine the price that the agency will charge for a service. This determination should be made by using the data developed in the cost-volume-profit analysis, the implications of the agency's pricing policy developed in the first step, and some consideration of other factors that may mitigate the price to be established.

Cost-volume-profit analysis provides data that enable a programmer to estimate the financial performance of a specific program. A program's financial performance can be classified into one of the following three cases: (1) the program's revenue may be less than its production costs (representing a loss to the agency); (2) the program's revenue may equal the cost of production—the break-even point at which the agency recovers all of its costs of production; or (3) the program's revenue may exceed production costs, which provides the agency with revenue in excess of its production costs. This excess revenue is known as a contribution margin; that is, a margin of revenue over actual production costs that may be applied to agency profits or retained income.

In addition to the actual cost data developed through cost-volume-profit analysis, the manager also needs to ascertain from the service category system whether a program is a merit, a private, or a public service. A public service one is offered at no cost to the public. A merit service is one offered at a price that is less than that required for full-cost recovery; the price enables the agency to recover some of its production costs. Often, the price charged for a merit program is based on recovering only the direct costs of a program, and no attempt is made to recover any indirect costs. A private service is offered at a price that will enable the agency to fully recover its production costs.

PRICING CONSIDERATIONS

Before establishing the price, one must also anticipate possible consumer resistance to a price. Howard and Selin (1987) have demonstrated

Exhibit 19-5: Program Cost Pricing Work Sheet

Programming Unit _____ Activity/Program Title _____

Fixed Costs	Changing Fixed Costs	Variable Costs (per unit)
Personnel (Total) $ _____	Personnel (Total) $ _____	Personnel (Total) $ _____
Services Contractual (Total) $ _____	Services Contractual (Total) $ _____	Services Contractual (Total) $ _____
Commodities (Total) $ _____	Commodities (Total) $ _____	Commodities (Total) $ _____
Materials (Total) $ _____	Materials (Total) $ _____	Materials (Total) $ _____
Other Expenses (Total) $ _____	Other Expenses (Total) $ _____	Other Expenses (Total) $ _____
Capital Outlay (Total) $ _____	Capital Outlay (Total) $ _____	Capital Outlay (Total) $ _____

Fixed Cost Total $ _____
Add $ __ for overhead rate*

Total adjusted Fixed Costs $ _____	Total Changing Fixed Costs $ _____	Total Variable Costs $ _____

*Optional—added to recover overhead or burden costs based on cost allocation studies and agency policy.

Establishing a Price

1. Total adjusted fixed costs $_____
2. Total changing fixed costs $_____
3. Total variable costs per unit ($ _____) x
   Expected number of participants (no.   ) = _____ $_____
4. Subtotal (add lines 1 + 2 + 3) $_____
5. Divide subtotal (line 4) by
   expected number of participants (no.   ) = _____ $_____
6. Multiply result on line 5 by
   _____% of desired cost recovery = $_____

   The last figure (the result on line 6) represents the price it is necessary to charge each participant in the program in order to achieve the desired level of cost recovery. "Percent of cost recovery" represents the contribution the agency wants an individual participant to pay toward the cost of providing a program. Percentage of cost recovery can range from 0% to an excess of 100%. The meaning of various levels of percentage of cost recovery are outlined below.

   0% A Public Good, totally subsidized service—the user contributes nothing to the cost of providing the service.
   1% to 99% A Merit Good, users contribute a percentage of the cost of providing a service—tax dollars are used to fund the remaining percentage of costs in excess of user fee contributions.
   100% A Private Good, users contribute the full cost of providing the service—no tax dollars are used.
   100% + A Private Good, users contribute in excess of actual costs for providing the program—excess income is used to subsidize other programs.

that there is a price tolerance zone within which a price may be established. Furthermore, this zone varies from activity to activity, which suggests that across-the-board price increases are a poor pricing strategy. A price must be set for each activity.

The price established must also take into consideration the attitude of the target market toward pricing. Kerr and Manfredo (1991) documented that intention to pay is most significantly influenced by past use and past fee paying. That is, individuals who are used to paying a fee for a given service and are frequent consumers of it will have the least resistance to price increases. Reiling, Criner, and Oltmanns (1988) have suggested that the two most persuasive arguments to influence attitudes about paying are to compare the price proposed with commercial rates for the same service, and to provide data about the cost of provision (data from the cost-volume-profit analysis outlined in this chapter).

An additional point to understand is price elasticity; that is, the relationship of the activity being charged to the overall price for participation. For example, when the agency operates tourist attractions, the prices at these are somewhat inelastic because the price of admission to the museum, for example, is a very small part of the total cost of a trip. Admissions to amenities constitute about 10 percent of the travel dollar. Thus, the $2.00 admission charge to a museum could probably be doubled without adversely affecting demand, because it would have a relatively small impact for a tourist on the overall cost of a trip to a museum. This is price elasticity, and the specific example provided is an example of an inelastic price. With information from these basic sources, the programmer determines the price to charge for a program. Exhibit 19-5 on page 355 includes a work sheet that brings together the data necessary for determining the price of program. A programmer faces many possible circumstances in establishing program fees. But remember, although quantitative data about the costs of production can be developed, the final price established must also take into consideration the agency's pricing policy, the target market's attitude toward pricing, and their ability to pay. Below are outlined some of these typical circumstances.

PUBLIC SERVICES

Public services are offered by the agency at no charge to the user. The agency does not recover any of its costs of production from a public service. Cost-volume-profit information for public services simply informs the programmer about the costs of producing the various services provided at no charge to the public. The data are useful for determining the comparative cost of the various public programs that the agency is offering free of charge. When the cost structure of public programs is examined, some savings and areas for cost reduction will often become apparent. Using cost-volume-profit analysis, then, is useful for documenting where the agency's resources are being spent, for identifying which groups are receiving subsidized services, and for determining the cost of each program service provided.

> *Cost-volume-profit information for public services simply informs the programmer about the costs of producing the various services provided at no charge to the public.*

> *Using cost-volume-profit analysis to examine the actual costs of producing merit programs establishes a base from which a price can be determined.*

Exercise 19-1: Cost-Volume-Profit Analysis

Complete the following problem outside of class, then discuss your solution in class. See Endnote 2 before you discuss the problem.

Background:
Consider the following information about a proposed watercolor painting class.

1. Fowler Community Arts Center has an arts and crafts room, which can be rented for $25 per hour. The room can accommodate 30 people.
2. The instructor to be hired makes $10 per contact hour and can teach 30 students. The instructor needs an aid to assist with any class exceeding 20 students. The aid makes $5 per hour.
3. Each participant will use an instructional book costing $5, painting tablet costing $6, and watercolor paint kits costing $11.
4. Each program operated in the arts division must absorb $100 in over head expenses for administrative and supervisory wages, advertising and marketing of the arts programs, and office expenses for handling registration.
5. The arts supervisor estimates that she will spend eight hours of her time on this watercolor class for hiring, training, and supervising the staff. The arts supervisor makes $15 per hour.
6. The program will operate for 10 weeks, two nights per week, two hours per evening.
7. There will be 40 hours of instruction time (two hours per night X two nights per week X 10 weeks).

Directions:
1. Prepare a Cost Data Table for this painting class.
   a. What are the overhead or indirect costs of this class?
   b. What are the variable costs of this program?

2. Prepare a Watercolor Painting Class Cost-Volume-Profit Table
   a. What is the break-even point for this program with 10 participants? 25?

MERIT SERVICES

Merit services are offered by the agency at a price that will permit a partial recovery of agency costs. Merit services can be thought of in two ways—either as programs that receive a partial subsidy or as programs that partly recover their costs of production. In reality, they actually do both. However, which component the agency chooses to emphasize can influence how these programs are thought about and treated in the agency. Using cost-volume-profit analysis to examine the actual costs of producing merit programs establishes a base from which a price can be determined. Knowing the cost of producing a program does not necessarily mean the agency will charge a price that permits a full recovery of its production costs. Merit services are one case in which production costs are simply the starting point in determining a price for participation.

The price actually charged for a merit service will be determined by production costs, the dollars available from other sources (primarily donations and tax dollars, depending on the type of agency) to subsidize the program, and the agency's policies regarding the type of program under consideration. Determining a price for merit services is clearly more complicated than simply using cost-volume-profit analysis to determine actual production costs and adding on a contribution margin. The process is somewhat the opposite of adding a contribution margin for profit; in this case, it involves subtracting a "subsidy margin" that reduces the actual price to the user. Through the subsidies allocated to merit services, the social welfare function of the agency is implemented, so allocation of these subsidies should occur with accurate cost data. Cost-volume-profit analysis provides the programmer with accurate data so that the actual dollar amount of a subsidy can be determined. In this way, the programmer and the agency know how much and for what programs their subsidy dollars are being used. Now complete Exercise 19-1 on page 357.

PRIVATE SERVICES

Private services are offered at a price that will enable the agency to recover all of its direct and indirect costs of producing the program. The use of cost-volume-profit analysis in private services provides the programmer with an accurate statement of the actual costs of production. These figures can be used as data for determining and justifying the price to be charged for a program. In a public or not-for-profit agency, obtaining full cost recovery for these types of services is important so that funds intended to subsidize public and merit services are not used to subsidize services that are supposed to be self-sustaining.

In a commercial recreation operation, knowing the full cost of production is equally important. If the agency is to make a profit and stay in business, it must make a margin of profit beyond actual production costs. It is normal practice to use cost-volume-profit analysis to determine actual production cost at an estimated level of volume and then to add on a margin of profit to production costs. In these cases, each program is expected to contribute a margin of profit to the overall profits of the agency. This increment is known as the contribution margin. For example, all programs may be offered at cost plus a 15 percent contribution margin to agency profit.

Public and not-for-profit agencies also use the contribution margin concept. Although these types of agencies are not profit making, they often develop retained income from some program services. This retained income is frequently used to help subsidize merit and public services, or to make up for losses incurred in the operation of less successful private services.

CONCLUSION

Methods of analyzing the relationship of cost to volume were discussed. The program management accounting system requires that each program service be isolated, and its costs of production and revenues matched so that its financial performance can be observed. Implementing the system will give the programmer factual cost data about each program service so that cost-based pricing decisions can be made. It will also enable accurate decision making regarding the subsidization of programs.

ENDNOTES

1. Variable costs are costs that increase an equal amount with each additional unit of volume. In most leisure services, the volume unit is the individual participant. However, this is not always the case. For example, in a band contest, variable costs may be dependent on the number of bands entered, not the number of band members. The same is often true for calculating the costs of athletic leagues and tournaments.

2. If you followed instructions and are reading this before discussing the cost-volume-profit exercise in class, you are indeed fortunate. The solution to the exercise is given in the website for the book: www. recreationprogramming.com! Please try to solve the exercise yourself before reading the solution.

REFERENCES

Howard, D. R., & Selin, S. W. (1987). A method for establishing consumer price tolerance levels for pubic recreation services. *Journal of Park and Recreation Administration, 5*(3), 48–64.

Kerr, G. N., & Manfredo, M. J. (1991). An attitudinal-based model of pricing for recreation services. *Journal of Leisure Research, 23,* 37–50.

Reiling, S. D., Criner, G. K., & Oltmanns, S. E. (1988). The influence of information on users' attitudes toward campground user fees. *Journal of Leisure Research, 20,* 208–217.

ADDITIONAL READINGS

Becker, R. H., Berrier, D., & Barker, G. D. (1985). Entrance fees and visitation levels. *Journal of Park and Recreation Administration, 3,* 28–32.

Crompton, J. L. (1981, March). How to find the price that's right. *Parks & Recreation,* 32–40.

Ellis, T., & Norton, R. L. (1988). *Commercial recreation.* St. Louis, MO: Times Mirror/Mosby College.

Manning, R., Calliman, E., Echelberger, H., Koenemann, E., & McEvan, D. (1984). Differential fees: Raising revenue, distributing demand. *Journal of Park and Recreation Administration, 2,* 2–38.

Stage D: Follow-Up Analysis

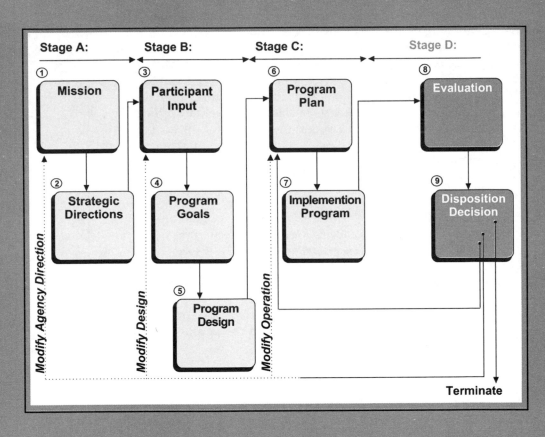

Follow-Up Analysis

In Part V, Follow-Up Analysis—Stage D, a program is evaluated and a decision is made about the disposition of the program. Programmers need to establish the worth of program services with systematically collected evaluation evidence. This evidence should be used to document program worth and to review program operations so that decisions can be made to manage program services properly.

This section includes three chapters. In Chapter Twenty, program evaluation techniques are explained, and a general plan for developing program evaluations is outlined. In Chapter Twenty-One, developing a comprehensive evaluation system is explained. How to make decisions about program services is discussed in Chapter Twenty-Two.

Model Boat Race
Photo courtesy of Long Beach Parks, Recreation, and Marine Department, Long Beach, CA

Program Evaluation Techniques

STEP 8 : EVALUATION

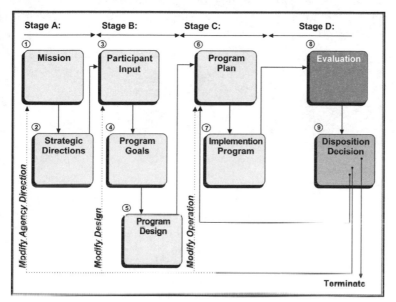

KEY TERMS

Evaluation
Evaluation
   Purposes
Steps of the
   Evaluation
   Planning
   Process
Research Design
Sample
Sampling
   Techniques
Evaluation Report
   Passages

Evaluation is an elastic concept that is used to describe many activities. Evaluating program services is the eighth step in the Program Development Cycle. It is the start of the follow-up analysis stage of the cycle and the antecedent to making a decision about the disposition of a program. With program evaluation data, the programmer makes a decision based on an analysis of evidence about the future of a program.

EVALUATION DEFINED

Suchman (1967) stated that "an evaluation is basically a judgment of worth—an appraisal of value" (p. 11). Suchman's central theme is that evaluation involves making judgments of worth. This definition of evaluation was further developed by Worthen and Sanders (1973), who state that "evaluation is the determination of the worth of a thing" (p.19). They also indicate that the determination of merit or worth is the touchstone of evaluation. This latter point is very important. Evaluation has not taken place until a judgment of worth or value has occurred. Evaluation is not simply collecting data; it also requires that a judgment of worth within the context of a value system be made with the data collected.

With program evaluation data, the programmer makes a decision based on an analysis of evidence about the future of a program.

Implementing Outcome-Based Programming

This chapter provides the necessary framework for evaluating the outcome component of outcome-based programming. In particular, Exhibit 20-1 outlines the critical steps to be addressed for an evaluation plan. The outcomes of outcome-based programming can best be documented with the use of a control group for comparative purposes. This chapter includes a diagram and description of the Classical Experimental Research Design, then explains how to use a control group.

The chapter also includes information about how first-line staff may conduct observations of leisure behavior. Becoming a good observer of behavior is a critical skill in documenting the outcomes provided by program services.

Finally, an outline of an evaluation report is provided. How the report is developed will play a key role in repositioning the agency in the minds of both stakeholders and community members.

Henderson (1995) describes evaluation in terms of "assessing where we are, where we want to be, and how we can reach our desired goals" (p. 5). Methods for addressing those questions are best represented in the form of a continuum, which ranges from casual, intuitive perceptions to more formal systematic approaches. The former does not require the use of systematic procedures or the presentation of objective evidence. The latter requires both and uses the scientific process to control the intrinsic subjectivity of everyday evaluation.

Many programmers evaluate their program services informally. An objective of this chapter is to help programmers move from informal to more formal evaluation procedures. The definition of evaluation to be used, then, is that *evaluation is judging the worth of program services, based on an analysis of systematically collected evidence.*

Evaluation is not simply collecting data...

PURPOSES OF EVALUATION

Evaluation is often imposed on programmers by a board, a third-party funding agency, or a higher-level administrator. As a result, evaluation is often viewed as an add-on responsibility imposed on the programmer or as a procedure undertaken with some trepidation, because it may result in an adverse view of the programmer's efforts. The viewpoint used in this book is that evaluation is part of the programmer's ongoing responsibility in operating and managing program services—it is not an add-on responsibility. Making judgments of worth about program services can serve the programmer and the organization in three ways: in program development, in organizational management, and in establishing accountability.

PROGRAM DEVELOPMENT

Evaluation data can be used in program development. With the data gathered in an evaluation, the programmer can help improve and refine programs by determining what works, what does not work, and why things work the way they do. Evaluation data can help analyze the value of the contribution of each part of a program, and thus facilitate program revision. Evaluation data can also boost staff morale. Although the results of an evaluation will sometimes indicate that a program is performing poorly, the majority of the services being operated are probably doing well and will receive a favorable evaluation. Staff morale is enhanced by favorable evaluation reports.

Evaluation, as it is currently conducted, will also result in new needs being discovered, even though this is not the purpose of evaluation. Needs identification is part of the needs assessment step of the Program Development Cycle. However, clients will often identify new needs on evaluation instruments, which leads to new program ideas.

ORGANIZATIONAL MANAGEMENT

Evaluation can help improve organizational management by using the information that evaluation generates. This information helps the programmer make informed decisions about how to modify programs, what services to drop, and which to continue. All of these alternatives can be made with systematically collected and analyzed evaluation data, rather than with individual perceptions or other less systematic methods.

Additionally, evaluation data will help the manager answer the ultimate evaluation question: Is this the best use of these resources in this organization at this time? The answer to this question is an important one for improving management of the organization and helping it move toward meeting its goals. It is an especially difficult question in a leisure service organization because leisure services often attract a committed core group of participants (Howard & Crompton, 1980). If one continues all programs that have a constituency, there will be few programs to cancel, even long after they cease to be useful to the organization. Leisure service organizations that have the benefit of annual increases can often ignore these issues and simply add new services with the additional resources received. In a recession situation, however, decisions to eliminate programs must be made. Evaluation data can provide the information and rationale necessary for determining which services to drop.

Another difficulty may occur if programs are continued each year without sufficient review and revision. When the organization's mission changes, these programs may no longer be included within the organization's current mission, even though they have a constituency. Evaluation data can provide the manager with the information and justification needed to terminate such programs.

Ultimately, the evaluation for each program operated must examine the question of whether the resources needed for the current program can be put to better use.

...the ultimate evaluation question: Is this the best use of these resources in this organization at this time?

ESTABLISHING ACCOUNTABILITY

Evaluation data can help the organization establish accountability by documenting program outputs. Documentation of benefits from pro-

Exercise 20-1: Comparing Purposes of Evaluation

In class, analyze and compare the three purposes of evaluation. Consider the following points:
- How do these three purposes differ?
- How are these three purposes similar?
- How do these three purposes complement each other in a comprehensive evaluation system?

gram services, discussed in Chapter Four, Outcome-Based Programming, is one example of evaluation data being used for accountability.

With these data, what is being accomplished in the agency's programs is documented with systematically collected evidence. This information can also provide evidence that the organization's goals are being met. The programmer can then effectively communicate these accomplishments to funding agencies and other publics, thereby justifying the expenditures necessary to continue services.

This evaluation provides evidence that the programmer is an effective manager and that the organization provides services important to a community.

The use of evaluation data in the management of the leisure service agency helps establish that the manager is involved in the ongoing review of program. It also helps the manager to take action to make certain that organizational goals are being accomplished. Evaluation, then, contributes significantly to the management of program services and the management of leisure service agencies. Now complete Exercise 20-1.

PLANNING AN EVALUATION

Evaluation is not a single activity or procedure. Most leisure service organizations will not have any one evaluation procedure that can meet all of the organization's evaluation needs. An agency will most likely have several procedures operating simultaneously to meet the diverse evaluation needs of the agency. Because of this diversity, programmers should understand how to plan an evaluation to address a specific evaluation problem and should know the issues inherent in implementing an evaluation. Grotelueschen, et al. (1974) provide an outline for planning an evaluation. A modified form of this outline, which is included in Exhibit 20-1, is used to organize the material that follows in this chapter. When an evaluation is planned, each of the steps outlined should be followed in the order presented.

Exhibit 20-1: Evaluation Planner

1. Purpose: Why evaluate?
2. Audience: Who is the evaluation for? What questions do they want answered? What will they do with the information?
3. Process: How will the evaluation be conducted?
4. Issues: What questions should the evaluation address?
5. Resources: What resources are needed to conduct the evaluation?
6. Evidence: What evidence should be collected?
7. Data-gathering: How is the evidence to be collected?
8. Analysis: How can the evidence be analyzed?
9. Reporting: How can evaluation findings be reported?

PURPOSE: WHY EVALUATE?

The first question to answer in planning an evaluation is to determine why the evaluation is being conducted. Three purposes for conducting an evaluation were outlined in the previous section. Although programmers may be able to address more than one of these purposes with a single evaluation, often they cannot do so. The point here is that in identifying a single purpose, the programmer is setting priorities that provide focus to the evaluation effort. Often, a single evaluation will serve only a single purpose. When the programmer attempts to serve several purposes, the focus necessary to actually answer the evaluation question, may never be achieved. The reason for specifying a purpose is to provide the necessary focus. In this way, the specific evaluation need identified as the reason for conducting the evaluation in the first place can actually be addressed. Rather than conducting one evaluation with broad, poorly focused purposes, programmers are best advised to conduct several well-focused evaluations specifically designed to fulfill a well-defined purpose.

The first step, then, is to determine whether the evaluation is being conducted to help in program development, organizational management, or organizational accountability. As precisely as possible, make a statement about the purpose for the evaluation. Following are three examples of such statements:

1. This evaluation is being conducted to determine participant-reported outcomes with program services.
2. This evaluation is being conducted to help make decisions about the disposition of program services.

3. This evaluation is being conducted to judge the worth of our agency's distribution of program services.

4. This evaluation is being conducted to document the benefits of participating in specific programs.

AUDIENCE: WHO IS THE EVALUATION FOR?

Evaluation data are not generated and used in a void. Patton (1997) has indicated that "people, not organizations use evaluation information" (p. 43). He further states that the two most important factors contributing to the use of evaluation information are political considerations and the "personal factor." Political considerations relate to members of the evaluation team. When assembling the evaluation team, the following criteria should be followed: (1) members must have an interest in the evaluation findings; (2) members should have the power to use evaluation findings for making decisions; (3) members should believe the evaluation is worthwhile; (4) members should be concerned with how the results are used; and (5) members should be willing to commit their time and energy to the evaluation.

The second most important factor, the personal factor, "is the presence of an identifiable individual or group of people who personally care about the evaluation and the findings it generates" (Patton, 1997, p. 44). Agency personnel use evaluation data to make a judgement of worth, and subsequently, to make decisions based on this judgement. Identifying who will actually use the evaluation data and what they will do with the information is an important step in planning an evaluation.

People use the results of evaluation, and unless it addresses their concerns, it will go unused.

House (1977) has suggested that evaluation is a persuasive argument, rather than a scientific proof, that must respond to a specific rather than a universal audience. As House says, "Thus the situation the evaluator faces is almost always an appeal to particular audiences that [he or she] can define with some precision. If [the evaluator] cannot define [his or her] audiences, the evaluation is indeterminate" (p. 9). When compared with the epistemological rules, methods, and justifications considered accepted practice in social science, the rules that evaluation audiences will accept are less well codified and not as universal. They are, in fact, situation specific. Part of any evaluation thus requires uncovering the rules of acceptance, which will establish the ultimate rationale for the asserted values of a program. To accomplish this, the programmer must define with some precision the evaluation audience who will actually use the information, and must determine what questions the evaluation audience believes are important and relevant to answer.

One's position in the scheme of a social program determines the types of information deemed relevant and therefore desired for evaluation (Weiss, 1973). For example, top administrators and boards generally are interested in a summary of broad issues and the impact of program services that will facilitate their decision to drop, modify, or continue a program. They are also interested in the data that establish accountability for the funds being used in providing services. Program directors and middle managers are most interested in strategies that are effective in achieving desired ends. Direct service personnel are usually most concerned with the effects of various face-to-face intervention techniques. Other possible users of information include external funding agencies, the public, clients, national associations, other providers of similar services, and so on. People's positions in an organization, then, determine to some degree the evaluation questions they will be interested in having answered. Although it is desirable to meet the evaluation needs of the entire organization with one evaluation, this often may not be possible.

Determining the evaluation audience, and consequently the evaluation data they desire, is the second step in planning an evaluation. Identifying a specific audience is a necessary part of any evaluation in order to focus information needs, guide the selection of an appropriate process for conducting the evaluation, identify salient values, and guide interpretation of objective data that will be gathered.

While planning a custom-designed evaluation, one must develop a priority of information needs and address as many needs as possible within the budget and other constraints. It will probably be impossible to meet all identified needs. Therefore, it is important to have first established those priorities that emerge from identifying the primary audience and the primary purpose for conducting the evaluation.

The answers to these first two questions about purpose and audience provide a framework for developing the remainder of the evaluation. Any process developed must fulfill the identified purpose of an evaluation and meet the information needs of a well-defined evaluation audience. Now complete Exercise 20-2.

PROCESS: HOW WILL THE EVALUATION BE CONDUCTED?

What specific techniques will be used to conduct the evaluation? Howe (1980) has identified six general techniques: professional judgment, measurement, discrepancy, decision-oriented, goal free, and transaction-observation. The technique one selects determines how the evaluation will be conducted. Each technique uses different methods and is best suited for a specific type of evaluation.

All techniques are either process models or preordinate models. Each type of model includes different preordained decisions and presents the evaluator with different choices and responsibilities.

Process models identify a procedure for conducting the evaluation but do not identify the criteria on which judgments of worth will be made. An example of a process model is the use of goals and objectives. Goal and objective technology explains very precisely a technique for writing goals and objectives, but the technology does not provide the original goals. Embodied in any set of goals and objectives is a point of view about what is important to accomplish and what may be ignored because it is less important. When using goals and objectives in evaluation, programmers must provide the original goals; in doing so, they provide a value structure for the evaluation. When choosing a process model, then, evaluators will need to provide the criteria on which judgments of worth will be made.

Preordinate models provide both the techniques for accomplishing the evaluation and the criteria on which judgments of worth will be made. An example of this type of evaluation process is the use of standards. An evaluation procedure that uses standards gives the programmer specific steps for collecting data and a set of criteria (the standards) on which the worth of program services will be judged. Programmers are often tempted to use preordinate models because the entire technique is explicated; therefore, the programmer has little to do except implement the pre-established technique. A caution programmers must exercise in using preordinate evaluation models is to make certain that the value system embodied in the preordinate model is consistent with the purpose of evaluation already identified, and that the data developed from the evaluation meet the information needs of the evaluation audience.

The evaluation planning steps that follow can be used in two ways. First, they can be used to analyze a preordinate model to make certain that the programmer understands how it deals with each of the planning steps. Second, they can be used as a planning agenda for determining how a process model or a custom-designed model will be implemented.

> *One must ensure that the value system embodied in a preordinate model is consistent with the purpose for evaluating.*

ISSUES: WHAT QUESTIONS SHOULD THE EVALUATION ADDRESS?

Determining the questions to be addressed in an evaluation is a critical step. In selecting the questions, the programmer must be concerned with validity and values. To be valid, the questions must be true indicators of the values asserted for the program. For example, programmers too often use attendance figures as an indicator of a program's worth. Attendance is a valid indicator of program impact; that is, how many and who were served. It is not a valid indicator of program quality, nor can it document program outputs; in other words, what actually happened to the individuals in the program.

Exhibit 20-2: Summary of Components of the Five P's of Evaluation

Participants
• Motivations/satisfaction
• Changes in attitudes as outcomes
• Changes in knowledge as outcomes
• Changes in skills and abilities as outcomes
• Carryover into other situations
• How individuals interact

    Program
    • Effective leadership
    • Promotion of program
    • If participants gained anything
    • Risk management

        Place
        • Safety concerns
        • Master planning
        • Adequate facilities

            Policies/Administration
            • Accountability of budget
            • Cost-benefit analysis
            • Cost-effectiveness analysis
            • Equitable provision of services

                Personnel
                • Performance appraisal
                • Assess training needs
                • Provide feedback for
                  improvement

From: Henderson, K. A. & Bialeschki, D. (1995). Evaluating leisure services: Making enlightened decisions (p. 31). State College, PA: Venture Publishing, Inc. Reprinted with permission.

Henderson and Bialeschki (1995), in the "Five Ps of Evaluation" (Exhibit 20-2), outline areas from which evaluation questions can be created. It is important to note that it is not advisable to evaluate everything at the same time; rather, programmers should select those areas that relate best to the program(s) at hand. A single evaluation may focus on one or more of the Five Ps of Evaluation. For example, a learn-to-swim program may contain questions about participants in terms of skill attainment and carryover into other areas (i.e., swimming in a lake or river). The same evaluation may contain questions about the program regarding how risk was managed in the aquatic environment and the effectiveness of the swimming instructors. Similarly, other items may address place, policies and administration, or personnel.

RESOURCES: WHAT RESOURCES ARE AVAILABLE FOR EVALUATION?

Every program manager must understand that evaluation costs money. At the very least, it will cost the staff time that could have been spent in other activities. Other expenses are also associated with evaluation: expenses for printing evaluation forms, collecting and analyzing data, and preparing and distributing the evaluation report.

One resource that may currently exist in the agency is data that are already routinely collected. At least part of the evaluation data needed may be obtained by reanalyzing or reinterpreting data that have already been collected by the organization. Evaluation does not always require new data to be collected. Other evaluation resources the agency may have access to are colleagues, universities, cooperative extension agencies, and consultants. All of these are potential resources for helping the agency conduct evaluations.

Once the decision to evaluate is made, the questions and issues to examine can quickly grow to a very large and unmanageable number. Each piece of information obtained adds incrementally to the cost of the evaluation. Because of this, it is important to provide focus to the evaluation with the procedures outlined in this section in order to avoid the expense of answering unimportant, irrelevant, or less important questions. It is also important to do some cost-benefit analysis of the answers to be obtained. To determine the potential benefit of possible questions, consider the following:

- If this question is answered, what could be done with the information?
- Is there some management implication in obtaining an answer to this question?
- Is this information worth the cost of obtaining it?

Although there are many questions it would be nice to have answered, program evaluation should remain focused on only those questions that enable the manager to improve program development and program management or those used to establish accountability in a meaningful way.

EVIDENCE: WHAT EVIDENCE SHOULD BE COLLECTED?

Evidence is any information that may be used in making judgments of worth about the issues raised in the evaluation. The evaluation effort is usually focused on the issues identified earlier in this process. Once these issues are identified, the search for evidence begins.

Evaluation does not always require new data to be collected.

...make certain that the evidence collected presents a balanced and comprehensive view of the program and its impact.

Exhibit 20-3: One-Shot Case Study Research Design

X	O

Exhibit 20-4: Pre-test–Post-test Research Design

O	X	O

Many types of evidence may be gathered, such as descriptions of personnel, participants, operational procedures, and processes; goals and objectives; costs; and program outcomes. Participant judgments about various components of a program may also be collected on open-ended or scaled questionnaires. What type of evidence is most appropriate will depend on the issues being investigated and the specific requirements of the evaluation audience.

A major consideration in this step of planning an evaluation is to determine the sources and quality of the evidence. Although much evidence may be collected, the evaluator should be sure to collect the most relevant and valid evidence.

A concern in gathering evidence is to make certain that the evidence collected presents a balanced and comprehensive view of the program and its impact. There is a tendency to give undue attention to forcefully or articulately presented, positive or negative, extreme views about a program. The evaluator should make certain that the final evaluation report is balanced and represents the typical or average view of the program. There is also a tendency to focus evaluation data on specific components of a program that may be positive or negative, rather than on judging the worth of the overall program and its components.

Establishing cause and effect is one of the most difficult social science problems.

The programmer should be concerned about the validity and reliability of the evidence collected. Evidence should be logically accepted as a measure or indicator of the issues being addressed in the evaluation. The validity of the evidence in evaluation studies is often not well thought out. Validity basically asks the question, "Is the evidence being collected a true indicator of the issue being addressed?" For example, if one issue of the evaluation of a swimming program is to document participant achievement, then a piece of evidence would be some measure of the participants' swimming skills.

Reliability of the evidence must also be assured. To be reliable, the evidence must be accurate and consistent. Reliable instruments allow one to obtain consistent results each time the instrument is used. For

Exhibit 20-5: Classical Experimental Research Design

R	O	X	O
R	O		O

Exhibit 20-6: Modified Classical Experimental Research Design

R	O	X	O		
R	O		O	X	O

example, a rubber yardstick would not yield consistent measurement of distance and would therefore be unreliable because it would not allow for consistent results.

At some point, the programmer will try to demonstrate that participation in a program led to certain outcomes. Establishing cause and effect is one of the most difficult social science problems. It requires that three propositions be dealt with simultaneously: time-order, co-variation, and control of rival causal factors (Denzin, 1979). To establish cause and effect, one must establish that the cause came before the effect; that is, in a time-order. In evaluating program services, this is usually accomplished because the program occurs before the observation or measurement of effect. Covariation between the presumed cause and effect must also be established: For every change in the cause, there should be a corresponding change in the effect. If the presumed cause leads to little or no change in the effect, one cannot assert a cause-and-effect relationship. The final proposition is that of controlling for rival causal factors. One must be able to demonstrate that participation in the program—not some other possible explanation—is what led to the observed change in the effect.

These three propositions are best controlled through the use of a good research design. Although this book is not intended to be a research text, some elementary knowledge of research design can enable the evaluator to develop better evaluations. A frequently used research design is schematically represented in Exhibit 20-3 on page 373. The X represents the treatment or program, and the letter O represents the observation or measurement. This research design is known as a one-shot case study (Campbell & Stanley, 1963). With this design, a program occurs, and then measurement occurs after the program. This is the typical scenario in many leisure service agencies in which program evaluations are completed at the end of a program.

Although this design does control for time-order—the treatment occurs before measurement of the presumed effect—it does not control for covariation or rival causal factors. Because there is no measurement before the program, there is no baseline data with which to compare the post-program measurement. It is therefore difficult to demonstrate that participation led to the observations obtained in the post-program measurements. In addition, without a pre-program test, it is difficult to assert that participation led to the obtained post-program measurements, because one does not know if participation led to the changes, or if some other rival causal factor led to the observed change. For example, the post-program scores could have been a result of participants' previously obtained skills and have nothing to do with their participation in the current program.

Some of the problems with a one-shot case study design can be addressed with a one-group pretest–post-test design (Campbell & Stanley, 1963), diagrammed in Exhibit 20-4 on page 373. In this design, a pre-test is introduced, and the programmer now has some baseline data with which to compare post-program results. This design enables programmers to better demonstrate the effect of the program because they can now document the change using measurements taken before and after participation. In this case, covariation is easier to demonstrate. The problem of possible rival causal factors accounting for the change rather than the program itself still remains, however.

Many of the problems associated with the previous research designs can be dealt with in the classical pre-test–post-test control group design (Campbell & Stanley, 1963), illustrated in Exhibit 20-5. This design features the addition of a control group (the group not receiving the treatment) to the previous design. It also features randomized assignment (R) of subjects either to the experimental group (the group receiving the treatment or participating in the program) or to the control group. If randomized assignment is not possible, one attempts to identify a matched control group in which control group subjects are matched as closely as possible with program participants on all variables that are considered relevant.

With this design, it is possible to control for time-order, to demonstrate covariation between the experimental treatment and the assumed result, and to document the possible effects of rival causal factors. For example, if the control group shows changes in the pretest and post-test scores similar to the experimental group, one would begin to question whether the experimental treatment (the program) was having any effect.

One problem with this design is that treatment or participation in a program is withheld from the control group. This is obviously a difficult set of circumstances to deal with in leisure service agencies. Participants register for programs to receive services, not to have them withheld! One can deal with this problem in the following manner. First, the research design diagrammed in Exhibit 20-6 can be used instead of the design diagrammed in Exhibit 20-5. The design in Exhibit 20-6 includes all of the features of the design in Exhibit 20-5, but treatment for the control group is added after the experiment. In this way, all who initially registered eventually receive the program. To administer such a scheme would require informing participants at the time of registration that they were participating in an experiment and that they would be randomly assigned to different groups who will receive the program at different times.

Programmers often get the impression that pretest–post-test social science studies must be conducted on each program operated in order to evaluate services. This is not the case. The effects of a program service should be documented initially, but once it is established that a specific program service leads to predictable outcomes, it is unnecessary to document these outcomes each time. After cause and effect have been established, one may return to using the first design outlined (Exhibit 20-3 on page 373) and simply document that participants have had the predicted outcomes. In this way, program outcomes are continuously monitored and documented.

A final concern regarding the collection of evidence is that of establishing the credibility of the programmer as an evaluator. When people evaluate programs they are responsible for developing, there are inherent conflicts of interest. The credibility of the programmer as an evaluator will be compromised if there is no ongoing critical review and analysis of program services. If only glowing successes are reported in evaluation reports, the programmer's credibility as an evaluator will be questioned.

Data-gathering practices currently used in agencies are not unacceptable, but the techniques can be improved.

DATA-GATHERING: HOW IS EVIDENCE TO BE COLLECTED?

In this section, we will discuss how the evidence may be obtained, how to actually collect data, when to collect data, how much to obtain, and from whom.

Techniques for Data Collection

There are many ways of collecting data for evaluation studies. Techniques that could be used include questionnaires, interviews, conversations, observation schedules, participant observation, anecdotal data, standardized tests, checklists, and rating scales. Programmers most frequently collect data by using questionnaires they have designed, talking to participants to obtain feedback about program services, and conducting on-site observation of programs. These three strategies produce a good assortment of data to use in judging program worth.

However, typical data collection practices have several flaws. First, the questionnaires are usually not instruments validated for data collection. The validity and reliability of the instrument is usually not established in any meaningful way. Second, discussions with participants and observations of ongoing programs are usually not guided by an interview or observation schedule. Often, a program supervisor in an agency conducts different interviews and looks for different items when observing programs in operation. Evaluation practices in agencies could be greatly improved by using validated instruments and by increasing the reliability of, the interview and observation methods.

Instrument validation is a technical matter beyond the scope of this book. However, validity begins with making a conceptual link between the issues being investigated and the questions asked on an instrument. When developing instruments, one should constantly review the rationale for including each question and determine how it logically links to and is a measure of the issues being examined.

Interviewing and Observations

Interviewing and observations are less formal methods of gathering data. Most programmers handle on-site visitations to programs as public relations exercises, in which they deal with any observed problems or emergencies and chat with participants, listening to any comments—good or bad—that the participant cares to make about the program. Often, each programmer in an agency tends to look for different items to judge how well the program is actually going. To be useful for evaluation, observations and interviews need to be handled more systematically.

When observing, the programmer may function in any one of the following modes: as a passive, covert observer; as an active, participant-observer; or as an overt, full participant (Howe, 1993). Each of these modes provides a variety of depths of involvement and access to the actual experiences of participants. In any case, the primary techniques are careful observation of peoples' activities and recording them; that is, taking field notes.

Interviews with individuals during these visits are not simply times to chat with participants. They should be considered guided conversations (Howe 1993) that are driven by a structured or unstructured interview schedule and use a conversational demeanor that establishes a rapport to elicit the information needed. Both of these naturalistic evaluation methods can be made more systematic and reliable by using the following techniques:

- Identify specific observation tasks or interview items.

All programmers involved in interviewing or observing programs should jointly develop the necessary interview forms and observation schedules. The result of this will be the development of comprehensive schedules that incorporate the collective wisdom of all program supervisors. Furthermore, everyone who conducts an interview or observation will be examining the same items. This increases the reliability of the process. Variations will no longer be the result of who conducted the interview or made the observation.

- Have detailed instructions about how to make observations.

Uniformity of practice in conducting an interview or observation also contributes to reliability. With good instructions, it should not matter who actually conducts the interview or makes the observation—the results should be similar.

- Train and prepare staff for making observations and conducting interviews.

Understanding random sampling is not complicated...

20

Have staff members make independent observations of the same event, using a jointly developed schedule, and then discuss and compare how and why they scored the event the way they did. The objective is to get consistency of results and inter-rater reliability.

- Require immediate and detailed reports.

Recording observations immediately is necessary in order to have accurate reports. Recalled observations are often less accurate than those recorded immediately.

- Validate the observations.

Information obtained through interviews or observations should always be validated. This is accomplished by seeking out additional verification of the information from other independent sources. Interviewers should try to discover if other participants hold the same view or should try to find additional observations. In either case, determine whether or not the reported or observed characteristic is typical of the program or is a single occurrence.

Data-gathering practices currently used in agencies are not unacceptable, but they should be improved. Improving them will result in more reliable and valid data on which to make judgments of worth.

Selecting a Sample

...samples selected through random selection procedures have the highest probability of being representative of the population from which they are drawn.

Gathering data almost always involves selecting a sample. There is an erroneous belief among program practitioners that selecting a sample means handing out questionnaires to whomever can be easily reached or whomever wants to complete them. Practitioners have little understanding of how to implement a random sampling procedure and even less confidence that doing so is necessary in the first place. Random sampling improves data in a number of ways. One of the most important is that it is the surest way to obtain a sample that is representative of the participant group you wish to characterize.

Given the question, "How can one characterize the views of a whole population by simply getting information from a few members of the population," the answer is random sampling. Understanding random sampling is not complicated, and once the rationale for drawing a random sample is understood, programmers will accept no substitute!

Population is a technical term for a cohort of individuals who are defined with some precision. For example, the members of a programming class could be defined as a population. In this case, because the class probably includes 20 to 30 individuals, one would probably not draw a sample, but would conduct a census to obtain data from the entire population. A population could also be defined as all freshmen at a university, all undergraduates at a university, or everyone registered at a university. As the population increases in size, conducting a census becomes increasingly difficult and expensive.

The sampling problem then becomes one of trying to find out the information that would have been obtained in a census, but by gathering data from a sample instead of from the entire population. When a sample is collected, one can never be sure of obtaining the true value that would have been obtained through a census. Actually, one obtains an estimate of what the population value might be. There are many ways of determining who might be included in a sample from the entire population.

A sample could include only those whose names begin with A. It could include only those whose social security number begins with an odd number. It could include the first 500 participants to come to a swimming pool on a Sunday. One can always devise a method for obtaining a sufficient number of individuals to make up a sample. The question is, "Are they representative of the entire population?"

Using random selection procedures increases the probability that the sample selected will be representative of the population from which it is drawn. This occurs because random selection is not a helter-skelter method, as is popularly believed. It is a precise method of selection in which every individual in the defined population has an equal and independent chance of being selected for the sample. Because of this, samples selected through random selection procedures have the highest probability of being representative of the population from which they are drawn. Three methods for drawing a random sample will be discussed: simple random sampling, systematic sampling with a random start, and matrix sampling.

Simple Random Sampling

Drawing a simple random sample involves several steps. First, it is necessary to have a consecutively numbered sample frame (a list) of the entire population. In leisure program evaluation studies, this is frequently possible because the programmer is often gathering data from individuals who have registered for a program. A list of registered participants can be used as the sample frame.

The second step is to determine how large a sample to draw. There is no simple answer to this question. However, as the size of the population decreases, the proportion of individuals to be included in the sample must increase. For example, to make certain there is good representation of a group of 15 individuals, it would be necessary to sample approximately 50 percent of the population of 15. Yet polling organizations will often use a sample of 2,000 to represent the entire population of the United States. A general rule of thumb is that for populations under 500, a sample of 50 percent of the population should be drawn; from 500 to 1,500, approximately 30 percent; from 1,500 to 2,500, 25 percent; and over 2,500, 400 individuals should be sufficient. The reader is cautioned that these figures are very gross recommendations, and that developing a sampling plan is a technical matter that depends on a number of factors. The help of a qualified statistician should be sought for recommendations on a specific data collection problem.

The third step is to randomly select individuals from the sample frame to be included in the sample. This is done by first identifying the range of digits needed in sample numbers. For example, a sample of 50 from a population of 100 would need 50 three digit numbers from 001 to

100. Fifty randomly selected numbers from these 100 would identify the individuals to be included in the sample. To sample from a population of 1,000, one would need four-digit numbers ranging from 0001 to 1,000, and so on for any size population.

A table of random digits is used to randomly select the sample (a table of random digits can be found in any statistics book). Determine in advance the direction in which to move through the table after selecting the first number, close your eyes, point to a number in the table, and then open your eyes. This is the first number, but it may not be usable if it does not include a number within the desired range. For example, if the first three-digit number selected was 301, it could not be used to select a sample of 50 from a population of 100. One must then systematically move through the table of random digits until the desired number of usable numbers is identified. Any duplicate numbers are simply ignored.

With this procedure, each person in the population has an equal and independent chance of being included in the sample. If one assumes that all information desired is distributed throughout the entire population, then a random sample is the best method of assuring that the data will also be randomly distributed throughout the sample.

This method works fine for small samples, but it becomes cumbersome with samples larger than 100. There are computer programs that can do this procedure. However, many times the sampling technique presented below is used instead.

Systematic Sampling with a Random Start

Systematic sampling with a random start is used to select a sample from a sample frame with many individuals. With this procedure, one actually selects only one random number and then every Kth individual from the sample frame. The Kth individual is determined by the sample interval, which is identified before the sampling procedure begins.

This method is useful in many situations encountered in evaluating recreation programs. For example, how might a sample be selected from a softball league with 1,200 participants? The league consists of 100 teams with 12 individuals on each team roster.

The first step is to determine the size of the sample to be drawn. With a population of 1,200, the sample should be at least 30 percent of the population, or 360 individuals (.30 x 1,200 = 360). The next step is to determine the sample interval, or the number between each player selected for inclusion in the sample. To determine the sample interval, divide the population by the desired sample size, thus 1,200 ÷ 360 = 3.33. This means that every 3.33rd individual would be selected. Because this is not possible, go to the nearest whole number, which in this case is every third individual. Generally, one would select the interval that would yield the larger sample, since one would not want a sample smaller than was originally determined.

The next step is to consecutively number individuals on team rosters. For example, each of the 100 team rosters would probably be numbered from 1 through 12. If all of the rosters were arranged in order, the individuals could be numbered from 0001 through 1,200. Arranging the

Exhibit 20-7: Sampling Matrix for Park Area

NUMBERING HOURS OPEN TO DEVELOP A SAMPLING PROGRAM
Days of the Week

Time	M	T	W	TH	F	SA	SU
6:00	1	2	3	4	5	6	7
7:00	8	9	10	11	12	13	14
8:00	15	16	17	18	19	20	21
9:00	22	23	24	25	26	27	28
10:00	29	30	31	32	33	34	35
11:00	36	37	38	39	40	41	42
12:00	43	44	45	46	47	48	49
1:00	50	51	52	53	54	55	56
2:00	57	58	59	60	61	62	63
3:00	64	65	66	67	68	69	70
4:00	71	72	73	74	75	76	77
5:00	78	79	80	81	82	83	84
6:00	85	86	87	88	89	90	91
7:00	92	93	94	95	96	97	98
8:00	99	100	101	102	103	104	105
9:00	106	107	108	109	110	111	112

rosters in this manner and consecutively numbering the team members develops a sample frame.

Then, a table of random digits should be used to select the first number to be included in the sample in the same manner as described for collecting a simple random sample. Once the first number is identified, then every Kth individual is selected for inclusion in the sample. In this case, every third number from the first number is selected. If the first usable number identified from a table of random digits is 1,195, then this individual is included in the sample. One then proceeds and includes every third individual away from this individual, including the 1,198, 0001, 0004, 0007, 0010, and so on until the entire sample is selected.

Although this technique technically violates the assumption of a random sample—that every individual has an equal and independent chance of selection—it is frequently used. With this technique, there is actually only one randomly selected individual. This technique is used because it is an expedient method for selecting a sample. However, because of inherent problems with the method, one must be cautious. It is especially important to understand how the lists being used to draw the sample are arranged. For example, if the first person on the roster is the team captain, and the first number randomly selected and the interval being used cause the first person on the roster to be continuously selected, it may be advisable to select a new starting point. If it does not matter that team captains are heavily represented in the sample, then the problem can be ignored. The point is that this method can create problems, and the programmer must be on guard against biasing results with the sampling method.

...some individuals are better situated than are others to know what actually happened in a program.

This technique is also useful for creating a sample from a population of unknown individuals. To do this, there must be a system for numbering individuals. For example, this method could be used to randomly draw a sample from all who were going to attend a garden show. The first step would be to estimate the total number of individuals who might attend the show, let us assume approximately 5,000. In this case, it would be necessary to draw a sample of 400 from the estimated 5,000 attendees. Assuming that entry to the garden show would involve purchasing a ticket at a controlled access point, one could consecutively number every individual who purchased a ticket, or sell consecutively numbered tickets in the first place. These tickets, numbered from 0001 through 5,000, are the sample frame.

Next, determine a sample interval: $5,000 \div 400 = 12.5$. Thus every 12th ticket purchaser will be sampled. One then proceeds as described above to identify the numbers of individuals who will be interviewed by randomly selecting the first individual and then identifying all remaining individuals by successively taking every Kth individual (in this case, every 12th individual). This technique can be applied in many situations that recreation programmers face and will result in data superior to other less systematic methods.

Matrix Sampling

Matrix sampling is also useful in many situations, especially for sampling from populations who use drop-in facilities with no controlled access point or ticket sales. For example, how does one randomly sample users of a park that is open from 6:00 a.m. to 10:00 p.m. daily? To do so, a sample frame must be established by creating a matrix of time blocks x days of the week and consecutively numbering the time blocks. Exhibit 20-7 on page 381 illustrates such a matrix. In this matrix, there are 112 possible times (16 hours x 7 days = 112) to collect data in this facility. One then decides what percentage of the total time blocks will be sampled. At this point, time slots during which individuals will be contacted are being discussed. Because people are the actual units of analysis, the numbers cited above can be used only as a rough guide for determining the sample size. Unless there are accurate data about when and how many people use the area, it will be necessary to sample rather heavily initially to make certain the sample obtained is truly representative of the typical users of the area.

In this case, it would be reasonable to begin with a sample of 40 percent of the time slots. This would result in 45 of the 112 possible time slots being selected for sampling (112 x .40 = 44.8). Once this is determined, it is a matter of using the method outlined in the section on a simple random sample to randomly select 45 time slots from the population of 001 to 112 time slots for inclusion in the sample.

Implementing randomized sampling methods will greatly improve the quality of data collected in program evaluations. Random sampling is the best method for assuring that the sample is representative of the whole population. Now complete Exercise 20-3.

Data Sources

When sources of data are being identified, information should be obtained from people who are in a position to have the information you desire. Many may have an opinion about the quality of a program, and it is important to obtain a variety of viewpoints. However, some individuals are better situated than others to know what actually happened in a program. For example, the program participants, the program leader, and the program supervisor who made occasional visits while the program was in operation, are all in a position to have firsthand information about what actually occurred. The evaluator should therefore identify the sources from whom the most knowledge may be obtained and make certain that evidence is systematically collected from these sources. Additional information collected from other sources can then be used to provide further insight and to validate the data obtained from the primary information sources.

...if the evaluation instrument cannot be completed in fewer than ten minutes, it is probably too long and needs to be further revised and focused.

Other Considerations in Data Collection

A final consideration in data collection is to decide when the data will be collected and how intrusive the collections will be. Programmers could collect pretest data at the time of registration, through a mail-out before the start of a program, at the beginning of a program, or at some other time. They can collect post-program data at the final program session, or through a mail-out shortly after a program has ended.

There are many possibilities for timing data collection. Different results will probably be obtained, depending on when the data are collected. Standard practice is to obtain pre-program data at the time of registration and post-program data at the final program session. There is some question about this technique, because those individuals who have dropped out of the program are not included in its evaluation. They may have some valuable insights into the program, however. A mail-out to all who originally registered for the program is a costly but more inclusive procedure.

Programmers must also be concerned with how intrusive the evaluation procedure will be. Participants register for programs to participate in them, not to complete evaluation forms. This is another reason that the evaluation instrument must be well focused in the first place. Participants may not be willing to answer all of the questions the programmer can develop. A general guideline here is that if the instrument cannot be completed in fewer than ten minutes, it is probably too long and needs to be further revised and focused. There is also an ethical problem: If programmers believe an individual's leisure is important, they will not want to intrude unnecessarily.

> *Analysis—placing data into a meaningful pattern that gives insight into the worth of a program.*

ANALYSIS: HOW CAN THE EVIDENCE BE ANALYZED?

After the data are collected, they must be analyzed to determine what they indicate about the program. In this step, the data are placed into a meaningful pattern that gives insight into the worth of the program being evaluated. There are many ways to conduct an analysis. The method chosen should provide insight into the concerns of the evaluation audience and should be appropriate for the type of evidence collected. In addition, the audience should be able to understand the analytical technique. For example, it is not useful to use statistical regression if the evaluation audience has no understanding of this statistical technique.

Because the data to be analyzed will be either quantitative or qualitative, the analysis should be appropriate for the type of evidence gathered. Statistical analysis is one method of placing quantitative data into a meaningful pattern. It should include reporting the distribution of scores (score tallies or percentages of responses in each category), measures of central tendency (mean, mode, and median), measures of dispersion (variance and standard deviation), and measures of association (correlations). Evaluation data analysis is seldom conducted to make predictions about future programs, but is focused instead on reporting current program outcomes and on interpreting the meaning of the documented outcomes.

Quantitative data analysis is useful in analyzing evaluation data, but much of evaluation data is qualitative, naturalistic evidence that must be pieced together into a coherent whole with rhetorical comment. When writing up this material, the programmer should remember that its primary purpose is to share the participant's leisure experience with the evaluation audience (Howe, 1993). The meaningfulness of qualitative data can often be made apparent by comparing evaluation results with some other known entity. Following are a number of possible comparisons that could make the data more meaningful:

- Time series data: Compare program results over time.
- Discrepancy comparisons: Compare intended versus actual program inputs, processes, products, outputs, and outcomes.
- Need reduction: Compare results obtained with the amount of need in the community. How much need was met (reduced) with the operation of this program?
- Standards: Compare program results with established standards, legal mandates, or administrative directives.
- Inter- or intra-agency comparisons: Compare program results with other programs in an agency, or compare the program with similar programs in other agencies.

Techniques that can be used in making these comparisons include critical review, journalistic accounts, historical review, and content analysis. In all data analysis, the primary objective is to develop information for the evaluation audience that provides meaningful insight about the results and impact of a program so the worth of the program is made apparent.

REPORTING: HOW CAN EVALUATION FINDINGS BE REPORTED?

Communicating the results of an evaluation can take many forms. During the early, formative stages of a program, oral reports and short written reports can be used effectively. Other reporting formats that have been used to give the evaluation audience insights into the program are testimony from participants, movies, still photographs, videotapes, slide shows, and actual participation in the program by the evaluation audience. All of these formats can be used effectively in various situations.

Even though there are many possible reporting formats, the use of a written, summative report with the familiar spiral binding seems to be the most common. This practice is likely to continue because of its universal understandability, its documentary value, and its ease of access. In preparing such a report, the practitioner is faced with many decisions about what to include and how to organize it. Following is a guide for organizing an evaluation report, along with an outline of the recommended content of sections that could be included in the body of such a report.

ORGANIZING THE EVALUATION REPORT

The typical evaluation report should contain the following sections and be organized in the sequence outlined below:

1. Title page
2. Author or authors and their affiliations
3. Evaluation audience—who is to receive the report
4. Executive summary—a one-page summary of the procedures and results
5. Table of contents
6. Lists of tables, figures, and photographs
7. Body of the report
8. Appendices: all items not likely to be available elsewhere, such as survey instruments, data tables, letters of testimony, and newspaper articles
9. References

CONTENTS FOR THE BODY OF THE REPORT

Item number seven, the body of the evaluation report, can contain many different sections. It is not recommended that all sections described in the following paragraphs be included in every report. What will be included should be determined by the purpose of the evaluation, the audience who will receive the report, and the specific process used in the evaluation.

Purpose of the Evaluation

Why the evaluation was conducted should be specified in all reports in order to conceptually outline the framework for the evaluation. Purposes can include program improvement, documenting accountability, improving planning, aiding policy analysis, assessing program impact, aiding managerial monitoring, and justifying continued funding.

Evaluation Questions

This section is the next logical extension of the "purpose" section. Here, the reader of the report should be told the major questions asked in the evaluation study and the criteria used to make evaluative judgments of worth. Content in this section should establish the content validity of the evaluation questions. How the questions relate to the purpose of the evaluation should be made apparent.

Description of the Program

The history of the program (if it has one) and the setting, including the location, the persons using the service, and the activities of the program, should be outlined. The person writing the report should attempt to portray to the evaluation audience the five Ws and the H of a journalistic story: the who, what, when, where, why, and how of the program.

It is the responsibility of the evaluator to present the evaluation audience with a report that is comprehensible to them.

Evaluator's Background

This section should be used to establish the credibility of the program's evaluator. Information presented should include the evaluator's affiliation, academic and professional background, a bibliography of other evaluation work or academic work, and an exploration of the evaluator's values and biases. Who the evaluator is and how he or she views the evaluation process should be exposed.

Summary of Regulations

A summary—and possibly an interpretation—of federal, state, local, professional, or administrative regulations and directives affecting or mandating the evaluation of the program should be included. Many evaluations undertaken today are mandated because of participation in some externally funded program. A brief explanation of such an arrangement would be in order.

Data-Gathering and Analytical Methods

Regardless of the data-gathering technique used, an accurate and complete description of how the data were collected should be included. Procedures for analyzing the data should also be reported. If social science techniques have been used, the conventions normally applicable for reporting them should be observed. However, depending on who the evaluation audience is, some additional interpretation beyond what is normally required in the academic press may be in order. It is the responsibility of the evaluator to present the evaluation audience with a report that is comprehensible to them.

Findings

Reporting the summarized data and interpreting their meaning should be completed in this section. Helping the evaluation audience understand the findings should be paramount in reporting them. It is very important that findings be conceptually integrated into the report. Organizing them around some of the key evaluation issues or questions identified earlier in the report is one very useful method. Others that have been used include organizing results along geographic areas, age groups, or program areas. Again, the only principle to follow is to use the method that leads to the clearest understanding of the findings.

Use of the Report

One problem interfering with the use of evaluations has been the lack of action based on evaluation reports. Evaluators can attempt to remedy this situation by making suggestions to the evaluation audience about how the results and the report can be used. Some possible uses would include the following: (1) to use the report as a beginning and collect the same evaluation information over time so that time-series data can be developed; (2) to release the whole report or sections of it to the press for a public relations program; and (3) to use the report as a catalyst for public action on an item of public concern that may have come out of the report. Evaluation takes scarce resources from agencies. The more potential payoffs there are from these expended resources, the more likely an agency is to engage in evaluation.

Contract

Any evaluation done by a consultant from outside an agency should be conducted with an appropriate contract. A copy of this document and a brief review of how the contract has been fulfilled through the final report is usually included in the final report.

Conclusions

This is the section in which value judgment questions are answered. What was the worth of the program? Evaluation has not occurred until these judgments are made—one has only gathered and reported data up to this point. No matter how scientific the data-gathering phase may have been, evaluation does not occur until the information is integrated with a value system and a judgment made about the program's worth.

In developing this section, stick to the original purpose of the evaluation and the data that have been generated. However, the unintended outcomes sometimes have more impact than the intended ones. Do not hesitate to cite additional findings beyond those mandated by some type of preordinate evaluation design. The report is strengthened if additional audiences that concur with the conclusions can be cited. Letters from participant observers and comments from the staff, the press, and other parties of interest should be used.

Minority Reports

Evaluation is not value free. Although one may start with objective data, during the process of evaluation those data are interpreted and a final judgment of worth made with subjective values. Often a significant divergence of opinion can evolve from such studies—issues can be simultaneously good and bad from different perspectives. These differing views may come from a minority of the evaluation team, the program participants, project staff, special interest groups, and so forth. Significant dissent should be accommodated in the final report.

Any evaluation study should include the evaluation purpose, questions, methodology, results, findings, and the rationale and logic of the conclusions. As does the scientist, the evaluator exposes the findings, as well as the logic used to reach conclusions, so the results may be challenged with alternate interpretations. Programs supported with public money in a free society should be open to this kind of scrutiny.

Credibility is built by sharing evaluation results of all types, including successes, modifications, and cancellations.

Recommendations

What kind of future action should be taken with the program? Usually only three alternatives exist: continue the program as is, continue the program with modifications (at either a higher or lower level than at present), or drop the program. During the investigation, if evaluators discover modifications they believe will strengthen a program, these should be identified in the report. Whether or not to recommend termination or continuation of a program will vary with each situation, and the evaluator will have to make the best decision possible, depending on prevailing circumstances. Either course of action should be accompanied by a rationale anchored in the purpose and findings of the evaluation.

Additional Considerations

20

By selecting appropriate sections from the above list, an evaluator should be able to assemble a logical and thorough report. Other points that may help in preparing evaluation reports include the following:

1. Know when decisions are to be made, and submit all reports on a timely basis.
2. Issue formal and informal reports as work progresses.
3. Make informal reporting sessions a time for problem solving.
4. Make the report descriptive so that those unfamiliar with the program can gain insights into its activities.
5. Prepare different reports for different evaluation audiences. Of course, different conclusions cannot be reported, but explanations of details may be different for different audiences.
6. Expand on your work by examining collected data to see if they could be reanalyzed and reinterpreted to answer other evaluation questions.

The evaluator, either in-house or out-of-house, must accept the responsibility for presenting the evaluation audience with a final report that is understandable in their terms and frame of reference. The foregoing discussion will give evaluation report writers a coherent framework that can be used in organizing an evaluation report.

The preceding outline for planning an evaluation is a useful guide for developing it. It is also useful for analyzing the suitability of an existing evaluation model for a specific evaluation project. There are many things to consider in planning an evaluation. The preceding discussion will help the programmer organize and focus the evaluation effort.

COMMUNICATING EVALUATION RESULTS

Reporting evaluation results and the managerial actions that are taken as a result of evaluation findings builds credibility with external publics. Through evaluation reports, the programmer will provide evidence of the benefits that resulted from participating in programs and provide evidence that the programming staff is engaged in ongoing managerial review and action while operating program services. As a programmer, ultimately you are demonstrating that you are a good steward of the resources entrusted to you.

Credibility is built by sharing evaluation results of all types, including successes, modifications, and cancellations. You should highlight

Exercise 20-4: Communicating Evaluation Results

Below are listed the three purposes of evaluation. Identify at least one evaluation report you would like to develop and send during the next three months for each purpose listed. Practice writing a paragraph or two of an evaluation report. Remember: WHO SAYS WHAT TO WHOM WITH WHAT EFFECT?

Program Development:
    To whom?
    What program?
    Target date?
    Questions to be answered?

Organizational Management:
    To whom?
    What program?
    Target date?
    Questions to be answered?

Accountability:
    To whom?
    What program?
    Target date?
    Questions to be answered?

---

evaluations of particularly noteworthy activities, modifications, and failures. In successful activities, stress documented program outcomes that are consistent with the benefits specified or the mission priorities. In programs that will be modified or cancelled, stress what managerial actions are being taken to improve or replace services.

Following are sample evaluation passages that may be used in the three outcome situations the programmer is likely to encounter. When writing these passages, keep in mind the communication axiom that asks, "WHO SAYS WHAT TO WHOM WITH WHAT EFFECT?" You, the program manager, are trying to communicate to the evaluation audience and external publics that you are a good manager who is constantly reviewing your services and improving them to make certain they are delivering the benefits promised. After reading these samples, complete Exercise 20-4.

SAMPLE EVALUATION REPORT PASSAGES

Each of these samples is written with a different assumption about the agency that will be preparing the report.

A Program That Will Be Modified—Military Recreation

(NAME), Morale, Welfare, and Recreation Director announced the results of the evaluation of the Base _____ program. Participants in the event reported that they valued the program because of the opportunities it provided them for (achievement, skill improvement, socialization, etc.).

Results of the evaluation also indicated a need to schedule the program at a more convenient (time, place, etc.).

OR

Results of the evaluation also indicated a need for better trained (officials, leadership, etc).

As a result of this evaluation, (NAME) said: "The _____ program is being revised to better meet participants' expressed needs. Specifically we plan to _____. I believe next year's participants will be very pleased with our revisions to this program. This is part of our ongoing evaluation of services that enables us to modify our programs to better meet mission and participant needs."

A Program That Will Be Continued—Public Recreation

(NAME), Director of Recreation, announced the evaluation results of the After-School Latch-Key program today. Participants in the event reported they valued the program because of the opportunities it provided them to (list opportunities).

Results of the evaluation indicate that significant benefits are being provided. Parents report that their children who participated had increased opportunities for personal development, to meet new friends, and to enjoy positive recreation activities after school with their classmates in a safe, supervised environment.

Because of the excellent evaluation report, the After-School Latch-Key program will be continued as it is currently being offered. This evaluation is part of our ongoing effort to evaluate services and enables us to document the benefits provided to our participants and the accomplishment of our mission in the community.

For a Program Cancellation—Private Golf Club

(NAME), Social Director, announced today the results of the annual evaluation of the Club's _____ program. Participants in the program reported they were not satisfied with this program because _____.

Club personnel reviewed and analyzed the program evaluation data for this program and have determined that the program is not meeting staff or customer expectations. (Give more specific reasons if you have them).

As a result of this evaluation, the _____ program has been cancelled and a new service will be designed. (Name the new service if you already know it.) This action is part of the Club's ongoing evaluation and review of services. According to (NAME), Social Director, "These evaluations enable us to eliminate programs that are no longer benefiting our customers and thereby enable us to introduce new, more beneficial programs."

CONCLUSION

Evaluations of program services are conducted by programmers to aid in program development, to help better manage the programming organization, and to provide accountability for program services. A nine-step procedure for planning an evaluation was outlined. These steps may be used for planning an evaluation or analyzing an existing evaluation model.

All evaluations can be improved by using better research designs, randomized methods of obtaining a sample, and schedules for obtaining observation and interview data. How to improve each of these techniques was discussed in the chapter. An outline for developing evaluation reports, suggested content for these reports, and sample publicity releases for completed evaluations were all discussed.

REFERENCES

Campbell, D. T., & Stanley J. C. (1963). *Experimental and quasi-experimental designs for research*. Chicago: Rand McNally.

Denzin, N. K. (1979). *The research act* (2nd ed.). New York: McGraw-Hill.

Grotelueschen, A. D., Gooler, D. D., Knox, A. B. , Kemmis, S., Dowdy, I., & Brophy, K. (1974). *An evaluation planner*. Urbana: University of Illinois at Urbana-Champaign, College of Education, Office for the Study of Continuing Professional Education.

Henderson, K. A., & Bialeschki, M. D. (1995). *Evaluating leisure services: Making enlightened decisions*. State College, PA: Venture.

House, E. R. (1977). *The logic of evaluative argument* (N.7) Los Angeles: University of California, Center for the Study of Evaluation.

Howard, D. R., & Crompton, J. L. (1980). *Financing, managing, and marketing recreation and park resources*. Dubuque, IA: Wm. C. Brown.

Howe, C. Z. (1980). Models for evaluating public recreation programs: What the literature shows. *Journal of Physical Education and Recreation, 51*(8), 36–38.

Howe, C. Z. (1993). The evaluation of leisure programs: Applying qualitative methods. *Journal of Physical Education, Recreation, and Dance, 64*(8), 43–47.

Patton, M. Q. (1997). *Utilization-focused evaluation* (3rd ed.). Thousand Oaks, CA: Sage.

Suchman, E. A. (1967). *Evaluative research*. New York: Russell Sage Foundation.

Weiss, C. H. (1973). *Evaluation research*. Englewood Cliffs, NJ: Prentice-Hall.

Worthen, B. R., & Sanders, J. R. (1973). *Educational evaluation: Theory and practice*. Belmont, CA: Wadsworth.

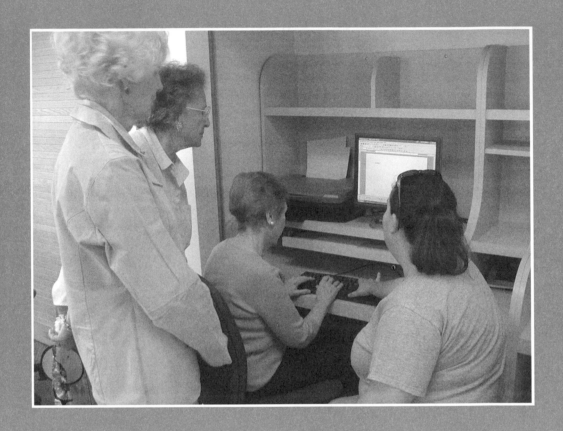

Seniors Computer Training Class
Photo courtesy of Long Beach Parks, Recreation, and Marine Department, Long Beach, CA

Developing a Comprehensive Evaluation System

STEP 8 : EVALUATION

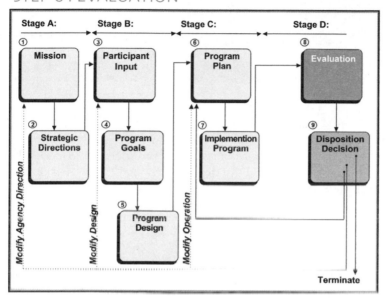

21

KEY TERMS

Comprehensive Evaluation System
Importance-Performance Evaluation
Service Hour Evaluation
Satisfaction-Based Evaluation
Goal and Objective Evaluation
Discrepancy
Triangulated Evaluation
Formative Evaluation
Summative Evaluation

No single technique will adequately address all evaluation questions. Comprehensive evaluation in an agency requires the use of several different techniques. To implement comprehensive evaluation in an agency, several things must happen. First, the agency must allocate resources, including staff time, training, and the materials and other resources needed to conduct the evaluation.

Second, agency managers need to create an open evaluation atmosphere. When an agency conducts evaluations, some evaluations will reveal inadequate programs. It is the responsibility of managers to create a sanction-free atmosphere so that problem programs can be identified and dealt with. If program managers want only good evaluation reports, they can get them by severely sanctioning the first programmer to deliver a report about a bad program. But if the agency hopes to identify programs that are performing inadequately, an atmosphere needs to be created in which programmers can report these programs without adverse sanction.

Third, the agency needs to assess how it is currently evaluating. Every agency makes judgments of worth about program services and makes disposition decisions with this evidence. Once the current system is identified, it needs to be made more

Outcome-based programming, such as BBP, assumes that the programmer will use the Goal and Objective method of evaluation. Because of this, it is important that the "performance objectives" be written in a manner that enables their achievement to be observed and thereby documented. As is pointed out in Figure 21-3, staff are searching for congruence between the performance objective designed and the outcome observed. During daily "process" discussions, staff will need to document the achievement of performance objectives based on actual observation of client behavior.

formal and systematic. Incorporating ideas developed in this chapter and Chapter Twenty into the system will help achieve this end.

If objectives were not achieved, staff will need to discuss whether this failure was due to a faulty design of the daily activities and procedures (animation plan) or inadequacies in other situating elements.

COMPONENTS OF A COMPREHENSIVE EVALUATION SYSTEM

An agency needs to consciously develop a comprehensive evaluation system. To be comprehensive, the system should be made up of the following five components: formative evaluation, summative evaluation, ongoing in-depth evaluation, an evaluation database, and strategic evaluation strategies. Each of these components fulfills a unique role in providing a comprehensive evaluation program for an agency.

FORMATIVE EVALUATION

Formative evaluation occurs while a program is being implemented; its purpose is to enhance new programs. The data produced must be readily available to facilitate the adjustments needed during the trial-and-error period of program development.

SUMMATIVE EVALUATION

Summative evaluation occurs at the end of a program to provide the data needed to make a final, summative judgment about the worth of a program and to assist with its future operation. Because a programmer may be responsible for evaluating many programs, summative evaluation procedures cannot be as cumbersome as the evaluation techniques used for in-depth analysis.

ONGOING IN-DEPTH ANALYSIS

Ongoing in-depth analysis of program services involves using evaluation techniques to thoroughly investigate and judge the worth of an individual program. In some cases, however, this component may be so time-consuming that only a portion of the agency's programs could be evaluated in this manner in any one year. In this case, it is recommended that all programs be evaluated on a rotating, scheduled basis, for example, every three years. The triangulated evaluation procedure is useful for accomplishing this analysis. An evaluation review committee can also be appointed to conduct an in-depth evaluation of a specific program, using evaluation techniques appropriate to the program. Evaluation committees can be made up of only staff, staff and board members, community advisory committee members, participants, or any combination of individuals who would be qualified to judge the worth of a program service.

EVALUATION DATABASE

An evaluation system must also provide the agency with an evaluation database. This database is a pool of systematically collected information about the worth of agency programs.

STRATEGIC EVALUATION

Finally, the database is used in preparing strategic evaluation reports. The agency may be required to develop these reports to answer unanticipated questions from a board, the public, or any other source. Too often, agencies cannot answer unanticipated questions because they have no database to analyze.

In this chapter, five models for conducting recreation program evaluation are outlined. The five models were chosen because they provide examples of a variety of approaches to leisure service evaluation and each implements specific components of a Comprehensive Evaluation System. Many other evaluation models are in use, but these five provide the reader with a good background in how recreation program evaluation may be approached. Each model is accompanied by the evaluation outline explicated in the previous chapter to explain the logic and technique of each model.

How the evaluation techniques discussed in this chapter fulfill the five components of a comprehensive evaluation system is outlined in Exhibit 21-1 on page 398.

IMPORTANCE-PERFORMANCE EVALUATION

Importance-performance analysis was reported by Martilla and James (1979) to be a useful technique for examining the desirability of product attributes. The technique is based on research findings demonstrating that participant satisfaction is a function of both participant expectations about attributes of a program they consider important and participant judgments about their experience with agency performance on these attributes. In importance-performance evaluation, participants are administered a test before their participation in a program to determine which program attributes are most important to them. Participants are also administered a post-program test with the same items as on the pre-program test. The purpose of the post-program measure-

Exhibit 21-1: Components of a Comprehensive Evaluation System

Formative Evaluation
    Program Observation Schedule (TRI)
    Patron Interviews (TRI)
    Other Data Bits (TRI)

Summative Evaluation
    Program Observation Schedule (TRI)
    Leader or Instructor Evaluation Forms (SAT and TRI)
    Participation Statistics (SH and TRI)
    Fiscal and Budget Data (TRI)
    Importance-Performance Data (I-P)
    Discrepancy Analysis (GO)

Ongoing In-depth Analysis
    Program Evaluation Summaries (TRI)
    Program Review Committees (Selected Techniques)
    Discrepancy Analysis (GO)

Evaluation Database
    Service Hour Summative Statistics (SH)
    Program Evaluation Summaries (TRI)
    Participant Outcome Reports (I-P and SAT)

Strategic Evaluation
    Analysis of Service Hour Data (SH)
    Analysis of Program Evaluation Summaries (TRI and SAT)
    Analysis of Participant-Reported Outcomes (TRI and SAT)

Key
    I-P   Importance-Performance Evaluation
    SAT   Satisfaction-Based Program Evaluation
    SH   Service Hour Evaluation
    TRI   Triangulated Evaluation Approach
    GO   Goal and Objective Evaluation

ment is to determine how well the agency performed in delivering the identified program attributes.

One of the most useful features of the technique is the method used for reporting results. Results of the pre and post measurements are plotted on a two-dimensional matrix, as illustrated in Figure 21-1. Importance data are plotted on the vertical axis of the matrix. The resulting quadrants are named (in clockwise order from the upper left-hand quadrant) "concentrate here," "keep up the good work," "possible overkill," and "low priority."

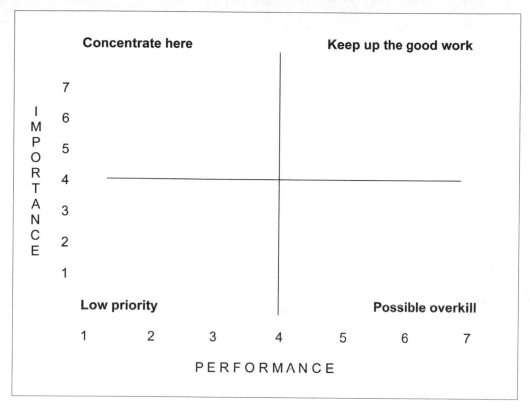

Figure 21-1: Importance-Performance Scoring Matrix

Where each piece of data is plotted is a function of both its importance to the participants and their judgment about how well the agency performed on delivering the attribute. Data reported in the "concentrate here" quadrant represent attributes that were important to participants but were not, in the participants' judgment, delivered well by the agency. Data reported in the "keep up the good work" quadrant were important to the participants, and in their judgment, were delivered well by the agency. Similarly, the logic of the remainder of the matrix can be ascertained.

IMPORTANCE-PERFORMANCE EVALUATION PLAN

The evaluation plan for importance-performance evaluation follows:

1. *Purpose:* The purpose is to judge the worth of agency performance in providing program services based on participant perceptions about the importance of program attributes and performance of the agency on selected attributes. This technique is particularly useful for formative evaluation of new, developing program services, or the evaluation of existing services whose attendance may have dwindled.

Exhibit 21-2: Importance-Performance Items

Importance

How important to you are the following features of our swimming pool program?

	Very Important			Important		Not Important	
1. Low admission for public swimming.	7	6	5	4	3	2	1
2. Opportunity to take swimming lessons to improve your swimming.	7	6	5	4	3	2	1
3. Cleanliness of pool.	7	6	5	4	3	2	1
4. Opportunity to meet new people.	7	6	5	4	3	2	1

Performance

How well were you satisfied with the agency's performance on the following items?

OR

Below are various features of our public swimming program. How well did the agency perform on these items?

	Very Satisfied			Satisfied		Not Satisfied	
1. Keeping the cost of admission for public swimming low.	7	6	5	4	3	2	1
2. Providing lessons for improving your swimming.	7	6	5	4	3	2	1
3. Providing a clean pool.	7	6	5	4	3	2	1
4. Providing opportunities to meet new people.	7	6	5	4	3	2	1

2. *Audience:* Program supervisors and administrators are the most likely audience for this evaluation technique. Importance-performance evaluation is very useful for program development and for monitoring how well the agency is meeting participant expectations. It is not especially useful for establishing agency accountability, nor does it produce a good comprehensive, summative evaluation.

3. *Process:* The first step is to develop a list of key program attributes to examine. There are three recommended sources for obtaining these attributes: a review of the literature for the program being evaluated, knowledgeable staff, and focus group interviews with

participants. Developing a list of pertinent program attributes on
which to judge the worth of program services is a very important
step in this evaluation model and one that should be given sufficient attention. The second step is to develop an instrument to measure how important these attributes are to potential participants
and to collect the importance data. The third step is to develop an
instrument to collect performance data from participants and then
to actually collect the data. The items included on the performance
instrument are the same items included on the importance instrument, but with some modification for verb tense and other gram-
matical adjustments to make the instrument read properly. See
Exhibit 21-2 for an example of importance-performance items. The
final step is to plot the data from the results obtained onto the matrix and interpret them.

4. *Issues:* The issues examined in importance-performance evaluation are participant judgments about how important key program
attributes are to their participation in and satisfaction with a specific program. The second issue is participants' judgments about
how well the agency performed in delivering the key program attributes.

One problem with importance-performance evaluation is the assumption that what is important to participants is static. Elsewhere in
the text, it has been established that a program is a dynamic, emergent
production. Because of this, participants may initially be attracted to a
program with a set of perceptions about what they consider important.
During the duration of a program, however, what is important to participants may change. Evaluators using this technique should remain
cognizant of this possibility.

5. *Evidence:* The evidence collected is participant perceptions of importance and performance on key program attributes.

*In impor-
tance-per-
formance
evaluation,
patrons are
adminis-
tered a test
before their
participa-
tion in a
program to
determine
which
program
attributes
are most
important
to them.*

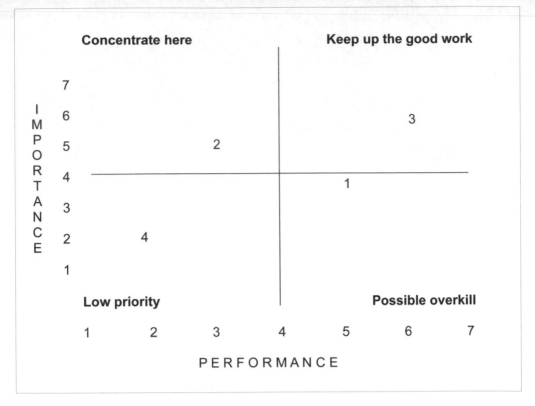

Figure 21-2: Analyzing Importance-Performance Items

6. *Data Gathering:* Data are gathered with the instruments developed before and after a program. Guadagnolo (1983) reported that the instruments can easily be administered on site and need not be mailed to participants. He also indicated that a questionnaire seems to be easily understood and is therefore easy to complete, which leads to high return rates.

7. *Analysis:* Data are analyzed on a matrix, with the vertical axis representing importance and the horizontal axis representing performance. See Figure 21-2 for an example of importance-performance analysis of the items included in Exhibit 21-1.

8. *Resources:* The resources needed to conduct this evaluation include instrument printing, time for instrument development, data collection, analysis, and reporting.

9. *Reporting:* From the analysis illustrated in Figure 21-2, one can interpret and report results of an importance-performance evaluation. In this case, it is evident that item #1 (a low admission price for swimming) is not an important issue to participants, but they believe the agency did a good job in keeping the price low. The agency may be doing an overkill on this item. Item #2 (providing lessons to help participants improve their swimming skills) was an important issue to participants, but they did not believe the agency did a good job in its instructional program. This is an item on which the agency needs to concentrate. Item #3 (providing a clean pool) was impor-

tant to participants, and they believed the agency did a good job. The agency needs to continue performing at its current level on this item. Item #4 (providing opportunities to meet new people) was not important to participants, and they did not believe the agency did a good job in helping them meet new people. Because this is not an important issue to the participants, the agency seems to be performing at an appropriate level, and no change in effort would be warranted.

Similarly, all items included in an importance-performance evaluation are analyzed and reported. The results are easy to interpret, and they provide the agency with clear managerial direction. Now complete Exercise 21-1 on page 401.

SERVICE HOUR EVALUATION

The service hour approach to program evaluation was developed to expand on the traditional "head count" attendance statistic. This expansion was accomplished by including the amount of time spent in a program, in addition to the actual number of participants. Because of the varying length of time programs are offered, the addition of the time variable enables the final statistic to reflect the amount of service delivered more accurately. For example, a service hour (SH) is one participant (P) in a program for one hour (H). The formula, then, is:

$$P \quad \times \quad H \quad = \quad SH$$

With this approach, a program with 30 children that lasts for one hour would be credited with delivering 30 service hours. A program with only 15 children that lasts for two hours would also get credit for delivering 30 service hours. With a "head count" system, the former program would be credited with 30 participants and the latter program with 15 participants. Failure to include the time variable can dramatically alter measurement of the quantity of the agency's service output.

In the service hour approach to program evaluation, both the number of participants and the amount of time they are served are collected. A service hour is the basic unit of output from the leisure delivery system, and it is the unit of analysis used in the service hour evaluation approach.

A classical issue of concern for publicly financed leisure service providers has been the distribution of services along designated variables. The public recreation literature is full of statements about the recommended distribution of services; for example, the program should serve all age groups; a variety of program areas should be offered; and programs should serve both sexes. As part of their statement of purpose, many agencies include statements about providing a variety of leisure opportunities to participants of all ages, income ranges, genders, races, and so forth in the community. However, few systems for recording and analyzing how program services are distributed have been developed. Therefore, most agencies have no system for evaluating how well their program distribution policy is being implemented.

Once service hour data are collected, the distribution of the service hours delivered can be analyzed along many variables. Analysis of this

In the service hour approach to program evaluation, both the number of participants and the amount of time they are served are collected.

distribution makes it possible to evaluate the distribution of agency services. Below are twelve variables that could be tracked in such a system. The first six are classical areas of concern that consistently appear in recreation programming literature as items that must be considered in designing a comprehensive program of services. Their inclusion in the system should be mandatory:

1. Age groups
2. Program areas
3. Program formats
4. Gender of participants
5. Geographic locations
6. Activity
7. Operating division
8. Ethnic backgrounds
9. Fee versus service programs
10. Special populations
11. Rank (military rank for use in military recreation)
12. Status, for example, active duty military, family of active duty military, or retirees

SERVICE HOUR EVALUATION PLAN

The evaluation plan for the service hour approach to evaluation follows.

1. *Purpose:* The purpose is to provide information about the distribution of program services to help improve organizational management and document compliance with agency policy.
2. *Audience:* Service hour data may be used in different ways by programmers, administrators, and policy makers.
3. *Process:* Service hour data are collected as a measure of recreation service output and analyzed along selected dimensions of organizational concern.
4. *Issues:* The issue being examined is the distribution of program services along any dimension selected for analysis. The major issue is the equity of distribution of program services along dimensions identified by the agency.
5. *Resources:* To operate the evaluation system requires instruments for collection, time to accomplish data collection, time and equipment to analyze data, and materials and time to report and interpret the information collected.
6. *Evidence:* The evidence collected is the service hour. The service hour is used as the unit of analysis in this evaluation technique.
7. *Data Gathering:* Data are recorded by program leaders and collected and analyzed by program supervisors or administrators.
8. *Analysis:* The distribution of program services along selected variables is documented. A variety of analyses that will provide insight into the distribution of services may be completed. In addition, service hour data accumulated over several years provides a database for additional analyses as needed.

Exhibit 21-3: Service Hour Evaluation Program Activity Report Form

1. Age Group

    01. Preschool (under 5)
    02. Elementary school (5–12)
    03. Junior high (13 and 14)
    04. Senior high (15–17)
    05. Young adult (18–20)
    06. Middle-aged adult (21–40)
    07. Older adult (41–60)
    08. Senior citizen (60–up)
    09. Mixed age group

2. Program Areas

    01. Arts and crafts
    02. Athletics
    03. Dance
    04. Drama
    05. Hobbies and clubs
    06. Language arts
    07. Music
    08. Science and nature
    09. Social recreation
    10. Volunteer services
    11. Special populations
    12. Other

3. Program Formats

    01. Open house
    02. Special event
    03. Skill development
    04. Competition
    05. Clubs and groups
    06. Self-directed, noncompetitive

4. Gender

    01. Males
    02. Females
    03. Coed

5. Geographic Locations

    01. Ace Recreation Center
    02. Banter Recreation Center
    03. Center Recreation Center
    04. Stevenson Recreation Center
    05. Fifth Street School
    06. King School
    07. Veterans Park
    08. Austin Gardens
    09. Maple Park
    10. Trip

6. Operating Division

    01. Athletics
    02. Cultural arts
    03. Maintenance
    04. Neighborhood recreation centers
    05. Senior citizen
    06. Special activities

7. Activity Number

Activity
Dates of operation
Leader
Reporting date

8. Number of leaders
9. Number of individuals enrolled
10. Number of hours of operation
11. Attendance at each session

Session ____ 1 ____ 2 ____ 3 ____ 4 ____ 5 ____ 6
____ 7 ____ 8 ____ 9 ____10 ____11 ____12
____13 ____14 ____15 ____16 ____17 ____18

Exhibit 21-4: Service Hour Evaluation Special Event Report Form

1. Age Group

    01. Preschool (under 5)
    02. Elementary school (5–12)
    03. Junior high (13 and 14)
    04. Senior high (15–17)
    05. Young adult (18–20)
    06. Middle-aged adult (21–40)
    07. Older adult (41–60)
    08. Senior citizen (60–up)
    09. Mixed age group

2. Program Areas

    01. Arts and crafts
    02. Athletics
    03. Dance
    04. Drama
    05. Hobbies and clubs
    06. Language arts
    07. Music
    08. Science and nature
    09. Social recreation
    10. Volunteer services
    11. Special populations
    12. Other

3. Program Formats

    01. Open house
    02. Special event
    03. Skill development
    04. Competition
    05. Clubs and groups
    06. Self-directed, noncompetitive

4. Gender

    01. Males
    02. Females
    03. Coed

5. Geographic Locations

    01. Ace Recreation Center
    02. Banter Recreation Center
    03. Center Recreation Center
    04. Stevenson Recreation Center
    05. Fifth Street School
    06. King School
    07. Veterans Park
    08. Austin Gardens
    09. Maple Park
    10. Trip

6. Operating Division

    01. Athletics
    02. Cultural arts
    03. Maintenance
    04. Neighborhood recreation centers
    05. Senior citizen
    06. Special activities

7. Activity Number

Activity
Dates of operation
Leader
Reporting date

8. Number of leaders
9. Number of individuals enrolled
10. Number of hours of operation
11. Attendance

9. *Reporting:* A written report summarized in various ways is used to document the distribution of services in a specific time period along a variety of dimensions. Reports that document changes over time may also be developed.

IMPLEMENTATION

Two forms are used in the system. One is the program activity report (Exhibit 21-3 on page 405) and the other is the special event report (Exhibit 21-4). The special event report is used on all activities such as special events, rentals, and club meetings that do not meet on a regularly scheduled basis as a class would meet. The program activity report is to be used on all programs that require a registration (paid or unpaid) and meet on a regular basis.

Each form contains 11 sections of information that must be reported accurately. The variables on which data are to be collected (items 1-6) can be chosen by the agency. The variables included in these example forms are for illustration purposes only, although they are considered by most administrators to be very important.

NUMBER 1: AGE GROUP

The agency can nominally define the age group categories it wishes to track. Once service hour data are collected with this tracking information, a report about the number and percentage of service hours delivered to each defined age group can be generated. In a similar way, reports about each additional variable included in the system can be developed.

NUMBER 2: PROGRAM AREAS

The program activity areas offered by the agency can also be tracked. There are many ways of nominally defining program activity areas, so the agency must select a method that results in a meaningful analysis for its operation.

NUMBER 3: PROGRAM FORMATS

How a program is organized varies from program to program. By tracking this dimension, the agency can ensure that it offers programs in a variety of formats.

NUMBER 4: GENDER

By tracking the gender of participants, the agency can determine whether it is providing an equal amount of service for males and females.

NUMBER 5: GEOGRAPHIC LOCATION

Examining the geographic distribution of program services is made possible by tracking the locations where service is provided. In this example, specific program sites are identified. If the agency operates so

Exhibit 21-5: Program Attendance Report Format

Activity (name)
Age group (name)
Program area (name)

Geographic location (name)
Program format (name)
Operating division (name)

A. Enrollment
B. Sessions (number of sessions)
C. Total attendance
D. Average session attendance
E. Percentage of attendance
F. Service hours
G. Staff hours
H. Efficiency ratio

Explanation:

A. Enrollment (given)
B. Sessions (given)
C. Total attendance (add attendance at all sessions)
D. Average session attendance (divide total attendance by the number of sessions)
E. Percentage of attendance (divide total attendance by potential attendance)
F. Service hours (normal session length x total attendance)
G. Staff hours (normal session length x number of staff x number of sessions)
H. Efficiency ratio (service hours - staff hours)

Exhibit 21-6: Special Event Report Format

(If enrollment was required for the program, the report will be identical to the Program Activity Report Format. If enrollment was not required, the report will be shorter.)

Activity (name)
Age group (name)
Program area (name)

Geographic location (name)
Program format (name)
Operating division (name)

A. Attendance
B. Service hours
C. Staff hours
D. Efficiency ratio

Explanation:

A. Attendance (given)
B. Service hours (attendance x hours of operation)
C. Staff hours (number of staff x hours of operation)
D. Efficiency ratio (service hours - staff hours)

Exhibit 21-7: Service Hour Report on an Individual Program

Recreation Center Girls Softball Tournament

Girls softball   Barrie Recreation Center
Elementary school   Tournament or leagues
Athletics   Athletics division
Females

A. Enrollment	21	E. Percentage of attendance	76%
B. Sessions	12	F. Service hours	288
C. Total attendance	192	G. Staff hours	18
D. Average session attendance	16	H. Efficiency ratio	16

many sites that the list would become too long, some other type of service area designation could be used.

NUMBER 6: OPERATING DIVISION

In this section, the relative output of various organizational divisions within the agency can be tracked and analyzed.

NUMBER 7: ACTIVITY NUMBER

All activities in an agency should be assigned a code number to be reported here. With this information, a report for a specific program could be developed if necessary.

NUMBER 8: STAFF

In this section, the number of staff members normally used for operating the program is reported. For most programs, this will be one or two. However, for special events it could be a larger number.

NUMBER 9: ENROLLMENT

In this section, the number of individuals enrolled in the program (paid or unpaid) should be recorded. For programs that meet regularly, the number reported here should be the number of people who have officially enrolled minus the number who officially withdrew. For special event programs, this section may or may not be applicable.

NUMBER 10: HOURS OF OPERATION

This section is used to report the normal length of a session.

Exhibit 21-8: Service Hour Activity Summary Report

Girls Softball Tournaments Summary

Girls softball (summary)   All locations
Elementary school   Tournament or leagues
Athletics   Athletics division
Females

A. Enrollment	145	E. Percentage of attendance	77%
B. Sessions	12	F. Service hours	2,016
C. Total attendance	1,344	G. Staff hours	126
D. Average session attendance	16	H. Efficiency ratio	16

NUMBER 11: ATTENDANCE

In this section, the count of the actual number of participants attending is reported. For programs that meet on a regular basis, the attendance at each session should be reported. For programs that meet only once, there is just one line for reporting the number of participants.

REPORTING FORMAT

Information developed from the service hour evaluation system for programs that meet regularly is reported as illustrated in Exhibit 21-5 on page 408. Information developed for special events is reported as illustrated in Exhibit 21-6 on page 408.

APPLICATION OF THE SERVICE HOUR APPROACH

Once the foregoing information is collected, an agency's services can be analyzed in many ways. Local needs would be the primary determinant of what reports would be developed. Below are examples of possible uses of the system.

Individual Program Report

It is possible to develop a report on an individual program, as is illustrated in Exhibit 21-7 on page 409. This type of a report is valuable in its own right. It can also be compared with reports of previous operations of the same program and with reports of the operation of similar programs within a community recreation system.

Activity Summary

It is possible to summarize all girls' softball tournaments and develop a report, as illustrated in Exhibit 21-8. This technique could be used for any activity tracked.

Other Summaries

It is possible to summarize your entire operation along any of the variables used for tracking. For example, the programmer could tell how many service hours were offered on an annual, monthly, or weekly basis to each age group or to which gender and at what locations. Through these comparisons over time and with each other, one can begin to see overloads and deficiencies in the distribution of program services. The major problem is to focus the reports that will actually be developed so that the agency is not overloaded with information.

Attention-Directing Uses

The percentage of attendance statistics and the efficiency ratio are both designed as attention-directing devices. These devices will alert the programmer to areas that may need further investigation. The percentage of attendance is calculated by dividing potential attendance (the number who enrolled in a class and should be attending) into actual attendance.

The second attention-directing device deals with staff efficiency. It identifies how many staff hours it took to produce the service hours delivered. The smaller the ratio number, the more staff time it takes to produce one hour of service. A ratio of 1 would indicate that it takes one hour of staff time to produce one service hour.

It is assumed that a community would, over time, identify an acceptable level of percentage of attendance and staff efficiency ratio. Any programs below a specified level would be examined further to try to ascertain if there is a problem. Both of these attention-directing devices achieve meaning only on a comparative basis within an individual agency.

The service hour approach to evaluation assumes that it is important to track the distribution of program service outputs along a number of different variables. The worth of an agency's distribution of services can be judged when using this system by the data developed. The system does not address program quality, and this is one of the weaknesses of the method. However, it does provide a quantitative measure of service output that can be analyzed to provide information to help improve the management of the agency. It can also provide data to use in helping the agency remain accountable.

SATISFACTION-BASED EVALUATION

Satisfaction-based program evaluation provides data about participant satisfaction with program services. These data can be used to judge the worth of program services. The assumption of the technique is that the worth of the programs can best be determined by identifying

Exhibit 21-9: Satisfaction Domains and Items

Achievement

I learned more about the activity.
It was a new and different experience.
I became better at it.
My skills and ability developed.

Physical Fitness

I enjoyed the physical exercise.
It kept me physically fit.

Social Enjoyment

I enjoyed the companionship.
Enjoying it with my friends.

Family Escape

Escaping from my family for awhile.
I was able to be away from family.

Environment

The area was physically attractive.
The freshness and cleanliness of the area.
I liked the open space.
The pleasing design of the facility.

Risk

I liked the high risk involved.
I liked the chance for danger.

Family Togetherness

Our family could do this together.
It brought our family together more.

Relaxation

It gave my mind a rest.
I experienced tranquility.
I got to relax physically.

Fun

I had fun.

Autonomy

I had control over things.
I was in control of what happened.
It gave me a chance to be on my own.

---

the degree to which programs have provided leisure experiences for participants.

Mannell (1999) has identified assessing satisfaction as one of the three social-psychological approaches to studying the subjective experience of leisure. He states, "The satisfaction construct is an 'after-the-fact' assessment or experiential consequence of an earlier involvement or set of involvements" (p. 238). Participant-reported satisfaction with leisure engagement is a well-accepted measure of leisure outcomes (Beard & Ragheb, 1979; Christensen & Yoesting, 1977; Driver, 1977; Driver & Brown, 1975; Hawes, 1978; Tinsley, Barrett, & Kass, 1977; Tinsley & Kass, 1978). Thus participant-reported satisfaction with leisure programs is used in this evaluation technique as a theoretically valid evaluation criterion that can be used to judge the worth of leisure programs.

The evaluation plan for satisfaction-based evaluation follows:

Exhibit 21-10: Leisure Program Evaluation Form

Listed below are statements that may reflect your satisfactions with this program. Please indicate by circling the appropriate number on each scale the degree to which each statement contributed to your satisfaction with this program. Statements that you believe do not apply to this program should be marked by circling the 0 in the Not Applicable column.

	Very satisfying		Satisfying		Contributes no satisfaction		Not applicable
1. I learned more about the activity	7	6	5	4	3	2	1	0
2. I had control over things	7	6	5	4	3	2	1	0
3. The cleanliness of the area	7	6	5	4	3	2	1	0
4. I enjoyed the exercise	7	6	5	4	3	2	1	0
5. I enjoyed companionship	7	6	5	4	3	2	1	0
6. I liked the high risks involved	7	6	5	4	3	2	1	0
7. I had fun	7	6	5	4	3	2	1	0
8. It gave my mind a rest	7	6	5	4	3	2	1	0
9. Our family could do this together	7	6	5	4	3	2	1	0
10. Enjoying it with my friends	7	6	5	4	3	2	1	0
11. I experienced tranquility	7	6	5	4	3	2	1	0
12. Escaping from my family awhile	7	6	5	4	3	2	1	0
13. It was a new/different experience	7	6	5	4	3	2	1	0
14. I liked the open space	7	6	5	4	3	2	1	0
15. I liked the chance for danger	7	6	5	4	3	2	1	0
16. The area was physically attractive	7	6	5	4	3	2	1	0
17. I became better at it	7	6	5	4	3	2	1	0
18. It keeps me physically fit	7	6	5	4	3	2	1	Not
19. It brought our family together more	7	6	5	4	3	2	1	0
20. I got to relax physically	7	6	5	4	3	2	1	0
21. I was in control of what happened	7	6	5	4	3	2	1	0

Exhibit 21-10: (continued)

22. My skills and ability developed	7	6	5	4	3	2	1	0
23. I was away from family awhile	7	6	5	4	3	2	1	0
24. It gave me a chance to be on my own..................	7	6	5	4	3	2	1	0
25. The pleasing design of the facility	7	6	5	4	3	2	1	0

Below are two statements about participating in this program. Please circle a number on each scale that best reflects your view.

1. Please compare this program with all of your other leisure pursuits. Compared with your other leisure, what priority would you assign this program?

One I would least like to give up						One I would give up first
7	6	5	4	3	2	1

2. Which of the following statements reflects your overall satisfaction with this program?

Delighted	Pleased	Mostly satisfied	Mixed	Mostly dissatisfied	Unhappy	Terrible
7	6	5	4	3	2	1

1. *Purpose:* The purpose of satisfaction-based evaluation is to provide theoretically valid measures of the outcome of leisure engagement. These data can be used to help develop program services and to help the agency account for the outcomes resulting from participation in its program services.

2. *Audience:* Program managers, program supervisors, and administrators are the primary audiences this evaluation technique will serve.

3. *Process:* The technique requires the collection and analysis of participant-reported satisfactions with programs.

4. *Issues:* The major issue investigated by the technique is whether programs are providing leisure experiences. This is determined by investigating the amount and types of satisfaction being met by a program.

5. *Resources:* The resources needed to conduct the evaluation are a valid and reliable instrument for data collection, and the time needed to analyze the data collected.

Exhibit 21-11: Calculating Satisfaction Domain Scores

Relaxation Domain	Subject 1	Subject 2
8. It gave my mind a rest.	7	4
11. I experienced tranquility.	5	7
20. I got to relax physically.	6	No score
	18	11
	$18 \div 3 = 6$	$11 \div 2 = 5.5$

6. *Evidence:* The evidence collected is participant-reported satisfaction with participation in a program.

7. *Data Gathering:* Data are gathered by having participants complete an instrument at the end of a program, thereby self-reporting their satisfaction with the program.

8. *Analysis:* Satisfaction domains are calculated and the resulting data are analyzed by time-series or program-by-program comparisons.

9. *Reporting:* Data can be reported on a program-by-program basis, in a summary report of a programming season, or in an annual report.

SATISFACTION ITEMS AND DOMAINS

There are currently 10 domains with 25 items. These are contained in Exhibit 21-9 on page 412. Some or all of the domains may be included in an individual evaluation.

The instrument used in the satisfaction-based evaluation technique is contained in Exhibit 21-10 on pages 413-414. The instrument is scored with a 7-point Likert scale. A "not applicable" choice is included in the instrument. This choice allows respondents an alternative when they believe the satisfaction items are inappropriate or not applicable to the specific program they are in. An item investigating the importance of the program to the individual is included in order to investigate the importance of a program in relation to all of the participant's other leisure pursuits.

It is assumed that as a matter of public policy, it is preferable to cancel programs that are less important rather than those that are very important to participants compared with all of their other leisure pursuits. An overall satisfaction item is also included to investigate participants' overall summative judgment about their satisfaction with a program. Previous use of this form has established that neither gender nor age biases responses to the items.

> *Satisfaction-based program evaluation assumes that the worth of programs can be best determined by identifying the degree to which programs have provided leisure experiences for participants.*

SCORING THE LEISURE PROGRAM EVALUATION FORM

A list of individual items and the domains in which they are included appear in Exhibit 21-9. Domain scores are calculated by simply averaging the items scored in each domain for each respondent. For example, the scores for two subjects on the relaxation domain are illustrated in Exhibit 21-11 on page 415. In this case, Subject 1 responded to all three items in the domain. Therefore, the number 3 was used as the divisor in calculating the domain score for Subject 1. Subject 2 responded to only two items in the domain, so the number 2 was used as the divisor in calculating the domain score for Subject 2.

To calculate a domain score across all participants in a single program, an average of all of the scores across all participants is calculated.

Data from the satisfaction-based program evaluation can be used in several different ways. First, the data can document participant-reported program outcomes. With a post-program administration of the instrument, data about what actually happened to participants in the program can be gathered. Programmers can use the data to document what is actually happening to participants in their programs and to establish accountability with their funding source. The technique provides systematically collected participant-reported outcome data resulting from participation in leisure services. With these data, the programmer does not need to assert the value of a program based on hearsay. Instead, data systematically collected from the participants themselves can be used.

Second, satisfaction data can be analyzed to determine if programmatic goals are being achieved. For example, in one administration of the instrument, the highest rated satisfactions on a Fall Foliage Tour were "fun," "environment," "social enjoyment," and "relaxation" (Rossman, 1983). Similar analyses of participant-reported satisfactions with different program services can aid the programmer in investigating whether program services provide appropriate satisfactions. This use of the technique aids in program development.

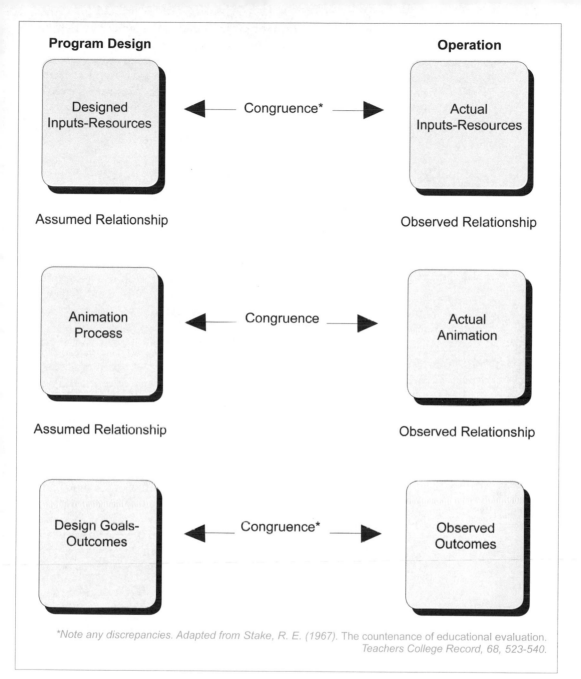

Program Design

Designed
Inputs-Resources

Assumed Relationship

Animation
Process

Assumed Relationship

Design Goals-
Outcomes

◄ Congruence* ►

◄ Congruence ►

◄ Congruence* ►

Operation

Actual
Inputs-Resources

Observed Relationship

Actual
Animation

Observed Relationship

Observed
Outcomes

*Note any discrepancies. Adapted from Stake, R. E. (1967). The countenance of educational evaluation. Teachers College Record, 68, 523-540.

Figure 21-3: Analytical Framework for Discrepancy Evaluation

Third, satisfaction data from various programs can be compared to investigate the differences in satisfactions provided by different program services. For example, the reported satisfactions summarized for all athletic programs could be compared with similar data for all cultural arts programs. In this way, differences in the types of satisfactions provided by different types of services can be documented. This analysis will help the programmer in organizational management by helping determine appropriate program directions for the agency.

Satisfaction-based program evaluation can be used in several different ways for various purposes. The data collected are participant-reported satisfactions with participation in agency program services. With this technique, judgments about the worth of program services are made using data collected directly from participants in the program. Now complete Exercise 21-2 on page 416.

GOAL AND OBJECTIVE EVALUATION

The process evaluation model, which uses goals and objectives to evaluate program services, is a logical extension of the use of goals and objectives for program management and design purposes, covered previously in Chapters Six, Eight, and Ten. The procedures recommended are based on the discrepancy evaluation method explicated by Stake (1967) and Provus (1971), and applied to the evaluation of therapeutic recreation programs by Peterson and Gunn (1984). Because it is a process model, the content of the goals and objectives are not specified. What follows, then, is a framework for the process.

There are three features to the model that make it a distinct method.

1. Goals and objectives are developed hierarchically. They end with precisely specified expected outcomes for participants, thus enabling a comparison of expected with actual outcomes (Peterson & Gunn, 1984). Therefore, the programmer must state exactly what is to be accomplished through the program.
2. The actual operation of a program is compared with its design (Stake, 1967). This specific feature requires one to examine not only outcomes, but also program inputs and processes. This expands the inquiry into possible causes of the discrepancies.
3. The program standards that form the basis of comparison should be derived from the program staff and the client population served (Provus, 1971). The evaluation audience and their value system are thereby incorporated in the evaluation.

Thus, implementation of a discrepancy evaluation model requires well-written and valid goals and objectives that may be used to determine the worth of a program. Furthermore, the technique admonishes us to take an expansive view of a program, including it inputs, processes, and outcomes, rather than a focal, microscopic one focusing on a single feature of the program. When implemented correctly, value inputs from the evaluation audience are incorporated into the overall evaluation plan.

GOAL AND OBJECTIVE EVALUATION PLAN

1. *Purpose:* The purpose is to judge the worth of program services by examining the discrepancies between the program design and its actual operation.

2. *Audience:* This method is amenable to almost every party of interest, provided that the goals and objectives are written to reflect their value perspective and interests. The process is very adaptable but is application sensitive; that is, it must be implemented correctly to provide the results desired.

3. *Process:* There are three steps to the discrepancy evaluation method: "(1) defining program standards; (2) determining whether a discrepancy exists between some aspect of program performance and the standards governing that aspect of the program; and (3) using discrepancy information either to change performance or to change program standards" (Provus, 1971, p. 183).

4. *Issues:* Goals and objectives can be developed to measure inputs, processes, or outcomes. Whether all of these should be developed depends on the specific program being evaluated.

5. *Evidence:* The specific content of the confirming evidence depends on the type of statement being examined. In each case, the terminal objective, the final one, and the hierarchy should be written so the evidence needed to confirm its accomplishment is evident to the staff and clients associated with the program.

6. *Data Gathering:* The techniques used are varied, again depending on the specific content of the terminal objectives. Techniques typically used are observations of participant behavior, evaluation surveys, attendance or other types of statistical data, interviews, and so on.

7. *Analysis:* The primary analytical framework is one of comparing intentions with actual results and noting any discrepancies. How well this can be accomplished is dependent on how clear, specific, and measurable the standards statements were written and on the thoroughness of the observations and data collections.

8. *Resources:* Two principle resources needed are staff time and expertise in implementing the method.

9. *Reporting:* The typical report is a written document presenting each objective and the data gathered about it. This should include an analytical statement about whether or not the standard is met, with a notation of any discrepancy observed and how it is to be reconciled.

IMPLEMENTATION

The use of goals and objective evaluation is predicated on well-written objectives that are used to determine if actual implementation is congruent with the intentions stated, or if there is a discrepancy. An example is provided in Box D of Figure 10-1. Included are three program design outcomes for a guitar class, with an example of the terminal performance objectives that will be used to measure the accomplishment of design goal #3, "At the end of the program, 90 percent of the students will be able to correctly identify the parts of the guitar."

The procedure, then, is to conduct the class, determine the percentage of students who can correctly identify the six parts of the guitar, and compare the observed level of performance with our stated objective. If 90 percent or more of the students can identify the six parts of the guitar correctly, there is congruence. If fewer than 90 percent can identify them, there is a discrepancy.

Determining congruence between intentions and actual performance and noting any discrepancies is the basic method of goal and objective evaluation. However, to thoroughly use the discrepancy approach requires one to not only state behavioral outcomes, but also to state program inputs and process goals. Figure 21-3 on page 417 outlines the basic analytical framework for discrepancy evaluation. One can observe in this figure that design goals with measurement objectives are developed for program inputs, processes, and outcomes.

Furthermore, there is an assumed relationship between the inputs to a program, the animation plan, and the outcomes desired. To conduct an evaluation using goals and objectives, then, one determines the congruence between intended versus actual observations of inputs, processes, and outcomes, and makes note of any discrepancies for further analysis. In addition, the assumed relationships between inputs, processes, and outcomes are examined to investigate their logic and validity. Any discrepancies are also noted for further analysis.

Discrepancies may be reconciled by changing the intended measure to be more realistic. For example, in the current case, one may modify the design goal so the desired result is that 80 percent rather than 90 percent of the students correctly identify the six parts of the guitar. However, omissions in inputs or animation processes may also account for failures in outcomes. For example, one intended input may have been a videotape for each student to take home that explained and showed the parts of the guitar. However, this feature may have been dropped due to budget constraints or to the late arrival of the tapes. Thus, the discrepancy in failing to reach the goal of 90 percent of the students being able to correctly identify the six parts of the guitar may be explained by defects in the designed inputs of the program.

A similar analyses may also be demonstrated in how a program was animated. The amount of time in the program devoted to identifying the parts of the guitar may have been too short, or this labeling activity may not have been reinforced in subsequent lessons. Each of these could account for the failure of 90 percent or more of the students being able to correctly identify the six parts of the guitar.

Thus, the use of goals and objectives for evaluation is a very flexible technique that can be applied in many situations. It requires well-written goals and objectives developed within a specific framework in order to facilitate making the judgments required to evaluate.

TRIANGULATED EVALUATION

Judging the worth of leisure services is a value-laden enterprise. A single program may be viewed as both good and bad at the same time from different perspectives. In addition, many evaluations use a single methodology to gather the data to be reported for evaluation purposes. The technique used in social science to deal with multiple perspectives and realities is triangulation (Bullock & Coffey, 1980; Denzin, 1978).

The triangulated approach to evaluation assumes that the data need to be gathered from multiple perspectives and with multiple methods.

...the use of goals and objectives for evaluation is a very flexible technique that can be applied in many situations.

The triangulated approach to evaluation assumes that the data need to be gathered from multiple perspectives and with multiple methods.

Exhibit 21-12: Leader or Instructor Evaluation Form

Program   Date

Leader or Instructor

Season

Please help us evaluate and improve our services by answering the questions below. Your feedback is important to our operation. All information is confidential. Please place an (X) on each line to indicate your opinion about the quality of service.

	Rating				
	Poor				Excellent
	(1)	(2)	(3)	(4)	(5)
Program Schedule					
1. Length of individual program meetings	( )	( )	( )	( )	( )
2. Time program met	( )	( )	( )	( )	( )
3. Day of week program was held	( )	( )	( )	( )	( )
Equipment and Supplies					
4. Material provided for program operation	( )	( )	( )	( )	( )
5. Equipment provided for program operation	( )	( )	( )	( )	( )
Facility					
6. Appropriateness of facility for program	( )	( )	( )	( )	( )
7. Safety of facility and equipment	( )	( )	( )	( )	( )
8. Cleanliness of facility	( )	( )	( )	( )	( )
9. Facility access and preparedness— was facility open on time and ready to go?	( )	( )	( )	( )	( )
Supervisor Support					
10. Supervisor provided adequate orientation training	( )	( )	( )	( )	( )
11. Supervisor provided ongoing cooperation and direction	( )	( )	( )	( )	( )
12. In the absence of your immediate supervisor, were other Bureau personnel helpful in solving your problems?	( )	( )	( )	( )	( )
Program Operation					
13. For this program, was the number of people enrolled appropriate?	( )	( )	( )	( )	( )
14. How well were the Bureau's goals for this program achieved?	( )	( )	( )	( )	( )
15. My performance in this program was . . .	( )	( )	( )	( )	( )
16. Do you believe there is sufficient demand to offer this program again?		Yes		No	

Additional Feedback
Please give us additional suggestions or comments you believe will help improve our services or help you do a better job serving our constituents.

Exhibit 21-13: Program Observation Schedule

Program_____ Location_____
Date Observed _____ Activities Observed _____
Time Observed From _____ : _____ To _____ : _____

Observation Checklist Rating Scale

4	3	2	1
Excellent No modification is warranted.	*Good* Could be improved if alternatives were available.	*Poor* Alternative arrangements must be made before the next program offering.	*Inadequate* Immediate action must be taken to correct the situation.

Facility
1. Is the facility adequate for this program? _____
2. Is the equipment adequate for this program? _____

Staff
3. Is there a sufficient number of staff on duty to handle this program? _____
4. Are the staff available to participants? _____
5. Are staff tactful and courteous to participants? _____
6. Are staff in control of the program; that is, no horseplay or loitering observed? _____

Program
7. Are adequate safety precautions being practiced? _____
8. Is the program being conducted consistent with the Bureau's advertised description? _____
9. Are the activities appropriate for the goals and objectives of the program? _____

Problems noted (list all 1s and 2s) Action taken (date)

Data Bits (Describe instances of behavior that either refute or confirm a program's accomplishments, or note any positive or negative comments from participants—get name and phone if possible.)

Get feedback on the following:

How important is this program to you in view of your other leisure pursuits?

Does this volleyball league provide you with an appropriate level of competition?

Signature _____

Exhibit 21-14: Participant Evaluation Form

Please help us to evaluate our programs by answering the questions below. Your feedback is needed to help us serve you better. Please indicate how strongly you agree or disagree with each statement by circling the response that most closely reflects your belief. All individual responses will remain anonymous and will only be used in a summarized form.

Recommended Questions

[Responses for all the items below are to be a 5-point Likert scale format with the following reponse categories:]

1	2	3	4	5
Strongly disagree	Disagree	Neutral	Agree	Strongly agree

[It is recommended that the following eight items be included on all instruments. Program supervisors will select other items from the Item Pool provided in the Chapter Twenty-One Addendum on pages 430-433 to complete the instrument.]

1. I had fun in this program.
2. I enjoyed this program because my skills and abilities developed.
3. I liked this program because of the chance for physical exercise it provided.
4. I liked this program because of the opportunities for social contact it provided; that is, making new friends or enjoying being with people.
5. I enjoyed this program because of the facility or setting in which it was held.
6. Overall, I am highly satisfied with this program.
7. My personal reasons for participating in this program were fulfilled.
8. In relation to all my other leisure activities, this program is very important to me.

Please feel free to comment further about this program on the back of this form. Please return the form to the program leader or mail to the Agency of Recreation and Parks. Thank you for your help!

Fuszek (1987) has adopted this strategy in conducting program evaluations in the parks and recreation department in Austin, Texas. Discussing the methodology used in Austin, he states that "the primary emphasis [is] placed upon pragmatic or qualitative assessment—i.e., how do all the parts/players fit [or not fit] together to achieve program goals—as opposed to relying solely on quantitative measurement or efficiency studies" (Fuszek, 1987). He then outlines seven methods to obtain data for use in judging the worth of program services. When this multiple perspective, multiple method approach is undertaken, it will more likely capture the true picture and worth of a program. The technique that follows is but one example of how the concept of triangulation may be applied to the evaluation of leisure services.

This example shows a triangulation of research methods and data sources. The research methods were developed from a series of

Exhibit 21-15: Program Evaluation Summary Format

Program _____ Location _____
Dates of Operation _____

I. Statistical Summary
    A. Participation Impact

        Number of Sessions (NOS)_____ Number of Enrollments (NOE) _____
        Potential Attendance (PA) = (NOS) X (NOE) _____
        Actual Total Attendance (ATA) _____
        Average Attendance (AVA) = (ATA) / (NOE) _____
        Percentage of Attendance = (ATA) / (PA) _____

    B. Staff

        Number of Staff (NBS)_____ Number of Staff Hours _____
        Staff/Participant Ratio = (AVA) / (NBS) _____

    C. Costs

        Salaries_____
        Equipment _____
        Supplies_____
        Facilities_____
        Total (TOTC)_____

    D. Revenue

        Agency Funds or Appropriated Funds _____
        User Fees or Nonappropriated Funds_____
        Total (TOTR) _____

    E. Cost Analysis

        Net Cost (TOTC)_____
        Average Cost per Participant (TOTC) / (NOE) _____
        Average Cost per Participation (TOTC) / (ATA) _____
        Percent Self-Supporting - (User Fees) / (TOTC) _____

II. Goals: Why was this program conducted? How does it fit in with the overall
     goals of the [agency name]? What were the specific goals of this program?

III. Procedures: Briefly describe what is involved in operating this program.

IV. Evaluation Data:
    A. Program Observations: Summarize reports from ongoing on-site
        supervision of the program. Number of visits and a general report of
        conditions found.
    B. Leader or Instructor Report: Summarize the leader's or instructor's reports
        about program operations.
    C. Participant Feedback: Report participant feedback about the program,
        including oral testimony, tabulated evaluation items, phone calls, and so on.
    D. Other Data Bits: Information from other data sources.

Exhibit 21-15: (continued)

V. Supervisor's Analysis of Evaluation:

What is this program accomplishing?
Who is the program serving?
Is this program the best allocation of these resources?
How does this program compare with other similar programs in the agency?
Does this program fit into the Bureau's mission?

VI. Program Disposition: This program should be:
   A.   Continued as currently operated.
   B.   Dropped (identify possible impacts below).
   C.   Modified as noted below.

Signature _____   Date _____

---

consulting interviews that one of the authors conducted with programmers in five agencies. In these interviews, it was revealed that the two
major methods used by programmers in evaluating their programs
were observation during on-site inspection of program services and interviews with participants. Both of these methods of data gathering are
legitimate, but neither is usually implemented in an appropriate fashion.

Often, different programmers in the same agency look for different
items when they make on-site visits. Therefore, there was no reliability
of observations. The first step in improving this method of data gathering is to have program supervisors jointly develop a single observation
schedule of what needs to be examined. Training program supervisors
in observation data-gathering methods, as discussed in Chapter Nineteen, is also necessary to improve this technique.

The second technique used by programmers was to talk to participants. Often these contacts were very informal public relations exercises rather than data-gathering sessions. Again, there were often as many
different interview agendas as there were supervisors. In many cases,
program supervisors simply chatted about whatever the participants
wanted to discuss. To improve this method of data gathering, an interview schedule was developed. Admittedly, it is somewhat intrusive
to have program supervisors with clipboards interviewing participants
in program services. At the very least, supervisors should have a few
focused questions they want answered in these discussions. In addition
to being viewed as public relations exercises, these discussions should
be considered opportunities to gather data about the quality of program
services from a primary data source—the participant.

Program supervisors should be prepared to validate unanticipated information they may gather in these interviews. Information

Examine the outline for the evaluation summary report and discuss the following questions:
- What does each section of the outline add to judging the worth of a program service?
- What additional questions may be added?
- Which items may be eliminated? How would the usefulness of the report be altered if they were eliminated?

is validated by pursuing and verifying or refuting information from additional sources, usually other participants. In either case, the information should be validated and verified from multiple sources.

The third method of gathering data is through a questionnaire. Two instruments are recommended, one administered to participants and the other to face-to-face leaders. Gathering data with instruments either through a census or a survey is the third method of data collection in this example of a triangulated evaluation approach.

In addition to triangulating methods, it is recommended that data sources also be triangulated. In selecting sources of information, one needs to identify individuals who are the most knowledgeable about what actually occurred in a program. Some experienced programmers believe they can assess the worth of a program service by their own observation and analysis. A triangulated approach assumes that in order to get a more complete picture about the worth of a program, one must obtain data from multiple perspectives. Furthermore, the approach assumes that some sources of information are better situated than others to have primary knowledge about what actually occurred in a program, so they are better sources of information. Part of triangulated evaluation, then, is identifying primary data sources and designing instruments and techniques for aggressively and systematically gathering information from these sources.

In the current example, the three most knowledgeable sources are assumed to be the face-to-face program leader, who has direct, first-line contact with a program; the program supervisor, who makes frequent supervisory contact with a program; and participants, who actually experience the service. They are therefore the three sources to be systematically pursued. Instruments and techniques for gathering data from these sources have been developed and are illustrated and discussed below.

TRIANGULATED EVALUATION PLAN

The plan for the triangulated evaluation procedure is outlined as follows:

1. *Purpose:* The purpose of the triangulated approach to evaluation is to help program supervisors in making disposition decisions about program services. The data gathered in this approach provide the programmer with information for determining whether to drop, modify, or continue a program service. The technique helps with program development and organizational management.

2. *Audience:* Program supervisors and program administrators are the primary audiences for this evaluation technique.

3. *Process:* The process involves the collection of evaluation data from three sources with three data collection techniques and the summary analysis of this information.

4. *Issues:* Program leader, program supervisor, and participant views about program outcomes, inputs, and process are examined.

5. *Resources:* Having instruments for data gathering, conducting training in how to use the instruments, and allowing time for data collection and analysis are all necessary.

6. *Evidence:* Leader observations, supervisor observations and interview data, and participant-reported satisfactions with outcomes and arrangements, as selected by the program supervisor, are all collected.

7. *Data Gathering:* Three instruments are provided, including the recreation leader or instructor evaluation form (Exhibit 21-12 on page 421), the recreation program observation schedule (Exhibit 21-13 on page 422), and the recreation participant evaluation form (Exhibit 21-14 on page 423).

8. *Analysis:* The data are analyzed on the program evaluation summary format (Exhibit 21-15 on pages 424-425).

9. *Reporting:* The final report is written according to the format outlined in Exhibit 21-15.

INSTRUMENTS

Three instruments are used in the triangulated evaluation procedure. The first is the recreation leader or instructor evaluation form, presented in Exhibit 21-12. This form is completed by the agency employee with direct contact in a program. The items on the instrument are examples of what might be asked of this type of employee. Questions are included that inquire about the adequacy of the program schedule, equipment and supplies, the facility, supervisory support, and program operation.

A second instrument is the recreation program observation schedule, presented in Exhibit 21-13. This is used to record observations of on-site visitations and inspections of program services by supervisors. The items observed can be altered to meet the needs of a specific agency. Note the rating scale included on the instrument. Each rating number is defined to try to improve reliability. Any item rated 1 should be taken care of immediately while the supervisor is on-site, and the action taken should be noted in the section provided. Items rated 2 should be taken care of before the next session of the program, and any action taken should be noted in the space provided. Items rated 3 should be taken care of as time permits and as alternative arrangements become available. Items rated 4 need no further action.

A designated area on the instrument is provided for recording additional data bits—unsolicited information gathered in the process of inspecting programs. In this section, specific interview questions that program supervisors may want participants to answer can also be added. Some examples are provided.

The third instrument used is the participant evaluation form, presented in Exhibit 21-14. What is presented is a format for the instrument. To use this instrument, the programmer selects items from the item pool presented in the addendum to this chapter.

To achieve some uniformity of evaluation data across all programs, it is recommended that the agency establish a list of five to eight questions to include on the evaluation instruments for all programs. An example of such a list is included in Exhibit 21-13. An individual program supervisor could then select an additional eight to ten questions from the item pool that would specifically apply to the program being evaluated. In this way, some data are unique to a specific program. The reader will notice that the questions included in the item pool deal with program inputs, processes, and outputs. Any instrument should include an assortment of each type of question.

The final instrument used in the triangulated approach to program evaluation is the program evaluation summary format, presented in Exhibit 21-14. This instrument includes various pieces of information that are necessary to evaluate a program comprehensively. The reader will notice that the outline includes a number of pieces of information that derive from evaluation techniques explained in previous sections of this chapter.

In Section I, the statistical summary, five pieces of statistical data are reported. These include data about participation impact, staffing requirements, program costs, program revenue, and a cost analysis of the program.

In Section II, program goals are assessed. Specifically, the programmer is asked to answer why the agency is conducting the program and how it fits in with the overall mission of the agency. In this way, each program must be justified with data each time it is evaluated.

In Section III, procedures, a brief explanation of what is involved in operating the program, is included in the report. One should not write the complete program plan in this section, but a much shorter explanation about what it takes to operate the program.

Section IV contains the summated evaluation data collected with the instruments recommended in the triangulated approach. In Section V, the evaluator is required to analyze the program by formulating responses to the questions using the evaluation data reported in the previous section. By using this outline, the programmer is required to analyze the program on the basis of evaluation evidence rather than on hearsay or other less reliable information. The analysis must be supported by the data. In a similar fashion, after completing the analysis, the programmer must make a program disposition decision based on the results of the evaluation data to either continue the program as currently operated, to drop it, or to modify it. If either of the latter two decisions is made, the programmer must provide the following information. For a program that is to be dropped, the programmer must speculate

To implement a comprehensive program evaluation, the agency must allocate resources, including staff time, training, and the materials and other resources needed to conduct the evaluation.

about possible effects that dropping it might have on the agency. For a program that is to be modified, the programmer must specify the modifications to be made.

The organization of the summary format requires that the evaluation report be developed in a logical manner and that the decisions be based on logical conclusions drawn from systematically collected data. Evaluation is thereby based on an analysis of evidence systematically collected from agency participants and programs. Now complete Exercise 21-3 on page 426.

The triangulated approach to program evaluation is a concept suggesting that multiple methods should be used to collect data from multiple sources. An example of how this technique may be used was presented, along with a rationale for why each method and data source was selected for inclusion.

CONCLUSION

Five models for use in leisure service evaluations have been presented. The theory behind each model and its assumptions were outlined. Each model was analyzed using the nine evaluation planning steps as an analytical framework. Before using the models presented or any other evaluation model, programmers must make certain that the model meets their evaluation needs.

Comprehensive evaluation in an agency should have five components. No single method can accomplish all five components. The contributions of each evaluation model to the components of a comprehensive evaluation were outlined.

REFERENCES

Beard, J. G., & Ragheb, M. G. (1979, October). Measuring leisure satisfaction. Paper presented at the Leisure Research Symposium, New Orleans, LA.

Bullock, C. C., & Coffey, F. (1980). Triangulation as applied to the evaluative process. *Journal of Physical Education and Recreation, 51*(8), 50–52.

Christensen, J. E., & Yoesting, D. R. (1977). The substitutability concept: A need for further development. *Journal of Leisure Research, 9,* 188–207.

Denzin, N. K. (1978). *The research act* (2nd ed.). New York: McGraw-Hill.

Driver, B. L. (1977). *Item pool for scales designed to quantify the psychological outcomes desired and expected from recreation participation.* Fort Collins, CO: Rocky Mountain Forest and Range Experiment Station.

Driver, B. L., & Brown, P. J. (1975). A socio-psychological definition of recreation demand, with implications for recreation resource planning. *Assessing the Demand for Outdoor Recreation.* Washington, DC: U.S. Government Printing Office.

Fuszek, R. (1987, October). Program evaluation in municipal parks and recreation. Paper presented at the National Recreation and Park Association Annual Congress, New Orleans, LA.

Guadagnolo, F. B. (1983, October). Application of the Importance-Performance Scale in Program evaluation. Paper presented at the Leisure Research Symposium, Kansas City, MO.

Hawes, D. K. (1978). Satisfactions derived from leisure-time pursuits: An exploratory nationwide survey. *Journal of Leisure Research, 10,* 247–264.

Martilla, J. A., & James, J. C. (1979). Importance-performance analysis. *Journal of Marketing, 41*(1), 77–79.

Mannell, R. C. (1999). In E. L. Jackson & T. L. Burton (Eds.). *Leisure studies: Projects for the twenty-first century* (pp.235-251). State College, PA: Venture Publishing Inc.

Peterson, C. A., & Gunn, S. L. (1984). *Therapeutic recreation program design: Principles and procedures* (2nd ed.). Englewood Cliffs, NJ: Prentice-Hall.

Provus, M. (1971). *Discrepancy evaluation: For educational program improvement and assessment.* Berkeley, CA: McCutchen.

Rossman, J. R. (1983). Participant satisfaction with employee recreation. *Journal of Physical Education, Recreation, and Dance, 54*(8), 60–62.

Stake, R. E. (1967). The countenance of educational evaluation. *Teachers College Record, 68,* 523–540.

Tinsley, H. E. A., Barrett, T. C., & Kass, R. A. (1977). Leisure activities and need satisfaction. *Journal of Leisure Research, 9,* 110–120.

Tinsley, H. E. A., & Kass, R. A. (1978). Leisure activities and need satisfaction: A replication extension. *Journal of Leisure Research, 10,* 191–202.

ADDENDUM: LEISURE PROGRAM EVALUATION ITEM POOL

The following items have been arranged by categories. Programmers are to select items most pertinent to their operation or specific program.

Staffing
• The leader (instructor, coach, etc.) was on time for the program.
• The leader was well prepared.
• The leader was knowledgeable about the subject matter.
• The leader was excellent.
• The leader made the class interesting.
• The leader was dynamic.
• The leader motivated me to get better at the activity.
• The leader was boring.
• The leader attempted to cover too much.

Price
• This program was too expensive.
• The fee for this program was reasonable.
• I would have paid more for a program of this quality.

Scheduling
• The length of individual class meetings was too long.
• The length of class meetings was just right.

- Class meetings were too short.
- This program was scheduled at a bad time for me.
- This program was scheduled at a good time for me.
- The day of the week the program was scheduled was good (bad) for me.
- I would have preferred that the program be held on a different day of the week.
- The facility the program was held in was too small.
- This facility was very enjoyable.
- This facility was inadequate.
- I had trouble getting to this facility.
- I would prefer a different location for this program.
- The facility was clean.
- The facility was dirty.

Program Structure
- The progression of this program was logical.
- This program was creatively planned.
- The level of this program was too difficult for me.
- Instructional materials for this class were excellent.
- This program went further into the activity than I desired.

Equipment
- There was not enough equipment available for this program.
- The equipment used in the program never worked properly.
- There was plenty of equipment to conduct this program.
- I had access to all of the supplies and equipment I needed for this program.

Club Organization
- I am an active member of this club.
- I seldom attend club functions.
- This club does not meet my needs.
- Club officers are doing an excellent job of running the club.
- The [agency] provides excellent support services to this club.
- This club's activities are one of my most important leisure pursuits.
- Club officers do not represent the desires of most club members.

League Organization
- This league involved too many games.
- League awards are overemphasized.
- League awards are important to me.
- League games were too long.
- The minimum number of players allowed on the roster was too small.
- The maximum number of players allowed on the roster was too large.
- Roster size for the league was adequate.
- The league entry fee was appropriate.
- Teams in the league were well matched according to ability.

- Game officials maintained good control of games.
- Game officials were knowledgeable about the rules.
- Game officials started play on time.
- Playing facilities were generally available at the scheduled starting time.
- Playing facilities were usually in excellent shape.
- This league was too competitive.
- Our team was not competitive in this league.
- [Agency] personnel were helpful.
- [Agency] personnel were available when needed.
- The league management system was adequate.

Future Intents
- I intend to continue in this program next session.
- I would attend a more advanced session of this program.

Program Outcomes—General
- This program was one of the best I've participated in.
- As a result of this program, I will participate in this activity more frequently.
- This program made me more aware of my own interests and talents.
- I looked forward to attending this program.
- I often remember my pleasant experience in this program.

Program Outcomes—Specific
- In this program, I developed skills and ability.
- This program introduced me to a new skill.
- Participation in this program increased my feelings of self-worth.
- This program gave me an opportunity to demonstrate my competence to others.

Physical Fitness
- This program kept me physically fit.
- I enjoyed the physical exercise I got in this program.

Social Enjoyment
- I enjoyed this program because it enabled me to be with others who have interests similar to mine.
- I enjoyed this program because I participated with my friends.
- I enjoyed the companionship of others in the program.
- I liked meeting new people in this program.

Exploration
- I enjoyed discovering new things in this program.
- I liked seeing new sights.

Autonomy
- I felt I had control over things in this program.
- This program gave me a chance to be on my own.
- This program helped me to get away from it all for a while.

Risks
- I liked the high risks involved.
- I liked the chance for danger in this program.

Family Orientation
- I liked participating in this program with my family.
- I enjoyed this program because it enabled me to be away from my family for a while.

Relaxation
- In this program, I enjoyed experiencing tranquility.
- The most satisfying aspect of this program was that it gave my mind a rest.
- This program pleased me because it relaxed me physically.

21

Bug Fest
Photo courtesy of Indy Parks and Recreation

STEP 9 : DISPOSITION DECISION

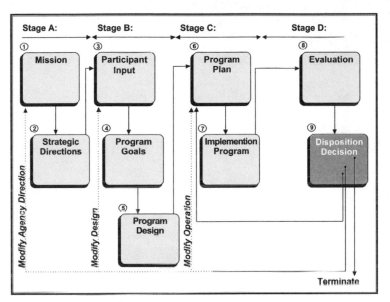

22

KEY TERMS
**Program Life
    Cycle
Introduction
Growth
Maturation
Saturation
Decline
Program
    Modification
Life Cycle Audit
Market Mix
    Program
Elimination**

The final step in the Program Development Cycle is to decide what will be done with a program—that is, what will be its disposition. The final disposition of a program should be made on evidence gathered during the evaluation phase. Only three choices can be made: to operate the program with no changes, to modify it, or to terminate it. Although this may seem like only three alternatives, one must remember that modification includes a broad range of alternatives. In addition, many scenarios for dropping a program must be considered.

It is somewhat of a misnomer to include in the Program Development Cycle a single stage called the decision-making stage. Program development involves a series of decisions. Ronkainen (1985) agrees with this view: "Product development is a sequential process involving not one decision point, but rather a series of go/no decisions" (p. 97). The programmer is faced with a series of decisions in developing programs; at each step in the cycle, a decision must be made about whether to proceed with the program concept or to abort it. Completing each step in the cycle also requires that the programmer make numerous decisions about the details of program development.

Furthermore, program development involves strategic decision making. Ronkainen (1985) points out that the central

The final disposition of a program should be made on evidence gathered during the evaluation phase. Only three choices can be made: to operate the program again with no changes, to modify it, or to terminate it.

Implementing Outcome-Based Programming

When used with participants in at-risk environments, the outcome-based programming model assumes that programs will be continued only if they clearly alleviate
the targeted social issue(s) that led to their implementation. Evidence that programs
help participants develop the protective factors identified would be a mid-level accomplishment that would warrant program continuation as well.

When used with other participants in difference service settings, evidence that a
program had delivered the benefits intended would be sufficient rationale for continuing the program as long as demand for the service continued.

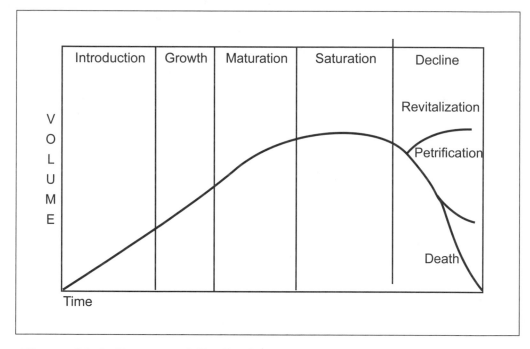

Figure 22-1: Program Life Cycle

element in strategic decision making is the "incomplete state of knowledge concerning the nature of the problem or the components which
must be included in a successful solution" (p. 98). Decision making in
program development is difficult partly because of the nonroutine nature of strategic decision making.

PROGRAM LIFE CYCLE

The ability to determine the disposition of a program will be influenced by the current position of a program in the program life cycle.
The program life cycle concept draws an analogy between a program
and the biological life cycle of animals (Crompton & Lamb, 1986). It as-

sumes that programs go through a transition analogous to birth, life, and death.

Figure 22-1 presents a diagrammatic representation of the program life cycle, which includes five stages: introduction, growth, maturation, saturation, and decline. Every program in an agency's program inventory will be located at a different stage in the cycle. Each stage has unique characteristics.

INTRODUCTION

The introduction stage is characterized by the considerable amount of programmer effort needed to introduce and successfully launch a new program. Grgen-Ellson (1986) reports that three factors lead to the successful introduction of new services: thorough market research, a well-planned implementation, and continual monitoring and ongoing support of the new service. Even with thorough preparations, however, the agency's cost per participant will probably be high during this stage because of the relatively small number of program patrons.

During implementation, programmers must monitor the new service very closely to make certain it is being delivered as intended by the program designer. Two marketing problems must be dealt with during the introduction stage: getting the target market to try the program for the first time, and getting the target market to continue using the service once they try it (Kotler & Andreasen, 1987).

Rogers and Shoemaker (1971) have identified a four-step process that individuals go through in adopting a new behavior pattern. The first step is acquiring knowledge about the new service and becoming convinced it has some usefulness to them. In the second step, the prospective client must be persuaded to participate; that is, to proceed from having an interest to being motivated to take action. In the third step, a person makes a decision either to accept the new program and participate in it or to reject participation. Often, the decision process is accompanied by either a vicarious experience or by an actual trial of the service. The final step is confirmation, during which an individual decides to become an ongoing participant or to stop participating in the service.

This latter step is often influenced by people's experience with a program during the third step when they tried the program. This is why it is very important to monitor the introduction of a new service.

GROWTH

During the growth stage, the number of patrons in a program increases most rapidly. There is demand and growth. The major task programmers face during this stage is to make certain that sufficient service is available to meet the demand.

How to deal with excess demand for a program service is somewhat problematic. In a public agency, there is always considerable political pressure on a programmer to meet all the demand for a service. In a commercial agency, there is also considerable financial pressure to meet demands for profitable services. In any agency, an inability to meet demand has the potential for eroding the credibility of the agency in the

The introduction stage is characterized by the considerable amount of programmer effort needed to introduce and successfully launch a new program.

During the growth stage, the number of patrons in a program increases most rapidly.

eyes of its consumer public. The agency must therefore anticipate potential demand and be prepared to meet it.

MATURATION

During the maturation stage, program growth slows, as does the rate of increase in new patrons.

During the maturation stage, program growth slows, as does the rate of increase in new patrons (Howard & Crompton, 1980). Usually, this is the longest stage for most programs. Thus, most programs will be in this stage and most marketing efforts will deal with mature programs (Kotler & Armstrong, 1993). It is important to continue to manage mature programs by altering their market mix, seeking new markets through further segmentation, or modifying the program as indicated from your analysis of the evaluation data.

SATURATION

When a program's growth slows and the number of patrons enrolled levels off, the program is in the saturation stage. During this stage, enrollments are made up of almost all repeat business. The management task in this stage is one of servicing an existing clientele. Additionally, because several other suppliers may be offering the same program service, the programmer is often competing for market share; that is, a portion of the total market.

During the saturation stage the program's growth slows and the number of patrons enrolled levels off.

There are four strategies the programmer may adopt during the saturation phase to help maintain a program's enrollments (Kotler & Andreasen, 1987):

• Market leadership: Take the leadership in program innovation. Try to maintain the agency's position as the best provider of this service.
• Market challenge: Take the offensive and challenge the market leader through any number of strategies, including price discounting, program innovation, improved service, and better distribution.
• Market follower: Try to maintain the current market share by duplicating the market leader. The market follower must know how to maintain its current customers by keeping its prices low and its quality high. It must also remain aware of market trends and be prepared to enter new markets as they open.
• Market targeting: Try to identify a unique segment of the market that can be serviced without threatening the larger suppliers. By finding a unique, profitable market niche, the agency can maintain a patron group for its services.

During the saturation stage, then, the programmer has an opportunity to make adjustments to the marketing mix of a program in order to maintain enrollments. Making adjustments during this stage may avoid having a program enter the decline stage.

The decline stage is characterized by falling enrollments.

DECLINE

The decline stage is characterized by falling enrollments. Decline can be rapid or slow. For example, specific types of craft activities can

Exhibit 22-1: Program Life Cycle Audit

Program _____ Program Manager _____ Date _____

Program Impact Data

	Actual			Estimated	
	2007	2008	2009	2010	2011
Enrollment	____	____	____	____	____
Attendance	____	____	____	____	____
Service hours	____	____	____	____	____
Annual growth rate	____	____	____	____	____
Staff hours	____	____	____	____	____
Staff/participant ratio	____	____	____	____	____
Average cost per participant	____	____	____	____	____
Revenue	____	____	____	____	____

Life Cycle

Introduction	Growth	Maturation	Saturation	Decline

VOLUME (vertical axis)

Revitalization

Petrification

Death

Time (horizontal axis)

Place an "x" where you believe the program is currently located on the life cycle. Use the stage indicators below to help you place the program.

Program Life Cycle Stage Indicators

Introduction Stage
1. Staffing costs are high—staff hours needed to operate the program are high and the staff/participant ratio is high.
2. Attendance and service hours are low.
3. Program enrollment is at one-half or below its capacity.
4. Average cost per participant is high.

Growth Stage
1. The number of staff hours needed for program operation goes down. Staff/participant ratio goes down.
2. Enrollment, service hours, and attendance increase substantially.
3. Average cost per participant goes down.

Exhibit 22-1: (continued)

4. Revenue goes up.
5. Enrollment is at 75 percent or greater of capacity.

Maturation Stage
1. Rate of revenue increase slows. Average cost per participant goes down.
2. Staff hours and staff/participant ratio decrease.
3. Enrollments are still at 75 percent of capacity but have fallen.

Saturation Stage
1. Revenue levels begin to decline. Average cost per participant begins to go up.
2. Enrollments and attendance have stabilized—there are no new patrons entering the program. Growth rate has stabilized.
3. Service hours level off and begin to decline.
4. Staff/participant ratio begins to increase.

Decline Stage
1. Staff hours increase. Staff/participant ratio increases.
2. Revenue declines significantly.
3. Average cost per participant increases.
4. Enrollment is below 25 percent of program capacity. Attendance has dropped significantly.

Adapted from a form used by the Anaheim Parks, Recreation, and Community Services Department as reported by Crompton J. L., & & Lamb, C.W., Jr. (1986). Marketing government and social services (pp. 226–227). New York: Wiley.

be popular in a given year, but the following year no one may be interested. Once a program begins the decline stage, the programmer will need to decide whether to try to revitalize the program, allow it to die, or allow the program to petrify. A program has petrified when there are a "relatively small number of enthusiastic participants remaining in the program, which may then run itself, providing no social or economic grounds for abolishing it" (Howard & Crompton, 1980). However, continuing a weak program can be very costly to an agency in both economic inefficiency and staff time. Weak programs often take an inordinate amount of staff time. For these reasons, the programmer should seriously consider eliminating programs in the decline stage.

To manage a program, programmers should be able to estimate its current position in the life cycle.

LIFE CYCLE AUDIT

To manage a program, programmers should be able to estimate its current position in the life cycle. Exhibit 22-1 on pages 439-440 illustrates a life cycle audit form that may be used to determine the current position of a program in the life cycle. Where a program is placed in the cycle should reveal typical program management problems.

Exercise 22-1: Altering the Market Mix

In class, select a program service and discuss how the market mix may need to be different at each stage of the program life cycle. Use the matrix below to guide your discussion.

Market Mix
Components   Life Cycle Stages

	Introduction	Growth	Maturation	Saturation	Decline
Product					
Price					
Promotion					
Place					

After completing your discussion, consider the following questions:
- In which stages can price seem to play the largest role?
- Does the usefulness of promotion ever wane as a strategy for obtaining additional patrons?
- When is it most likely that the programmer would alter the product in order to influence the life cycle of a program?
- In which stage(s) is place or distribution most likely to be used to alter the life cycle of a program?

RESEARCH UPDATE: USING VISUALIZATION TO SOLVE PROBLEMS IN PROGRAMS. Approximately 40% of programmers use visualization to solve problems in programs.

Females	42.7%
Males	41.0%
Experienced programmers (eight+ yrs)	44.0%
Less experienced (<eight yrs)	39.8%
Certified	39.1%
Not certified	44.8%

ALTERING THE MARKETING MIX

Conventional marketing wisdom suggests that each stage of the program life cycle requires a unique market mix. At each stage, different components of the marketing mix (product, price, promotion, and place) will need to be changed so that they can help to continue the life of a program. Explore this idea by completing Exercise 22-1 on page 441.

PROGRAM MODIFICATION

One of the most difficult programming decisions is to know how and when to modify a program. Although a program may need to be modified any time, the later part of the saturation stage and the early part of the decline stage are almost always critical times.

An understanding of leisure theory provides the best guidance about how to modify a program (Little, 1993). The leisure theory discussed earlier in the book suggests that, for a program to provide a leisure experience to constituents, it must continue to be a novel experience. Programmers must modify a program to keep it novel and enticing. One way to monitor this is to closely watch patrons' reported outcomes. Another, according to recent research conducted by the authors, is to use visualization to experience a program vicariously, searching and experimenting with possible modifications.

Remember that a service can be altered by changing any one of the six situating elements of a program. As outlined in Chapter Three, it is not necessary to alter the entire program, only one or more components of it. Often, then, at the end of the saturation stage or during the decline stage, the programmer must modify a program. Patron feedback is the best source of data about any modifications that may be necessary.

IMPLEMENTING PROGRAM MODIFICATIONS

Almost all programs will have a core group of participants who like things "just the way they are." Thus, programmers must understand the situations they are facing in recommending modifications to a program. How difficult it will be to implement change in a program will depend on two variables: the degree of change, and the amount and type of information available about the advisability of change. The degree of change can range from small, incremental changes to large, major changes in the program. The information the programmer may have about the advisability of change, or to justify the change, can range from a large amount of pertinent, detailed, quantitative information to a small amount of intuitive, qualitative, judgmental information derived from experience or casual observation. The quality and quantity of information will vary greatly and will affect how easily the programmer will be able to implement change.

Figure 22-2 is a graphic representation of four decision situations created by various combinations of information availability and the degree of change contemplated. Included in the matrix are the mode of change to be recommended, which implies the degree of change that will result, and the basis or rationale for making change.

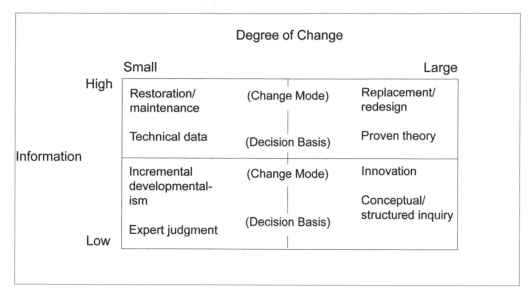

Figure 22-2: Decision Matrix

In the first decision mode, restoration/maintenance, a small degree of change is proposed. Technical information about the program is the basis for recommending this change. Restoration decisions are characterized by the use of technical information to implement small, incremental changes that restore a program to its original design. Because the change is small and the information available is great, this is usually an easy change to implement. An example of this would be increasing the number of staff at a day care operation to comply with a new child care law. This change would continue the program as designed and keep it within the minimal requirements of the law.

In the second mode, a program is completely replaced with a new service or a completely redesigned service. The rationale for this is a proven theory or method. Although the change implemented is great, the information base for the change is also substantial; thus, the change is usually easy to implement. The only block may be a lack of understanding for the change by the patrons who will be affected. This situation will require that the programmer communicate the basis for the change to the patrons. An example of this would be replacing a traditional summer playground program with specialty camps, such as sports or arts camps, scheduled so that they may also serve as day care programs. The information base for such a change could be declining enrollments in the playground program, the success of similar camp programs in other communities, the expressed need in the community for summer day care, and an expressed desire for program services with a more defined focus.

The third mode is incremental developmentalism, which involves small changes based on a small amount of information. The rationale for these changes is the experience and expert judgment of staff. Usually these changes are so small that the experienced practitioner is allowed the leeway to make them. Because the changes recommended are small, they are relatively easy to implement. This type of a decision is typical of the modifications made in many recreation programs that are developed through trial and error, with only small adjustments at each iteration.

Little (1993) provides several examples of modifying programs with this type of decision strategy. For example, in observing the operation of a summer day camp, she noted that varying levels of camper ability led to the need to alter certain activities so all of the children could feel competent. With a similar technique, she determined that a drama skit activity included in a weekend program operated for incarcerated mothers and their children could be retained if its implementation were changed from requiring the mothers to create the skits to simply acting out canned skits. Both of these were small, incremental changes that could be made because of her understanding of leisure behavior and how it constrained participation in the current programs. It is important to point out here that although the changes were small and the information used to justify the changes seemed minimal, the knowledge base and analysis required to identify them were not. Previous experience with programs and a knowledge of leisure behavior that was directly applicable to the current programs were both necessary to successfully modify these programs. Changes of this type are easier to implement if the programmer's credibility has built up over time with a record of successful changes.

The final decision mode is innovation, which is characterized by a low level of information being used to recommend a substantial change. Creative thinking and innovative design techniques discussed in Chapters Eleven and Twelve are the typical methods used to develop the data needed for this type of recommended change. These techniques produce a low information level because these data are often considered "soft," since they are not derived from quantitative analysis. This is one of the most difficult changes to have accepted. A successful track record of implementing innovative programs will help the programmer have this type of a change accepted. An example of this type of change would be the recommendation to begin a major new special event or program service never tried in a community.

Modifying programs is an essential part of program management. The programmer must develop the skills necessary to analyze programs, to note their deficiencies, and to be able to recommend and have accepted the modifications that will keep them viable. Understanding the resistance one is likely to face in implementing modifications is important to successfully accomplishing them.

THE BIRTH AND DEATH OF PROGRAMS

An important implication of the life cycle concept is that in a healthy organization, some new programs will be introduced and some existing programs terminated each year. Introducing and terminating programs is a normal event in managing the program inventory of a leisure service organization. In addition, eliminating programs will be an economic necessity in a recession situation. With static economic resources, the programmer can obtain the resources necessary to introduce new programs only by eliminating some of the old ones.

It is therefore critical that a leisure service programming operation have a formal procedure both for identifying new program services to launch and for eliminating program services that have outlived their usefulness to the organization. The first two stages of the Program Development Cycle (pages 98-99) provide a formal procedure for developing and launching programs. A formal elimination strategy will be discussed below.

PROGRAM ELIMINATION

Programmers tend to add programs, not eliminate them. Adding only new programs to an organization's inventory will lead to a deterioration of service quality. Eventually, the professional staff will simply be spread too thin to do a thorough job on each program. Even the best programmers have a limit on the number of programs they can successfully manage.

In most leisure service organizations, three primary forces work against eliminating programs: staff, patrons, and organizational political forces. First, staff members too often develop an "ownership" of programs they have created. They are therefore reluctant to eliminate a program because they consider its elimination a personal or professional failure. Programs have life cycles, and the useful life of almost all good programs will eventually end. Often this termination has nothing to do with the competence of the professional staff—it is a predictable consequence of beginning a program. The only question is when it will occur.

Professional staff members need to realize, then, that eliminating some programs each year is a normal and necessary part of program management. All viable organizations must constantly search for new products and services to bring to the marketplace.

Not-for-profit organizations, municipal leisure service agencies, church recreation operations, and other similar leisure service organizations with a third-party funder encounter two additional forces that make it difficult to eliminate programs. Patrons who make up a core group of participants will lobby against eliminating a program. These groups are very committed to the continuation of a specific activity. Although these groups often are very small, the intensity of their commitment is great, and they will attempt to ensure continuation of "their" activity, regardless of its economic efficiency.

The second force is board members and higher-ranking administrative personnel, who will often respond to the efforts of groups lobbying for the continuation of a program recommended for elimination by the professional staff. Because leisure services in these types of organizations are often subsidized, it is therefore possible to continue economically inefficient services.

These latter two cases can best be dealt with by having program criteria established and accepted by the various parties before actually making disposition decisions. Making decisions from an economic profitability model is much more objective and easily determined. Because of this, commercial recreation operations have clearer decision criteria, and the elimination of unprofitable services is required.

22

"Even the best programmers have a limit on the number of programs they can successfully manage.

Professional staff members need to realize, then, that eliminating some programs each year is a normal and necessary part of program management."

Once the decision is made to eliminate a service, the programmer must determine an elimination strategy. How will the service be eliminated? Following are three possible strategies for eliminating a program service:

- Retrenchment: A program can be continued with reduced expenses. Often, because the retrenched service is not the same service originally provided with a higher level of funding, enrollments decline.
- Staged: A reduction of a program service can be staged. Such a strategy can be phased in over a period of time so that current participants can find alternate services to meet their needs.
- Sudden: A service can be simply be eliminated immediately. This is often possible with services that have outlived their useful life.

CONCLUSION

The final step in the Program Development Cycle is to make a decision about the disposition of a program. It is important that decisions be warranted by the evaluation data collected about the program. The current place of the program on the program life cycle will partly determine the disposition of a program. The programmer must decide whether to modify, eliminate, or continue a program. All healthy programming organizations should add some new programs and eliminate existing ones each year.

REFERENCES

Crompton, J. L., & Lamb, C. W., Jr. (1986). *Marketing government and social services*. New York: Wiley.

Grgen-Ellson, N. (1986). Increasing the probability of new product success. *Journal of Retail Banking, 8*, 25–28.

Howard, D. R., & Crompton, J. L. (1980). *Financing, managing, and marketing recreation & park resources*. Dubuque, IA: Wm. C. Brown.

Kotler, P., & Andreasen, A. R. (1987). *Strategic marketing for nonprofit organizations*. Englewood Cliffs, NJ: Prentice-Hall.

Kotler, P., & Armstrong, G. (1993). *Marketing: An introduction* (3rd ed.). Englewood Cliffs, NJ: Prentice-Hall.

Little, S. L. (1993). Leisure program design and evaluation. *The Journal of Physical Education, Recreation, and Dance, 64*(8), 26–29, 33.

Rogers, E. M. (with Shoemaker, F. F.). (1971). *Communication of innovations*. New York: Free Press.

Ronkainen, I. A. (1985). Using decision-systems analysis to formalize product development processes. *Journal of Business Research, 13*, 97–106.

Index

Index

Index

About the Authors

J. ROBERT ROSSMAN has been associated with programming for over 35 years as a practitioner, scholar, and consultant. Early in his career, he served as a recreation leader, program supervisor, and program administrator. During his tenure as a faculty member, Dr. Rossman taught undergraduate and graduate courses on recreation programming and delivered scholarly papers on programming at national and international meetings. He has consulted with municipal and military recreation organizations about designing and staging program services and has conducted workshops for military and community recreation programmers around the world. Although retired from university appointments, his career continues as an author, speaker, and consultant about designing, staging, and managing programmed experiences. He is a member of the American Academy for Park and Recreation Administration and the American Leisure Academy.

BARBARA ELWOOD SCHLATTER brings 25 years of programming experience to the profession. As an outdoor educator, she specializes in hiking and whitewater canoeing experiences for people of all ages and abilities. In the Peace Corps, she designed and implemented community youth development programs in Guatemala. Her scholarly work has been published in the *Journal of Recreation and Park Administration*; *Research Quarterly for Sport and Exercise*; *JOPERD*; and the *Cyber Journal of Applied Recreation and Leisure Research*. An associate professor, she directs the Recreation and Park Administration program at Illinois State University. She has presented educational sessions on program-related topics at conferences around the world. Schlatter also offers her expertise in fund raising, sports programming, and program evaluation to the local Boys and Girls Club, where she serves on the board of directors. Her teaching specializations are in recreation programming, outdoor recreation, and human resource management. She is a member of the American Leisure Academy.